TURN! TURN! TURN!

the '60s folk-rock revolution

by Richie Unterberger

Backbeat Books
San Francisco

Published by Backbeat Books
600 Harrison Street, San Francisco, CA 94107
www.backbeatbooks.com
email: books@musicplayer.com
An imprint of the Music Player Network
United Entertainment Media

Distributed to the book trade in the US and Canada by
Publishers Group West, 1700 Fourth Street, Berkeley, CA 94710

Distributed to the music trade in the US and Canada by
Hal Leonard Publishing, P.O. Box 13819, Milwaukee, WI 53213

Text Design and Composition by Leigh McLellan
Cover Design by Doug Gordon
Front Cover Photos: Michael Ochs Archives.com
Production Editors: Amanda Johnson and Michael Baughan

Library of Congress Cataloging-in-Publication Data

Unterberger, Richie, 1962–
   Turn! turn! turn! : the '60s folk-rock revolution / by Richie Unterberger.
      p . cm.
   Includes discographical references (p.), bibliographical references (p.),
   and index.
   ISBN 0-87930-703-X
   1. Folk rock music—History and criticism. I. Title.
   ML3534.U57 2002
   781.66'093—dc21   2002016097

Printed in the United States of America

02 03 04 05 06   5 4 3 2 1

contents

groups like the Blue Things record great folk-rock far from Hollywood and Greenwich Village; ambitious folk-rock records like "Eight Miles High" and "Society's Child" fight media censoship, as the establishment fights back; Dylan peaks in mid-1966 with Blonde on Blonde *and a world tour with future members of the Band, but retreats after a motorcycle accident; folk-rock's first golden age comes to a close, setting the stage for new offshoots that will help shape rock for the rest of the 1960s.*

foreword

What makes a classic record? It's one of life's imponderables. There are lots of answers that seem to contain an element of truth, but no single satisfying definition that enables you to say, "Yes, that is a classic, but that is merely good." I think it's something to do with crossing cultural boundaries and surviving changing tastes and styles. If that's right, then the folk-rock boom of the mid-'60s had its fair share of classics.

Think about the Byrds' version of Bob Dylan's "Mr. Tambourine Man," to take just one example. It is not just a smash hit from the '60s, a quaint period piece, a golden oldie. It's an era-defining record, definitely, but there is even more to it than that. There's a sense in which it *lives*, so you feel compelled to talk about it in the present tense. The chime of Roger McGuinn's 12-string guitar and the singers' incandescent harmonies transcend the time and circumstances in which they were recorded and continue to exude a joyous vitality that retains the power to enthrall and inspire. I've been listening to it for 25 years and it still gets me every time I hear it.

There are other classic folk-rock records, and plenty of merely very good ones as well. This book tells you about most of them. It also tells you about the bandwagon-hoppers, opportunists, and people who just didn't quite get what was happening—people common to all musical genres. The subplot of their lesser contributions only serves to clarify the achievements of the main players.

"Turn! Turn! Turn!" takes its title from a Pete Seeger song, the lyrics of which are based on a passage in the Old Testament book of Ecclesiastes. That passage can be paraphrased in one statement: There is a time, a *right* time, for everything. That's certainly true of the story of the emergence of folk-rock. With hindsight the musical and broader social forces that converged in its making have a look of inevitability about them, as if everything was conspiring to produce that one outcome at that point in history. It was the *right* time because rock music had reached a stage in its life when it needed to make decisive steps from youth into adulthood. Folk-rock was one of those steps. It was a step into greater lyrical depth, whether poetic and introspective or political and outward-looking. It was a step into new instrumental possibilities. It was a step into melody. In fact, it was more than a step—it was a giant leap.

Mark Brend
London, April 2002

Mark Brend is the author of *American Troubadours:*
Groundbreaking Singer-Songwriters of the '60s.

introduction

"Folk+Rock+Protest=An Erupting New Sound." So blared the headline in *Billboard* magazine on August 21, 1965, trumpeting the onslaught of a new way of making music that was shaking the foundations of the industry to its core. The Byrds and Bob Dylan had started it, with huge hits that summer that married the lyrical content and integrity of folk music with the visceral power of rock. Many more such artists were on their way to the same destination, bearing messages that would change the world, from Simon & Garfunkel, the Lovin' Spoonful, and the Mamas & the Papas to Buffalo Springfield, Donovan, and Jefferson Airplane. By the end of the 1960s, when Crosby, Stills, Nash & Young carried the folk-rock flame forward into the next decade, it was so entrenched within popular music that hardly anyone was even bothering to call it folk-rock anymore. The erupting new sound had become, to a large extent, *the* sound of rock music and its generation of listeners.

As that *Billboard* headline signified, at the time the industry thought of folk-rock as a craze, one of many that periodically come and go, enabling the music business to keep marketing new performers and selling tons of records. By the end of 1966, the folk-rock craze, or boom, was over, its most talented performers permanently accepted as part of rock's mainstream. Often they moved on to psychedelic rock or new experiments in sound, and even if they never forsook folk and folk-rock as a base, the mere mingling of folk and rock elements was no longer reason for excited commentary. It was now a cornerstone of rock, persisting to this day, and responsible to a great degree for a huge elevation in the overall lyrical intelligence of all rock music. In that sense, it never went away, and was one of the most successful crazes of all.

Yet as the initial folk-rock boom faded further and further into history, music historians became keener to dismiss it as a passing fad, an awkward hybrid, or a necessary, temporary phase that rock needed to pass through as it grew into an art form. Too often, it was simplified as something that Bob Dylan had invented almost single-handedly, even if it took the Byrds to popularize folk-rock with covers of Dylan songs. As it diversified, and as different critics brought infinitely different perspectives to the form in the following decades, folk-rock's definition became so wide and flexible that at times the term seemed almost meaningless. To some, any singer-songwriter singing about personal concerns with a guitar style that owes anything to acoustic folk strumming is folk-rock. Others adamantly apply far narrower guidelines, echoing the very dogmatic mindset that the first folk-rockers were so eager to escape. It's all served to blur folk-rock's image and, in the eyes of some, diminish its importance.

But it *was* important, indeed about as important as any stylistic evolution of popular music in that most turbulent of decades, the 1960s. So much of what we take for granted in popular music today—lyrics (often, though certainly not always) with a personal and/or universal message, artistic hunger to break down barriers between different styles, performers who write and record their own material their own way, and the hope that music means more than record sales—all can be partially attributed to folk-rock. Less tangibly, much of the socially conscious progress set in motion by young people in the 1960s—antiwar activism, championship of civil rights, personal and sexual liberation, a questioning of authority, and a determination to enjoy life rather than merely get on with it—was fueled, directly or indirectly, by folk-rock. Folk-rock was particularly effective at spreading its messages because it marked one of those rare instances where social activism and mainstream commercial interests merged, each furthering the agenda of the other.

Though inextricably linked with the events of its era and the generation that produced it, the music of the original folk-rock epoch has proved to be as timeless as the traditional folk music that inspired many of its artists. You don't need to have experienced the period firsthand to feel the sound's impact just as deeply as anyone did in 1965 or 1966. There was the sense of musicians mixing forms to produce something greater than the sum of its parts, something that pushed them beyond what they thought was possible, something that neither folk nor rock could have created on its own. Even as a suburban 17-year-old in 1979, I could grasp this at once, if only intuitively, playing the Byrds' *Mr. Tambourine Man* over and over, 14 years after its release, long after the Byrds had disbanded, long after they had regular airplay. *Mr. Tambourine Man* was different from what was on the radio, for the most part, in the late '70s. This was Music With Meaning. If that seemed pretentious to those who thought of rock 'n' roll as a party music that should never be taken too seriously, well, the gains certainly outweighed the losses. Folk-rock, by the Byrds and others I was discovering long after their heyday, was music to feed both the body and the mind.

It would take much longer to fully appreciate the mammoth seismic cultural and musical shifts that had made folk-rock possible, even after I'd acquired most of the greatest folk-rock records in my late teens and early twenties. Folk-rock did not start as a result of a bold, solitary act of courage by Bob Dylan, risking all by deciding to play his lyrically complex folk songs on an electric guitar. This is a myth—one I encountered, in print, yet a few more times while writing this book—perpetuated by pundits anxious to seize upon one particular figure, and one particular action, as an axis upon which history turns.

It is in no way undermining Dylan's crucial contributions to point out that he was but one of hundreds, if not thousands, of musicians from his generation engaged in the same collective, largely unconscious simultaneous move from folk to rock in those heady days of 1964 and 1965. Some of those others, like the Byrds, have received due recognition for their own groundbreaking achievements. Yet many of those vital to this transformation never have been given the credit they deserve, because they did not make hit records, or sometimes did not even record.

So who invented folk-rock? In general, everyone; in particular, no one. The forces steering its birth were wild, unpredictable, inevitable, and beyond the control of any one individual or group of individuals.

Which was, naturally, what made it so exciting. It was a crazy-quilt of connective threads between musicians, styles, generations, politics, the record industry, and the mass media. It was envisioned by virtually no one in 1963, yet within two years—after unforeseen thunderbolts like the JFK assassination, the arrival of the Beatles in the United States, the British Invasion, and the Byrds drawing overflow crowds with their folk-based music played on loud electric guitars—folk-rock had overrun the Western world. It might not have been as loud and crude as rockabilly, the early Rolling Stones, or punk. But within the context of its own time, it was equally rebellious and controversial.

The 18 months or so from the beginning of 1965 to the summer of 1966 were an especially frenzied crucible of mad invention, a time when its performers and listeners were riding a wild horse, both hanging on for dear life and exhilarated beyond belief at its reckless speed and unexpected bucks and turns. By mid-1966, the Byrds, who recorded the first major folk-rock hit with "Mr. Tambourine Man" in January 1965, were already deeply into psychedelic rock; Bob Dylan, an acoustic folksinger when the Byrds covered his song, was an electric rock superstar, backed by what might have been the loudest band in the world. The en masse shift of an entire generation from mild, short-haired folk musicians to uninhibited, long-haired rockers within a year or two is almost unparalleled in its speed, decisive as a karate chop that literally split one generation from another. The more I found out about it—starting as a teenager in the 1970s, then wading through hundreds of records and books, and ultimately talking to some of the front-line messengers themselves—the more I was convinced that the story of the entire 1960s folk-rock movement was one that needed to be told.

The roots of folk-rock stretch back to before the birth of rock 'n' roll, before the dawn of the recording era, even before the twentieth century, to the folk music that arose in the United States, often derived from the British Isles and African origins. The precise definition of folk-rock was the cause of much debate in 1965 and 1966, and continues to be today, among both fans and historians. To some, folk-rock is embodied by early Byrds hits like "Mr. Tambourine Man" and "Turn! Turn! Turn!": a folk song, or a folk-like song, played on electric instruments with an electric rhythm section, combining prominent features of both folk and rock. To others, it's anything from the mid-'60s with an electric 12-string guitar, conscientious harmonies, and a bashing tambourine to help keep the rhythm, even if the song and lyrics are those of a conventional romantic pop tune.

To those using the broadest criteria, folk-rock is rock music that borrows strongly or even just noticeably from folk, whether in the vocal harmonies, guitar strums and picks, or song composition. To those using the narrowest of definitions, it's a traditional folk song played with rock instrumentation. Just about the only thing that everyone who listens to early folk-rock can agree upon is that the Byrds and Bob Dylan were folk-rock. That is, at least some of the time, perhaps, or maybe.

So what *was* folk-rock when it started? All of the above, in my estimation, if to varying degrees. Mid-'60s folk-rock was a wide umbrella, enveloping the Mamas & the Papas and such strongly pop-informed, slickly produced groups at its poppiest edge; the avowedly underground, raw, subversively left-wing agitprop of the Fugs at its most radical extreme; young folksinger-songwriters like Judy Collins, Phil Ochs, and Ian & Sylvia who were barely starting to dip their toes into electric folk-rock, as if for fear of drowning if immersed too quickly; and the Byrds—the Beatles of folk-rock, if there was such a thing—in the center. There was room for artists who some would soon consider psychedelic, such as the early Jefferson Airplane. There was even room for groups who have been sometimes classified as garage bands (like the Leaves) or pure pop acts (like the Turtles).

I have covered it all in this book, and also given substantial space to artists who may never have been defined as folk-rockers, but were strongly influenced by folk-rock, like the Beatles, to use the most obvious example. I would rather err on the side of caution than be too exclusive. That's particularly important to do, I feel, since one of folk-rock's greatest accomplishments was its influence upon rock and pop as a whole—one of many things that distinguished it from the insular folk scene that produced many folk-rockers. The barriers between the hip and unhip, and between performers of apparently different genres, so rigidly codified by rock historians after the fact, were actually much more fluid at the time than has been commonly acknowledged.

Sometimes boundaries do need to be drawn, though. Acoustic folk performers of the 1960s, whether from the folk boom that preceeded folk-rock or from the folk-rock era itself, are here noted mostly for how they impacted the course of folk-rock. As much as the history of 1960s folk-rock encompasses, it should not be misconstrued as half the history of '60s folk music, and half the history of '60s folk-rock music. Folk-rock was *not* the same as folk music; that was central to the whole point of its existence. *This* is a book about folk-rock itself, with one chapter laying out the roots of its genesis in folk music from 1960–63.

One truly major boundary needed to be drawn to keep this history from approaching the size of a telephone book. The original intention was to cover the whole of 1960s folk-rock, a movement that if anything got more diverse and interesting between mid-1966 and the end of the decade. Folk-rock was a flower whose tendrils infiltrated almost every facet of rock music in its first five years, and in fact largely shaped several of its offshoots. Psychedelia, the singer-songwriter movement, country-rock, the late-blooming heyday of British folk-rock—retroactively named mini-genres like acid folk—even the birth of the rock festival: all either were grounded in, or owed a great deal to, the original flush of folk-rock.

It was quite a challenge to fit all of folk-rock's branches from the years 1964-69 into one volume. More than 100 interviews and a quarter of a million words later, it proved impossible to fit into one book, but not impossible to tell the entire story. This led me to *Eight Miles High: Folk-Rock's Flight from Haight-Ashbury to Woodstock*, the sequel to this book, also published by Backbeat Books, in 2003. *Eight Miles High* follows the continued evolution of many folk-rock performers detailed in the book you're holding—the Byrds, Bob Dylan, Donovan, Judy Collins, Buffalo Springfield, and many others—as well as the entrance of such giants as Joni Mitchell, Jefferson Airplane, and Fairport Convention onto folk-rock's main stage, and the prime of more cultish figures such as Tim Buckley, Skip Spence, and Nick Drake.

But *Turn! Turn! Turn!: The '60s Folk-Rock Revolution* is devoted to the story of the first groundbreaking generation of folk-rockers, and particularly to the years 1964 to 1966, in which folk-rock originated, flourished, and peaked. It covers not so much folk-rock's maturity as its birth and first full-force impact, stopping in mid-1966, when a motorcycle accident precipitated Dylan's year-and-a-half withdrawal from the public eye, leaving other folk-rock originators and newcomers to forge new directions all over the folk-rock map.

Like its sequel, this book gives much weight to the perspectives of those who were there, drawing upon firsthand interviews conducted mostly with musicians, but also with producers, record label executives, managers, club owners, and journalists. I spoke to key innovators like Roger McGuinn of the Byrds, John Sebastian of the Lovin' Spoonful, Judy Collins, and Donovan, and not only about their hit records, though they had plenty of those. I was also concerned with highlighting the lesser-known, and often overlooked, forces that shaped their unique contributions to the folk-rock mix. Toward that end, I sought out many behind-the-scenes figures (to the public, at any rate), such as Elektra Records president Jac Holzman, Byrds manager Jim Dickson, and Bob Dylan producer Bob Johnston. Budding singer-songwriters like Arlo Guthrie and Janis Ian, folk boom stars like Peter Yarrow of Peter, Paul & Mary, elder statespersons like Pete Seeger, even British Invasion pop stars like Manfred Mann: all had much to contribute.

Physical landmarks that had played such a forceful role in folk-rock were unavoidable as I traveled to New York, Los Angeles, London, and Liverpool during my research. Washington Square Park in New York City still teemed with activity on weekends and hot summer nights, including some of the kind of music that had launched the early-'60s folk boom when folkies gathered there to jam. In Los Angeles I stayed just a mile from the Troubadour, often driving past the still-open club where Roger McGuinn, Gene Clark, and David Crosby had formed the nucleus of the Byrds. Overseas, Liverpool's Mathew Street is still thronged with reminders of the group that more than any other incited folk musicians to go electric—even though the street's original Cavern Club, where the Beatles played in the early '60s, has been demolished. Back in San Francisco, where I live and work, I and thousands of others attended the summer 2001 memorial service for Mimi Fariña, where Judy Collins and Joan Baez sang, and early folk-rockers such as Jefferson Airplane's Paul Kantner dotted the crowd of mourners.

For some of the people I interviewed, particularly the musicians, the term "folk-rock" remains a source of not just hazy definition, but occasionally one of vexation. There was sometimes no surer way of getting someone's back up—then and now—than to refer to him or her as a "folk-rock" musician. The term folk-rock itself, after all, almost certainly originated in the record industry, not among musicians, and was beyond a doubt popularized into a catchphrase by the media. Many of the innovators we think of as folk-rockers prefer to think of themselves simply as musicians, and not ones constrained by any labels. Often they insist that what they were doing was not a conscious blend of folk and rock, but simply an organic process that came naturally and should not be subjected to microscopic analysis.

In part that's because, I believe, barely anyone thought this music would still be so popular 35 years later, or ever expected it to be the source of such intense critical scrutiny. Yet folk-rock *has* become as much of a bedrock of the popular music of the Western world as traditional folk music was back when most of the first folk-rockers were picking up their guitars. More time, in fact, separates the birth of folk-rock from the writing of this book than separated the first folk-rockers from the Depression-era folk recordings that gave them much of their early repertoire. Even as one too young to have heard folk-rock when it was first performed and recorded, that realization, as I spoke to many of the first-generation folk-rockers, was stunning, and a little sad. It was much sadder when I referred to Donovan in a freelance piece on the Beatles and the Maharishi, only to be greeted with this earnest query from an editor: "Donovan who?"

After all that time, however, most of those pioneers are still alive, well, and performing. And their occasional reluctance to be categorized is understandable in light of the spirit that drove them to create folk-rock in the first place, sometimes risking ostracism from the socially progressive—yet often artistically stultifying—folk community in which they often first honed their craft. If the folk-rock revolution had any overriding messages, they were to disobey unwritten laws, be willing to crash barriers, and refuse to be pigeonholed into any one bag. That's part of the reason there are so many interpretations of "folk-rock," and why it's impossible for any one musician or listener to define it. Folk-rock was a music of change, not tradition. A music that, as the Byrds sang in one of folk-rock's biggest and greatest hits, continued to turn, turn, turn.

Richie Unterberger
March 2002
San Francisco

prologue

the great
folk-rock clash

the 1965 newport folk festival

It was billed as the Newport Folk Festival, and for the most part, folk music was what an estimated 75,000 people heard at the event over the course of several days in July 1965. What it's remembered for, however, is a chaotic 25 minutes or so of—mostly—rock 'n' roll that may be the most controversial performance in the history of twentieth-century popular music.

On the night of July 25, 1965, Bob Dylan took the stage at Newport, Rhode Island to play electric rock music in front of a live audience for the first time since beginning his career as a recording artist. A mere three songs were presented before he went offstage, returning to sing a couple more alone, accompanied only by his own acoustic guitar and harmonica. One of the five songs from his set had just topped the charts, though in a version recorded by a different act. Another was on its way to stopping just short of the #1 position, and remains his biggest hit to this day.

Yet Dylan was booed. Or some people booed, while others cheered. Or some booed and some cheered, while others were totally baffled. Or no one could really hear what was going on anyway.

Considering that a complete tape of the performance survives, along with a partial film of the show, it is astonishing how many widely varying accounts of the performance have circulated since 1965. It is rock music's equivalent to *Rashomon*, the classic Akira Kurosawa film in which four characters give different, often contradictory versions of the same murder. It is tempting to view Dylan's appearance at the 1965 Newport Folk Festival as one in which the telling similarly varies, according to the musical and social tastes, values, and prejudices of the narrator. There are few other incidents that set the fusion—and conflict—of tradition and innovation, young and old, and art and commerce, in such bold relief.

The objective truth of what really occurred that night will never be possible to determine. What is certain is that it will endure as the defining symbol of the emergence of folk-rock—the hybrid of acoustic folk and amplified rock 'n' roll that would do more than irrevocably alter the course of popular music. It would irrevocably alter the shape of twentieth-century culture and society as a whole.

he brouhaha over Dylan's electric debut at the 1965 Newport Folk Festival was as unexpected as it was volatile. Yet if only in hindsight, it brought to a head crosscurrents, tensions, and alchemies that were years in the making.

For most of the ten years since rock 'n' roll had become massively popular among the world's youth, it had traveled an almost entirely separate path from folk music. To roughly summarize the overgeneralizations of the more vigilant champions of folk music, rock 'n' roll was disposable, commercial trash, marketed to immature teenagers. Folk music, by contrast, represented the authentic expression of the people, attracting a sophisticated, literate audience as concerned with changing the world for the better as it was with being entertained.

Yet folk music and popular success were not mutually exclusive. Indeed, the first half of the 1960s had seen a folk boom that expanded its listenership by the millions. The boom did not only encompass the liberal intellectuals and college campuses that had comprised the core of the folk community for decades. By the early '60s it was also crossing over to the pop charts in unprecedented fashion. At the same time, folk was a growing factor in progressive social activism, providing anthems for the mushrooming civil rights and antiwar movements.

Bob Dylan and the Newport Folk Festival were among the most potent symbols of the folk scene. Cofounded in the late '50s by George Wein and Albert Grossman, the first Newport Folk Festival was held in the usually sedate seaside Rhode Island town in 1959. Held again in 1960, and put on hold for the next two years, it returned in full force in 1963, attracting growing numbers of folk fans and becoming the preeminent showcase of folk talent in the United States. Folk music's biggest stars could usually be counted upon to appear, and live recordings of festival performances, issued on Vanguard Records, were crucial to boosting the careers of numerous newcomers and old-timers. And there was no bigger star in the world of folk music, and no more esteemed spokesperson for the folk movement, than Bob Dylan in the mid-'60s.

Since his arrival in Greenwich Village from Minnesota as an unknown 19-year-old in early 1961, the former Robert Zimmerman had blazed a meteoric trail through the folk world. Four years earlier he had been a Woody Guthrie wannabe. In 1965 he was perhaps the most idolized songwriter on the globe. He had established himself as the foremost protest and topical composer in the folk idiom with "Blowin' in the Wind," "A Hard Rain's A-Gonna Fall," "With God on Our Side," and other biting commentaries on injustice and military madness. In the past year or two he had proved himself the master of more poetic and personal ruminations such as "Chimes of Freedom," "Gates of Eden," and "Mr. Tambourine Man."

The Newport Folk Festival had been instrumental to his rise to folk superstardom, particularly in 1963. That was the year he had dueted with folk's biggest record-seller, Joan Baez, on "Blowin' in the Wind"; shared vocals with folk's greatest living legend, Pete Seeger, on the satirical Dylan composition "Playboys and Playgirls"; and joined hands with Seeger, Baez, Peter, Paul & Mary, and other folk figureheads for "We Shall Overcome," the unofficial civil rights anthem of 1960s political activism. By that time, he and several other leading folk acts were managed by festival cofounder Albert Grossman. But by the summer of 1965, Dylan was not a folksinger anymore, at least not to anyone with an open ear.

To get a sense of why some felt Dylan was committing sacrilege at Newport that year, it's necessary to understand that the festival was viewed by many not just as a series of performances, but as a mini-community unto itself. It was administered by the nonprofit Newport Folk Foundation, whose mission, according to *Billboard*, was "supporting research and exposure of folk music," with "artists paid only expenses." Its evening concerts presented the participating musicians with the highest profiles. But much of the daylight hours were given over to workshops—no less than 15 of them, in fact, on the day before Dylan's set—on wide-ranging and sometimes esoteric facets of the folk tradition, including blues guitar, bluegrass banjo, ballad swapping, psaltery, and (as noted in *The New York Times*) "Negro group singing and rhythm patterns." The barrier between artist and listener narrowed, giving those just learning their instrument a chance to play along with their heroes, and the artists an opportunity to swap tales with and mentor their followers.

In the days when rock festivals were unknown, folkfests also served as the largest mass gatherings of the burgeoning youth counterculture, Newport being the biggest. In the shots accompanying the credits to Murray Lerner's *Festival*, a documentary comprised of footage from the 1963–66 Newport Folk Festivals, you're greeted with a seemingly endless march of bohemian young adults trudging to the festival grounds. Add a few inches of hair, more flamboyant dress, and color, and it's not hard to imagine many of the same men and women in the audience at Woodstock four years later.

Bob Dylan was the biggest attraction on the bill of the 1965 Newport Folk Festival, his slot scheduled for the closing set of performances on Sunday night. Intense debate over his stylistic focus and role in the folk community, however, had begun the year before with the release of his fourth album, *Another Side of Bob Dylan*. That record marked a shift in focus from songs of social commentary to songs about relationships and romance, and increasingly complex, sometimes abstract wordplay. On "My Back Pages" he seemed to wave farewell to his days as a protest singer. He devoted his appearances at Newport in 1964, both at a workshop on topical ballads and in the main performance area, to this new breed of composition. And he played, for the first time, a newly written song called "Mr. Tambourine Man."

Not all of his audience applauded his new direction. It had already been something of a matter of contention within folk circles as to whether topical songs should be emphasized at folk festivals at all. "Topical ballads became the word for what Dylan did," explains *Festival* film director Murray Lerner. "Creating new folk songs, and using—changing—the words to old ones. It was part of my thesis in the film, that the tradition was changed to express something new. I imagine it's happened throughout history. Of course, there was a lot of controversy about that.

"There was definitely controversy within the administration of the festival about what should be presented, and what was folk music. There was a lot of late evening discussion about who should be on. And there was a lot of vehement opposition to anything that wasn't pure folk music." And here was Dylan, having just helped establish the topical song as a major vehicle for folk performers, spinning wheels and changing gears even while the merits of topical ballads had yet to be fully accepted. In *Broadside*, which along with *Sing Out!* was the most influential folk music magazine in the United States, Paul Wolfe declared: "His new songs, performed at Newport, surprised everyone, leaving the majority of the audience annoyed—some even disgusted, and in general scratching its collective head in disbelief."

A year later, the debate between folk "purists"—a word that would appear, over and over again, as folk-rock became the rage—and less tradition-bound musicians and listeners had accelerated beyond anyone's expectations. "Mr. Tambourine Man," the song that Dylan had introduced at the topical ballad workshop in 1964, had topped the American charts just a month before Newport '65, in a fully electric rock 'n' roll version by a bunch of ex-folkies called the Byrds. Dylan was becoming as much a pop star as a folk one, not just in the marketplace, but in demeanor and image as well. With his growing hair and mod clothes, he not only looked like a rocker, but *was* a rocker. One side of his last LP, *Bringing It All Back Home*, had been hard-driving rock 'n' roll. That album was hovering just outside the Top Ten, and an electric single from the album, "Subterranean Homesick Blues," had made the Top 40. And now "Like a Rolling Stone," his hardest-rocking song yet, had just entered the Top 100, seemingly confirming that Dylan's conversion to rock music was complete.

I t was in this highly charged atmosphere that Dylan arrived at the Newport Folk Festival in July. Today, with 35 years' hindsight, it may seem odd that Dylan was not necessarily expected to perform his latest hits, with similar instrumentation to that on the records, at such a major showcase. This was, however, a *folk* festival, not a rock one—rock festivals as such didn't really exist yet—or even a pop one. The concert program listed an astonishing variety of folk performers, and not just acknowledged stars such as Joan Baez and Peter, Paul & Mary, progressive folk artists Ian & Sylvia, emerging singer-songwriter Gordon Lightfoot, and folk icons Odetta and Pete Seeger. There were country bluesmen Mississippi John Hurt and Reverend Gary Davis; bluegrass masters Bill Monroe and the Charles River Valley Boys; elderly Appalachian musician Roscoe Holcomb; fiddler Eck Robertson, who had made his first record in 1922; more specialized ensembles presenting folk dance, work songs, and fife and drum corps; and even an entire Sunday morning concert of religious music.

Additionally, though Dylan had been recording with rock musicians for about six months, he had not performed live with a rock band since he was a teenager known as Bobby Zimmerman. He had not even formed a working group for such occasions, and had toured England in the spring as a solo acoustic act, even as *Bringing It All Back Home* and "Subterranean Homesick Blues" were ascending the charts there.

Dylan had only an acoustic guitar with him when he participated in a songwriters' workshop on Saturday, July 24, performing "All I Really Want to Do"—another song, incidentally, that was on the pop charts, via cover versions by both the Byrds and Cher. Captured on the *Festival* film, it was rewarded with an enthusiastic standing ovation. Never mind that it was a prominent example of the nontopical songs Dylan had recently written, and a folk-rock hit for Hollywood-based stars. The crowd certainly did not seem to be holding that against him. Which makes the more volatile reception of his performance the following night yet more intriguing.

Elsewhere on the festival grounds that Saturday, tensions between traditionalists and the new guard were already coming to a boil. Playing at the blues workshop was the Paul Butterfield Blues

Band, whose lead guitarist, Mike Bloomfield, had recently recorded with Dylan, playing on the "Like a Rolling Stone" single. Introducing them was Alan Lomax, probably the most esteemed American folklorist. Lomax had been recording folk and blues musicians in the field since the 1930s, and vigorously championing them and other folk musicians from Europe and the Caribbean via numerous channels, including radio broadcasts, Library of Congress collections, and album releases. Yet when presenting workshops, wrote Robert Shelton in *The New York Times*, he could be an "articulate, illuminating, fluent, but sometimes maddeningly pedantic host-narrator."

The exact words that Lomax used to introduce the band cannot be tracked down, and form a sideplot mini-legend to Dylan's '65 Newport affair. Everyone who was at the Butterfield set seems to agree, however, that it did not present the young, integrated, electric Chicago blues band in the most flattering light. In Jan Mark Wolkin and Bill Keenom's *Michael Bloomfield: If You Love These Blues*, veteran Chicago blues musician Nick Gravenites paraphrases Lomax's speech as: "Well, they've got this band from Chicago. Some people feel that white people can't play the blues, and some people feel they can—you make up your own mind. Here they are."

Albert Grossman, who was in the process of adding the Butterfield Blues Band to his artist roster, was not amused. Angry words were exchanged—again, the exact words have been lost to time, even to bystanders like occasional Dylan session guitarist Bruce Langhorne, who remembers helping to break up the ensuing fight, with assistance from singer-songwriter Richard Fariña. The two stocky, middle-aged men were "rolling around like a couple of bears in the dust," according to Geoff Muldaur of the Grossman-managed Jim Kweskin Jug Band, as onlookers observed the brief struggle with disbelief.

Not that Lomax's intro dampened Butterfield's reception: "He downplayed their legitimacy, and then they got up and tore the place to shreds," declares Muldaur, still rankled by the memory decades later. "Legitimate, le-shmit-a-mate. Fuck you." Adds Murray Lerner, "I thought the Butterfield Blues Band was going to be something else totally. And the minute they got on and started playing, I really got excited. Without any preparation, I jumped on the stage and photographed them quite intensely. I thought that electric music had this other quality of being hypnotic. [It was] a new way of experiencing music, and put you on its spell in a different way." It was a taste of the vanguard-vs.-old guard conflict that would play itself out on a much larger stage the following evening.

"Alan Lomax, who tended to be kind of outspoken, probably said something [that] Albert—who was very, very loyal to Bob [Dylan], *extremely* loyal to Bob—just didn't cotton to," Langhorne speculates. "Feelings were very strong. Because there were a lot of people who were very heavily invested in the traditional folk music. With the folk music revival, these were people who had been playing folk music for years and years and years in obscure venues, and suddenly they saw their time had come. They probably saw electrification and rock 'n' rollation as total co-option."

It's Dylan who's gotten the lion's share of retroactive attention for bringing rock to Newport, but the changes being wrought by folk-rock in the outside world were in fact already being heard before his Sunday night concert. The magazine *Boston Broadside* (a regional publication that was a separate entity from the New York-based folk periodical *Broadside*) had reported that "the Newport Folk festival announced that they had relaxed the ban on amplified instruments for [Butterfield's band] only, so that they might play at the Festival," but if such a ban was in effect, it was in the process of getting somewhat relaxed. In addition to the Butterfield Blues Band, there were also the Chambers Brothers, a gospel-folk crossover band using electric guitar and drums (excerpts from shows by both groups can be heard on *Newport Folk Festival: Best of the Blues 1959–68*). Filling in for an ill Josh White, the Chambers Brothers played "Time Has Come Today," three years before it became a psychedelic rock hit. "People jumped, and broke down fences, and ran and rushed the stage—it was incredible," remembered Joe Chambers in a 1994 *Goldmine* interview. "Newport had never seen or heard anything like that. And after we finished, and the crowd finally settled down, the emcee came back up and said, 'Whether you know it or not, that was rock 'n' roll.'"

Performing on the first evening was Donovan, already fending off charges of Dylan imitation in the wake of his first two hit singles, "Catch the Wind" and "Colours." Although the Dylan-wannabe charges were unwarranted, further Dylan-Donovan parallels were generated when he sang at Newport with Joan Baez on "Colours." Duets with Baez, at Newport and elsewhere, had been crucial to Dylan's rise to stardom, and to some it must have seemed that Donovan was trying to follow the same path that Dylan had blazed as a folkie troubadour.

It was not widely known that the British singer, still in his late teens, had actually already performed, on television, with an electric rock group three months earlier, though his 1965 recordings were mostly in the acoustic folk style. He would not play electric rock at Newport, but put his own two cents into the rising debate in a discussion at the festival with revered British folklorist and folksinger A.L. Lloyd. As reported by *The New York Times* that weekend, "Donovan and Mr. Lloyd differed about whether to keep folk and pop music separate. Donovan said he would like to see everything fused, but Mr. Lloyd said: 'Much of pop commercial music reflects instability, despair and loneliness. I have the feeling our kids are attracted to folk song because it speaks of a more stable society than ours is today.'"

Richard Fariña, who like Dylan had already released folk-rock recordings (as half of a duo with his wife Mimi), had ideas of beating Dylan to the punch himself with his afternoon set on Sunday. Barry Tashian, guitarist in Boston's hottest rock band, the Remains, had already jammed with the Fariñas off-record, and was invited by Richard to appear with them onstage at Newport. "When we got to Newport and it was time for the Fariñas to do a soundcheck, I got my amp and stuff on stage," recalls Tashian. "Peter Yarrow [of Peter, Paul & Mary] was acting as a stage manager/audio man. He said that the electric guitar wouldn't work. Said it was impossible to mix it into their sound with any success on stage. So I bowed out."

His story's corroborated by a 1965 interview of Fariña by Ed Freeman on the Cambridge, Massachusetts radio station WMBR, in which Fariña stated, "There was a terrible microphone hassle, because they were intensely concerned with balancing. They had four microphones on just Mimi and me. One for each of the instruments, one for our voices." (Oddly, Fariña is heard introducing Al Kooper, who had recently played rock with Dylan in the studio, from the stage during a tape of their performance. Kooper does not remember if he played with them, but does recall seeing a backstage pre-show rehearsal photo of himself playing acoustic guitar with the Fariñas and washtub bassist Fritz Richmond.)

Their set further impeded by a massive downpour, the Fariñas made the best of the situation by carrying on regardless. Pete Seeger gave this backstage report a few months later when he had the Fariñas as guests on his *Rainbow Quest* television show a few months later: "Seven thousand people were getting soaking wet, and they said, 'What the heck, let's get wet.' They started stripping off their clothing and dancing to the music. It was a real rocking number with wonderful rhythm going. And there were people waving their shirts in the air and dancing all kind of dances, women had stripped off their shirts, dancing in their bras. It was pandemonium. Seven thousand people dancing in the thundering rain, and Dick and Mimi pounding on. It was wonderful." Despite the absence of electric guitar, as *The New York Times* noted, "Their 'House Un-American Blues Activity Dream' was of the protest-folk-rock-style."

These little-known anecdotes in the buildup to Dylan's appearance are notable not so much as a who-went-electric-first-at-Newport tally, as they are illustrations that electric, danceable, rock-influenced music would have been making inroads into the folkfest scene whether Dylan was there or not. They also cast doubt as to whether black-and-white divisions between the heroes and villains of the event were truly as wide as they've sometimes been portrayed. Seeger, cast as the axman ready to pull the plug on rock 'n' roll that evening, could have hardly been more enthusiastic in his on-screen endorsement of the Fariñas (and, on a slightly later episode of *Rainbow Quest*, of Donovan, who performed on the program accompanied by Shawn Phillips on sitar). Yarrow, credited in the Dylan fanzine *Telegraph* by festival production manager (and soon-to-be leading British folk-rock record producer) Joe Boyd with getting the festival's board to add Butterfield to the weekend lineup, seemed queasy about Tashian plugging in with the duo. (This is Tashian's recollection; Yarrow does not remember giving the Fariñas that specific advice.) If muddy sound was his concern, those fears would be more than confirmed by another show a few hours later.

Richard & Mimi Fariña

t's been mooted that Dylan was not intending to play an electric rock set in his featured spot, only deciding to do so in the stormy aftermath of Butterfield's performance. In some respects, a superstar deciding to assemble a band the day before an important, highly visible concert, one bound to draw controversy and criticism should the music not be up to par, seems unlikely. On the other hand, Dylan had never been (and still is not) one to give much forethought to his band arrangements. "Like a Rolling Stone," after all, had featured an upfront organ part by a musician, Al Kooper, who had barely played keyboards before, and only got on the session by sneaking onto the instrument just before a take while no one was looking. Onstage, however, there would be no second takes if the songs fell apart.

The first and last conversation ever to take place between Dylan and Barry Tashian indicated that Bob may have been taking the matter with less than total seriousness. "I must have known he would have a band, because I remember asking him who was going to be in his band," points out Tashian. "His answer was a total put-on: 'Oh well, I'm gonna have Jack Teagarden on trombone and, like, a full trumpet section, and Mongo Santamaria on congas, do you know him?' That's not a quote, but it was something along those lines."

Dylan was not about to make a jazz jam out of his show, and did select, whether beforehand or on the spot, musicians that played standard amplified rock instruments. The nucleus comprised players from the Paul Butterfield Blues Band: Bloomfield, bassist Jerome Arnold, and drummer Sam Lay. Pianist Barry Goldberg, who played live with Butterfield sometimes, had come to Newport at Bloomfield and Butterfield's invitation, but Butterfield producer Paul Rothchild nixed the idea of Goldberg playing with Butterfield at the event. That did leave him available for Dylan's band, and Kooper, who was at the festival anyway, completed the lineup after being informed by Grossman that Bob was looking for Al. Kooper, indeed, remembers Dylan saying that he had been trying to call him for days, indicating there might have been some forethought to having an electric band playing backup prior to that weekend.

At least two of the musicians, then—Bloomfield and Kooper—had played with Dylan before, albeit in the studio. And, according to Kooper's version in his autobiography *Backstage Passes and Backstabbing Bastards*, the musicians then rehearsed in a Newport mansion that Saturday night until dawn. Contrary to some rumors that have circulated over the years, there *was* a soundcheck, as evidenced by daylight shots of the band (Dylan sporting a loud mod polka dot shirt) playing without an audience in *Festival* (the concert took place after dark). Nevertheless, only three songs were prepared, and an all-night rehearsal may have been inadequate considering the unfamiliarity of some musicians with the material. Drummer Sam Lay, in fact, admits he "had never heard of Bob Dylan before. I was told, 'Hey, they want you to play with Bob Dylan.'" To which Lay responded: "Who the hell is Bob Dylan?"

Lay continues the story with unembarrassed relish: "They said, 'Well, you said you liked that song we heard in such and such a place. *That's* Bob Dylan.' And the fellow that was playing guitar on that record was one of our band members, Mike Bloomfield. Even today, that song would still have to be #1 to me. It was 'Like a Rolling Stone.'" An African-American blues drummer, utterly unfamiliar with Dylan's name, yet already captivated by the "Like a Rolling Stone" single: this was in itself an indication that Dylan's impact had reached far beyond—and could not be contained by—the folk world.

When the band did hit the stage in Newport's Freebody Park on July 25, it was in the midst of the closing evening concert of the festival, in the company of acts that were definitely not going to consider using electric rock bands. Many in the 15,000-strong crowd were there to see Bob Dylan, certainly. Yet an advance flyer for the festival also lists Peter, Paul & Mary, dulcimer player Jean Ritchie, Ronnie Gilbert of the Weavers, country bluesman Mance Lipscomb, Kentucky fiddler Cousin Emmy, and the Ishangi Dance Troupe among the night's entertainment. In the midst of this mixed bag, Dylan was given this curiously worded introduction from Peter Yarrow: "Coming up now, is a person who in a sense has changed the face of folk music to the large American public, because he has brought to it a point of view of a poet. Ladies and gentlemen, the person that's gonna come up now has a limited (chuckle) amount of time. His name is Bob Dylan!" The audience responded with an appropriate roar.

A folk festival sound system, much less effective for large crowds in 1965 than a comparable setup would be in 2000 anyway, was not prepared for the different requirements of balancing and projecting electric instruments to a large crowd. Dylan, sporting a black leather jacket and red shirt, and his ad hoc band did not approach these obstacles timidly. They puttered around on their instruments for a few seconds before blasting into a frenetic "Maggie's Farm," one of the songs from the rock side of the *Bringing It All Back Home* LP.

Bootlegs of fairly good fidelity have circulated of the three-song performance almost since the night it took place. If one were unaware of the historical significance of the surrounding event, it's fair to say that it would not attract overwhelming interest or praise, even within the hermetic clique of Dylanologists. The band, frankly, sounded ragged, compensating for their under-rehearsal with a certain brash, careless yank-the-tablecloth-off-the-Thanksgiving-banquet energy.

In "Maggie's Farm," the sole electric number from the set to appear in the *Festival* film, there was, particularly in Mike Bloomfield's busy, stinging blues guitar riffs, an amphetamined jitteriness missing from the slower studio version. On the bootleg tape at any rate, Kooper's organ is all but buried in the mix. In the *Festival* clip, the cameras focus almost solely on Dylan and Bloomfield, the sparse lighting making them appear almost as ghostly apparitions in a field of darkness. If there's any sense of nervousness on the part of the performers for broaching folkie etiquette, they're hiding it well, delivering the music with apparent zest and confidence.

"Maggie's Farm" was not exactly the most tuneful curtain-raiser Dylan could have chosen, and following it with the new hit single "Like a Rolling Stone" should have given him and his deckhands momentum. Indeed he and the band acquitted themselves respectably on the classic. Dylan's singing was committed and inspired, if hard to decipher on some of the more speedily uttered lines in the verses. Kooper's swirling organ was well to the fore, even if Butterfield's rhythm section played with a tentative feel that betrayed its unfamiliarity with the material. The song, however, crashed to a discordant conclusion that could have hardly sounded less disorganized if the power had been cut. And as with all three electric tunes that night, the demarcation between the band's opening warm-up strums and the actual commencement of the song was so slim as to be virtually nonexistent.

Dylan's final number with the full band, "It Takes a Lot to Laugh, It Takes a Train to Cry," was unfamiliar to virtually everyone in the audience, as it would not appear on record until his *Highway 61 Revisited* album was released at the end of August. At this point, the frail glue holding the band together was seriously cracking. The musicians rushed through the tune with an inappropriate speed, and wound down with a particularly undignified halt, like a racecar running out of gas just short of the finish line. It was not the wisest choice for a curtain-closer, Bloomfield compensating for the slim melody by jamming oodles of notes into both his solos and responsive licks to Dylan's vocal lines. Those vocals were speed-rapped (in contrast to the slow, bluesy studio version with honkytonk piano) so blurrily as to likely be uncodable to an audience that not only had never heard the song, but had spent most of the weekend listening to music with lyrics that were not competing with loud electric instruments.

Then, the singer muttering "let's go, man, that's all," the band's performance was over, about 15 minutes after it started, even if Dylan wasn't quite done for the evening. Heard in isolation, it's certainly not the best of his live music, nor the worst. The performance has taken on a mythical aura not so much due to the music as to what was happening backstage, among some of the festival's power brokers and performers, and in the audience, where reaction to what had transpired could have scarcely been more divided.

Speculation is still rampant as to whether the audience booed Dylan's rock set; whether there were just a few scattered boos; whether there were half boos and half cheers; whether any boos were because of disgust at his conversion to rock music, or at dissatisfaction with the sound system; or whether what's been reported as boos were in fact audience complaints that they couldn't hear the music well. On the bootleg tape of the set, the audience sounds restless and edgy. But there are certainly not loud boos, though the mix might not have been able to capture much crowd noise.

A film of the event might help settle some of these arguments, but Lerner admits he's not even sure whether he filmed all three electric songs, and whether the footage still exists. As for those looking for truth-at-24-frames-per-second in the *Festival* sequence with "Maggie's Farm," Lerner points out that "we didn't have the kind of lighting where we could film the audience at night. We weren't really photographing the audience; we were photographing Dylan. The booing of the audience, I didn't hear. On the soundtrack we have, there's very little booing. It could be our recording wasn't set up properly for the audience."

More trenchant, perhaps, than the ratio of boos to cheers was the visceral reaction of listeners to the show. Lerner, filming Dylan from just a few feet away, was in a better position to gauge that than almost anyone. "I was stunned, actually. I had a sociological reaction, in addition to a musical reaction—it was that intense for me. It felt like I was entering a new world, and I didn't know what it was going to lead to. I'd heard electric music with Butterfield, but it was different. It was like I could sense that something new was being created, [with Dylan's] look and method of singing and the response of some of the people around me. It was exciting and scary."

Joe Boyd, who had helped set the amp levels for the band, does not underestimate the divisive effects of Dylan's appearance. "It was completely schismatic. There were a lot of people who were upset about the rock band, but it was pretty split. I think, probably, more people liked it than didn't. But there was certainly a lot of shouting and arguing, and a sound which you can hear in a lot of ballparks. You used to get this confusion when Bill Skowron used to come up to the plate for the Yankees, 'cause his nickname was Moose. Everybody used to go, 'MOOSE!,' and it sounded like they were booing him. Because you don't get the articulation of the consonant, a crowd shouting 'more, more, more' at the end of Dylan's three songs sounded very much like booing.

"I've heard, recently, a recording of that night, and it doesn't sound to me like booing so much as a roar, just a kind of general hubbub between songs, and during Yarrow's attempt to get Dylan back onstage. I really wouldn't be prepared to say it was 50-50, or two-thirds/one-third, or whatever. But I think there was a segment of the audience, somewhere between a quarter and a half, that was dismayed, horrified, or varying-degrees-of-unhappy about what he was doing."

"I heard 'em booing," insists Paul Nelson, then the young managing editor for *Sing Out!* magazine, and later an editor for *Rolling Stone*. "I was in the photographer's pit right under the stage, about ten feet away from the band. I *heard* them boo. It was full-flowered, blasting rock 'n' roll, and to hear it back, it's really quite tame compared to what he went on to. It's not all that earthshaking. But it was then." According to Michael J. Carabetta, writing in *Boston Broadside* magazine a few weeks later, it wasn't just standard wordless boos raining onstage either, as "some ignorant jeerers were still yelling for Dylan to get his 'folk' guitar."

"It wasn't warm at all," says a bemused Sam Lay, well-positioned to judge audience response from the drummer's seat. "It's hard to say, because you had applause and boos combined. I ain't talkin' about whiskey booze either! You know what kind of boos I'm talking about. At the same time, I have to admit, I could care less. I didn't know what Bob Dylan was all about at the time. I didn't know what the hell I was doing up there, no way." Dylan himself made one of his few direct comments on the matter in December 1965, at a televised press conference for KQED in San Francisco: "I didn't know what was going to happen, but they certainly booed, I'll tell you that. You could hear it all over the place. I don't know who they were though, and I'm certain whoever it was did it twice as loud as they normally would."

In his report on the concert later in 1965 in *Sing Out!*, Nelson was unequivocal not only about the negative audience response, but in his view of a great continental divide emerging that forced listeners to choose sides: "Newport 1965, interestingly enough, split apart forever the two biggest names in folk music: Pete Seeger, who saw in Sunday night a chance to project his vision of the world and sought to have all others convey his impression (thereby restricting their performances), and Bob Dylan, like some fierce young Spanish outlaw in dress leather jacket, a man who could no longer accept the older singer's vague humanistic generalities, a man who, like Nathanael West, had his own angry vision to project in such driving electric songs as 'Like a Rolling Stone' and 'Maggie's Farm'...

"Make no mistake, the audience had to make a clear-cut choice and they made it: Pete Seeger. They chose to boo Dylan off the stage for something as superficially silly as an electric guitar or something as stagnatingly sickening as their idea of owning an artist.... It was a sad parting of the ways for many, myself included. I choose Dylan. I choose art. I will stand behind Dylan and his 'new' songs, and I'll bet my critical reputation (such as it may be) that I'm right."

In the same *Sing Out!* article, Nelson's sentiments were seconded by Jim Rooney, a folk musician from Cambridge, Massachusetts: "It was disturbing to the Old Guard, I think, for several reasons. Bob is no longer a neo-Woody Guthrie, with whom they could identify. He has thrown away his dungarees and shaggy jacket. He has stopped singing talking blues and songs about 'causes'—peace and civil rights. . . . He screams through organ and drums and electric guitar, 'How does it feel to be on your own?' And there is no mistaking the hostility, the defiance, the contempt for all those thousands sitting before him who aren't on their own. Who can't make it. And they seemed to understand that night for the first time what Dylan has been trying to say for over a year—that he is not theirs or anyone else's—and they didn't like what they heard and booed. They wanted to throw him out."

It's important to recognize, though, that several of Dylan's listeners, and musical peers, who were fully supportive of his move into electric rock were dissatisfied or even distraught with the performance. The main objections were to the quality of the sound, and the unpolished execution. Even if the sound quality is fair on the bootleg tape and the *Festival* clip, it must be remembered that what the audience was hearing could have sounded quite different from how the musicians heard it onstage, depending on where you were in the crowd. And by most reports, the sound did not do justice to either Dylan's music or his words. In an August interview with the *New York Post*, the singer himself claimed, "They twisted the sound. They didn't like what I was going to play and they twisted the sound on me before I began."

"It was *terrible*!," exclaims Sylvia Tyson, then part of the top folk duo Ian & Sylvia, who had known Dylan since the early '60s, and been among the first artists to cover Dylan songs. "I'm sure you'll find people who will argue with me that it was brilliant. It wasn't. It could have been great, and it wasn't. It was all over the map, and the sound levels were totally fucked. It was not [that] they hadn't rehearsed it, because Dylan doesn't like to rehearse anything. They played *badly*. They played so loud you couldn't hear him.

"It was a mixed reaction, about 50-50. The people who really hated it *really* hated it, were quite volatile about it. I think it was certainly a visceral reaction against Dylan doing anything that wasn't acoustic. But Paul Butterfield had played at the festival. They knew his band. Dylan wasn't up there with a bunch of strangers."

"'Maggie's Farm' was really quite extraordinary," enthuses Yarrow. "But they didn't have a decent monitor sound system where they could really hear each other. So it was kind of a difficult circumstance in which to really make music that was coherent. And it was very difficult to mix it out there, because it was, idiomatically, not something that was expected."

"It really *stunk*," chimes in Muldaur. "It stunk to high heaven. Bloomfield's energy and note-salad approach to blues, which he could pull off with Butterfield . . . it just was atrocious with Dylan. It had nothing to do with breaking any barriers. It's just, like, rehearse your fucking band and get some better players! Other people may not have that feeling, but a few of my friends do.

"The music sucked. You gotta understand why that meant something to me. I knew that a lot of sucky music was about to come our way, where people [who] could just play six chords and play the same fucking notes over and over again were gonna play electric instruments, start playing all this shit all the time. And that's what happened."

NEWPORT FOLK FESTIVAL

Bob Dylan playing electric rock at the 1965 Newport Folk Festival. Playing onstage, left to right: Mike Bloomfield (playing white guitar), Sam Lay (on drums, partially hidden), Jerome Arnold, Bob Dylan, and Al Kooper

In *Broadside*'s report of the event, eyewitness soundbites weren't much more favorable. Manager Jack Soloman: "Dylan was out of his own element. Butterfield [Paul Butterfield himself, it should be noted, was not playing with Dylan, just some members of his band] isn't a performer. He just lays down music." Joan Baez: "Tonight Bob was in a mess. He's really very good. People just don't understand his writing." Copywriter Carol Adler: "This is the most hostile audience I've ever seen. I don't understand it. Dylan completely knocked them out wherever he went in England." (Though of course Dylan had been playing as a solo acoustic singer in Britain.) And venerated folksinger Theodore Bikel: "You don't whistle in church—you don't play rock and roll at a folk festival."

Yet the same performance is recalled with almost diametrically fervid enthusiasm by others. "I was there in the front pit when Dylan went electric at Newport," says Rick Turner, a guitarist accompanist in the mid-'60s for Ian & Sylvia, and soon to go into flat-out rock himself in the New York band Autosalvage. "The booing has been greatly overexaggerated by many people who were not there. Yeah, there was some negativity. Some of the diehard old-time folkies backstage were having a problem with it. But most of us who were there were lovin' it and blown away. But, I'm sorry, this whole thing of him being roundly booed and all that—I was *there*, man. I didn't hear it. I heard a few catcalls. But I was in fucking row three, boogying. Yeah, the sound wasn't set up for electric. But it was fucking great."

"We loved it," affirms Arthur Gorson, attending the festival in the company of a singer-song-writer he managed, Phil Ochs, who was considered Dylan's closest rival in the art of protest folk. "It was killer. It was pushing the limit again. Audiences that tried to keep their artist locked in some moment need to be rebelled against anyway. The element in the audience that was booing and didn't like the electric was a close-minded audience that needed to be moved along." Dono-van echoes Gorson's sentiments that the Newport hordes were far from the cutting edge, despite their bohemian image: "The audience at Newport Festival were not hip, and reacted like straight bigoted squares would to new developments, even though they banged a bongo or two, and wore sloppy jumpers and berets at weekends."

Still, Gorson qualifies, "It sounded terrible because the facility wasn't equipped to deal with it, and the soundcheck was fucked up, and didn't get a really good chance to balance things. Also, half the time, Dylan sounded terrible anyway, because he never played what he rehearsed and changed things."

"My overall impression was that more people were offended than were enchanted," muses Bruce Langhorne. "Some people were going, 'What the hell's that?!' And some people were going, 'Oh wow!' But I liked it. I thought it was excellent," he delightedly laughs. "Because I believe in innovation." Also among the yay-sayers was rocker Barry Tashian, his lost opportunity to plug in with the Fariñas a few hours before notwithstanding: "I was in the first row in the press area directly in front of center stage. I don't remember any booing. I was digging it and thought most everyone else was too. I thought the folk artists were finally coming around to *my* point of view."

To Al Kooper, the response was not so much a matter of bringing conflicting audience philoso-phies to a head, as a more mundane dissatisfaction with the bang they'd gotten for their buck. "Most were upset that the headliner of a three-day festival performed only three songs for 15 minutes. Many had traveled great distances and sat through music they didn't care for to hear Bob. The aver-age set ran 45 minutes to an hour, so 15 minutes was particularly jarring to those people. They were, in fact, incredulous."

Adds Kooper: "The 'anti-going electric' vibe was not fully realized at Newport. It was much more prevalent backstage; i.e. the Board of Directors; the Alan Lomaxes, George Weins, and Pete Seegers—the old guard who couldn't deal with the changing of the times." Therein lies perhaps the biggest controversy in a night of confusion.

oyd has remembered (in *Telegraph*) fielding complaints from Alan Lomax and Pete Seeger about the extreme volume of the set, and being strongly implored to turn it down (though Paul Rothchild, producer of several Elektra Records acts, including the Paul Butterfield Blues Band, was the one responsible for mixing the sound). That imbroglio, in turn, gave rise to stories, still sometimes repeated as fact today, that Seeger and/or Lomax—usually Seeger—actually attempted to cut the power with an ax, conveniently lying nearby after having been used in a demonstration of work songs. In Eric von Schmidt & Jim Rooney's *Baby Let Me Follow You Down*, Paul Rothchild quotes Seeger, ax in hand, declaring his intention to chop the power cables if the show wasn't halted, Theodore Bikel cooling Pete out with admonition, "You can't stop the future." Which doesn't sound like the words of the same man who told *Broadside* that "you don't play rock and roll at a folk festival."

However, there's no watertight evidence that the "ax" story actually happened. Seeger, understandably weary of deflecting questions about the incident for the past 35 years, at this point declines specific comment about what was on his mind that evening. He refers instead to a 2001 interview in the *Whole Earth Review*, where he told David Kupfer, "The sound was distorted. I ran over to the guy at the controls and shouted, 'Fix the sound so you can hear the words.' He hollered back, 'This is the way they want it.' I said, 'Damn it, if I had an ax, I'd cut the cable right now.'"

In an unpublished 1988 interview with Tom Erikson, he elaborated, "They had, I felt, turned up the volume, and got so much distortion that I couldn't hear anything. The funny thing is that I don't mind distortion when a singer will distort a voice and get a rough-sounding voice, or when a trumpeter gets a dirty sound out of a trumpet. And I didn't mind Bob snarling, and the rough voice.

"But I did want to hear the words, and they had the thing blasting so that I couldn't hear the words. I wanted to go and pull the plug on it. I was real mad. I think the song he was singing was 'Maggie's Farm.' I think it's one of his best songs. But I couldn't make out the words." The evening was quite likely turning into something quite different than he had envisioned when, as Rooney wrote in his *Sing Out!* account, Seeger had "begun the night with the sound of a newborn baby crying, and asked that everyone sing to that baby and tell it what kind of a world it would be growing up into."

Those who have known Seeger for a long time have a hard time visualizing the well-known spokesperson for peace and tolerance actually picking up an ax with intentions of cutting the power. Interestingly, *Broadside* did claim in its coverage of the spectacle, "One of the Festival board members became so upset at Dylan's electric guitar as to threaten to tear out the electrical wiring system. This member is said to have been dissuaded only when it was pointed out that such an act would plunge the whole shebang into darkness and God knows but what riots might ensue." In Jac Holzman and Gavan Daws's *Follow the Music*, Rothchild places eight people on either side of the cable, with more on the way, ready to either cut the power or defend against the ax's blow.

Anna Chairetakis, Alan Lomax's daughter, was present for the festivities at Newport that weekend, and dismisses the ax story: "The actual cutting of cords did not happen." She's more interested in placing the concerns of Seeger and her father—neither of whom held blanket objections to rock 'n' roll or electric music per se—in the context of the event. Lomax had already devoted much of his life to recording and documenting the music of folk musicians, many of them poor southern ones. With the early-'60s folk revival, she feels, Lomax hoped that some such musicians with whom he had worked, like the Georgia Sea Island Singers, Bessie Jones, and Hobart Smith, "could really break through and make an impact. He was trying to get them to Newport and help them to get record contracts. And he also wanted to see them make money, because they were poor and really needed it. He'd been working on this particular angle since he got back from Europe in '59.

"I never heard him ranting against Dylan, in particular. I think, as he saw it, the entrepreneurial aspect of the folk movement, especially as manifested at Newport, won out, and got everyone's attention, instead of the Hobart Smiths and the Mississippi John Hurts. Today they are legends. But when they were alive and still able to perform, they had to compete, in their own forum—Newport—

with people who had more drive, ambition, and know-how. And they couldn't deliver the impact that Dylan did when he merged folk and rock, speaking as he did to the ambivalence I think many young people had about their identity and position as middle-class people, articulating as he did a kind of romanticized cynicism which was very appealing. Dylan was something of an opportunist, in my opinion. He used Newport and the folk revival movement, which was becoming quite tuned in to the traditional artists, as a way to advance, to make his big breakthrough.

"It was frustrating for [people such as Lomax], because here was this guy who's coming in with his own individual special message and style. It was exciting. The issue was that the traditional artists would get pushed to the sidelines again. It wasn't just the fact that Dylan's music was electric or not. I believe there was another electric band at Newport. The situation was what it was later represented to be. And even if Alan had cut the cord, or if he and Pete cut the cord together—though they did not—it didn't mean that he opposed pop and rock. The fact is that he loved early rock 'n' roll. He loved the Everly Brothers and Jerry Lee Lewis, and later Bobby Darin, among other white performers of that early period; later on, he fell utterly in love with soul music."

Sing Out! editor Irwin Silber, who with Seeger and Lomax completes the unholy trinity of supposed old-guard purists who have been unreasonably blamed for standing in the way of progress along the folk-rock highway, was also at Newport. "It certainly created great consternation and great enthusiasm on both sides. And not too many people were left neutral in the middle. Although there probably *were* people who said, 'Okay, wait and see, let's see what he does, let's see what happens.'

"Even if you were appalled by it or against it, too much has been made of the fact that it was about electricity. There were people who were playing electric guitars at the Newport Folk Festival who were not treated that way. So there was a sense that there was something else that was going on.

"What *is* true is that he came back without an electric guitar, and sang some of his older songs, and there was a very positive reaction to that. So it looked like, 'Oh, okay'—sort of breathing a sigh of relief—by a number of people."

It's not certain what Dylan himself thought as he and his backup musicians left the stage, and whether he was intending all along, as a gesture of compromise or not, to end his set with acoustic numbers. The fever pitch of emotion and conflict that some have ascribed to the performers and festival personnel is not necessarily a folk legend. Not long after the event, Eric Andersen, a singer-songwriter and friend of Dylan's, wrote in *Broadside*: "I wasn't at Newport last year but people who were backstage told me that after Bob Dylan got booed off the stage two people cried…Pete Seeger and Bob Dylan, both for totally different reasons. Seeger because Dylan had 'sold out,' and Dylan because he thought the kids didn't like him anymore. They were at opposite ends of the stage, both crying at the same time. It must have looked ridiculous." Yet in *Boston Broadside*, Ed Freeman insisted, "Bloomfield was standing next to Dylan onstage and did not hear any booing, and is reasonably certain that Dylan didn't hear any either…[Dylan] looked disgusted because he hadn't been able to get together with the band on stage, not because of the audience reaction."

"He seemed flustered," says Lerner. "Peter Yarrow kept saying to the audience, 'Come on, let's ask for Bobby to come back and continue.' It took him a while to get that done. Maybe it was

Dylan who was hesitating. But then Dylan came back." Probably Dylan was *not* intending to end his set with acoustic material, or he would not have needed to borrow Yarrow's guitar when he returned to face the audience. In a 1996 interview in *Goldmine*, Yarrow told William Ruhlmann, "It seemed as if he always took delight in shocking people with his new incarnations, and when he went onstage some people say that it was warmly received. My recollection is that it was anything but, that people were in shock and they were amazed and they were upset and Bobby knew that...he was very disturbed by it when he got offstage, and I gave him my guitar, and I said, 'Go back on,' which he did." (Some accounts have Dylan borrowing the guitar from yet another unpredictable entrant into the drama, Johnny Cash.)

On the bootleg tape, restless displeasure from the crowd at this point is much more evident than it had been at any gap between the electric songs, giving credence to Kooper's speculation that the audience was mostly peeved at the brevity of Dylan's appearance. "Bobby was—yes, he will do another tune, I'm sure," said Yarrow, by now sounding just as flustered as Dylan was. "We'll call him back. Would you like Bobby to sing another song? I don't know...listen, it's the fault of the...he was told that he could only do a certain period of time. Bobby, can you do another song, please? He's gonna get his axe." (Meaning his guitar, not the mythical ax wielded to chop the power cord!)

"He's coming. He's gotta get an *acoustic* guitar," noted a progressively anxious Yarrow with emphasis, the crowd's impatient chants of "We Want Bob!" adding to the havoc. "Bobby's coming out now, yes, I understand. But who cares, we want Bobby, and we do...The time problem has meant that he could only do these two [sic] songs. He'll be out as soon as he gets his acoustic guitar." The crowd erupted into applause when Dylan finally did return to continue his performance sans band. The song he chose after several more minutes of farting around, believes Kooper, provided "the true galvanizing moment of the festival—Dylan singing 'It's All Over Now, Baby Blue' to the board of directors, the audience and the world."

If the song, from the acoustic side of the *Bringing It All Back Home* LP, was intended as an ironic kiss-off, it was nonetheless sung and played quite well, and received with far more wholehearted enthusiastic cheers from the throng than his electric set had been. Contrary to some recounts of the evening, however, it was not Dylan's final number, delivered as the ultimate slam-the-door-on-the-past statement. There was one more half-chaos, half-comedy interlude before the closing song, when Bob called out after strumming a few chords, "Does anybody have an E harmonica? An E harmonica, anybody? Just throw them all up!" Dylan stopped, changed keys, and, as seen in the *Festival* film, picked up a harmonica that had been thrown to him from the front rows, bouncing onstage in the darkness.

Dylan launched into a hearty "Mr. Tambourine Man," which had just replaced "Blowin' in the Wind" as the most famous song in his catalog, courtesy of the chart-topping cover by the Byrds. The crowd reacted with a lusty ovation that left no doubt—whether or not they had been booing during the electric part of the program—that this particular audience, at any rate, preferred the older-fashioned, acoustic version of their favorite singer.

Certainly the leading American trade papers of the time viewed the acoustic songs as the ones that redeemed Dylan in the eyes of his followers. Reported Lee Zhito in *Billboard*, "For a brief moment it seemed that he had lost the support of his followers. Shouts from non-Dylan attendees that he go back to the 'Ed Sullivan Show,' or that he shun the electric guitar, brought tears. The indication was that many in the audience felt he wasn't the same Bobby of a year ago—that perhaps he's turned too commercial for the folk purists. Dylan, with the air of one who relishes controversy, soon had the crowd in his palm. A particularly moving rendition of his 'Tambourine Man' brought it to its feet with cheers for more." *Variety* was more taciturn: "Dylan came on Sunday night, backed by a rhythm trio [sic], and performed in typical [sic] rocking style. That, however, was not what his fans expected and they let him know it. He returned later by himself and delivered his current click, 'Mr. Tambourine Man,' which restored him in favor with the crowd."

It might have made sense to schedule Dylan as the final performer of the festival, but in fact his set took place shortly before the interval. The second half of the night's program, dominated by traditional folk performers, stood in stark contrast to the preceding melee, supplying an anti-climactic footnote to a memorable evening. Even Irwin Silber took offense to the closing finale in his *Sing Out!* summary of the festival, as he observed "hordes of singers, musicians, self-appointed participants, and temporary freaks take over the stage in a tasteless exhibition of frenzied incest that seemed to have been taken from a Hollywood set.... It seemed as though everyone wanted to make sure they were in on the big 'civil rights act,' and a moment that might have become the high-point of the entire weekend was suddenly turned into a scene of opportunistic chaos—duplicated once again after the inevitable Peter, Paul & Mary finale and reducing the meaning of Newport to the sense of a carnival gone mad."

The evening concert left both performers and attendees drained and nonplussed at its close. "The whole audience was in a very unsettled state," says Sylvia Tyson. "The organizers didn't know what to do. They turned off the stage lights, and that whole audience was sitting there, not knowing which end was up. That was when Mel Lyman [of the Jim Kweskin Jug Band] went out with his harmonica, in the dark, and played 'Amazing Grace' [remembered in other accounts as 'Rock of Ages'], and settled down the whole audience, totally cooled them out." At a post-concert party for performers that night, the Chambers Brothers played, carrying the new electric sounds even into the post-mortem discussions. In *Baby Let Me Follow You Down*, Maria Muldaur, a singer in the Jim Kweskin Jug Band alongside Geoff Muldaur (to whom she was married in the '60s), remembered asking Dylan to dance. She was answered by his oft-quoted aphorism, "I would, but my hands are on fire."

The reaction of Dylan himself in the wake of the storm is uncertain. In his Dylan biography *No Direction Home*, *New York Times* music critic Robert Shelton remembers how when he saw Dylan a couple of times the following week, "he still seemed stunned and distressed that he had sparked such animosity." But in the *Chicago Daily News* later that year Dylan added, "I wasn't shattered by it. I didn't cry. I don't even understand it. I mean, what are they going to shatter, my ego? And it doesn't even exist, they can't hurt me with a boo." He'd have to get used to wearing such emotional armor. From the summer of 1965 to the summer of 1966, listeners around the world would greet his rock sets with varying degrees of hostility (and enthusiasm), even though he habitually split his show into acoustic and electric halves, offering something for everyone and still managing to displease many.

Tom Rush at the Newport Folk Festival, mid-1960s

The 1965 Newport Folk Festival, and Dylan's segment in particular, has passed into history as the ultimate Armageddon between commercialism and authenticity. At the time, however, it was not considered a newsworthy event on the order of the Vietnam War, or even the 1969 Woodstock rock festival. Curiously, longtime Dylan friend Robert Shelton, perhaps constrained by early evening deadlines in those days before faxes and modems, did not mention Dylan's set in his coverage of the final day's events for *The New York Times*. In Britain, Donovan's on-the-spot reporting for *Melody Maker* simply stated, "Dylan's concert was on Sunday night and I left Sunday afternoon so I didn't get a chance to hear what he was doing." *Sing Out!* and *Broadside* heatedly debated Newport '65's ramifications later in the year, but those were specialized publications with relatively low circulations, read mostly by folk enthusiasts rather than more pop-oriented fans. Much of the luster attributed to the show has likely been awarded in retrospect.

Yet the impact on those who were there—particularly fellow musicians and movers and shakers in the industry—was substantial. Jac Holzman, founder and president of Elektra Records, America's hippest folk label, was standing next to Paul Nelson as Dylan played. In his autobiography *Follow the Music*, Jac Holzman viewed Dylan's appearance as nothing less than an epiphany: "This was electricity married to content. We were hearing music with lyrics that had meaning, with a rock beat, drums and electric guitars, Mike Bloomfield keening as if squeezing out his final note on this planet. Absolutely stunning. All the parallel strains of music over the years coalesced for me in that moment. It was like a sunrise after a storm, when all is clean…all is known." His close friend and associate, Elektra producer Paul Rothchild, went as far as to declare in the same volume, "To me, that night at Newport was as clear as crystal. It's the end of one era and the beginning of another. There's no historical precedent."

In 2001, Holzman remains absolutely certain that Newport was a dividing line between eras, for him and others. "We got it instantly. I'm a little dense sometimes. But I got it, and I smiled, and I wanted to go in that direction. And from that moment on, that's what I did. Did I sign folk artists? Sure. But I was looking for groups at that point."

Some historians have painted Dylan's Newport appearance as a bolt from the sky that pointed the way to the future. Many have given him the lion's share of credit for fusing folk and rock into the style that became known as folk-rock. Some have even intimated, or outright declared, that he invented it. Had Dylan's gig at Newport been as sudden and brilliant an action as one member of a pack lurching in an entirely different direction, it would have been much easier for the purists to roll back the tide. But while he was undoubtedly an important and central figure in the folk-rock fountain, he was in fact just one of many making the move that would combine the best of both styles. In the process a new music was created that was greater than the sum of its parts, simultaneously heralding the death of the resurgence in traditional folk music. That would have been evident to anyone paying attention to events in the outside world that weekend, or in the weeks leading up to it.

In fact there was already no turning back. The Byrds had made folk-rock the hottest trend in contemporary pop with "Mr. Tambourine Man," still in the Top Ten. Soon they would take folk-rock to England, touring as America's response to the Beatles. By the end of the year, their rock adaptation of a Pete Seeger song, "Turn! Turn! Turn!," would follow "Mr. Tambourine Man" to #1. Dylan's "Like a Rolling Stone" would become the biggest hit of his career, reaching #2, a remarkable achievement in 1965 for a six-minute single. The Beatles themselves were bringing Dylan's influence into their own music on *Help!*, both in the confessional title track (another #1 hit) and their world-weary ballad "You've Got to Hide Your Love Away." Entering the charts the week of the festival was not only "Like a Rolling Stone," but also the We Five's pop-rock treatment of an Ian & Sylvia song, "You Were on My Mind," soon to become one of the year's most popular singles. In August, the Lovin' Spoonful, a group led by Greenwich Village folkie-turned-rocker John Sebastian, would climb the charts with their first hit, "Do You Believe in Magic," the definitive celebration of the healing powers of rock 'n' roll.

The same month, Barry McGuire would take protest and blunt discussion of nuclear holocaust and civil rights disturbances onto AM radio coast-to-coast with P.F. Sloan's "Eve of Destruction." The first electric rock singles by folkies Judy Collins and Simon & Garfunkel had appeared by the end of 1965, opening the floodgates for dozens of folksinger-songwriters to plug in during the following year. And in California and New York, ex-folkies who had never reached iconic status were forming the nucleus of the bands—Jefferson Airplane, Buffalo Springfield, the Youngbloods, the Fugs, the Mamas & the Papas, and many others—that would take folk-rock into psychedelia and beyond. American involvement in the Vietnam War was escalating; drug intake and sexual promiscuity were on the rise; campus unrest over the right to free speech was building; and a louder, brasher soundtrack for dissent, rebellion, and celebratory liberation would be needed than could be supplied by acoustic hootenannies. It was a revolution that had been a decade in the making, really, but had become an unstoppable steamroller in the past 18 months, from the time the Beatles took over America's airwaves at the beginning of 1964.

"The times they are a-changin'" Dylan had proclaimed in one of his early, most overquoted protest songs. But actually, Dylan's electric rock debut at Newport did not change the world so much as announce that the world had changed.

1

before the revolution

W alking around the intersection of Bleecker and Macdougal Streets in Greenwich Village on a hot summer night in 2000, you might not suspect this area was the launching pad for the folk music boom of the early '60s. If it still pulsates with energy, it's a high-tech commercial current. The crowded streets are dominated by tourists, weekend car cruisers from the suburbs, cheap falafel shops, overpriced bars and restaurants, and omnipresent loud conversations on cell phones. Strolling north a couple of blocks toward Macdougal and 4th Street gets you away from the beehive, past an artist displaying his posters for sale on a fence. "Remember the '60s?" says the logo on one.

Cross 4th into Washington Square Park, and you're greeted by rap music, blasting from portable radios and tape machines as chess players hunker down at their tables. Continue for a few paces, though, and you begin to get a sense of the artistic community that has fostered folk music and art in the park for decades.

At the southwestern end, a Shakespeare play is in progress on a small concrete knoll. African drummers congregate in a circle further along the south end, on your way to the large open area and circular wading fountain in the park's center. Here a bespectacled African-American guitarist sits, alone, intently playing his acoustic guitar, listening just as intently to the playback of what he's just done on his portable tape deck. A religious speaker has drawn a small crowd nearby, and continuing to the north part of the space, there's a jazzy, mellow guitarist practicing licks. At the north entrance to the park, next to the grand (but currently fenced-off) Triumphal Arch, two more acoustic guitarists trade bluesy riffs as a sort of accompaniment to a small integrated gathering of cardplayers.

It's a faint echo, perhaps, of the bustle of the park during the day on weekends, when skateboarders can drown out the clangs of the assembled instrumentalists. But even now, you can sense the melting pot of cultural influences and urban stimuli that, in the 1950s and early '60s, brought together acoustic guitar, banjo pickers, and harmonizing singers in such places.

Then Washington Square Park and Greenwich Village were the epicenters for a music based on American folk traditions and participatory ethos. Its homes were the clubs and coffeehouses around the intersection of Bleecker and Macdougal. Folk-rock pioneer Fred Neil was even inspired to name his mid-'60s debut album after those crossroads and pose with his guitar at the very juncture of those streets for *Bleecker & MacDougal*'s classic cover photo, capturing its nightlit frenzy of activity at its most romantic (even if its title misspelled Macdougal Street with an incorrect capital D).

The folk music heard throughout Greenwich Village in the five years or so before that photo was taken posed an alternative to the slicker, more manufactured pop stars and recordings dominating the mass media. There were similar satellite communities across North America, in Cambridge, Berkeley, Toronto, Los Angeles, Chicago, Coconut Grove, Austin, Minneapolis, and less celebrated crucibles. With substantial differences, like-minded clans were forming in Britain, at folk clubs and bohemian hangouts in London, Edinburgh, Birmingham, and elsewhere. Together, they would provide the foundations for a generation of folk-rock performers that would shake the world.

The folk-rock they eventually devised would be equal parts folk and rock, if not more rock than folk. The influences that folk-rock combined, however, were coalescing in the early-'60s folk revival, for a good five years or so before "Mr. Tambourine Man" made #1 and gave birth to the term.

Many of the singers and songwriters who created folk-rock began their professional careers around the beginning of the 1960s, as adolescents or young adults in spaces like Washington Square Park or Greenwich Village coffeehouses, strumming acoustic guitars and singing traditional folk songs. In doing so, they became part of a crest of a popularization of folk music, particularly among urban audiences, that had been building in the United States since the beginning of the twentieth century. The seeds of its alliance with progressive politics and championship of the underdog reach back at least to the 1910s, when union activist Joe Hill adapted folk songs and hymns into pro-labor pieces that could be used to rally workers.

American folk music, then as now, got its true lifeblood from singers and instrumentalists playing for their own satisfaction, apart from any notions of making money at it. It thrived in the backwoods of Appalachia, where families would gather to sing in their homes, in their fields, on their porches, and at their churches. It thrived, despite severe poverty and repression, among the descendants of African slaves in the deep South, where the form known as blues began to prosper. It blossomed among cowboys establishing settlements in western territories, and immigrants keeping alive the rhythms and melodies of their homeland in polka, Tex-Mex, and klezmer music. And it often flowered, less romantically, among middle- and upper-class Americans, whether housewives playing on the parlor piano, or doctors relaxing with their banjos.

By the 1920s, with the advent of mass-produced recordings, much of this music was reaching millions more homes and ears than it could possibly have at the beginning of the 1900s. Often companies aimed it at the "race" market, a somewhat condescending term at best, demeaning at worst, that served as a code word for ethnic minorities and poor rural listeners. Many of the first country, folk, blues, jug band, and Cajun records were made during this era, by musicians performing in a manner little different, or no different at all, to how they played in their own homes and social functions. Some of these artists, like early country pioneers the Carter Family and Jimmie Rodgers, sold phenomenal numbers of records, not all of which could have been bought by poor people.

In some ways, this was the time when roots folk music, performed mostly by rural residents, achieved its highest level of popularity. It wasn't necessarily thought of as "authentic," or an expression of the working people. It was just folks doing what they did, the results getting captured on shellac and enjoyed by many like-minded folks, usually from similar backgrounds. The high times came to an end, though, at the beginning of the 1930s with the onset of the Depression. Record sales plummeted, and record labels' specialty or "race" rosters suffered especially severe cuts.

While less roots music would be recorded in the 1930s, such recordings, and the evolution of these sounds, hardly underwent a deep freeze. In the midst of the Depression, the entire work of the most influential country blues artist of all, Robert Johnson, was recorded. Bill Monroe made his first records in 1936, on his path to becoming the most important originator of bluegrass music. The Delmore Brothers made close-harmony country records that anticipated the innovations of rockabilly and the sound of the Everly Brothers. Bob Wills was mixing cowboy music, swing jazz, pop, and blues into western swing. When combined with other popular styles and increased reliance on more sophisticated electric technology in recording and instrumentation, these and many other musicians were planting the seeds for rhythm and blues, electric city blues, and a smoother, more urban brand of country music.

At the same time, a different strain of folk music was gaining momentum that emphasized preservation more than evolution, authenticity more than popularity, and politics more than economics. Although the term "folk revival" is most often associated with the commercial folk boom of the early '60s, the folk revival had really started in the 1930s, particularly among ethnomusicologists, academic scholars, and urban intellectuals. New York City, with its strong traditions of both intellectualism and large pockets of left-to-radical (at least by American standards) citizens, was its stronghold from the outset.

It might seem strange that this most urban of cities would champion folk music that was usually rural in origin. Its relative tolerance of dissident thought, however, made it something of a safe, or at any rate safer, haven for those who had tried to use folk music in conjunction with political activity far from the madding crowd. Lee Hays of the Weavers, who had taught at the radical Commonwealth College in Arkansas; Sis Cunningham and Gordon Friesen, future founders of the folk magazine *Broadside*, who had organized for progressive causes in Oklahoma; Woody Guthrie, the great Oklahoma folksinger and itinerant minstrel—those and others ended up in New York City by the 1940s, often after being hounded for their political beliefs and sympathies. After author and folk song collector John Lomax and his son Alan discovered the great folk-blues singer Leadbelly in a Louisiana prison in 1933, setting off events resulting in his pardon, it was to New York that he relocated, knowing it was there he would find his most appreciative audiences.

The notion of using song to mobilize the masses had taken root in New York earlier in the 1930s with the Composers Collective. These couple of dozen classical composers (including Pete Seeger's father, Charles Seeger) wanted to use their works to advocate leftist causes and trade unionism, although as Peter D. Goldsmith noted in his book *Making People's Music: Moe Asch and Folkways Records*, "the results were songs that were largely unsingable." Far from New York, some folk performers had tried to ally their music with work for social change. Aunt Molly Jackson (another figure who would move to New York in the 1930s) and others put folk songs to political lyrics to support striking miners in Appalachia, and organizer-musicians like Hays and Cunningham had employed folk songs as integral parts of their work.

The marriage of folk and politics in New York itself was bolstered in the early 1940s by the formation of the Almanac Singers, whose shifting membership included future Weavers Lee Hays and Pete Seeger, as well as Woody Guthrie. Even as they came from considerably different backgrounds— Seeger had recently dropped out of Harvard—they were singers and songwriters gifted at utilizing the best of folk traditions, while crafting rousing lyrics pertinent to burning social issues of the day. Other major New York–based folk and blues singers like Jackson, Josh White, Burl Ives, and Sonny Terry would sing with the group. They even made, with considerable courage, recordings of pro-union and antiwar songs. Their impetus was derailed, as was the impetus of the American Left as a whole, by America's entry into World War II. There was no call for antiwar or anti-union songs in the mobilization of the US war effort, and the Almanacs broke up in 1942.

The Almanac crowd resumed its activities after the war, and was instrumental in the formation of People's Songs at the end of 1945. According to Seeger's own report to members in the organization's *People's Song Bulletin*, it would "create, promote and distribute songs of labor and the American people." People's Songs, as was true of folk circles throughout the 1930s and 1940s, included numerous members with Communist and socialist affiliations, and came under increasing heat as anti-Communist sentiment built up in the United States. It folded in 1949, and its cause was taken up by the similar and smaller People's Artists. That outfit was deflated when an outdoor concert they put on in Peekskill, New York that summer (featuring Paul Robeson) ended before it started, at the hands of a large, violent right-wing mob.

Remnants of the Almanac Singers—Seeger and Hays, teaming up with the younger singers Fred Hellerman and Ronnie Gilbert—were at the core of the Weavers. The foursome rocketed to superstardom in 1950 with their revival of the folk tune "Goodnight Irene" (previously popularized by Leadbelly). It sat on top of the *Billboard* charts for an unbelievable 13 consecutive weeks, followed by hits like "On Top of Old Smoky" and "Kisses Sweeter Than Wine."

Their success was a major leap in introducing folk music to the American masses, though even at this juncture, tension between commercial success and purist pressures surfaced. The Weavers recorded their big hits with intrusive pop orchestration, wore tuxedos onstage, and gigged for more than $2,000 a week in Broadway theater. This was bound to draw criticism from those cherishing the ideal of folk songs as tools to inspire the proletariat. Any debate of their success became moot when their left-wing associations began to catch up with them and land them on the widening McCarthy-era blacklist of entertainers. Less than three years after "Goodnight Irene" was a smash, the Weavers, facing insurmountable obstacles in securing gigs and airplay, disbanded.

By this time folk performers in general were associated with subversive left-wing politics in the eyes of some. Several folkies were caught up in the Communist witch-hunts of the House Un-

American Activities Committee (HUAC), and Seeger, White, Ives, and Oscar Brand were all questioned by the committee. The damage inflicted on many careers, not just in folk music but in film and other entertainment industries as well, was enormous. It would take Seeger until 1962 to clear himself from legal troubles spawned by HUAC's investigation, and he remained unofficially blacklisted from network television until the late '60s. Many on the Left never forgave White for his responses to questioning, which were seen by many as too compromising. On top of everything else, while all this was going down, Woody Guthrie was diagnosed with Huntington's chorea, leading to his slow and painful incapacitation and eventual death 15 years later.

Even at this low ebb, the folk revival could not be stopped. John and Alan Lomax, and others, had already done much to elevate the preservation of folk music to a pursuit worthy of academic study and cultural significance. Some Lomax field recordings, such as those of a pre-electric Muddy Waters in Mississippi in the early '40s, had already been assembled for the Library of Congress. In 1952 eccentric folklorist Harry Smith compiled a series of three double LPs for Folkways, *Anthology of American Folk Music*, that were the first archival reissues to restore many seminal folk, hillbilly, blues, and Cajun 78s of the 1920s and 1930s to wide availability. John Cohen and Mike Seeger of the New Lost City Ramblers even made copies of partial tapes of Smith's collection, taken out of the New York Public Library (where Seeger and Ralph Rinzler were cataloguing them) on the sly, to send to musicians all around America.

As the LP or long-playing record format gained popularity in the early '50s, it became more economically feasible to issue such recordings for the commercial market. Among the small, New York–based labels specializing in such catalogs were the aforementioned Folkways, run by middle-aged Polish immigrant Moe Asch, who had the fortitude to record Seeger at the height of the singer's struggles with the blacklist. At the other end of the spectrum was the infant label Elektra Records, founded by teenaged college student Jac Holzman in 1950.

On other fronts, People's Artists, despite its difficulties, had managed to start a new publication after the demise of *People's Songs Bulletin*. Called *Sing Out!*, it was on its way to establishing itself as the most widely distributed American folk magazine, and a crucial forum for the folk revival movement in both the 1950s and 1960s. European tours by US bluesmen, with Big Bill Broonzy in the lead, ignited interest in American folk and blues across the Atlantic, particularly in Britain, where some performers began working toward a curious mixture of Dixieland jazz, folk, and blues called skiffle. British interest in American folk was also piqued by the arrival in the mid-'50s of US expatriate Ramblin' Jack Elliott, a younger disciple of Woody Guthrie, who based himself in the UK for much of the '50s. And near the end of 1955, the Weavers reunited for a triumphal concert in Carnegie Hall, recorded and issued by another adventurous independent label, Vanguard Records.

McCarthyism was on the wane by the time of the Weavers' reunion, and the American musical landscape was also changing. Quite apart from the community of urban folk enthusiasts, a new kind of popular musical movement had coalesced. It was rooted in many of the same folk, hillbilly, and blues traditions folkies held dear, yet was vastly different. It was brasher, louder, more rhythmic, and unabashed in its quest for commercial success, particularly in its targeting of the exploding teenage market. The cross-breeding of country and western music with rhythm and blues was the backbone of the new sound, yet strong echoes of gospel, Tin Pan Alley, swing jazz, and pop vocal groups could be heard as well.

It was, of course, rock 'n' roll. African-American rhythm and blues, close to but not quite the same as rock, had been wildly popular in black communities since the late '40s. It had already been crossing over into the white teenage audience for several years, via adventurous listeners who restlessly span the radio knob in search of something more exciting than the corny, mainstream ballads and pop tunes dominating the airwaves in the early '50s. Bill Haley had been the first white to take a hybrid of country and R&B to huge sales levels, particularly with 1955's chart-topping "Rock Around the Clock."

It was Elvis Presley who truly kicked the rock 'n' roll craze into overdrive, combining the best of white and black music into something new, while grabbing bits of pieces of all manner of eclectic influences—Bill Monroe's bluegrass, Dean Martin's slurry, velvety vocals, southern gospel—to fill out the picture. That he was able to be so eclectic and artistically adventurous, and at the same time become the most popular singer in the world bar none, was remarkable. Elvis was embraced by future folk-rockers such as Bob Dylan, and in some ways he foreshadowed the similar double feat of popularity and unpredictable innovation that would be duplicated nearly ten years later by the Beatles, who gave popular culture a similar jolt. One difference is that many future folk-rockers who were barely teenagers or sub-teenagers when they heard Elvis were, by 1964, performers able to quickly absorb the Beatles' influences into the creation of their own different kind of music.

Rock 'n' roll was well suited for an America that had emerged from World War II with unprecedented economic prosperity, steadily rising standards of living and disposable income, and a yearning for energetic, rebellious outlets in a society that was in many ways conformist and repressive. It was a musical and social climate that was simultaneously confusing and thrilling, and occasionally terrifying. Most 1960s folk-rock musicians came into adolescence in this environment in the mid-to-late '50s, the time at which most of them first began to sing and play instruments—in most cases years before they turned professional.

The great majority of the vital folk-rock musicians made a transition from acoustic folk music to electric rock 'n' roll in the mid-'60s, often to the surprise, and sometimes to the indignation, of their peers and elders in the folk world. But in fact, in many and perhaps most cases, the folk-rockers had grown up as rock 'n' roll fans in the 1950s, sometimes even playing rock as teenagers prior to their conversion to folk music. On rarer occasions, some had even already made rock records. Perhaps some of the anger and controversy targeted at early folk-rockers could have been averted had the extent of their rock roots been realized; perhaps not. But the reality was that in the mid-'50s, they were children of their time. When rock 'n' roll became a supernova and the defining music of its era, these teenagers naturally latched onto it as *their* music, unaware as yet of the countercultural or sociological implications of choosing this bastardized stew over more authentic, politically correct folk forms.

As the son of one of the most revered folk musicians of the twentieth century, and one who grew up in a household in which both folkies and lefties were constantly visiting, one might think that Arlo Guthrie was about the least likely folk-rocker to be a rocker in his early years. Yet when he was 12 or 13, he emphasizes, "the first guitar that I bought myself was an *electric* guitar.

"Popular music in those days wasn't really separated for marketing purposes like it is today. On one radio station, you could hear the Kingston Trio and the next minute you could hear the Everly Brothers, as well as Perry Como or somebody else. I grew up, like everybody in those days, listening to the radio.

"Folk music—probably I had a broader appreciation for what it could be, just because of my own personal background. But I could never really distinguish between the history of it and the modern application of it, whether it was from the Carter Family, which everybody agreed was traditional folk music, or the Everly Brothers, which everybody agreed was pop. It all sounded like it came from the same place to me, and that the talents and abilities that it took to perform it weren't much different in one genre or the other. A lot of my friends were playing *all* these different kinds of music at one time. The same guy could pick up a banjo and play a bluegrass tune, then pick up a slide guitar and play a blues, and then pick up an electric guitar and play an Everly Brothers song."

Some major folk-rock figures now view early rock as not being that far removed from folk in any case. As Donovan notes, "Elvis, [Buddy] Holly, and [the] Everlys used acoustic guitars and double bass in the beginning. Elvis's first single sounds folk-blues now when you hear it." Even back in 1955, *Country Music Round-Up* called Presley "a real 'Folk Music Fireball.'"

The young Jac Holzman, founder and president of Elektra Records

It is by now well known that Bob Dylan was not just a rock 'n' roll fan, but a rock 'n' roll musician, before he switched his focus to folk music at the end of the 1950s. Then known as Bob Zimmerman (and sometimes using the stage name Elston Gunn), he played piano and sang with local bands in Hibbing, Minnesota. The inscription under his high school yearbook photo read, "to join Little Richard." He cited Elvis Presley and Carl Perkins as influences on the sleeve notes to his first album (issued in early 1962), by which time his image was that of a solo acoustic guitar player with a repertoire devoted largely to traditional folk. He even played a couple gigs on piano in North Dakota in 1959 backing Bobby Vee, the teen idol with the watered-down Buddy Holly sound. Dig deeper into the pre-histories of noted folk-rockers, and a love for rock that was at least equal to their subsequent passion for folk seems more the rule than the exception.

Take Roger McGuinn, the leader of the Byrds, and (along with Bob Dylan) the most influential folk-rock musician. When he met the Beatles in 1965, their mutual love of early rock greats was crucial to cementing their friendship. "I found out that George Harrison and I learned how to play the same lick on the guitar at the same time," he told television interviewer Bob Costas on *Later* in 1991, in the wake of the Byrds' induction into the Rock and Roll Hall of Fame. "It's a thing [from] Gene Vincent's record, called 'Woman Love.' It was the back side of 'Be Bop a Lula.' And John Lennon and I talked about it, 'Be Bop a Lula,' and he said that was his favorite record. And I said, yeah, I *loved* that record."

There were numerous other figures with a rock performance history predating their involvement with folk and folk-rock, some surprising, and not all of them teenagers at the time. There was John Phillips, the main songwriter of the Mamas & the Papas (and already in his early twenties when Elvis had his first hit), singing doo wop in Alexandria, Virginia with the Del Ray Locals. Fellow Mamas & the Papas singer Denny Doherty was in a mid-'50s rock 'n' roll band in Nova Scotia. Lovin' Spoonful leader John Sebastian was playing in rock bands at his prep school in New Jersey. Ian Tyson, years before becoming half of Ian & Sylvia (and already approaching his mid-twenties), played rockabilly in Canada as part of the Sensational Stripes, sharing a bill with Buddy Holly, Eddie Cochran, LaVern Baker, and Paul Anka in 1957. Richie Havens sang doo wop on the street corners of the rough Bedford-Stuyvesant neighborhood in Brooklyn. Gram Parsons covered Little Richard and Everly Brothers songs as part of the Legends, a Florida group also including future country-pop-novelty star Jim Stafford and MOR pop singer Lobo. While Peter, Paul & Mary would only tentatively move into folk-rock, even one of their members, Noel Stookey, had played an electric guitar in groups before selling it and taking up a Martin acoustic in his early twenties.

In some cases, the nascent young rock fans even got to make records. The most famous of these were Paul Simon and Art Garfunkel, still in high school when their respectable fusion of pop-rockabilly and the Everly Brothers, "Hey, Schoolgirl," actually made the middle of the *Billboard* Top 100 in 1957, prompting their appearance on *American Bandstand*. In the late '50s Fred Neil made some excruciatingly rare teen idol and rockabilly-type singles, as well as cowriting the Buddy Holly track "Come Back Baby," and playing guitar on the demo of Bobby Darin's hit "Dream Lover." Jefferson Airplane guitarist Jorma Kaukonen recorded a 78 as a member of the Washington, DC rock 'n' roll band the Triumphs. As part of the Squires in Winnipeg, Neil Young recorded Shadows-type instrumentals on an extremely rare local 1963 single, a couple of years prior to his brief attempt to make it as an acoustic folksinger. Marty Balin of Jefferson Airplane did pop-rock singles in the early '60s, such as the Del Shannon-styled "I Specialize in Love," before going folk with the Town Criers. There were even a handful of bona fide 1950s rock stars—namely Dion, the Everly Brothers, and even Bobby Darin—who would eventually make their own excursions into folk-rock in the 1960s, without much of a prior catalog of acoustic folk music in their discographies.

For many of the musicians who would eventually enter folk-rock, though, professional gigging and certainly recording were nothing more than wishful thinking at this point. It was a time for listening to the new rock 'n' roll on the radio, the phonograph, and new music programs like *American Bandstand* on a still-new medium, television. The young enthusiasts spent hours learning to master instruments, as well as picking up on country and blues sounds that, while not exactly rock 'n' roll, were closely related to its source: Hank Williams, Muddy Waters, Howlin' Wolf, Johnny Cash. The entrees on their menu, however, were usually the early rock titans that still cause them to sigh with ecstasy in middle age: Elvis, Buddy Holly, Carl Perkins, Jerry Lee Lewis, Chuck Berry, Little Richard, Bo Diddley, and vocal groups like the Coasters and the Drifters.

It was a golden age, whose impact was felt not just in North America but across the globe, particularly in Britain, where teenagers were forming bands that would be the nucleus of the British Invasion in the mid-'60s. No one doubts the depths of youngsters' devotion to the early rock icons. As it relates to the incubation of folk-rock, the question now becomes why so many rock 'n' roll fanatics abandoned the music for folk in the late '50s, not to reenter rock history—as performers, at any rate—for a good five years or so.

As Arlo Guthrie observed, it should be remembered that back in the 1950s, rock was just one of several styles of popular music. It didn't dominate record stores or radio playlists nearly as much as it would in subsequent decades. Other forms, including mainstream pop vocals, easy listening instrumentals, crossover country music, and novelties, continued to enjoy considerable shares of the market. Folk music was certainly still very much a minority taste, selling far fewer records than rock did. Yet it was continuing to make inroads into the mainstream, a huge and amorphous body that now contained a higher percentage of teenagers than at any prior time in American history.

One underrated performer who did his bit to increase US awareness of folk music, if just a bit, was Harry Belafonte. Now thought of more as an all-around entertainer than a music star, his pop-calypso records of 1956 and 1957, often based around traditional folk songs of West Indian origin, were simply massive. Five of his albums reached the Top Five during those years, with "Banana Boat (Day-O)" making #5 on the singles chart. There were even predictions—in hindsight, by an industry desperate for the wild rock 'n' roll beast to disappear as quickly as it had arrived—that calypso would replace rock 'n' roll as the hottest trend in contemporary music. That didn't happen, though at least one artist with a folk-rock tangent in his future, Vince Martin (an early duo partner of Fred Neil), had dallied with calypso when he sang with the Tarriers, who had their own Top Ten hit with "Banana Boat Song" in 1957. And the Kingston Trio's Dave Guard had previously been in a calypso group (Dave Guard & the Calypsonians) before the Kingston Trio was formed in Palo Alto in 1957.

It took the Kingston Trio to truly make folk music a fad, with far more of an impact than occasional one-shots such as "Banana Boat Song" could deliver. Yes, the group are often roundly disparaged, or even despised, for its whitebread brand of carefully harmonized acoustic folk; its clean-cut image, down to the striped shirts; and its commercial success, of course, based on material that was performed in a gutsier manner by people of poorer backgrounds. The fact remains, however, that it was able to take "Tom Dooley," an Appalachian folk ballad of murder and love, taught to folk song collectors Frank and Ann Warner by Appalachian musician Frank Profitt, to #1 for two weeks in the fall of 1958. The members of the Kingston Trio were themselves far removed from the Appalachian source, having learned the song from an unnamed singer while auditioning for the Purple Onion nightclub in San Francisco. Nor was it even intended as a hit single, only being lifted from their first album after a couple of radio DJs in Salt Lake City started playing it as an LP cut.

No matter. "Tom Dooley" popularized—and introduced—folk music to millions of people who would never have listened to a Folkways LP. The Kingston Trio was amazingly successful (and prolific) over the next few years, with ten additional Top 40 singles, sometimes derived from traditional folk ("A Worried Man"), sometimes written by contemporary songwriters such as Hoyt Axton and Billy Ed Wheeler. Some of them had overtones of social comment and protest, whether expressing concern for the fate of the world (Pete Seeger's "Where Have All the Flowers Gone") or objecting to the Boston transportation system (the sardonic "M.T.A.").

The group was even more of a powerhouse in the album market, landing five #1s between 1958–1960, thus doing a great deal to expand the LP market as a whole—something that could only help struggling folk labels like Folkways. Following in the Kingston Trio's footsteps were more commercial folk groups. Usually white and male, they scored hits with a wholesome and harmonized approach. Middle-of-the-road folk stars included the Highwaymen ("Michael Row the Boat Ashore"), the Brothers Four ("Greenfields"), and the Limeliters, while country artists crossed over to pop radio with a mini-vogue of folky mini-epics, such as Johnny Horton's "The Battle of New Orleans" and "North to Alaska," and Jimmy Dean's "Big Bad John."

The Weavers had already had pop-folk crossover fame at the beginning of the 1950s, but the Kingston Trio were creating, and reaching, a somewhat different audience. "We probably single-handedly created the college market," boasts Frank Werber, who met the group as a publicist for the Purple Onion and hungry i clubs in San Francisco, subsequently becoming the group's manager. "'Cause I'll tell you, when we went out on the road, there was nothin' out there. You'd come to venues, they never heard of lights or a decent sound system. Or [they'd say], 'What, we gotta let blacks in?'" The group reacted in a way that both professionalized and expanded the folk circuit, as well as making an overlooked contribution to desegregation. "We started having all these addendums on our contracts: give us adequate lights, a sound system, and no racial restriction."

Mass acceptance of acts with a style based in roots music always generates interest in the sources of their repertoire. There is no doubt that the hits by the Kingston Trio and its compatriots sent the more passionate and curious of their listeners scurrying for rawer, more "authentic" interpretations of such material. Songs which, more likely than not, would be found on labels like

Folkways, Elektra, Vanguard, the British company Topic, or Prestige, the last of whom was developing a strong country blues catalog.

The Kingston Trio, and even folk groups in the same mold like the Chad Mitchell Trio that didn't have big hits, were cultivating a need for venues to play in across the country. That need was being filled by the appearance of more and more clubs featuring folk music, whether relatively commercial-minded ones such as San Francisco's hungry i and the Gate of Horn in Chicago, or more bohemian coffeehouses like Club 47 in Cambridge, Massachusetts. There was enough of a folk audience to merit the creation of folk festivals, the most prominent being the Newport Folk Festival, which staged its first program in July 1959. The Kingston Trio and Pete Seeger were performers at that event, as was a newcomer, Joan Baez, whose set there would put her on the road to early-'60s superstardom. Folk had built up enough steam to be labeled a craze by a June 1960 feature in *Newsweek*, which noted that artists like the Weavers, Seeger, Odetta, and Theo Bikel were now filling concert halls holding one to four thousand listeners.

At the same time folk was in commercial ascension, rock 'n' roll was in artistic decline. The mammoth energy of the first big boom of rock 'n' roll in 1956 and 1957 had already begun to fade slightly in 1958, as the industry began to predictably react by grooming malleable artists who offered a watered-down counterpart to the wilder sounds of the initial explosion. Then began a chain of events, oft-recited to the point of staleness, that found many of the best early rock singers dying, retiring, imprisoned, or neutered. Jerry Lee Lewis, scandalized by a marriage to his 13-year-old cousin that effectively killed his career for years; Elvis Presley, inducted into the US Army in 1958, emerging two years later, only to retire from the stage to concentrate on silly movies; Little Richard, retiring from the business to devote himself to religious study; Chuck Berry, convicted of bringing an underage girl across state lines for immoral purposes, and then imprisoned. The death of Eddie Cochran in a car wreck during a British tour, and the near-exile of a surviving passenger in that same car, Gene Vincent, to Europe. The deaths of Buddy Holly, Ritchie Valens, and the Big Bopper in an airplane crash in February 1959 were the cruelest blows of all. (Bob Dylan, incidentally, had seen Holly perform in Minnesota just two nights before that crash.)

Roger McGuinn speaks for many performers of his generation when he opines, "I think the rock 'n' roll scene changed from the Memphis sound with Sun Records—rockabilly, Carl Perkins, Gene Vincent, Elvis. Around the time I started getting interested in folk music, rock 'n' roll became more bubblegum. It had less integrity. Folk music offered a good alternative, because the stories were good, the melodies were good, there was a lot of folklore behind the songs. Plus it just had sort of a cool factor to it."

From the time rock histories started being written in the late '60s, a virtual party line has solidified maintaining that rock 'n' roll died in the five years between Buddy Holly's death and the maiden arrival (almost five years later to the day) of the Beatles in the United States. Some would have it that the era was dominated by sappy teen idols, many from the Philadelphia school, like Frankie Avalon, Fabian, and Bobby Rydell. That theory, while containing some elements of truth, is in dire need of re-examination. In fact, although rock 'n' roll was going through a fallow period in many respects, in some ways it continued to thrive and, indeed, move forward and innovate.

These five years, from 1959-1964, saw soul music begin to crystallize with some of the greatest work of Ray Charles, Sam Cooke, and the Drifters, while James Brown, Curtis Mayfield, and Jerry Butler began to ramp up to their own peaks. It was also the heyday of instrumental rock, which retained much of the fire of early rock without much dilution; the birth of both instrumental surf rock and, via the Beach Boys, vocal surf music; the peak of the Brill Building team of songwriters who brought pop-rock to new levels of sophistication; the prime of the girl-group sound, often abetted by Brill Building songwriters; the chief stretch of hits by masterful orchestral rock producer Phil Spector; and the rise of modern pop-soul in the Motown empire. Not to mention some of the best work (at least at the very beginning of the 1960s) of the Everly Brothers, and the salad days of Roy Orbison, the Four Seasons, and Dion.

Clearly there was more driving young musicians to folk music than a perceived decline in the quality of rock 'n' roll. First there was, as McGuinn aptly puts it, "the cool factor." Those raised in subsequent generations of sensory overload may find it hard to comprehend that quiet acoustic folk, which sounds so tame to many twenty-first century listeners, was once considered *the* countercultural music. In part that was because, beneath the layer of the Kingston Trio and the like, folk was still fairly underground, and in-the-making bohemians are always attracted to movements in which the mere discovery of obscure records and books helps set one apart from the mainstream. In part it was also because of its lingering associations with egalitarian political activism, which was implicit (and sometimes explicit) in the humane concerns voiced by many of the songs, whether traditional or newly penned. With anti-Communist hysteria dying down as the 1950s turned to the 1960s, there wasn't as much real or imagined danger in hanging around with the likes of Pete Seeger, who was continuing to tirelessly advocate social justice. He did not allow his political agenda to get in the way of his music, which directly inspired many musicians—network ban be damned—via a busy concert schedule.

"To a greater or lesser degree, we fashioned ourselves as folk purists," feels Barry Melton, a folkie for years in Southern California before he went the folk-rock and psychedelic route as guitarist for Country Joe & the Fish. "Part of the folk movement was from the purist point of view. When I was young and coming up in the folk music movement, I didn't want to learn music from records. I only was interested in learning through the oral tradition. Because that was what kept folk music pure, right? You didn't learn it off records. You learned it from *people*, which is the way it had been passed down for the entire history of humankind. I don't think it makes intellectual sense in retrospect," he laughs. "We were victims of that mindset. Rock music was something that was played on the edge of town by people who didn't have mufflers on their cars, usually in some place like the armory or something. Folk music was played in coffeeshops somewhere near the university campus."

Turning more serious, Melton adds, "Folk music was legitimate, it was something you could discuss, it was music of real working people." He again chuckles in facetious recognition that most folk enthusiasts were not working class, but middle class. "I wouldn't describe myself as upper-middle-class, probably lower-middle-class. But, certainly not deprived by any means. But this was our mind-set. I was playing the blues by the time I was a teenager, and I was interested in playing the blues because it was wrapped in a whole series of political beliefs in which I was involved, which revolved around the civil rights movement. Here was the authentic music of the oppressed black rural South, and that's what I wanted to play. I wasn't interested in playing bluegrass music, 'cause"—he adopts a tone that makes it clear he no longer feels this way— "[it was] the music of the racists who were picking on people who were part of the black rural South, although for various anomalous reasons I played Carter Family songs. But you don't have to be intellectually consistent."

Reawakened fascination with folk music often went hand-in-hand with the birth of a political consciousness. "I was very protected, coming from a Republican small town upbringing," says Steve Gillette, who in the 1960s would write songs for Ian & Sylvia and Linda Ronstadt & the Stone Poneys, in addition to doing his own folk-rock recording for Vanguard. "I didn't really understand anything about class struggle, or about the labor movement, or any of the things that really, I did think, create folk music—what Tom Paxton calls the folk scare.

"But kids in the suburbs were starting to learn to play Roscoe Holcomb–style clawhammer banjo. I had Pete Seeger's first banjo book, and had a five-string banjo in 1958, which I got because I was influenced by Dave Guard. But I went from the Kingston Trio to the New Lost City Ramblers and there discovered all the old Depression songs and labor songs. That started a process of radicalization that's really moved me a long way away from my Republican suburban upbringing. A 15-year-old friend of mine, Dan Paik, came over to play folk music with me, and was a liberal, radical folk kid, the first person I ever knew who had a subscription to KPFK, the [community supported, noncommercial] Pacifica station in Los Angeles. He was talking about the House Un-American Activities Committee, and I had *never* heard anybody talk about the House Un-American Activities Committee. The perspective I had was so whitebread and backward that all of that was some sort of untouchable political taboo."

As Gillette discovered, political naiveté could even be an obstacle to career advancement. "My first manager took me up to the Ash Grove [in Los Angeles] to audition for Ed Pearl. Pearl made a big show of putting me onstage with a microphone, then walking across the room and climbing this little ladder that led up to the light booth. [He] told me to go ahead and start singing, and then came down that ladder and walked out of the room, and didn't come back. It was kind of an obvious putdown. I didn't honestly understand why, but the basic feedback I got back [was] that he felt I was one of those kind of more commercially oriented performers, not involved with labor, not involved with protest issues. And he was right. I was kind of a sheltered kid from the suburbs, just learning to play, not really the real thing."

Whether newly tuned-in folk musicians were political or not, however, the expanding folk community offered a support system at a time in their lives—often their late teens or college years—at which such slightly odd and artistic misfits were hungriest for a bohemian self-image. The burgeoning coffeehouse scene offered a forum for individuality, whether onstage or in the audience, in a period where such outlets were not easy to find. It was no accident that many coffeehouses were concentrated around colleges, and were especially numerous in liberal towns dominated by large universities, such as Cambridge and Berkeley. Even in the late '50s, college students still often endured stultifying regulations such as dress codes, curfews, strict limits on visits to dorms housing the opposite sex, and obligatory ROTC duty. Coffeehouses were refuges against the citadels of conformity, made all the more alluring by their associations with the beatnik scene and controversial author-poets. Even some who would quickly drop out of college would find their true milieu in the university bohemian scenes, as Joan Baez did in Cambridge, and Bob Dylan did when he drifted into Minneapolis's haven for fringe types, the small Dinkytown neighborhood, after semi-attending the University of Minnesota.

Playing folk music, and particularly playing folk guitar, could serve as a badge of sorts for outsiders (the word "freaks" would not come into vogue for years) to identify each other. And it sometimes seemed no accident that folk musicians and fans first found each other when they discovered mutual bonds of outsiderdom, only subsequently realizing that they shared an interest in the same sound and songs too. Debbie Green, who with her friend Joan Baez became a pillar of the Cambridge folk scene, has several times recalled how she and Joan met as two of the only three students among several thousands at a Boston University freshman orientation to refuse to wear beanies. Five years later, Lowell Levinger would meet fellow guitarists Rick Turner and Michael Kane when *they* were the only three people at a BU orientation not to wear their beanies; Levinger (as "Banana") and Kane would go on to play in the folk-rock group the Youngbloods, while Rick Turner would play on Ian & Sylvia's first folk-rock outings.

The urge to get in on the university/coffeehouse action still doesn't fully explain why so many creative rebels chose folk rather than rock as their vehicle for self-expression. The fact is that folk, particularly as its audience widened by the end of the 1950s, offered more and quicker opportunities to carve a niche and make a living than rock did to many of the white, comfortably middle-class youngsters that would form the crux of the folk-rock generation. There was no way that most of them could have been teen idols, even artistically respectable ones like Ricky Nelson or Dion, given their unconventional looks, voices, and personal idiosyncrasies. No one was going to give Bob Dylan a contract as a rock singer in 1960, so nasal and harsh was his vocal tone. And even if he had *sounded* like his brief associate Bobby Vee, Dylan's looks were plain and disheveled enough to ensure that no promoters or record companies would have tried to *make* him into a star like Vee.

Not everyone in such a position was Paul Simon, willing to spend literally years hanging around New York pop-rock studios and chipping away at the margins of the Brill Building in search of a break (and even he would, after about five years of trying, enlist in the folk scene for a better chance). For many, particularly those with a developing social consciousness anyway, folk music offered a much greater opportunity to play music professionally and attract immediate notice. It was even within greater economic reach than starting or joining an electric band, with its costly guitars and amplifiers. All you needed was an acoustic guitar, a harmonica if you wanted to be more versatile, and a neck rack if you wanted to play both at once. "The thing about acoustic music was, you could enthrall an audience with just one guitar," says Eric Andersen, who had learned to play by listening to Buddy Holly, the Everlys, Chuck Berry, and Little Richard. "You could create atmospheres just with language."

All that said, there were those who seemed to meet all the prerequisites for making the move from rock to folk who never did. There was Lou Reed, for example—a sharp, middle-class kid from suburban New York, Jewish (as were a high proportion of young folk musicians and entrepreneurs), rebellious, and literary, studying literature with poet Delmore Schwartz at Syracuse University. He never did stop trying to be a rocker, recording a doo wop single as a teenager in 1958 as part of the Jades, playing in bands in Syracuse in competition with future members of the Blues Magoos and Rascals, working as a songwriter for a cheap rock exploitation label after graduation. Like others in his mold, though (such as folk-rock session keyboardist supremo Al Kooper), his own time for being influenced by folk, as filtered through electric folk-rock, would come by the mid-'60s.

The proliferation of folk venues and grassroots interest in the music also meant that it was easier than ever to get quality instruction in playing the instruments, as Roger McGuinn received in the late '50s at Chicago's Old Town School of Folk Music. When the Limeliters passed through town in need of an accompanist, McGuinn was in a position to accept their offer just after graduation from high school, an opportunity he was unlikely to receive in other popular music mediums. In the early '60s, the startling success of Joan Baez's first two solo albums, consisting of traditional folk songs delivered with acoustic guitar and voice—which made the Top 20 and stayed in the chart for about a year each—no doubt made innumerable others realize that youthful near-overnight stardom in the field was not an impossibility. Baez, after all, had just reached her twenties herself, and had built her own audience in Cambridge coffeehouses.

As difficult as it might be to acknowledge decades later, mercenary motivations also played a part. "Folk music was just a vehicle to get out of Nova Scotia, because it was a popular form of entertainment at the time," Denny Doherty admits without shame. "I had a rock 'n' roll band that I fronted back in Nova Scotia, before folk music came along. On the weekend, you'd make 30 or 40 bucks. Folk music? Hah! Had a television show, we're playing frat houses, let's go to Montreal, play in clubs. It was like a cabaret act, and you could get away with it.

"You couldn't do that with rock 'n' roll. It was, 'Let's have some folk music, let's get a little class to it, we can put that in the room, and we can charge a three-dollar cover charge.' And *that's* why I got involved in folk music. Folk music was a passing fad that a lot of people got involved in because they *could* do it. It was simple and easy enough. You didn't play anything, except a guitar or a banjo, and sang."

areerist aspirations might have been common, but this should not diminish the genuine enthusiasm that many of the musicians shared for the music. It was more than dreams of fame and fortune that caused Dylan, for example, to trade his electric guitar and amplifier for a flat-top Gibson acoustic after hearing an Odetta record— "the first thing that turned me on to folk singing," he recalled in a *Playboy* interview. Even in 2000, when asked by *MOJO* to name the record that changed his life, McGuinn chose not Gene Vincent, or Elvis Presley, but Bob Gibson and Hamilton Camp's *At the Gate of Horn*, taped at live early-'60s folk sets that he attended as part of the audience.

It wasn't even necessary for young hopefuls to get immersed in the urban coffeehouse vibe to catch the folk bug. Remembers Sylvia Tyson, later to team up with Ian Tyson in Ian & Sylvia, "I came to folk music through a very different process than most of the people who were part of the folk era, in that I was from Chatham, a small southern Ontario town. There were no records. There was nobody I could listen to. So I got all of my songs from books. So I didn't have any preconceived notions about how they should be performed."

Tyson's avaricious collecting of songs by whatever means possible was part and parcel of the vital first steps toward becoming a folk professional after developing minimal instrumental and/or vocal competence. A large repertoire of tunes, preferably traditional in origin, was needed, and the more extensive the better. Such a repertoire required much industriousness to develop. The songs were not easily found on the radio. Folk LPs—the more authentic of which were not always well-distributed in any case—were not always easily found and accumulated, particularly for college-aged neophytes without much discretionary income.

Consequently songs were learned via several different channels besides radio and records. There was sheet music, as well as songs published in scholarly books, and more secular-minded magazines—*Sing Out!* being the most prominent. They were gleaned not only from all facets of American folk, blues, and country, but also British Isles sources originating from several centuries back, with some other traditions from around the world tapped as well. Songs were taught to each other face-to-face in dorms, homes, on lawns and beaches (where the acoustic guitar's portability came in especially handy), clubs, cafés, and backstage. The lengthy liner notes to numerous early-'60s folk releases now seem stilted in their minute details of the multitudinous sources of ballads, blues, and broadsides from North America and around the world, like entries in an unspoken competition to determine who could span more territory. They do, however, serve as evidence of just how deeply artists scoured for songs.

Of the records that passed down folk classics to the new generation, the Harry Smith–compiled *Anthology of American Folk Music* volumes are the most celebrated. Arguably their importance has been overemphasized, particularly in the wake of a Harry Smith revival of sorts that saw the albums reissued by the Smithsonian on a CD box set, to considerable brouhaha, in the late 1990s. It's true that songs from the Smith collections showed up in the live and recorded repertoire of Baez, Dylan, and later the Grateful Dead and Big Brother & the Holding Company—psychedelic bands with ex-folkies in their lineups. It's also true that some of these same songs, such as the oft-recorded "Coo Coo" (done by Clarence Ashley on the *Anthology* box, and later by Janis Joplin and Big Brother), could have been learned from numerous other folk albums, or from hearing them done live, either informally or at a show. Still, the impact of such volumes could be not just considerable, but enormous, as Alan Lomax's daughter Anna Chairetakis testifies: "I used to play it over and over and over again. I learned all the songs on one of the albums at one point."

Peter Stampfel of the Holy Modal Rounders does say that Dylan "went through the Smith anthology, made up a whole bunch of songs to Harry Smith anthology tunes when he was starting, just as a way of teaching himself to write songs." Chairetakis adds that "my father loved the anthology. At one point he handed Dylan the record and said, 'Look, if you want to learn to be a folksinger, immerse yourself in this.'" Dylan authority Clinton Heylin, however, pointed out on his Web site that although the singer was taped doing more than 100 traditional folk songs between 1960 and 1962, "only seven come from the *Anthology* (three in arrangements clearly taken from non-Smith versions)." Clearly Dylan and others were gathering songs, sometimes obsessively, from everywhere. Not least among those were recordings overseen by Lomax himself, who, after spending much of the 1950s in Europe, returned Stateside to do a wealth of important field recordings in the American South in the late '50s and early '60s.

Sometimes the hunger to hear and absorb was acute enough to result in what some would view as breaches of ethics. Debbie Green endured the spectacle of watching Joan Baez go through an entire set of songs she had learned from Green, with the same arrangements, at one of Baez's early appearances. Bob Dylan took, without permission, records from the collection of Jon Pankake, a fellow University of Minnesota student who, with Paul Nelson, founded the folk magazine *The Little Sandy Review*. Dylan only returned them after a tense, threatening visit from Pankake, Paul Nelson, and fellow Minneapolis folkie Tony Glover. Among the records poached by Dylan were discs by Ramblin' Jack Elliott and Woody Guthrie, the latter especially serving as his role model for the next three years or so. Pankake and Nelson did know what it was like to lust after Elliott and Guthrie recordings. Confesses Nelson, "One of the main objectives of starting [*The Little Sandy Review*] was to get free records, 'cause we couldn't afford to buy them."

Dylan was certainly taken by Guthrie's music, and maybe even more by Guthrie's image. He devoured Guthrie's autobiography *Bound for Glory*, entranced by the tales of hoboing around the country during the Depression. In his obsession with Guthrie, he was not alone. Ramblin' Jack Elliott, a man a generation younger than Guthrie, had become almost a living incarnation of Woody's style, relaying Guthrie's earthy tales of the road and common folk in much the style of Woody himself. Both Elliott and Dylan took admiration one step further into emulation, adopting the speech and rural appearance of their idol.

Essentially, this allowed them to reinvent themselves into entirely different personalities. Elliott, like Dylan, was not always a rambling cowboy, but of a middle-class Jewish background, born a doctor's son in Brooklyn under the name Elliott Adnopoz. Robert Zimmerman, of somewhat humbler yet still middle-class Jewish roots as a shopkeeper's son in Hibbing, Minnesota, became Bob Dylan, wayward wanderer of no fixed roots and mysterious past, sometimes claiming to be an orphan from New Mexico. For both Elliott and Dylan, their true backgrounds would emerge in due course. But in the meantime it allowed them to spin self-mythologizations that did their part to ensure recognition in the folk world. To varying degrees, the persona of the wandering troubadour with a murky past, fueled by fascinating and sometimes contradictory rumors, would also be exploited by other folk-rockers who started as folksingers in the 1960s, such as Richard Fariña, Dino Valenti, Tim Hardin, and Fred Neil.

For all his naiveté in imitating his hero, Dylan already had some innate talent that would set him apart from others under the spell of Guthrie and his ilk. "When he started out singing, he didn't write songs," says Nelson. "He was just singing Belafonte and Odetta songs, and things like that. You couldn't tell him from 20 people. But the change was overwhelming and extremely fast.

"It's kind of well known that he took a bunch of Jon Pankake's records, and among them was a Jack Elliott Topic recording. We saw him somewhere playing, and he'd gotten that style down in about two days. He went from being a very average interpreter to what he sounded like on [his] first record, blandness to sounding like Guthrie and Elliott, almost overnight. That's when I knew: 'This guy's special.' I've never seen anybody find a style that quick. And he could make it his own. This is long before his first record."

Icons such as Guthrie, and indeed the originators of many songs in the day's folk repertoire, were sometimes made all the more romantic if they were dead and long gone. But Woody was in fact still alive, if in alarmingly declining health, in a hospital in New Jersey, not far from New York. Dylan determined to meet his inspiration in person. For him, as for many young folksingers with exceptional talent, all roads were pointing to New York City.

By the early '60s, there were thriving clusters of clubs and coffeehouses featuring folk music throughout North America (and sometimes beyond). Some were more famous than others, like the hungry i and Purple Onion in San Francisco, the Ice House in Pasadena, the Ash Grove in Los Angeles, the Gate of Horn in Chicago, Club 47 in Cambridge, even another Purple Onion in the Yorkville district of Toronto. There were many others in centers that were not nearly as strong magnets of media attention: Judy Collins emerged from the Denver circuit, Eric Andersen was in company with struggling folkies like John Kay (later of Steppenwolf) and Jackson C. Frank in Buffalo, and Robin Williamson (later of the Incredible String Band) and Bert Jansch kicked around in various dives in Edinburgh, Scotland. But nowhere boasted nearly as strong a concentration of folk venues, and indeed interest in folk in general, as New York, particularly in Greenwich Village.

Gerde's Folk City, the Cafe Wha?, the Gaslight, and the Bitter End were just the most renowned of the Village folk clubs at the time. There were many others, including relatively swank places like the Village Gate that put on some of the more high-rep acts, down to tiny ones near the corner of Bleecker and Macdougal that had starving singers pass hats and baskets through the crowd for subsistence. Izzy Young's Folklore Center on Macdougal might have been the hippest place in the country for picking up folk books, records, instruments, and magazines, and also staged its own performances, including early ones by Dylan and, much later, Tim Buckley and Joni Mitchell.

"I created a place where everybody was equal, in my mind," says Young. "I knew everybody in the audience, I knew everybody on the stage, and there was no separation between the audience and the musicians. No dressing room, no coffee, very narrow benches. People were *suffering* when they sat through an hour and a half, or two hours, of my concerts. Not even a Coke machine. You couldn't even get water."

Folk also boomed on a less commercial, amateur level, with musicians flocking to Washington Square Park to play and trade songs, especially on the weekends. There was also the hootenanny. In his "Johnny Appleseed" column in *Sing Out!*, Seeger recalled first coming across the term in the summer of 1941 while touring in Seattle with Guthrie, where the pair were invited to a "hootenanny"—a community gathering with food, drama, film, music, and singing. By 1951, *Webster's* dictionary was listing one of the word's meanings as "a gathering of folksingers." In New York, hootenannies, whether thought of as such or just informal home parties, were bulwarks of the folk revival.

"It was the most cosmopolitan city in the world," says Art D'Lugoff, who put on both folk and jazz at the Village Gate. "I point it out again and again that Dylan came to New York, and not to Washington or Atlanta, or Philadelphia. They didn't even come to any other borough but Manhattan. That's where people came. Not only for folk, but for many things. It had a very strong leftist-liberal tradition, which en masse was important."

A business structure that both supports and exploits artists is going to sprout around any growing musical movement, no matter how grassroots it is. New York, long the center of American commerce and media (and music publishing), was where much of the business machinery behind the folk boom was located. In addition to the clubs, there were the chief American labels specializing in folk: Folkways, Elektra, Vanguard (which also had an extensive line in classical recordings), Prestige, and Tradition. Major labels, particularly but not exclusively Columbia, were taking a growing interest in expanding their folk rosters, and the best recording studios were in New York, whether affiliated with these companies or not. New York was also the seat of the most dedicated print coverage of folk, with *Sing Out!* magazine and *New York Times* critic Robert Shelton.

Plus there were managers that were realizing that folk was outgrowing its niche to become a big money-earner. These included Harold Leventhal, who handled Pete Seeger and the Weavers, and would pick up Judy Collins (and later Arlo Guthrie). Albert Grossman, after entering the field as part owner of the Gate of Horn in Chicago, had moved into management and moved on to New York. His growing clientele included Odetta, Bob Gibson, and Peter, Paul & Mary, though he lost out to Boston-based Manny Greenhill in his attempts to woo Joan Baez.

Labels and managers were spending increasing resources trying to find and develop new folk stars in the wake of Baez and the Kingston Trio. The industry then, as always, was geared more toward youth than veterans, and rather than focusing on longtime mainstays of the folk revival, was casting nets for young artists in the latest wave. Briefly it seemed as if several labels, envious of the paydirt Vanguard had scored with Baez, were trying to cultivate their own woman singers of traditional ballads with high, pristine voices: Judy Collins on Elektra, Bonnie Dobson on Prestige, and Carolyn Hester on Tradition (and slightly later, Columbia). Albert Grossman combined aspects of the harmonizing pop-folk groups and the lissome folk maiden by teaming Mary Travers with two men in Peter, Paul & Mary. To variable extents, all of these singers (particularly Collins) would outgrow the virginal Madonna image. But even at their outset, their approaches (and sales) opened the possibilities for recordings encompassing a wider and more idiosyncratic range of new folk artists.

For, as most folksingers drew from the same deep well of repertoire rather than writing some or any of their own material, their primary means of distinguishing themselves from the pack would be interpretive skills. Many of them, after all, performed and even recorded many of the same songs, as evidenced by the surplus of versions of staples like "John Riley," "Man [or Maid] of Constant Sorrow," "House of the Rising Sun," "Donna Donna," "Worried Man Blues," "Cuckoo," et al. When folk revivalists began to record such material for the LP market in the 1950s, there was an over-reverent stiffness that bleached out much of the inherent expressiveness of the material.

The purist de-emphasis on individuality could reach, if only in retrospect, comical extremes: folklorist and Folkways producer Kenneth Goldstein, wrote Peter D. Goldsmith in *Making People's*

Music, "believed that [Paul] Clayton was an ideal singer of folk songs because his voice was altogether lacking in color. The very blandness of his singing allowed the songs to speak for themselves without the distraction of the singer's interpretation." This isn't to discount the important contributions that singers like Clayton, Cynthia Gooding, and Theo Bikel made in getting the folk revival off the ground, or the political courage of Richard Dyer-Bennet, the ballad singer who did a benefit concert for the American Labor Party as the Red Scare was gaining force. But there is a reason why barely any of these records have been reissued: they sound not only dated, but often hokey, even prissy.

"The purist attitude at the time was that this golden age was gone, and the right way to do it was to try to re-create it down to the pop and scratch on the old 78 RPM record," chortles Peter Stampfel. "That's certainly a valid viewpoint, but it wasn't mine." He wasn't alone in feeling that the time had come to inject a little more personality, even irreverence, into the old tunes. "I don't think you can go very far with just replicating something that already happened," says Jesse Kincaid, a Cambridge folk musician before helping form (with Taj Mahal and Ry Cooder) one of the first Los Angeles folk-rock bands, the Rising Sons. "Your times are forcing you towards reflecting the sounds and the technologies available in that time."

"There were traditionalists—and they're still around, by the way—who absolutely refused to accept that anything newer than John Jacob Niles or somebody like that could be considered folk music," says Arlo Guthrie. "There were some to whom even my *dad* couldn't be folk music, because their definition of it didn't encourage much expansion."

Nor did everyone take any given version of a folk standard as gospel, since, as Judy Collins observes, traditional folk songs are in fact in an ongoing state of evolution, rather than immutably sacred objects. "We all know that there are many different versions of 'Maid of Constant Sorrow,'" she says by way of illustration. In fact, both she and Bob Dylan recorded that song on their respective debut albums, Dylan singing it as a "Man of Constant Sorrow." "Many classic traditional songs throughout the world have been altered and changed by the folk process. The folk process is a *living* process."

The angelic voices of Baez, Collins, and others brought a vigor and freshness to the idiom. At the same time, the general cleanliness of their approach left room for earthier, bluesier, rawer counterparts, more in line with the grit of Woody Guthrie's dust bowl ballads and the country blues of the rural South. Huskier, smokier woman singers were around, such as Barbara Dane, Odetta, and (simultaneous to the emergence of Baez and Collins) Judy Henske, who invested her vocals with a dash of cabaret belting. On his Prestige releases of the late '50s and early '60s, gravel-voiced Dave Van Ronk gave an immediate urgency to familiar blues and folk material that lifted him far above the usual standard of the era. Earthy performers like Van Ronk could instill the same can-do philosophy in admirers as the Kingston Trio or Baez could. "When I was 16 years old, I went to the Caffe Lena in Saratoga, New York, to hear Dave Van Ronk," remembers Steve Lalor, later to sing and play guitar with Seattle's best folk-rock group, the Daily Flash. "I was both amazed and impressed at how attainable his guitar style was. It did not *look* as impossible as it sounded on his records. The next week, I went to hear Rev. Gary Davis and had the same reaction. I got busy practicing my guitar playing."

When he first arrived in New York in January 1961, Dylan was not far removed from Van Ronk in his style, though his vocals were high and whining where Van Ronk's were down in the gutter. Dylan soon achieved what he set out to do in meeting and befriending Woody Guthrie at Greystone Hospital in New Jersey, though at this point Guthrie was barely able to strum a guitar. He wasn't the only ambitious upstart seeking the elder's blessings. "Dylan and Dino Valenti had both gone to see Woody Guthrie in the hospital," recalls an amused Stampfel, who had only recently relocated to New York from the Midwest himself. "They both felt that Woody would hear them play and say, 'Yes, you have learned your lessons well and you will carry on my glorious life when I am dead and gone.' Bob Dylan once did this tirade about 'how dare Dino Valenti say that and feel that about Woody Guthrie.' I basically agreed with him."

Yet even at this point, Stampfel recognized that Dylan was not merely a Guthrie imitator. "He was the first person that really knew traditional stuff, whose phrasing was rock 'n' roll. In 1961. When I first heard him, that knocked me out. I thought that folk music and rock 'n' roll were the two paths that could never converge. The idea of them converging was completely out of the question, like a boy and girl that you admire hugely, that you wish they'd get together, but you knew they'd kill each other if they came close. But he'd been listening to rock'n'roll since he was about eight years old. He was the first person that had both those things down cold."

What Dylan was singing in New York clubs in 1961 and recording for his debut Columbia LP at the end of the year, however, was not rock 'n' roll. His repertoire, as wide as it was, remained almost wholly traditional, and his singing was accompanied by nothing other than his guitar and harmonica. Apart from any other reluctance he might have had to even think of playing rock music at this point, it would have been considered the apex of impropriety within the folk world to do so. Rock 'n' roll was still viewed by much of the folk establishment as the ultimate in gauche, consumer-driven infantilism, the diametric opposite of the humanistic and communal values folkies revered.

His citation of Presley and Perkins on the sleeve of his first LP notwithstanding, there are indications that Dylan himself was eager to keep any associations with rock at arm's length for the time being. In one of his first radio interviews in 1962 on New York's WBAI, Cynthia Gooding remembered seeing Dylan previously in Minneapolis, inquiring, "At that time you were thinking of being a rock 'n' roll singer, weren't you?," to be met with the nonresponse "Well, at that time I was just sort of doin' nothin'. I was there." On an earlier radio appearance in July 1961, Dylan dueted with Elliott—the fellow Guthrie acolyte, whom Dylan had also befriended—on a savage parody of rock 'n' roll doo wop/teen idol songs, "Acne," written by Cambridge folkie Eric Von Schmidt. There is little or no genuine affection for rock in the not-so-brilliant or subtle performance (now available on the soundtrack to the Elliott film documentary *The Ballad of Ramblin' Jack*), which now sounds less like a loving satire than an affirmation of the folk audience's distaste for the medium. Rock and folk had never seemed as far apart.

Where Dylan made his most radical break from previous generations was not so much through his style as through his songwriting. Just as Paul Nelson had been amazed by Dylan's ability to absorb and imitate Woody Guthrie within days, the Village folk crowd was flabbergasted by his ability to take that further and begin pouring out original songs in the Guthrie pattern at a staggeringly pro-lific rate. Noel Stookey has told the story of how he gave the young writer an article from *The New York Times* about a disrupted boat cruise, to be astounded when Dylan returned the next day with a completed song based on the incident, "Talkin' Bear Mountain Picnic Massacre Disaster Blues." This, like numerous early Dylan outings, was a basic talking blues, but over the course of 1962 his writing matured both lyrically and melodically. His second album, *The Freewheelin' Bob Dylan* (re-leased in May 1963), was comprised almost wholly of original material, in itself a bold step for a folksinger who had yet to secure a national reputation.

The very issue of whether artists identifying themselves as "folk" musicians should be writ-ing songs at all had been an issue of some controversy in the folk community since the onset of the folk revival (and continues to engender less heated debate even now). If pressed for a definition of what constituted a "folk" song, many would have classified it as a song of no known certain author or origin, having been shaped by collective forces and passed down through the generations.

It got to the point, remembers Judy Collins with some amusement, where songwriters would even try to slip their own tunes into circulation by claiming they were traditional numbers. "John Jacob Niles wrote a song called 'Black is the Color of My True Love's Hair'"—a song that became one of the most-covered staples of the folk revival, and one of the first ever recorded by Joan Baez— "[and] passed it off as a traditional song. He was too embarrassed and too righteous to ever allow anybody to think he'd written the song. Same thing with Burl Ives, who wrote 'I Met Her in Vene-zuela,' and claimed that he passed it off as a song he collected from some woman with a basket on her head."

Collins also suggests that the economics of releasing LPs with traditional copyrights might have suited the labels just fine. "When Elektra started, when Vanguard started, when these little folk music companies started, one of the reasons that they were able to stay alive is that they took the copyrights on the traditional songs, and put them in their own pockets. People like me didn't know any better. I didn't know I was supposed to copyright a version of a song. Fortunately I learned by the time I re-corded 'Amazing Grace' [a huge international hit for her in the early 1970s]; I had learned that les-son. But this is how the pockets of a number of these companies were lined, and how they were able to put out the songs. They got the two pennies, or the four pennies, or whatever it was, from who-ever was publishing."

Seeger, Guthrie, and others may have written effective songs of social commentary and per-sonal experience, albeit often based on old folk melodies (as, indeed, many of Dylan's early tunes were). There were substantial numbers of absolutists, though, who viewed folk that had been shaped by the folk process as its only true manifestation. Songwriters could be dismissed as being outside of the music's realm, or even desecrators of the tradition.

On *The Freewheelin' Bob Dylan* and his third album (*The Times They Are A-Changin'*, re-leased at the beginning of 1964), Dylan nudged folk closer to the mainstream of popular culture— and hence, though no one could have foreseen it, rock music—by writing both personal songs that tapped into his generation's zeitgeist, and observational ones that directly or allegorically com-mented upon social issues. "Blowin' in the Wind," its pensive angst reflecting an uncertain world that had tottered to the edge of self-immolation, was the most famous. There were others, particularly what were labeled protest songs, like "Masters of War," which attacked warmongers in the bluntest terms possible, and "A Hard Rain's A-Gonna Fall," which lamented nuclear fallout in far more poetic terms. There were also more romantic songs with as much heart as mind, such as "Girl from the North Country" and "Don't Think Twice, It's All Right." *The Freewheelin' Bob Dylan*'s ripples through folk and indeed pop music were immediate, and much more far-reaching than its good but unspectacular peak of #22 in the charts might indicate.

Stampfel: "No one really thought much about writing songs until Dylan came along, although Tom Paxton was writing songs, and of course Pete Seeger was also. But it was very uncommon. It seems that a lot of people, watching Dylan make up songs, suddenly felt that *they* had to do it, or felt that it was alright to do it, or that [it] was expected of them. Whereas people didn't have that feeling when hearing Tom Paxton songs, which preceded Dylan's by a couple of years. When I started writing songs, I mostly did it the way Dylan started writing songs in 1961, which is putting new words to old songs, which of course is what Woody Guthrie did a lot before Dylan.

"One problem a lot of people had with rock 'n' roll is that the lyrics were stupid"—frequently as stupid, one might interject, as the lyrics heard in the parody "Acne." Feels Stampfel, "When Dylan came along, his premise was you can write about anything. And you don't have to write stupid."

"When he came to the Village, he was initially thought of more as a performer giving homage to Woody Guthrie, in the sense that certain white urban educated young people were making homage to black blues singers," explains Peter Yarrow. "What began to evolve, particularly in Bob's writing and singing, was something that of course incorporated music and influences from the past, but became uniquely his own poetry. And [he] introduced the kind of lyric and intent that was unprecedented. Because it was never difficult to understand the intent of, let's say, Pete Seeger's songs, or Woody Guthrie's songs. But Bobby brought it to a different place."

"We all thought that Bob was phenomenal," says Tom Paxton. "Songwriters love to hear good songs, and it really had the effect of spurring us to keep trying to improve our writing. It just happened that a lot of the good songs we heard were from Bob. The first time I heard Ian & Sylvia sing 'Tomorrow Is a Long Time,' which is a not widely sung Dylan song, I remember thinking, 'That song is utterly beautiful.' I remember my excitement at hearing 'Where Have All the Flowers Gone' for the first time; a guy named Len Chandler sang it at the Gaslight one night. They made me want to write great songs myself."

Buffy Sainte-Marie looks back on the genesis of a new songwriting consciousness with affection, and sees how the folk revival spawned a new audience and performance environment that made such compositions possible: "Our early-'60s generation had the great benefit of a network of coffeehouses which attracted students. My songs—because of that special window of student-powered coffeehouse communication—could be about anything, and still have an audience. Early-'60s songs were real, beyond the old Sinatra/Eisenhower Tin Pan Alley themes. As a songwriter I had the benefit of hearing real folk songs, and tried to write songs that would last for generations (like an antique) and be universal in appeal. That is, (typical college girl approach) I did real research and had no familiarity with the business part of the music business, so I wasn't 'aiming at a market.' The songs were original, unusual, well-researched, and most of all true to what I was seeing around me, which rang true to student audiences and other artists across a wide range of styles."

Broadside magazine was an important agent in fostering a new, socially conscious generation of writers—"topical" songwriters, as they were called at the time. Its impact was felt not so much through the magazine itself, which began as a mimeographed seven-page job with a print run of a mere 300 in February 1962 (by the mid-'60s, circulation was still only a thousand, and even at its peak would not exceed 2,500). Its contribution was providing a forum for new songwriters who usually had yet to land big record deals, or record at all. The issues were centered around printed lyrics and rudimentary sheet music to new compositions, aiming to—as issue #2 declared—"distribute topical songs and stimulate the writing of such songs. Our policy is to let each songwriter speak freely—even though we may not agree fully with the sentiments expressed—and let each song cut its own trail."

Broadside published (in print form, rather than administering in the legal sense) songs by Dylan, Paxton, Phil Ochs, Eric Andersen, a 12-year-old Janis Ian, and less remembered figures like Bonnie Dobson, Gil Turner, and Mark Spoelstra, alongside the tunes of elder statespersons like Pete Seeger and Malvina Reynolds. The words and music to "Blowin' in the Wind" emblazoned the cover of issue #6 in May 1962, long before Dylan had released his version on Columbia, and he was listed as a contributing editor through early 1965.

Sometimes the magazine would even make its own primitive recordings in Folkways' studio, or on a cheap reel-to-reel recorder in the apartment of *Broadside* editors Sis Cunningham (herself a musician) and Gordon Friesen, some of which found release through the Folkways label (including some cuts by Bob Dylan under the pseudonym Blind Boy Grunt). The editorial content expanded to include interviews and provocative essays, such as one on "The Need for Topical Music" by Phil Ochs, who would contribute several lengthy pieces to *Broadside* over the coming years. "I think there is a coming revolution in folk music as it becomes more and more popular in the US, and as the search for new songs becomes more intense," wrote Ochs. "The news today is the natural resource that folk music must exploit in order to have the most vigorous folk process possible."

Cunningham and Friesen were hardened old Left veterans who, as members of the Communist Party, had left Oklahoma in the early 1940s after that state's party leadership was arrested. Journalist Friesen suffered the worst of the McCarthy-era blacklist, unable to secure steady employment after 1948, and the middle-aged pair were not in good economic or physical health as they entered the 1960s. They nonetheless put their all into *Broadside*, run from the front room of their apartment in the projects. The family (including two daughters) also ate in that room, held monthly meetings of songwriters in the apartment (they moved to a larger one in 1964), and even let some newcomers to the city, like Eric Andersen, stay with them for a while. Their hand-cranked mimeograph machine had been handed down to them when the neighborhood branch of the American Labor Party closed. They had no telephone throughout most of 1962 and would not have been able to keep *Broadside* going without financial support from Pete Seeger and his wife Toshi. They were living examples of willingness to sacrifice almost everything for the sake of their ideals and art.

Phil Ochs, the singing journalist

Many of the songs they recorded for Broadside/Folkways releases, and/or printed in the pages of *Broadside*, in the early and mid-'60s can be heard on the Smithsonian Folkways five-CD box set *The Best of Broadside 1962–1988*. The execution and melodies can be plain and dry, the lyrics more blunt than poetic. But even at their most ham-handed, they were targeting maladies of the contemporary world, and not just promoting remnants of Depression-era American radicalism. There were songs about fears of nuclear war, critiques of US imperialism, cries for justice for African-Americans, and rage at media manipulation.

In some cases they were strong enough to outlive their immediate use as agitprop and become perennial standards. Among those compositions were "Blowin' in the Wind"; nuclear fallout allegories whose lovely melodies and gentle lyrics clothed devastating implications (Bonnie Dobson's "Morning Dew" and Malvina Reynolds's "What Have They Done to the Rain"); and Janis Ian's early acoustic version of her teen interracial dating tale "Society's Child." All of those songs would become big sellers when rerecorded by others (and in the case of "Society's Child," by Ian herself) for the pop and rock audience. In such a fashion, the influence of *Broadside*—and, by extension, the Communist- and socialist-rooted progressive politics of Americans like Cunningham and Freisen—spread far beyond its tiny circulation base.

"They helped to foster that sense of community," says Ian. "Otherwise it just would've been a bunch of people running around the Village trying to make it. Sis and Gordon had something more noble in mind. They really mentored two generations of songwriters. If you look at the amount of people who were published there for the first time, from Dylan and Phil Ochs to me, it's extraordinary how people gravitated to them. They were there when you were in trouble, they were there when you were celebrating, they were there to listen to anything new that you wrote and offer their opinions, they were there if you needed to sleep on their couch. You don't find that anymore.

"They had the vision to put on things like the *Broadside* hootenanny series at the Village Gate [with performers like Paxton, Ochs, Seeger, Andersen, Sainte-Marie, and Patrick Sky], and start putting out private records at a time when no one was doing that. You knew when you went to the hoots, you would see good people. You wouldn't be wasting your money. They built up a reputation for encouraging young talent. I mean, I was first published in there when I was twelve and a half. There's not a lot of magazines that would be willing to do that."

"It was a place where we could write songs, have them actually appear in print, and learn from each other," adds Paxton. "And be part of something that was bigger than ourselves. In the context of those years, the civil rights movement and then the war in Vietnam, it was very important to us to have a place where songs on those and related topics could appear. Songs that had, really, very little or no commercial possibilities, nevertheless were appearing in print."

Yet some of those songs *did* have commercial possibilities, as did some of those performers. The signing of topical songwriters to proper record labels (Broadside, and its distributor Folkways, didn't have the muscle to sell many units) really didn't get underway in a big way until 1964. But when it did, many of the better singer-songwriters whose early work can be heard on the *Broadside* box were recording for the biggest independent folk labels, and sometimes even major ones like Columbia. Elektra got Paxton, Ochs, and Spoelstra; Vanguard took Richard Fariña (as part of a duo with his wife Mimi), Sainte-Marie, and Andersen. Columbia already had Dylan, and even prior to signing Dylan had added Seeger, who views his association with a wing of a large corporation pragmatically: "I was trying to break out of the blacklist. And I discussed with [Moe] Asch at Folkways, 'John Hammond wants me to record for Columbia. Do you think I should do it?' And Moe thought only five seconds. He said, 'I think you should. It would be good for you, and good for us.' In other words, if I could show that my songs could sell for Columbia, then they could sell on Folkways too. He had a problem of just staying alive, you know. It was a two-horse company."

Pete Seeger even had a small hit with Malvina Reynolds's anti-suburban blandness ode "Little Boxes" for Columbia, though he continued to be unofficially banned from network television channels like CBS. As it happened, Columbia, in an overlap that worked against its interests in some ways in such cases, was a wholly owned subsidiary company of CBS. The silliness didn't stop there, as the producers of CBS's *The Ed Sullivan Show* told Dylan he couldn't sing "Talkin' John Birch Society Blues" for a scheduled appearance in May 1963. Dylan, who had yet to be on national TV and could have greatly benefited from the exposure, put his principles before his career, and walked off the set. That song never did get a wide hearing, as it was one of the casualties when the track listing for *The Freewheelin' Bob Dylan* was revised at the last minute.

That highlighted at least one disadvantage to recording protest songs for a record label that was a branch of a large corporation, and an advantage to associating with smaller, less powerful ones with more backbone (and less to lose). It was a point of pride to Jac Holzman, as he stressed in a letter to *Broadside*, that Phil Ochs had never been subject to "censorship of any kind," and Elektra also issued material harshly critical of government and social institutions by other topical songwriters on its roster, such as Tom Paxton. "I lived through the blacklist," he says. "The blacklist was an onerous and terrible thing, and all of us were scared by it. I was scared by it. There were all kinds of threats and stuff. I was pleased I didn't cave when there were some people who would have liked to have had me cave, and I just went ahead and did what I wanted to do."

The surge in topical songwriting was not solely a New York or even US phenomenon. "Morning Dew" author Dobson and Buffy Sainte-Marie, composer of the antiwar standard "Universal Soldier," were both Canadian, for example. In Britain, where a somewhat different form of folk revival was taking place that would in turn create different sorts of folk-rock in the British Isles, there were also writers such as Ewan MacColl and Alex Comfort (yes, the *Joy of Sex* author) using the folk idiom to create songs addressing contemporary issues. Seeger was particularly impressed with such material during his British tour in late 1961, writing in *Sing Out!*: "Whereas here in America our new songs either are strictly fly-by-night satirical, or sentimental, or flat-footedly earnest, there the best songs, like those of Woody Guthrie, seemed to capture glints of humor in the middle of tragedy."

At that point, it would have been difficult for many of the topical songwriters to sell great quantities of their own records. It was more than a matter of the odds Vanguard and Elektra faced when competing against bigger labels (though Vanguard was already selling massive quantities of Baez's LPs and hit it big in the singles market with the Rooftop Singers' "Walk Right In"). Dylan's voice was just too grating for most singles-buyer's ears at that point, and he sounded positively saleable next to the wavering pitches of Reynolds, a gray-haired singer in her sixties who hadn't even begun to write songs until her mid-forties. Song publishing, in addition to record sales, is where much of the real earning potential lies in the music industry. Labels, managers, and publishers knew that some of the new breed's songs could be far bigger if they were given the right interpretation. Sainte-Marie might not have been "aiming at the market," as she puts it, but she'd find out just how profitable her protest songs were the hard way: "The Highwaymen were coming off 'Michael Row the Boat Ashore' and they heard me sing 'Universal Soldier' at the Gaslight Cafe in the Village. They asked who was the publisher. A guy at the table said he could help and wrote up a contract making himself the publisher. The recording made tons of money and ten years later I bought the copyright back. Never made that mistake again!"

One of those visionaries on the lookout for songs to publish and record was Albert Grossman. He had engineered the formation, after considering various possible members (including Bob Gibson), of the two-man-plus-one-woman vocal folk trio Peter, Paul & Mary. Their work has not worn well with rock-oriented critics, who scorn the tame, clean-cut precision of their arrangements; their broad cross-generational appeal, which got their album into the hands of many parents who could have never stomached Dylan records; and their dilution of songs that were recorded in more cutting, emotional versions by their composers.

There is no denying, however, the enormous impact of Peter, Paul & Mary's self-titled 1962 debut album, which went to #1 and stayed on the chart for two years. And there were real reasons for their popularity that went beyond clever managerial strategy. Their harmonies were ebullient, with a far greater sense of rhythmic joie de vivre than the standard pop-folk act. Their personas interacted dynamically, with the sex appeal of Mary Travers, the comic interjections of Noel "Paul" Stookey, and the more serious musicianship of Peter Yarrow. Their choice of material, often under the guidance of Grossman, was astute. And if they weren't the most down-home port of entry, they nonetheless did their share to turn many on to the riches of traditional folk music. "Peter, Paul & Mary brought a lot of fairly esoteric folk music to the public attention by playing a quite bland version of it, that then could direct you toward something a little stiffer," believes John Sebastian, "in the same way that Paul Butterfield and Mike Bloomfield had the effect of bringing B.B. King off the chitlin circuit."

The Top Ten hit off their first LP was Pete Seeger and Lee Hays's "If I Had a Hammer" (first recorded as a single by the Weavers in 1949), a rallying cry for brotherhood, sisterhood, justice, and freedom. To get a folk song into the Top Ten was difficult enough in 1962. To do so with a song that had first been performed at a benefit for Communist Party leaders that had been prosecuted under the Smith Act was nothing short of astounding, though no doubt many if not most of those buying Peter, Paul & Mary singles were unaware of its origins and socialist, pro-labor overtones.

The group seemed to be taking a greater risk by putting out a single of Dylan's "Blowin' in the Wind," which they first heard as an acetate passed on to them by Grossman, and which had already been released by the New World Singers (on a *Broadside* compilation) and the Chad Mitchell Trio before they put it on a 45 in June 1963. Dylan was, after all, at this point still a far less famous and acclaimed songwriter than Seeger. Yet the single made #2, greatly advancing not just the career of both Peter, Paul & Mary and Dylan, but also the overall crossover of folk to the pop audience. Another Dylan cover by Peter, Paul & Mary, "Don't Think Twice, It's All Right," followed "Blowin' in the Wind" into the Top Ten later in 1963. In helping expose the trio to fellow client Dylan, Grossman was, in Yarrow's estimation, "giving a gift of a possibility of discovering extraordinarily written material to us. We were *all* a family."

It might be tempting to accuse the musicians and their manager of financial self-interest in their raids of the Dylan catalog. Since he handled both Dylan and PP&M (as they were often abbreviated), and took fully 50% of Dylan's publishing income, Grossman had much to gain by getting Dylan's songs to be hits. Hit covers made Dylan more famous and brought substantial publishing revenue for both Grossman and Dylan. Peter, Paul & Mary were hardly unwitting pawns in Grossman's game, however. Not only was their enthusiasm for Dylan's music genuine, but so was their commitment to the progressive humanism espoused by "Blowin' in the Wind" and "If I Had a Hammer." It was backed up by appearances at events such as the summer 1963 March on Washington for civil rights, at which Dylan also played.

Peter, Paul & Mary's recordings of Dylan material were indicative of a new eagerness throughout contemporary folk in general to broaden repertoire from a traditional base and encompass new, emerging songwriters. Cover versions of Dylan songs expectedly multiplied after "Blowin' in the Wind" charted. Sometimes they marked the first recordings of contemporary material of any sort by a folk artist, as on Baez's 1963 album *In Concert, Part 2*, on which she sang Dylan's "Don't Think Twice, It's All Right" and "With God on Our Side" (Baez at this point was also boosting Dylan's career by having him sing with her on stage).

On Judy Collins's third album, *#3* (from late 1963), she took the then-daring step of devoting most of the set to contemporary material. There were a couple of Dylan tunes, but also work by Hamilton Camp, Bob Gibson, Shel Silverstein (an accomplished folk songwriter, though he's better known as a *Playboy* cartoonist and composer of Dr. Hook's "The Cover of Rolling Stone"), Mike Settle, and Pete Seeger. The closing song was Seeger's "Turn! Turn! Turn!," arranged, as was most of the album, by Roger McGuinn, then a young session musician known as Jim McGuinn (he would change his first name to Roger in 1967), who also played second guitar and banjo.

"I had made two albums which were basically traditional," says Collins. "We sat down and said, wait a minute. There's a whole raft of these wonderful writers—the city singers, the city writers, the music coming out of the contemporary folk scene. I was aware of, and surrounded by, these great writers, including of course Dylan. I saw Pete Seeger all the time, heard him, went to his concerts. Same for Bob Dylan and Tom Paxton and the others that were people that were in the Village. So I was very attuned to the music, and I loved it. I think that my third album was an important album in the folk process, because I think it did bring people's attention to a lot of these songs that were being written by the singer-songwriters of the time." When she recorded her next album in concert in March 1964, she would draw deeper from the surging well of new songwriters, doing songs by Dylan, Paxton, Fred Neil, Billy Wheeler, and future Mamas & the Papas leader John Phillips.

The switch to contemporary material was generated not only by the quality and relevance of the new songs, but also by a certain restlessness with the aesthetic limitations of traditional ones. Collins, unlike many folkies and ex-folkies, is bold enough to state one of the problems bluntly, using one revered source of traditional material, the English and Scottish popular ballads collected by Francis James Child in the late nineteenth century, as an example. "The problem with the Child ballad collection is that it doesn't have melody. You can't collect language without melody. Song is not poetry, and vice versa. I firmly believe that lyric and melody belong together, and cannot be separately presented, or separately studied. And so the real deficit of the Child ballad collection is that there are basically no melodies. Poems are not songs, and lyrics are not poems. And unless they are hand in hand, and respect it as such, they don't do justice to the real point of the folk tradition, which is to carry the melody with the lyric."

She continues, "I can understand the sense of the scholarly approach to adhering to what was. But it was a precious and a kind of narrow, self-protective environment. And there are still people who believe that this is an inviolate sort of tradition that must be expressed in a certain way."

Judy Henske, as is still her wont, describes her frustrations in a particularly colorful manner, when recalling her enthusiasm for the work of Fred Neil, the super-low-voiced singer who was crossing folk with blues, country, and pop. "Remember, these are the old folk days. People are running around singing things like 'Green Broom'—'I went to the woods to cut broom, green broom.' Now how interesting is that? It was the longest folk song ever written; it, like, lasted 20 minutes. And it was the most *boring* song that was ever written. I used to sing it to punish audiences. But if you had a Fred Neil song to sing, you weren't punishing the audience. You were rewarding them for sitting there, because it was an inevitably really great song. When he wrote 'The Other Side of This Life,' it was a very well-considered and musically well-written piece of philosophy."

Ian & Sylvia, the harmonizing duo whose songlist was more diverse than almost anyone's, were catching on to freshly minted songs as well. Now transplanted from Toronto to New York, and under

Grossman's management, they put Dylan's "Tomorrow Is a Long Time" (which Dylan himself didn't release until the early 1970s) on their second album for Vanguard in 1963. Just as crucially, they, and some others who had begun to cover new songsmiths, were in turn inspired to begin writing themselves. In their case, it was almost as if the years of immersion in all shades of folk was immediately distilled into something that took the best ingredients, yet sounded distinctly different. Ian Tyson's first composition (also on their second album) was "Four Strong Winds," which tapped into on-the-road wanderlust as effectively as any ageless folk number. Sylvia Tyson's first composition, released in 1964, was "You Were on My Mind." Both remain the respective writers' most famous songs, and both, particularly "You Were on My Mind," would play an unforeseen role in the gestation of folk-rock when they were covered by rock bands. They and Collins (who would not begin writing songs for a few years) would continue to popularize barely or never-recorded songwriters throughout the 1960s, including fellow Canadians Gordon Lightfoot and Joni Mitchell.

Sometimes the competition for new material could get comically cutthroat. "Ian & Sylvia were really the ones who discovered Gordon Lightfoot as a songwriter," says Rick Turner, who played guitar on the duo's 1966 album *Play One More*. "There was an incident at the Grossman office regarding 'Early Morning Rain,' which Peter, Paul & Mary wound up with the big hit on. Well, the demo had come into the Grossman office, done by Ian & Sylvia. Ian really wanted that to be released as a single, and suddenly Peter, Paul & Mary had the big frigging hit with it. Ian was *pissed*. He went to, I think it might have been Stookey, and basically accused him of stealing the demo and ripping off the song. Upon which the reply was, 'No no, man, we never even heard it.' To which Ian said, 'Well, how come you changed exactly the same words I changed?'"

Yarrow, who says that the only version of "Early Morning Rain" he heard was Gordon Lightfoot's, observes that "it wasn't a question of people racing for hits. Basically, we were all for each other. When you were in the Village, you walked around from place to place and watched other performers and heard their songs. Nobody was secretly keeping their songs. People weren't even copyrighting their songs. It wasn't about money. It was about the work, the excitement, the feeling, and the response to the music. So everybody was sharing with everybody else. And everybody was *borrowing* from everybody else in terms of spirit, form, and experimentation."

By late 1963, folk music was at its greatest level of acceptance and popularity within the pop world. Peter, Paul & Mary and Joan Baez were selling more LPs than almost anyone. PP&M had made Top Ten singles, and other acts were taking occasional songs into the top of the chart, as did the Rooftop Singers (with Erik Darling, who had been in a later Weavers lineup) with their #1 "Walk Right In," an adaptation of a song first issued in 1930 by the Memphis jug-blues band Cannon's Jug Stompers. Trini Lopez somehow managed to get to #3 with another version of "If I Had a Hammer," only a year after Peter, Paul & Mary. The New Christy Minstrels made the Top 20 with "Green, Green," featuring the hoarse lead vocals of Barry McGuire.

Time had put Joan Baez on its cover in November 1962, beginning its story with the memorable intro "anything called a hootenanny ought to be shot on sight, but the whole country is having one." The same magazine followed up with a major feature on topical folk songs the next summer. By that time ABC television had a show devoted to folk music, *Hootenanny*, and that once-esoteric word was now part of everyday vocabulary. An August *Billboard* headline trumpeted "Hoots Name of the Game This Year," and Hollywood even tried to get in on the act with an exploitative 1963 MGM film *Hootenanny Hoot*, featuring Johnny Cash, Judy Henske (singing in a bathing suit), and the Brothers Four (singing from trained seal bandstands).

On top of its commercial presence, folk was more in tune with the mood of the American audience than it had ever been. The crumbling of the worst aspects of McCarthyism and the Cold War had led the way for new freedom of expression. There was overdue advocacy for civil rights for African-Americans, a cause with which many folk musicians, white and black, allied themselves. College-age political activists were making their own break with outmoded tradition by building a New Left in the Students for a Democratic Society. President John F. Kennedy, for all his considerable flaws, kindled hope for progressive social change and decreased discrimination with the more liberal aspects of his agenda, as well as projecting youthful energy that many young liberals felt mirrored their own. "Why are we in the midst of a folk boom?" asked Dylan in the *New York Sunday News* that October. "Because the times cry for the truth and that's what they're hearin' in good folk music today."

"Do you realize the power of folk music?" queried Peter Yarrow in a *Saturday Evening Post* cover story on the folk boom. "Do you realize the power of PP&M? We could mobilize the youth of America today in a way that no one else could. We could conceivably travel with a presidential candidate, and maybe even sway an election. Not that we're going to use this power. It's enough to know that we have it. . . . I'm part of a group and a movement that is saying to people, 'We care about you, we want you to feel our love, we're not trying to feed you placebo tablets'. . . . We're not out to protest anything. Our purpose is to affirm. We get up on stage to show how beautiful it is to open your heart, to feel pity, to cry, to get involved."

"Folk music had become the dominant music on the airwaves in America around 1963," says Yarrow now. "What it brought to the scene was the full legacy of folk music as an expression of social consciousness, a way to create community, and really be a part of social change. When I say part of social change, I don't mean just as the trimming, but a kind of exchange of hearts connection that really energized and reflected the feelings of people, and ultimately their determination to forge a fairer and more just society. This music was filled with a sense of honesty that was untainted by the simple desire to make money, which was not necessarily the prevalent motivation for writing and singing music prior to the folk renaissance in the 1960s."

The times seemed ripe for folk music to act as an important vehicle for changing society. If only subconsciously, perhaps some were also thinking that the spirit and values of folk could reach even more people if it merged with elements of rock music. For in 1963—even though rock 'n' roll had supposedly died in Buddy Holly's 1959 plane crash—it was still the most popular music in the English-speaking world.

Rock had intimately interwoven strands of folk music into its fabric since coming into being, and there are innumerable examples of early rock songs, going back to the 1950s, based partly or almost wholly on folk material. Even laying aside the many rock covers of blues songs, there was Elvis covering Bill Monroe's bluegrass classic "Blue Moon of Kentucky" on the flip of his first single in 1954; Ritchie Valens adapting the Mexican traditional tune "La Bamba" for his most well-remembered smash; and the Fendermen making an outrageously silly rockabilly version of Jimmie Rodgers's "Mule Skinner Blues" into an off-the-wall Top Five hit in 1960. In the late '50s another, now-seldom-mentioned, Jimmie Rodgers (no relation to the Depression-era country great) had hits that matched vaguely rockabillyish pop with folk songs, including "Kisses Sweeter Than Wine," which the Weavers had done with some success earlier in the decade. In 1961 the Tokens took "Mbube," a traditional Zulu song that had previously been done by the Weavers as "Wimoweh," gave it a doo wop pop arrangement, retitled it "The Lion Sleeps Tonight," and had a #1 single.

There were more subtle examples, such as Lloyd Price's "Stagger Lee," a murder tale with origins in African-American folklore that had been recorded in variations by Woody Guthrie, Cisco Houston, Mississippi John Hurt, and others. Part of the lyric of Chuck Berry's "Reelin' and Rockin'" had appeared in "Right Now Blues" in the late '20s by Memphis blues minstrel Frank Stokes. And in the late '50s, the Everly Brothers—revered by rockers-turned-folkers as much as Buddy Holly was, and then at the peak of their superstardom—made the daring move of releasing an entire album of acoustic country and folk material, sometimes traditional in origin. Titled *Songs Our Daddy Taught Us*, the LP included some songs, like "Barbara Allen," that were standbys in many a folk set, though the record was really a detour to pay tribute to the siblings' Appalachian roots, rather than an attempt to merge folk and rock 'n' roll.

Folk-rock, at least as it sounded and was usually defined by the media in its 1960s heyday, differed from such material. It would mix the fully developed form of rock 'n' roll with what folk had evolved into by the early-'60s folk revival; it was not a less-conscious integration of aspects of folk as rock 'n' roll matured. While strikingly obvious attempts to concoct such a blend would not become evident until 1964, the roots of its approach ran deeper than many realize.

For one thing, while most of the crowd in the Village and like-minded scenes were sticking wholly to acoustic folk in their gigs and recordings, it was becoming more apparent that many of them harbored a closet love of classic rock 'n' roll. "Rock 'n' roll had really gone into a tailspin in 1958 and 1959," offers Stampfel. "I'm sure everyone is aware of the details. But one thing that people don't notice that much is that it turned around again by 1962. That's the year that the Beatles had their first hit [though only in England, with "Love Me Do"], the Stones formed, the Beach Boys had their first hit. All the wonderful girl groups were coming in. Phil Spector started his whole string of hits.

"When I first played the Gaslight in '61, after-hours people would start to do Everly Brothers songs and obscure Chuck Berry songs. We'd go, 'This is great stuff. You think so too? Yeah, I think so too.'" Such after-hours sessions were not solely Village phenomena. Steve Lalor was in the early '60s roaming West Coast clubs like the hungry i with "Hey Joe" author Billy Roberts and Lynn Shepard as the Driftwood Singers. "Folk music was politically incendiary but artistically whitebread," Lalor feels. "My folk trio did 'Midnight Special' the way Chuck Berry might do it. It was received as 'refreshing.' There was a lot of 'Kumbaya' energy around folk music. In our trio format, it was also limiting. We had no rhythm section. Our guitars were amplified only by mics. We created dynamics and tension, but it was difficult to attain the groove of blues, gospel or rock. When we played in Vancouver's Cave, Billy introduced us to the after-hours scene, and we sat in with [soul-rockers] Bobby Taylor and the Vancouvers, featuring Tommy Chong [later of Cheech & Chong] on guitar. Lynn and I would do Jimmy Reed, Bobby Blue Bland, and obscure Chuck Berry tunes to the wee hours of the morning."

"The negative attitudes toward rock 'n' roll, which a lot of people had, were actually changing by '61 or '62," adds Stampfel. "Even people that had a negative attitude toward rock 'n' roll [would] basically still like Chuck Berry and Little Richard." And some of them were already beginning to make tentative moves toward letting a little rock 'n' roll into their own records.

It is still little known that in the late '50s, Buddy Holly and early-'60s folk revival notable Carolyn Hester did some recording together, a connection fostered by sharing Norman Petty as producer. Jerry Allison, from Holly's band the Crickets, contributed brushes on a cardboard box to a song on Hester's rare 1957 album *Scarlet Ribbons*, and in 1958 Holly and the Crickets did some still-unreleased material on a Hester session in Clovis, New Mexico. Hester herself is unsure of what songs were completed, though she believes one of them was the Holly-Petty tune "Take Your Time," which Holly recorded on the B-side of his classic hit "Rave On."

Hester believes the influence might have gone both ways. "Many years later, a German magazine interviewer for *Rock 'n' Roll Times* told me that as a youngster he had been mad for Buddy Holly," she says. "He said he persuaded his parents to let him go with a group of friends to London, because Buddy Holly was going to come there from America. It was 1958, and the London theater had a fabulous pipe organ. When Buddy was introduced the curtain was raised, but neither Buddy nor Crickets were anywhere to be seen. Then the crowd heard the mysterious sounds of an organ being played, and as the pipe organ, in all its magnificence, emerged, rising from the pit, there was Buddy sitting and playing. He sang a song from my first album: 'Black Is the Color of My True Love's Hair.' So all through those early years, I thought it was Buddy influencing me when critics said I was the most rhythmically inclined of the folksingers. It was 1996 before I found out that Buddy not only had been there when I was recording, but that he must have 'let it [Hester's folk influence] in.'"

A mutual enthusiasm for Holly's work would help lead to the presence of Dylan in September 1961 on harmonica for some cuts on Hester's self-titled Columbia album (a session which in turn helped Dylan catch the attention of Columbia producer John Hammond, who signed him to the label). "Dylan's being there was sparked by my meeting him one night at Gerde's and the fact that he, a Buddy Holly fanatic, couldn't get over my singing [Holly's] 'Lonesome Tears,'" says Hester. "He came up after my set and said, 'That's a Buddy Holly song. He's one of my heroes.' Of course, I had to tell him I had known Buddy, and that is the basis of my friendship with Bob ever since.

"A few months later, in Boston, Bob asked me about helping him get some gigs, so I said that coming up next were these sessions. I said, 'I wouldn't need any guitar help because Bruce [Langhorne, later to play on dozens of folk-rock sessions by Dylan and others] is playing, but would you want to come play harmonica? My dad played harp for me on a record one time.' Bob replied, 'Just let me know where and when.'

"Of course, I had already been in a recording studio with Buddy Holly and the Crickets. So even though I was a folksinger, I was really looking forward to stepping up and stepping out with my hand-picked 'band.' I knew exactly where we were going with this even if John Hammond wasn't sure. He demanded and received an in-person rehearsal, and, bless his heart, he saw the light. This was BIG folk music, and even better, I thought I was taking a page out of Buddy Holly's book—that even though we were young, we were roots. We weren't rockabilly, we were folkabilly. If I could just say that we 'swung' I think that would come close."

While *Carolyn Hester* and some other progressive folk albums of the early '60s do not sound close to rock music to modern ears, they often did have a rhythmic verve and fuller arrangements that were helping to slide them closer to a rock sensibility. With the exception of bluegrass or old-timey bands such as the New City Ramblers, contemporary folk albums usually stuck to a plain acoustic guitar accompaniment, perhaps with acoustic string bass as well. Just as some purists wanted to keep folk material traditional, so were they determined to keep accompaniment traditional, or what they thought was traditional.

As Rodney Dillard of the bluegrass band the Dillards (later to upset the traditional apple cart with their own use of electric instruments and nonfolk influences) notes, purism could be taken to ludicrous excess. "I came from a rural area, grew up on a farm with no electricity and no bathroom, until I was fourteen. We were coming out of that music, which had been around just like the dogs in a yard; I grew up with it. These intellectuals who discovered bluegrass music were coming from an intellectual/educational/social approach. At that time, everybody was wanting to put it in a museum, keep it the way it was, and just look at it once in a while, and protect it so it didn't change.

"Our first album, *Back Porch Bluegrass*, had echo on the record. And one of the guys from one of the little back-east rags said, 'Since when did they have echo chambers on back porches?' Well, that guy'd probably never been off his block. Because you sit back here on my back porch right now, and you get nothing but echo, because I live up on a side of a mountain. That kind of flippant statements by people who have no frame of reference of which to judge something like that got me sort of at odds with these people at the time."

Ian & Sylvia made underrated contributions in beefing up folk arrangements without yet venturing into electric instruments, underscoring the earnest exuberance of their stirring harmonies with Sylvia's own autoharp and skilled second guitarists such as John Herald. The punch and finely sculpted tenor of their music were not accidents, stresses Sylvia Tyson: "The norm at that point was not to rehearse a lot. Once you got down the chords, you just kind of played it. We were aware that we probably put a lot more time into arrangements, of double lead lines and things like that." Adding oomph on albums by Ian & Sylvia, Hester, Odetta, and others was Bill Lee, a jazz musician (and filmmaker Spike Lee's father) who became the top New York folk session acoustic bassist.

Just as Judy Collins's *#3* album was a significant landmark in the shift of repertoire from traditional to contemporary, so was it a key step in the expansion of instrumental color on an album by a major folk artist. Those colors were provided in large part by second guitarist, banjo player, and arranger Jim McGuinn. The two Pete Seeger songs, "Turn! Turn! Turn!" and "The Bells of Rhymney," would be done within a couple of years by the group McGuinn would soon found, the Byrds, in rock versions so full and powerful they would make the Collins tracks seem like unplugged dressing room warm-ups. For that reason alone, *#3* would be an important root of the folk-rock sound. The very manner in which McGuinn got involved was symptomatic of a growing interaction between the supposedly pure folk world and the blare of the larger commercial pop one.

"I had a musical director who knew Jim [as he was then known] McGuinn, Walter Raim [who arranges and plays on a few songs on *#3*]," recalls Collins. He said, 'I want you to go hear Jim. Because I want to think about a little bit more expanding in terms of instrumentation on this album.' And I said, 'That sounds good to me.' We wanted some interesting sounds. So I went, actually, to Las Vegas to hear Jim McGuinn play. He was in the band and on the show with Bobby Darin, and would play backup for Bobby Darin on the banjo. A wonderful banjo player, of course. And then he would do his little solo set. I saw him and said, 'Oh, this'd be fun, to work with Jim. He's got the kind of feel that I like.'

"When I put the album out, it was wonderfully received. In fact, 'Turn! Turn! Turn!' became a bit of a minor hit out of that album. It was the first time that the *Gavin Report* [*Bill Gavin's Record Report*, a top music industry tip sheet] took any notice of me; they wrote about 'Turn! Turn! Turn!,' and how terrific it was. People were playing it and listening to it, and it became certainly a very important part of my repertoire."

These recordings by Collins, Ian & Sylvia, and Hester nonetheless were well shy of actually introducing electric instruments. This was the biggest no-no of all to folk purists, though actually there were some little-noted cases of respected folkies playing with full bands that included electric guitar, as on Bob Gibson's 1960 Elektra novelty folk LP *Ski Songs*. Gibson, seldom mentioned in the media these days, is often cited as an influence by folk-rock musicians for the harmonies he did in his short-lived duo act with Hamilton Camp (especially heard in the work of Simon & Garfunkel, who used a cover of Gibson-Camp's "You Can Tell the World" to lead off their debut LP).

John Sebastian feels that Gibson's 12-string guitar work was especially influential on a moodier, bluesier brand of folk troubadours beginning to make the rounds of Village clubs in the early '60s: Fred Neil, Dino Valenti, and Richie Havens. "Gibson was the first guy to take a 12-string knowing what Leadbelly had done with it, knowing how to jazz up a folk strum a little. Gibson was a masterful strummer with a very, very light and agile touch. When he played, he sang very light and easy, but the 12-string was really slammin'. He wasn't using drums, but he was getting the effect by just the use of accents and things in his guitar style." The full, reverberant sound of the 12-string could be judged as another sign on the road to the fuller sound of folk-rock.

Prior to 1964, little evidence of the new 12-string slingers exists on record. An unreleased 1961 demo acetate of seven traditional folk songs by Valenti survives, demonstrating his skill at combining chunky 12-string guitar strumming, somber and biting vocals, and haunting minor chords to build a tense mood unlike the generally far more polite folk recordings of the time. Playing an acoustic 12-string to build up a wall of sound is not the same thing as doing rock 'n' roll, however, and it would take Bob Gibson fan Roger McGuinn to fully realize the electric possibilities of the instrument.

Happy Traum, who would go on to edit *Sing Out!* in the late '60s and record with Dylan in the early '70s, has an anecdote from personal experience that explains how the purist mindset helped undermine a little-known early attempt to match folk with electricity. Traum was in the early '60s a member of the New World Singers, who had recorded "Blowin' in the Wind" for *Broadside*. He had also played and sung with Dylan on a *Broadside* version of another Dylan composition, "Let Me Die in My Footsteps." Around that time the New World Singers were signed by Atlantic Records.

"We were fairly purist in our approach to electric stuff at that point, as were a lot of people," he says. "It was kind of like a point of honor in a way not to sort of go commercial with what was considered some of the more rock 'n' roll kind of instruments. When the New World Singers did our Atlantic album, we were produced by Ahmet Ertegun [the legendary Atlantic executive who helped nurture the careers of dozens of great R&B and rock acts of the 1950s and 1960s]. We kind of knew that this was kind of a big deal, but didn't know quite how big a deal it really was at the time, because we were so into the folk thing.

"Ahmet was trying very hard to get us to add electric bass and maybe a little drums, or maybe a little Fender guitar in there. And we were extremely resistant, and kind of fought him a lot. We were trying to make a commercial record; we were trying to sell records. But we felt we had to sell the way the Weavers might have sold, or other kind of groups that were more in the folk world [would have]. But he didn't really understand where *we* were coming from, and we certainly didn't understand where *he* was coming from, which was this really deep knowledge of R&B and black music," as demonstrated by Ertegun's work with stars like Ray Charles.

It was also apparent that those thinking of adding electricity to rock from the other side of the control room might not have been ready to meet the folk world halfway. Continues Traum, "To just put in perspective where he was at in terms of folk music, when we first got signed, the most exciting song that we knew—and the one that we most wanted to record for him—was 'Blowin' in the Wind.' I think it was after we had done it on *Broadside*; it was close to that time. I remember [being] in the empty studio, with Ahmet sitting in a chair. We were standing, the three of us, in front of him singing 'Blowing in the Wind.' When we finished, he said, 'Well, it's nice, but if you could change the words so it was a love song, it would be fine.' And we said, 'But don't you understand? This is written by this amazing poet.' And he said, 'Well, it'll never sell.' And then of course Peter, Paul & Mary's version came out." Atlantic was scooped again by Peter, Paul & Mary when the New World Singers put out a cover of Dylan's "Don't Think Twice, It's All Right" on Atlantic in May 1963, only to see PP&M's version become the Top Ten hit.

The most notorious pre-1964 attempt by a folkie to go electric was Bob Dylan's "Mixed Up Confusion," recorded in the fall of 1962 and issued as an extremely rare Columbia single. The track was like an anachronistic blip from the future, its rambling lyrics of alienation and basic, repetitive blues melody bearing much similarity to his rock records of the mid-'60s, albeit with more pronounced Jerry Lee Lewis and Little Richard influences. The music and words were not nearly as strong as they would be on his 1965-66 releases, lacking, as some other Dylan originals admittedly

Ian & Sylvia, in 1962

did, virtually anything in the way of a catchy tune. Too, he and the session musicians seemed ill at ease with the whole enterprise of creating a rock record. The drums (by well-known New York sessionaire Herb Lovelle) and piano clattered away at a tempo suggesting they were rushing through the takes as quickly as possible, and the guitars were barely audible in the mix.

Much confusion still surrounds "Mixed Up Confusion." Izzy Young wrote in a notebook he kept (quoted in Anthony Scaduto's *Bob Dylan*) that Dylan wrote the song on the way to the session, did three sessions for the number, and was disgusted by the results. John Hammond told Scaduto that Albert Grossman had the idea that Dylan should be recorded with a Dixieland band for the single, although the song sounds anything but Dixieland. It's also been suggested that Dylan walked out of the final "Mixed Up Confusion" session after finding that a Dixieland horn section had been booked to embellish his latest attempt at the song. In the liner notes to the 1985 box set *Biograph*, Dylan curtly dismissed the whole enterprise: "I didn't arrange the session. It wasn't my idea."

What's more, Dylan did three other songs that autumn with a band backup, including covers of "That's All Right, Mama," which Elvis had sung on his first single, and "Rocks and Gravel." These also had a tentative feel, as if the musicians were holding back for fear of playing too loudly or uninhibitedly on a folk album. (Still unreleased, these attempts, as well as different versions of "Mixed Up Confusion," appear on bootlegs.) Another, a quite nice rendition of "Corrina, Corrina," actually came out on *The Freewheelin' Bob Dylan*, though the drums were so light as to inspire no comment or outrage among purists. Perhaps Dylan was simply dissatisfied with his attempts to record with a band, or he and Columbia felt or realized that putting out rock at this point might alienate some of his constituency. In any event, the "Mixed Up Confusion" single was withdrawn soon after its release at the end of 1962, and it would be a couple of years before he recorded with a band again.

From the most commercial side of the music industry, there were odd rumblings suggestive of a desire, though perhaps purely exploitative, to mate rock and folk. The folk boom was big enough that record labels wanted ways to capitalize on it, even with performers who had no real roots in the form, if only to give them an excuse to fill out full-length releases they were cranking out for the LP market. There was a spurt of folk—or vaguely folk-themed anyway—records by rock singers well into 1964, some of them ludicrous from every angle, such as twist king Chubby Checker's *Folk Album*.

More artistically credible artists made tentative ventures into the folk repertoire. The Four Seasons' *Born to Wander*, subtitled "Tender and Soulful Ballads (Folk-Flavored)," included a got-to-wander road song, "New Town," by an all-but-unknown Phil Ochs (who would never release a version himself). There were also some attempts to give folk artists quite mild drum backing, as Chess subsidiary Argo Folk did on Dean DeWolf's 1963 effort *Folkswinger*, and the Rooftop Singers did on their hit "Walk Right In." There were LPs of session musicians doing rock-ish instrumental versions of folk hits, like Billy Strange's *12 String Guitar*, with covers of "Walk Right In," "Tom Dooley," "If I Had a Hammer," and the like, the backing crew including top Los Angeles rock session drummer Hal Blaine. But for the most part, these ventures were somewhat in the novelty vein, with the aim of broadening the appeal of mainstream entertainers, or squeezing some juice from the folk boom before the bubble burst.

Some of these experiments were nonetheless more interesting than others. Bobby Darin, a Mr. All Things To All People who had done rock, show tunes, straight pop, and more (including a cover of Leadbelly's "Rock Island Line" in 1956), had introduced a 15-minute folk interlude into his concerts, with Roger McGuinn on 12-string guitar. Jackie DeShannon, a promising soulful pop-rock singer-songwriter in Los Angeles with a growing curiosity about folk, did a 1963 album of traditional and contemporary folk songs including Dylan's "Blowin' in the Wind," "Don't Think Twice, It's All Right," and "Walkin' Down the Line," the last of which Dylan never released in the '60s. DeShannon, deeply impressed after seeing Dylan in concert at Town Hall in New York, had actually wanted to do a whole album of Dylan songs, which might have been a first in 1963. "I said, 'He's going to be the James Dean of rock. He's it!'" she told Steve Escobar in a Jackie DeShannon Appreciation Society newsletter in 2001. "And they just didn't see it. And I've said this many times, if I had been with John Hammond at Columbia . . . had I been with a visionary, I think my career would've been very different."

Trini Lopez, after years of scuffle as a pop-rock singer, became one of the biggest LP sellers in the world with 1963's *At PJ's*, a live-in-L.A. nightclub set with faintly Latin go-go rhythms. Lopez played electric guitar on the rocked-up versions of "If I Had a Hammer" and Woody Guthrie's "This Land Is Your Land," and Mickey Jones, later to play with Bob Dylan on his 1966 world tour, was on drums. "I took the song, and I made it not only listenable, but I also made it danceable," claims Lopez regarding his hit cover of "If I Had a Hammer." "Folk music was really in; I liked the melodies, I liked the lyrics. But I didn't do 'em the way they were being written. I did 'em *my* way. I changed them around for my own satisfaction, my feeling of the songs, and *my* beat. I bet you people that weren't too much into folk got into it more, because I brought a freshness to it." If the thought of Trini Lopez as a folk-rock progenitor sounds heretically far-fetched, consider that Marty Balin of Jefferson Airplane cited him as an influence in the liner notes to the *Jefferson Airplane Loves You* box set, telling Jeff Tamarkin: "I remember when Trini Lopez was doing folk music to electric instruments and it was very tacky, but the idea was cool."

Another surprising early-'60s act that some folk-rockers view as having helped to jump-start the folk-rock connection was a British group, the Springfields. Featuring a young Dusty Springfield, they had an American Top 20 hit in September 1962, more than a year before the British Invasion got underway, with "Silver Threads and Golden Needles." They also did versions of folk songs like "Lonesome Traveler" and "Allentown Jail" with full band accompaniment, even if the arrangements owed more to middle-of-the-road pop orchestration than rock 'n' roll. Still, says Jerry Yester—then in the Modern Folk Quartet, which would make its leap into folk-rock soon enough—he and Barry McGuire, then in the New Christy Minstrels, would "listen to that stuff, and it blew our minds. 'Cause we were still flat-out in folk music, and to hear this John Barry-[type] band behind the Springfields . . . we loved it."

Of all the pre-British Invasion records that toyed with folk and rock simultaneously, the most effective was the title track of the second album by Yester's future wife and musical partner Judy Henske, *High Flying Bird* (released at the beginning of 1964 on Elektra). As originally written, "High Flying Bird" was definitely a folk song, penned by Billy Ed Wheeler (who had cowritten the

Kingston Trio's hit "The Reverend Mr. Black"), with an arresting minor-keyed melody and brooding lyrics contrasting the freedom of a bird to the singer's earthbound misery. Henske's magnificently bluesy, down-and-dirty vocal was given a full band backup, with electric guitar by Jack Marshall, 12-string by John Forsha, and drums by Earl Palmer, veteran of countless New Orleans and Los Angeles rock and R&B sessions. Worthy of being a hit single, it wasn't, though the song was incredibly influential, showing up in the early repertoire of several key folk-rockers, including Stephen Stills (who recorded it with the Au Go-Go Singers) and Jefferson Airplane (who did it at one of their first recording sessions in late 1965, and onstage at the Monterey Pop Festival in 1967, with Marty Balin and Grace Slick trading lead vocals). A similarly successful grafting of full-band rockish backing to a low-voiced woman folksinger, this time with wicked blues-jazz organ, can be heard on Judy Roderick's treatment of "Brother, Can You Spare a Dime?," though that didn't come out until May 1964.

"I wanted drums," booms Henske, who believes she influenced later husky women singers such as Cher and Janis Joplin (Elektra boss Jac Holzman also cites Cass Elliot of the Mamas & the Papas as someone who borrowed from Henske). "And they said, 'Well, you can't have drums. Judy Collins doesn't have drums. Or Joan Baez doesn't have drums.' I said, 'But they're sopranos and I'm not. And *I* want drums.' I think that's how it started. I had that very heavy backup rhythm; that was John Forsha. When I went out on the road, I finally did have drums, with a full band: piano, bass, drums, guitar." As for "High Flying Bird," adds Forsha, "I agree that the song could be called folk-rock, although that wasn't our intent. We took a country-folk song, head arranged it, and gave it to a jazz combo. Although hindsight is 20/20, I don't believe anybody was thinking rock at the time."

S eismic shifts were in the works, though, that would have everyone thinking about rock soon enough. It might not have been readily apparent in the summer of 1963, but the folk boom was soon to run out of steam. Perhaps nothing is as emblematic of its decline as the swift rise and fall of *Hootenanny*, the TV series launched in early 1963 by ABC to showcase folk music. Filmed in half-hour segments on different college campuses, the show to surface appearances was a breakthrough initially, getting good ratings and featuring top performers Judy Collins, the Clancy Brothers, the Limeliters, the Journeymen (with John Phillips), the Big Three (with Cass Elliot), Bonnie Dobson, and Bob Gibson. It was the vehicle for a further modest breakthrough by including an interracial group, the Tarriers, on one episode. Naturally its tight mass-oriented format also meant an over-reliance on whitebread performers, and other compromises, as Collins found when two verses of her interpretation of "John Riley" were cut to fit time constraints.

Yet the show ran into problems when it almost immediately emerged that Pete Seeger was not going to be invited to perform, as his unofficial blacklist from network television was still in effect. The list of artists who consequently boycotted *Hootenanny* reads like the top drawer of acts that the show *should* have featured, including Peter, Paul & Mary, Bob Dylan, Joan Baez, the Kingston Trio, Tom Paxton, Barbara Dane, Ramblin' Jack Elliott, and Carolyn Hester. ABC's Manhattan studios were picketed; when Jack Newfield of *West Side News* pressed the show for an explanation, he was told, unbelievably, by executive producer Richard Lewine that Seeger and the Weavers "were not invited because we wanted better folk singers....We used the Smothers Brothers because they are far better than the Weavers." The ACLU declared that ABC's refusal to allow Seeger to appear was an "arbitrary censorship of the citizen's right to see and hear," and the *New York Post*'s James Wechsler urged ABC to "call off its holy war against Seeger." *Hootenanny* would only capitulate to the point of offering to give Seeger a slot if he would sign a loyalty oath; Seeger, naturally, refused.

Says Hester, who appeared on the program before becoming aware of Seeger's predicament and subsequently helped organize the boycott: "ABC called me several times to come back to the show, stating that Pete Seeger would have this problem on any network in America because of his testimony before the House Un-American Activities Committee. To me, it was black and white. It was the spirit of Senator Joe McCarthy against the spirit of Pete Seeger. No contest. The boycott, in effect, broke the back of the successful run that folk music had enjoyed."

Seeger summarized the situation in *Sing Out!* a few years after *Hootenanny*'s cancellation: "I never knew the real power of TV till 1963. For 20 years we had used the word 'Hootenanny' to describe a democratic kind of songfest where homemade music of many kinds could be swapped, where racism would receive short shrift, where the whole audience, young and old, could join in on union songs, old spirituals, and sharply pointed new songs. But in six short months 99 percent of the nation received a whole new definition of the term. The old definition was almost obliterated. A hootenanny was now a gay variety show where nothing controversial would ever be presented."

The folk boom's demise was more than a matter of dilution of the talent pool willing to appear on one program (which, though it expanded to a full hour for the following season, went off the air in late 1964). Just as Roger McGuinn had felt that rock 'n' roll was going the "bubblegum" route in the late '50s, now he saw that the wheel had turned full circle, with folk getting watered down as well. "Folk music, by around '63, had kind of run its course," he says. "It had gone from being an obscure art form back in the '40s and '50s to a tremendously commercial medium. And the genre had become overdone. *Hootenanny* was exploiting folk music to the point that it turned it into bubblegum. What had happened to rock 'n' roll had happened to folk music, and it was time to change gears and get into something with a little more interesting . . . a little more integrity, something that had more meat to it."

What that something might be was not clear. In keeping with the trend among some progressive folk artists to diversify their instrumentation and flesh out their arrangements with more players, some felt that the growing number of jug bands might provide a clue to the new direction. Inspired by large ensembles of the 1920s and 1930s that had mixed blues, folk, and vaudevillian humor on all manner of odd instruments, jug bands like those of Jim Kweskin were forming, injecting some needed irreverence into the folk scene. Predicted Izzy Young in *Sing Out!* in late 1963, "The jug band will be the next phase of American folk music to become commercially popular and will cause a tremendous run on old jugs, kazoos, washboards and similar items."

Young was right that there would be a tremendous run on a new arsenal of instruments by young folk musicians. As for what kinds of instruments they would be, he was dead wrong.

2

meet the beatles

....

oger McGuinn, like many folk musicians of his generation, still remembers the immediate and indelible impact of the first time he heard the Beatles.

"It was probably a 30-second commercial that Brian Epstein had put together that had the Beatles onstage with screaming girls. They were playing, I guess, 'She Loves You' or one of their early songs." [Possibly this was a clip of the Beatles doing "She Loves You," aired on *The Jack Paar Show* on January 3, 1964, which was the first widely publicized and viewed footage of the group on American television.]

"I thought that was really interesting. I loved the beat, I loved the harmonies. So I went to the record store on 8th Avenue in Greenwich Village, and found *Meet the Beatles*. I took it back to where I was living in the Village, and listened to it over and over and over again. I learned *all* the songs," he laughs. "And really got into it.

"They put together the rockabilly scene . . . they mixed it with blues and bossa nova and classical and all kinds of influences. They kind of made a stew of all these different forms of music. Quite unconsciously, I'm sure. It was tremendously appealing to someone who had been in folk music and heard all these chord changes in folk music, and then heard them put into a different beat. They made it into, like, a heavy 4/4 beat.

"They borrowed the Phil Spector beat that was happening a little bit earlier than they were, like 'Da Doo Ron Ron' and that sort of thing. The beat from those songs got into the Beatles, and they repackaged it with more folk music chord changes. By the time I heard it, I went, 'Ah! This is really cool.' I loved their modal fourth and fifth harmonies. I thought they were really wonderful.

"So I started incorporating the beat that they were doing into the folk songs I was doing in Greenwich Village. And that was really the beginning of what turned into folk-rock and the Byrds."

David Crosby, then living with a British friend named Clem Floyd while playing solo at a folk club in Chicago, had almost the same reaction. "Clem walked in one afternoon with that first Beatles album, *Meet the Beatles*," he told *Goldmine*. "He put it on, and I just didn't know what to think. It absolutely floored me. 'Those are folk music changes, but it's got rock and roll backbeat. You can't do that, but they did! Holy yikes!' I ate it for breakfast."

In February of 1964, Jerry Yester was part of the Modern Folk Quartet, one of many wholesome young groups singing cheery, harmonized acoustic commercial folk. He and his bandmates were poised for nationwide exposure after landing a contract with Warner Brothers, the label of Peter, Paul & Mary, before something utterly redrew their road map. "A couple of months before, we had our album cover taken, and these kids came up and said, 'Are you guys the Beatles?' We said, 'Who?' And Henry [Diltz, the group's banjo player] said, 'Oh yeah, I read about those guys in *Newsweek*. They grow their hair long, and they're real big in England.' We were just hearing little things, and then heard they were gonna be on *The Ed Sullivan Show*.

"We rented a motel room just to watch *The Ed Sullivan Show* when the Beatles came on, 'cause we wanted to know who the hell these guys are. We watched the show, and it was like, this bolt of electricity went through everybody's brain. That was *it*. No more haircuts. Within a month, all the pawn shops were cleaned out of electric instruments. The group was like a tadpole that started growing legs, and then got arms. Chip got an electric bass, I got an electric guitar, and in less than a year, we were a rock band. And all those little folk clubs became little rock clubs.

"When the Beatles happened, it was a very magical thing for so many performers. It was like, 'That's the direction, boys! That way!' Folk music *died*, I think, a month after *The Ed Sullivan Show*."

Roy Marinell, later to write or cowrite songs for Warren Zevon like "Werewolves of London" and "Excitable Boy," was in 1963 just another struggling young folk musician from Chicago, where he had known the teenaged McGuinn. "In the first week of July in '63, I heard 'Please Please Me' by the Beatles on the radio, driving through some obscure part of Arizona, New Mexico. 'What is *this*?' We cranked up the volume, and thought it was black guys, to be honest. I never heard it again until the following year.

"There's two moments in music that I remember hearing. When I was a kid I heard Elvis, 'Heartbreak Hotel.' I remember going 'What?,' jumping up, running over, and cranking that thing up." The other was on December 26, 1963, the official release date of the Beatles' "I Want to Hold Your Hand"—Marinell can still quote the exact day. "I was home for Christmas in Chicago, driving on Lakeshore Drive, going north, right where the Lakeshore Drive ends. I heard 'I Want to Hold Your Hand.' That was a turning point for me. When they hit that lick"—he mimes the riff George Harrison plays during the verses— "'Oh my god, what is that?' That was when it changed for everybody. Everybody starting playing Beatles songs."

And, he could have added, everybody started *listening* to Beatles songs, bohemian folk purism thrown to the dogs. "A few days after that first performance on the Sullivan show I spent the evening with some friends in a cafe in my hometown," wrote Greil Marcus in *The Rolling Stone Illustrated History of Rock & Roll*. "It was, or anyway had been, a folk club. This night one heard only *Meet the Beatles*. The music, snaking through the dark, suddenly spooky room, was instantly recognizable and like nothing we had ever heard. It was joyous, threatening, absurd, arrogant, determined, innocent and tough."

I t is no exaggeration to claim that the Beatles changed everything, and not just for young folk musicians, but for young
people of all sorts throughout North America, Britain, and
much of the world. It was not just the freshness of their
music, which as McGuinn noted synthesized the best of the
first decade of rock 'n' roll and turned it into something new
with their relentlessly inventive melodies, vocal harmonies,
and tremendous energy and beat. It was also their attitude,
challenging conformist attitudes with their long hair, outspoken cheekiness, and irrepressible humor.

Some have postulated that their phenomenal success in
the United States, starting from the release of "I Want to Hold
Your Hand" at the very end of 1963, was in part due to American youth's need for new heroes after the assassination of
President John F. Kennedy just one month earlier. The Beatles
were also youthful (well, much more youthful) idealists,
capable of mobilizing millions with hope, optimism, and the

*A poster for the Beatles' first full-scale
North American tour, with Jackie
DeShannon among the supporting acts*

promise of a better world. Social analysis of the Beatles phenomenon began almost immediately, with
Harvard professor David Riesman surmising in *US News & World Report* that the group's popularity was "a form of protest against the adult world. These youngsters are hoping to believe in something, or respond to something new that they have found for themselves."

The impact of the Beatles, though, went beyond any supposed subconscious collective cultural longings, and would have been inevitable regardless of who was in charge of the government.
They had already become the biggest sensation in twentieth-century entertainment in Britain over
the course of 1963, with four gigantic hit singles. The last two of those, "She Loves You" and "I Want
to Hold Your Hand," as well as their two debut albums, were already among the highest-selling records in British history. Indeed, the second of the LPs, *With the Beatles*, was the first British album
ever to sell a million copies, and "She Loves You" remained the best-selling single issued in Britain
for nearly 15 years. There were also the unprecedented scenes of fan hysteria accompanying the
group wherever they played and appeared in public. The United States had been resistant to Beatlemania throughout 1963, the singles coming out on independent labels and attracting hardly any
airplay. That changed when Capitol finally took up its option to release Beatles product Stateside.
"I Want to Hold Your Hand" reached #1 in January 1964, a feat duplicated immediately on the LP
charts by *Meet the Beatles*, both releases setting industry sales records of their own.

The statistics corroborating the Beatles' dominance of the American market in early 1964 still
have the capacity to amaze. At one point that winter it was estimated that they were responsible for
60 percent of all singles sold in the country. On April 5, 1964, they occupied all top five positions
in the *Billboard* singles chart (and had the top *nine* singles in Canada), as well as the top two slots
in the LP listings. Their first appearance on *The Ed Sullivan Show*, days after their arrival in New
York on February 7 for their first American visit, broke ratings records with an audience of around

70 million. And the fan hysteria surrounding their brief tour of the US was even more fervid than it had been back home.

It would be exaggerated to claim that the Beatles single-handedly caused the death of folk music, which by definition will never disappear. But they did act as the true death knell of the folk *boom*, at least on record. In fact, all areas of American music were reeling from the Beatles' takeover, even more so when equally unsuspected hordes of British acts followed them into the US charts throughout 1964. The British Invasion, as it was dubbed (in the UK it had been called the Beat Boom), blindsided the whole business.

The repercussions were immediate. Sam Charters had been the folk producer for Prestige for about a year when he heard his first Beatles record while driving to work. In his notes to the compilation *The Prestige/Folklore Years Vol. 1*, he wrote, "I pulled the car over to the curb a few blocks from the office and sat listening to the sound that I realized would, in a very short time, make my job obsolete." Prestige virtually discontinued its folk department by 1965, focusing on jazz for the rest of the decade. Vanguard (for whom Charters would subsequently work as a rock and blues producer) and Elektra didn't react that radically, but would need to bend with the trends to survive. For though folk music was dead, commercially speaking, a new form of music was already being born among folk musicians that might have been impossible to conceive of had the Beatles not cleared the deck.

As Bob Dylan famously explained to his biographer Anthony Scaduto in 1971, "I had heard the Beatles in New York when they first hit. Then, when we were driving through Colorado we had the radio on and eight of the ten top songs were Beatles songs. In Colorado! 'I Wanna Hold Your Hand,' all those early ones.

"They were doing things nobody was doing. Their chords were outrageous, just outrageous, and their harmonies made it all valid. You could only do that with other musicians. Even if you're playing your own chords you had to have other people playing with you. That was obvious. And it started me thinking about other people.

"But I just kept it to myself that I really dug them. Everybody else thought they were for the teenyboppers, that they were gonna pass right away. But it was obvious to me that they had staying power. I knew they were pointing the direction of where music had to go. I was not about to put up with other musicians, but in my head the Beatles were *it*. In Colorado, I started thinking it was so far out that I couldn't deal with it—eight in the top ten. It seemed to me a definite line was being drawn. This was something that never happened before. It was outrageous, and I kept it in my mind. You see, there was a lot of hypocrisy all around, people saying it had to be either folk or rock. But I knew it didn't have to be like that. I dug what the Beatles were doing, and I always kept it in mind from back then."

The spell the Beatles cast was not limited to folkies, of course. There was an explosion of teenage groups in the United States, labeled (after the 1960s) garage bands, that emulated British bands in a rawer and more basic fashion, often crudely. Guitar sales, already at a new peak at the tail end of the folk boom, doubled between 1963 and 1965. In Britain itself, the Beatles had already, and continued to, inspire hundreds of other groups that took their basic repertoire from American rock 'n' roll and rhythm and blues. Those fellow British Invaders were inspired to write their own material as the Beatles had, often with a similar attention to catchy melodies, harmonies, and furiously rhythmic guitars. The effect they had on American folk-makers would be somewhat different.

The magnetic pull between the Beatles and their folkie fans could be partly explained by some similarities in backgrounds and tastes. The Beatles, born between 1940 and 1943, were close in age to the folkies and part of the audience that had grown up during rock 'n' roll's birth and glory years. The Beatles, Dylan, McGuinn, and others shared many of the same early heroes: Elvis, Gene Vincent, Buddy Holly, Chuck Berry, the Everly Brothers, et al. And as personalities, the Beatles shone with a similar independence and distrust of established authority, though delivered with a mischievous smile rather than the blatant sneer of a Dylan protest song.

The case could be made that there were some elements of folk in the Beatles' music. McGuinn and others picked up on the likeness of some of their chord changes and vocal harmonies to those heard in folk, and the Beatles, in a limited sense, had actually started as folk musicians. They had their roots in a Liverpool high school group, the Quarry Men, that had formed and first performed in 1957 as a skiffle band. Skiffle, that strange mix of folk, blues, and trad jazz, had just been popularized by Lonnie Donegan in Britain with his cover of Leadbelly's "Rock Island Line"; Donegan would even sometimes use electric guitars on his skiffle records. Uncounted skiffle bands were formed by British teenagers in its wake, its appeal guaranteed by the do-it-yourself ethic that would fuel American garage bands in the '60s and punk acts in the '70s: you didn't need much skill or knowledge to play. And, in a country where the standard of living was lower than it was across the water, you didn't need much in the way of equipment either. Acoustic guitars, banjos, tea chests for bass, and washboard for percussion would do.

From their inception, the Quarry Men were playing some rock 'n' roll. John Lennon was singing the Dell-Vikings' doo wop classic "Come Go with Me" when Paul McCartney, from the audience, first caught sight of his future bandmate at a Quarry Men gig on July 6, 1957. Folk tunes, however, continued to be part of their repertoire as they evolved into the Beatles, and this was not merely something they did to satisfy their audience. A 1999 Sotheby's auction of Lennon memorabilia revealed that the teenaged Beatle's collection included 78s of Donegan's "Lost John," "Don't You Rock Me Daddy-O," and "Cumberland Gap," along with the expected Presley and Holly records. Yet it would be misleading to infer that the Beatles' folk inclinations ran as deep as those of young Americans in the '60s folk boom. Folk was just one part of the many strands of popular music they drew upon for their unique fusion, and was always far subordinate to rock in their personal tastes.

They *were* more aware of folk even at this early stage of their recording career than some have realized. In *Many Years from Now*, Paul McCartney told biographer Barry Miles that a chord change on the B-side of "She Loves You," "I'll Get You," was lifted from Joan Baez's version of "All My Trials." And the group did a one-off version of "Walk Right In" onstage one night in January 1963, during their first British tour. Yet a year later, Ringo Starr was grousing in *Melody Maker* (when asked to rate Peter, Paul & Mary's version of "Stewball" for the "Blind Date" celebrity review column), "They keep telling us there's going to be this big thing with folk stuff but I can't see it…. It goes on and on. I suppose they all have a meaning somewhere, but it's lost on me."

American folk musicians fell in love with the Beatles—even with Starr, in spite of his sour take on "Stewball"—for much the same reasons as everyone else did: the giddy irresistibility of their songs, melodies, and performances. It was apparent even to those from the hootenanny crowd who were lucky enough to hear them by accident in 1963, months before Beatlemania swept the States. There was Roy Marinell, stunned by what he heard on the radio while driving across the Southwest that summer, and Steve Gillette, who still remembers hearing and loving "Love Me Do" on the jukebox of *The Queen Elizabeth* on a trip to Europe that September (he, like Marinell, mistook them for a black group). Gene Clark, who in 1964 would found the Byrds with Roger McGuinn, was touring Canada as part of the New Christy Minstrels the previous year when he first heard "She Loves You," later finding it on a jukebox in Norfolk, Virginia. As Sid Griffin quotes him in his liner notes to Clark's *Echoes* compilation, "I might have played it 40 times in the two days the New Christy Minstrels were playing that town. I knew, I *knew*, that this was the future."

These testaments don't wholly explain why Clark and others were stopped in their tracks and made an about-face change in direction. Folk music had been adopted by young people, in part, because of its superior lyrical intelligence. As great as their early music was, and adept as Lennon-McCartney were even at this stage at devising clever turns of the phrase within the pop format, their words were still largely portrayals of basic teen and young adult romantic situations. What the folkies might have sensed, if only subliminally in early 1964, was how the Beatles' eclecticism might be the vanguard of a new kind of rock music. It was a music that, instead of being ground into a formula as rock 'n' roll had in the late '50s, could continue to evolve and renew itself into more sophisticated and unpredictable forms. The Beatles would indeed fulfill this promise throughout the 1960s, in ways more exciting and accomplished than even the most besotten fan could have anticipated in early 1964. But the glimmers of that possibility were there.

"This is an era when a record company was not fond of the idea that *any* of their artists would evolve," points out Cyrus Faryar, once a part (with Judy Henske) of Dave Guard's post-Kingston Trio group the Whiskeyhill Singers, and by 1964 a bandmate of Jerry Yester's in the Modern Folk Quartet. "What a record company of that era really demanded was that an act would gain prominence and then repeat itself over and over and over again, singing and doing the same kind of material. The phenomenon of the Beatles was that no two songs were the same. And no two *albums* were the same. They delivered this evolutionary blow to the perception of what popular music was."

McGuinn has said that his intention at the outset of the Byrds was not so much to combine folk and rock as to play the kind of music the Beatles were doing. Among him and like-minded peers, there was not so much a conscious attempt to absorb the British Invasion into their own music as to imitate the British Invasion itself. It was something like a parallel to America's entry into the space race, a panicked response to the realization that the Russians had pulled ahead with the launch of Sputnik while they weren't looking. North America had been similarly caught off guard by a phalanx of British rockers, their seizure of the airwaves as unexpected as an invasion of aliens from another planet. There had to be at least as many good musicians on the American side of the pond. Why couldn't young Americans be doing the same thing too?

In the race to catch up, though, visionaries like McGuinn and Clark—and those who would become part of the stampede to electric rock but never quite make it to stardom, like Yester and Faryar—faced a long, hard slog simply to get to the starting line. They didn't even have electric instruments, for one thing. Even after they raided the pawn shops, as Yester remembers doing, they didn't necessarily have the *right* instruments, or the most suitable ones. Even if they had good ones, they had to almost relearn their playing from scratch, few of them having used electric instruments extensively, or at least much in the recent past. Many of them didn't have recording contracts, or had ones with labels that expected them to, as Faryar says, keep churning out the same old thing. And they didn't even have the right haircuts—a laughable obstacle to read about now, maybe, but a considerable worry when the Beatles had made long hair the vogue for hip males. For the guys, in what was still a mostly male-dominated field, it would take several months to catch up even on *that* front.

The transition from folk to rock—or folk to Beatles, as some thought at the outset—was an exhilarating yet painstaking process. As much as they might have wanted to be the Beatles, attributes of their folk background crept in inevitably, chiefly in the harmonies, the finger-picking and chord-strumming techniques, the mournful and exultant multi-part harmonies, and the thoughtful lyrics. "There was no way around it, 'cause that was all of our influences," agrees Yester. "We approached it differently in terms of the chords in the songs, a lot more minors, a lot of suspended notes. We played it like we played folk music, except it was electric. And it really sounded different." It took all of 1964, and much of 1965 for some, for musicians in the forefront of the shift to work out the kinks. While such experiments were taking place everywhere, the most important of them would be in clubs and recording studios of the two cities that were now the undisputed centers of the US music industry, New York and Los Angeles.

In New York, folk-rock's infant breakthroughs were achieved by a loose circle of musicians, including future members of the Lovin' Spoonful and the Mamas & the Papas, who played and recorded with each other in various permutations before settling into the lineups that would make them stars. The strongest link between them, ironically, might have been a musician who never would achieve fame as a recording artist. Erik Jacobsen was a folkie who had been just as bowled over by the Beatles as anyone. Unlike most of his friends, however, he saw his future in different terms than joining a rock band of his own.

In the early '60s, Jacobsen had been one of those young banjo-slingers traveling to New York in hopes of getting noticed by a label like Elektra. His bluegrass band, the awkwardly named Knob Lick Upper 10,000, jammed in Washington Square Park. It was in the park itself that they got noticed by Albert Grossman, who got them signed to Mercury, where they did a couple of fair bluegrass-folk LPs. In early 1964, Erik was "traveling around with the Knob Lick Upper 10,000 when the Beatles had just come out. We were trying to promote our record, 'Rocky Mountain Water Tastes So Fine' or something. We went to some radio stations, and they were just total ga-ga over the Beatles." Jacobsen checked out a Beatles single on a jukebox after a gig in Washington, DC, and heard not just the death of the Knob Lick Upper 10,000, but the birth of a new opportunity.

"I'd been trying to help arrange for our group, and I always thought about bass lines. When I heard McCartney's bass playing…I mean, I loved the whole band, but the thing that really stuck in my mind was the bass playing. I started thinking, 'Wow, I hear a whole 'nother thing that's possible with this electric bass.' It was just so different from what anybody else was doing. It was so melodic, [with] nice syncopations; it was fabulous. So I decided, kind of then and there I think, by the next morning, that I was gonna quit the Knob Lick Upper 10,000, and go to New York City, and produce electric folk music. One of the first guys I met was John Sebastian, who was playing folk accompaniment with various sessions. John electrified the autoharp, and he started buying electric guitars. He was trying to play things that he had heard as a kid, and was really the first guy that I saw playing with electric guitar."

Sebastian picks up the story: "An amazing coincidence, some of these things that happened. I took an apartment on the fifth floor of some destroyed building in Lower Manhattan. The guy that lived next door moved out, and Erik moved in. I guess I had maybe shook his hand in some other setting, but really, we didn't know each other at all. Every night, I would come home from my little run around the Village, where I'd be playing as an accompanist, and Erik would be playing unfamiliar records next door. Eventually he'd knock on my door, or I'd knock on his. It was either me saying, 'God, that's good, whatever that is you got playing there,' or it would be him calling up to say, 'Come over to listen to this.'"

Their bonding was sealed by a more exotic mutual interest. "We had in common that…at that time, not too many people smoked pot in Greenwich Village," says Jacobsen. "It was not something that everybody did, as they later did. 'Cause we had to go to very bad places to get it.

"So I asked John: 'Why don't we get together and try to make some records?' He and I recorded two or three records—'Warm Baby' and 'Rooty-Toot.'" Jerry Yester recalls that he, Jesse Colin Young, and Sticks Evans also played on "Warm Baby."

Neither of those tracks came out, though Sebastian's band the Lovin' Spoonful would put a version of "Warm Baby" on their 1966 album *Daydream*, with Jacobsen producing, and Sebastian would put a solo version of "Rooty-Toot" on an early-'70s live album. But they did represent some of the first attempts of folk musicians to come to grips with the new form of full-band rock music. As Sebastian remembers the 1964 recording experiment with Jacobsen, "'Warm Baby' is a total quote of [blues great Robert Johnson's] 'Come on in My Kitchen.' It's sort of exercising the Robert Johnson muscle in any way that we could. Now, it was silly; it wasn't particularly good or anything. But we were experimenting in some pretty interesting 'it'll be five years before this makes it' kind of ways. We had these African hair drums to get a little bit of a different drumming sound, and some chromatic bongo drums that I don't think had been picked up by studio instrumental rental. Also, I played a sitar on that [1964] record"—nearly two years before George Harrison made the first widely noted use of sitar on a rock track, on the Beatles' "Norwegian Wood."

As Jacobsen and Sebastian tried to work out their ideas, they connected with several other folkies who were thinking along similar lines. Two of them were Canadians Zal Yanovsky and Denny Doherty, who'd been in the Halifax Three, one of the many folk threesomes to spring up in the aftermath of the Kingston Trio. Jacobsen had already met both of them when playing in Toronto as part of the Knob Lick Upper 10,000, and "asked them if they knew any good singer-songwriters around. They said, 'Well, there's this guy up in Boston, Tim Hardin.' I called him up and said, 'Some guys were hyping me on you.' He said, 'Send me $100 and I'll come down.' He came down, and I remember the first question he said was like: 'Where can I get some shit?'" Meaning much stronger stuff, it should be said, than what Jacobsen and Sebastian were smoking in their apartments.

Hardin, an ex-Marine in his early twenties, had already bounced around the Village and Cambridge folk circuits, as well as hoboing around the country with other young troubadours like Shawn Phillips. He was at the forefront of a group of singer-songwriters—also including, most notably, Fred Neil—who were mixing folk with rhythm and blues. The growing blanket of the British Invasion was giving such artists more license, if only a little, to use electric guitars. That's what Hardin plays on his first 1964 demos (some of which would appear years later on archival releases like *Tim Hardin 4*). While Jacobsen had been told that Hardin was a songwriter, at this point he in fact was usually covering R&B and folk songs like "Bo Diddley," Willie Dixon's "Seventh Son," and "House of the Rising Sun," or writing songs that were thinly disguised rewrites of same. Still, it was an electrified folk-blues that, particularly due to Hardin's soulful and mournful vocals, had the germ of something new.

"He'd go all night without even opening his eyes," enthuses Michael Ochs (soon to become his brother Phil's manager) about one of Hardin's early shows in the Village at the Night Owl. "Him on electric guitar, and behind him would be Freddie Neil on backup guitar, Peter Childs playing a dobro or something exotic, John Sebastian on harmonica. They would go all over the place. They would do a Bo Diddley song, one of Dylan's songs. They had no idea where it was going to go next. You'd be going, 'Christ, this is everything I love about music.' It was the best singing in the world, [and] the best playing."

When Jacobsen had five or six Hardin demo tunes, says Sebastian, Erik called up his next-door neighbor to say, "'Come over and listen to this. I know you're playing down there [in the Village] with John Hurt and Fred Neil, tell me what you think of this.'" After hearing Hardin, Sebastian responded, "'I think the guy is the next Elvis. I think this is huge.' And Erik would say, 'I do too, and I can't get anybody from a record company to acknowledge this at all, to think that there's anything different or anything unusual or unique about this guy.' And I'd tell him, 'No, they're wrong. They're all wrong. This guy is a genius.'

"Tim looked to us like the next big thing. We were still getting to know him. We didn't understand the profoundness of his drug addiction. But what we were hearing from him was this wonderful stir of the pot of R&B and country. He was way ahead of his time. His singing was so heartfelt and yet so swinging. He was incorporating some of these people that we idolized, like Mose Allison and Ray Charles, in his singing. His guitar style was a kind of early R&B approximation that was very much his own. Slowly I began to make friends with Tim and Erik enough that when the next call for sessions came up, both of them wanted me to come along."

Jacobsen, no older than the musicians he was producing, was operating with little money and no track record. Acting as Hardin's manager and publisher in addition to hoping to be his producer, he had his hands full trying to advance the mercurial singer's career. He was hindered as much by Hardin's own disorganization, and bad actors in the crowd Tim ran with, as he was by the inability of record labels to recognize that the singer was something out of ordinary. At an audition for Columbia that is dated as May 1964 in the CD reissue *Hang on to a Dream: The Verve Recordings*, Jacobsen recalls that the label "wouldn't accept me as a producer; you know, I had never produced anything. So they assigned some guy to it. The whole thing just disintegrated right in front of me.

"Tim was higher than a kite. He nodded out. Zal [Yanovsky] I think was there, and Cass [Elliot], laughing, kind of saying, 'C'mon, Tim, wake up, play something.' But he used to nod off. He'd get to a turnaround, and he would kind of just quickly jump into it, so that the musicians were watching him like cats, like, 'When is he gonna start again?'

"Everybody was smoking pot in the hallway. The guy from Columbia was just freaked. We were in there for 12 hours, and come out; not one single movable thing was left in the waiting room. One of Timmy's friends was a klepto, and started with the Rolodex and typewriter, and all the contents of all the drawers in the secretary's thing . . . took her chair, pictures off the walls, even unscrewed the men and women's signs off the doors. That was an old-line New York recordist who did that. I was having to pay the bill for all these session guys, which was hard to [come] up with.

"But that session produced some great shit, boy. We had [top jazz musician] Gary Burton on vibes, Sticks Evans on drums, and a really good bass player. 'Green Rocky Road,' 'Airmobile,' and all those blues things, funky things, were cut in those very early sessions with Tim Hardin. He had such a wonderful sense of timing, in terms of his vocal lines. The darn guy could start almost anywhere, and he could never do the same thing twice."

Whether the label doubted the music was salable, or didn't know if it could handle a musician as tempestuous as Hardin, Columbia didn't issue any recordings by the artist at the time. Hardin's first proper LP wouldn't come out until 1966 (on Verve), though literally several dozen pre-Verve demos were later issued. In a sense, this might have been a blessing in disguise, as Hardin's songwriting would improve immensely in the interim, and the market would be far more accepting of his originality within a couple of years. In the meantime, Jacobsen's New York clique kept making tentative stabs at some sort of rock-folk fusion. Among them were two musicians that had been at the Tim Hardin session, Cass Elliot and Zal Yanovsky, and Yanovsky's Halifax Three bandmate Denny Doherty, all thrashing about for a means of survival after the Beatles had put their previous folk groups out to pasture.

1963 was the year that the Halifax Three broke up, the Journeymen broke up, the Big Three broke up, everybody broke up," says Doherty. "It seemed that everybody came off the road after the Kennedy assassination, and folk music was sort of over. Zal and I wound up playing as two-thirds of a surf trio, just instrumental stuff. By the time we got back to New York, Cass had broken up with the Big Three [a group that had also included two folk-rockers in the making, Tim Rose and James Hendricks]. Everybody was sort of bivouacked at the Albert Hotel"—famous for harboring on-the-way-up and down-and-out musicians throughout the 1960s.

The Big Three had recorded a couple of albums for the tiny FM label in 1963 and early 1964, the second of which used some fairly low-key electric guitar and drums on tracks like "Grand-

The Mugwumps. Left to right: Denny Doherty, Cass Elliot, James Hendricks, Zal Yanovsky

father's Clock" and "Wild Woman." These were sung by Rose and Elliot respectively in full-throated low, bluesy vocals at odds not just with much other commercial folk, but with most of the group's other material. Rose now says that he was pushing for them to go electric even then. "We had these vicious arguments in our last year together, about, 'It's gotta go rock. Let's just put electric guitars [in], and let's get a drummer.' I wanted to get a blues guitarist. We used a guy on our second album, a fucking jazz drummer, Panama Francis, didn't know from shit. We added electric instruments and drums; they were added incorrectly. Cass didn't want to do it, I wanted to do it, so we kind of added it. So there was no flow to it. But at least the inkling was there, [that] this was the way to go."

After Rose left in the spring of 1964, resumes Doherty, "Cass, Jim Hendricks, Zally, and I started a group called Cass Elliot and the Big Three. We went out and played a few gigs around New York, but that didn't really cut it, 'cause it was still folk music. Without management getting involved, we all just said, 'Let's go electric. This is not cutting it.' So we got some electric instruments. That still wasn't far enough, so we got a drummer, Art Stokes. We changed our name to the Mugwumps, started rehearsing old Drifters songs and some original stuff we were doing. Went back to Washington, DC, because our managers had a club there which we were the house band for.

"But we looked and sounded too frigging weird. We had a black drummer, Cass with her chiffon dresses, and we're doing rock 'n' roll. It just looked too friggin' bizarre for words. We didn't think about it, but it must have looked and sounded like some kind of weird hybrid. And we were having a great time. We were doing all rock 'n' roll songs and evolving without actually saying, 'Let's go this way, let's do this.' It wasn't a conscious effort. We didn't say, 'Let's go out and do some folk-rock.'"

The Mugwumps got to open for the Beach Boys once and release one single for Warner Brothers in the latter part of 1964, as well as record about an album's worth of material. The album was not released until 1967, after most of the group had become famous in the Mamas & the Papas or the Lovin' Spoonful. Its eclecticism was not so much a strength as indicative of a lack of focus. There were pedestrian covers of '50s rock oldies like the Coasters' "Searchin'," and Bo Diddley's "You Can't Judge a Book By the Cover," as well as uncertain fusions of Merseybeat and Tin Pan Alley pop (such as the single "I'll Remember Tonight"/"I Don't Wanna Know"). The group was not so much a cross between rock and the best traits of the members' folk training as it was a second-tier rock band. The exceptions were the two Elliot-Hendricks originals, especially the lovely "Here It Is Another Day." Its lilting, folky Beatlesque melody and spidery electric guitar speckles hinted at the formula to be perfected by the Mamas & the Papas by the end of the following year.

By the end of 1964 the Mugwumps had split. Perhaps it was too soon for their approach to take hold. But it also could have been a matter of musicians, still new to rock and pop, needing a while to find their optimal partners. Near the year's end Doherty was already, unwittingly, in the process of finding his true metier by joining the Journeymen, about to play out the string of commercial folk as the New Journeymen, under the stewardship of John Phillips. And throughout 1964 there was a musical chairs of sorts as Erik Jacobsen made recordings, in various combinations, of Yanovsky, Elliot, Hendricks, and Jerry Yester and Henry Diltz of the Modern Folk Quartet.

A couple of these tracks, rocked-up takes of "Tom Dooley" and "Oh Susannah," surfaced on the 1999 CD compilation *The Magic Circle*. They're impressive prototypes of the folk-rock sound in their treatment of traditional folk standards with not just electric rock arrangements, but some real guts. "Oh Susannah" is anchored by a growling John Barry–type bass line, choppy rhythm guitar, and a gravelly blues vocal by Yanovsky in a style that sounds remarkably close to Tim Rose's. "Erik['s] recordings were taking folk material and making it rock 'n' roll," enthuses Yester. "[It] was really, as far as I can remember, the earliest overt folk-rock that I ever heard. 'Oh Susannah' with a rock band is about as classically folk-rock as you can get." Jacobsen is more diffident about these early outings: "I was just experimenting, casting around with a bunch of people, looking to try to make records. There was no real mold as to what those records should be like, or what they should sound like. So they never came to anything."

There were other Village refugees from commercial folk, or even guitarists stuck for the moment in one of the country's dwindling number of commercial folk ensembles, using any opportunity they could to sneak a little rock 'n' roll onto studio tape. The Au Go-Go Singers were one such ensemble, its nine-strong membership including guitarist-singers Richie Furay and Stephen Stills. Like many such groups, the Au Go-Go Singers' repertoire, stage outfits, and arrangements seemed to have been selected with a greater eye to playing Midwestern high school assemblies than hip Village clubs. Their sole album, 1964's *They Call Us Au-Go-Go Singers*, was largely given over to unbearably wholesome interpretations of folk staples like "Gotta Travel On." Amidst the folk songs-cum-cereal commercials, a lone, whiskey-stained voice cut through the crap. It was Stephen Stills, singing "High Flying Bird"—the same song done to great effect by Judy Henske earlier that year—with genuine fire and commitment, and actual electric guitar and drums, though the effect was tarnished by more glee club backup vocals. The young upstart got his comeuppance by having his track placed immediately before an a cappella rendition of "What Have They Done to the Rain" that made Malvina Reynolds's nuclear warfare warning safe enough to sing for the most conservative of rotary clubs.

John Sebastian's chance to sing on folk-rock records was yet to come, but he too at least got some valuable experience in the studio as a session musician, often on harmonica, on progressive folk records by Fred Neil, Jesse Colin Young, Judy Collins, and others. He was also part of the Even Dozen Jug Band, an unwieldy clump of players who did a one-off LP for Elektra in 1964, that also included Maria Muldaur (then Maria D'Amato), Steve Katz (later of the Blues Project), David Grisman, and Stefan Grossman. Joe Boyd, later to move to England and become one of Britain's top folk-rock producers with Fairport Convention and others, even remembers that he and producer Paul Rothchild had notions of putting together a folk-rock group featuring Sebastian and others around the spring of '64. According to Boyd, the lineup would have also included Young, Yester, and Yanovsky, though Yester himself has no memory of this.

Sebastian was pulled into the Mugwumps' camp as well. He played harmonica with them (though not on their recordings), and hit it off especially well with the flamboyant Yanovsky, whom he had met at a gathering at Cass Elliot's apartment to watch the Beatles' debut on *The Ed Sullivan Show*. With the dissolution of the Mugwumps, the path was clear for them to form their own band. "The writing was on the wall already," says Sebastian. "Roger McGuinn and I played the same club as solo artists before either one of us had a band. He was playing Beatle tunes, I was playing jug band tunes. To me and Zally, it seemed logical that electrifying some of this material and this mood would come up with something that was somewhat unique. It was only another step or two to get aware of things like electric autoharps and electric 12-strings."

It would not be until well into 1965 that Sebastian and Yanovsky's group, the Lovin' Spoonful, would begin to release records. Before that, they'd have to do their rock 'n' roll apprenticeship in rehearsals in the dank Albert Hotel basement, as well as gigs in Village clubs, especially the Night Owl. At least they wouldn't have to worry about competition from McGuinn, who by that time had also cottoned onto the possibilities of electric 12-string guitars. For he, like a growing number of folkies from New York and all over North America angling for a break, had moved to Los Angeles.

L.A., more so than New York, might have seemed another unlikely base of a folk revival, even an urban one. If there was ever an American city where tradition was less valued, it was this metropolis, which had only been a major population center for half a century or so. By the time of the folk boom, the region was engulfed in an ever-expanding sprawl of suburbs. The rampant construction, of both bland housing and superhighways, stifled the growth of intimate, pedestrian-friendly neighborhoods that one might think necessary to harbor the kinds of communities to support folk music.

But Southern California was also the land of opportunity and promise in many fields. Throughout the twentieth century, it had drawn droves of refugees from hard times in the South, Texas, and Oklahoma, including many low-income whites and blacks that brought their roots music with them. Country, bluegrass, and blues musicians were plentiful in the area by the beginning of the 1950s, and the drive to record many of them was an underrated factor in the emergence of Los Angeles as a prime beachhead for both independent labels and branches of major record companies. Hollywood's longtime reign as capital of the movie business made entertainment itself a big business in L.A., with the attendant mushrooming of clubs and music venues. Folk music was not the biggest scene in live sounds, having to compete with jazz, R&B, and rock shows. But its popularity was well-established in Los Angeles years before the Beatles made their first records.

"Southern California has never gotten its just due," feels John McEuen, a teenage folk multi-instrumentalist in the mid-'60s who was soon to join the Nitty Gritty Dirt Band. "Orange County in particular had clubs called the Paradox, the Mon Ami, the Prison of Socrates, the Golden Bear; McCabe's Guitar Shop in Long Beach was doing concerts for a while. After the Newport Folk Festival album[s] came out, people started being aware of Doc Watson, bluegrass and Appalachian music. A lot of the players that I knew in this area would also go to the Ash Grove and the Troubadour [in Hollywood], or the Pasadena Ice House. Between all these clubs, there was always something cool going on. Either Mance Lipscomb, or Lightnin' Hopkins, or Merle Travis, or the Stoneman Family, or Flatt & Scruggs, even." The hootenannies at the Meeting Place in the relatively remote suburb of Claremont, remembers Chris Darrow (later of Kaleidoscope), would draw participants as disparate as emcee Terry Kirkman (later of the Association) and Frank Zappa.

"There were two clubs in Los Angeles back then, the Troubadour and the Ash Grove," says Chris Hillman, then a teenage bluegrass mandolinist who had already recorded albums as part of the Scottsville Squirrel Barkers and the Hillmen, but soon to learn electric bass as part of the Byrds. "The Troubadour catered to a more commercial folk sound—Hoyt Axton, [David] Crosby would sing there. We all would do the hootenanny night there. The Ash Grove, about a quarter of a mile away, would have Bill Monroe and Lightnin' Hopkins and people like that. Very roots-oriented. I was drawn to the Ash Grove, as [David] Lindley was drawn to the Ash Grove, and Ry Cooder was drawn to the Ash Grove. The guys in the Byrds—the other guys—were more into the Troubadour set." Barry Melton, then in L.A. before moving to the San Francisco Bay Area to help form Country Joe & the Fish, sees the Ash Grove–McCabe's axis as "a real nursery for musical ideas and young musicians. That cross-blending ended up in rock with a little Doc Watson, B.B. King, Lightnin' Hopkins all mixed together, which you hear so much of in the folk-rock idiom."

Of Troubadour owner Doug Weston, Larry Murray (later of Hearts and Flowers) says, "People had love-hate relationships with him. But he really held that thing together in a subtle manner, and really made things happen. For example, if you were an unsigned act and he could kind of spot if you were gonna do something, he'd hire you, and you'd have to sign this deal with him that you owed him two to three more engagements at the same price. So you worked for $25 a night. Like three years later, you were making $2,500, and Doug would go, 'Oh, by the way, on the Saturday of Easter, I would like to exercise my option.' Managers, mainly, hated him for it."

For those on a budget, or performers without enough clout to land a Troubadour gig, there was also the New Balladeer coffeehouse near Santa Monica Boulevard in West Los Angeles. Twenty-year-old Morgan Cavett, by day a liquor store delivery man, was by night manager of the modest West Los Angeles establishment, so modest that in fact the "manager" was the sole employee other than owner Angelo DiFrenza. "The New Balladeer was kind of a weekday hangout place for a lot of people," he remembers. "There was no charge, they could sit and nurse a cup of coffee all night and sit around and play guitars. And maybe somebody would have a little pot or something."

Among the coffee-nursers and young girls from nearby University High School were teenagers who would be recording electric folk-rock within a year or two, including Bryan MacLean of Love and Tim Buckley. Among the performers was a young, struggling David Crosby, who "played quite regularly for money. We'd pay him five or ten bucks a night and all he could eat." Cavett eventually handed over the managerial reigns to John Kay, then still a folkie, but later to front Steppenwolf: "John, on purpose, would run the espresso machine during David's songs, which would piss him off. They'd start yelling and screaming back and forth."

It was a time for innocent hijinx between musicians who were still barely out of their teens, or sometimes still in their teens. The innocence, as well as some of the purist party lines separating these hangouts, began to dissolve as the British Invasion started to unveil a new world of both musical and financial possibilities. Kenny Edwards, a college student who would soon play with Linda Ronstadt in the Stone Poneys, had a part-time job selling guitars in the small shop in the Ash Grove's lobby. Like many of the Ash Grove habitues, he considered the Troubadour crowd a more commercial, impurer counterpart to the more ethnic tradition-minded Ash Grove clientele. "Both worlds couldn't have been more widely disparate, almost like hip-hop and folk now. To the outside observer, it would have been a fine distinction indeed. But at that time we went, 'Oh, those people are over there, and we don't know anything about them, and nor they us.'

"The thing that actually broke that barrier down was everybody sort of looked up from their folk page and heard the Beatles and [were] going, 'Wait a minute. There's something *very* interesting happening there.' There was a lot of real dyed-in-the-wool folkies who still weren't particularly interested in rock 'n' roll in that way, who kept their bluegrass purity, or their blues purity. But for the most part, that sort of broke down the barriers between the so-called commercial folk people and traditional folk people. 'Cause everybody went, 'Hey, this is too exciting. We all have to get involved in this.'"

The Troubadour was (and remains) on the main drag of West Hollywood, Santa Monica Boulevard, on the stretch of road with the heaviest traffic between Beverly Hills and the Sunset Strip. More than the Ash Grove, it would serve as the primary meeting ground for the musicians who would shape the sound of Los Angeles folk rock. "There's a little outside room at the Troubadour, which has been many things over the years," says Roy Marinell. "At that time, it was called the Folk Den. There was no liquor there, it was just coffee and soft drinks and what have you. You could hang out there without having to pay to go into the club, and pick guitar or just socialize. That was the first time I saw McGuinn and Crosby and Clark. Michael [Clarke, the Byrds' drummer] was using the sticks on a table or something like that, and they were starting to sing harmony. And it was pretty amazing."

McGuinn had started to play the Troubadour regularly by the time he turned 22 in the summer of 1964. Opening for Hoyt Axton and Roger Miller, he performed—as he had started to do in Greenwich Village—Beatles songs on a 12-string guitar. It was the latest stage of a career that had gone through several disparate phases, even though the young musician had yet to make anything like a national reputation. As an accompanist, he had toured and recorded with the Limeliters and the Chad Mitchell Trio, and also contributed to several compilation albums of instrumental folk and banjo songs. He had backed Bobby Darin in the folk portion of the all-around entertainer's set. Judy Collins, as previously noted, hired him as an arranger on her #3 album after seeing him perform with Darin in Las Vegas.

He had not entirely turned a blind eye to pop-rock ambitions, either. In early 1963, Darin's publishing company hired McGuinn as a songwriter, and he worked in the Brill Building for $35 a week. (That was not a unique distinction among budding folk-rockers; Paul Simon and Fred Neil were also writing songs in New York for consideration by pop-rock artists in the early '60s.) One song he cowrote with Frank Gari, the surf-rock trifle "Beach Ball," actually found release on a Capitol single by the City Surfers. McGuinn even played on the track, which also featured drums by Darin. It was a flop, but he would soon cross paths again with the pianist on the session, Hollywood producer-in-the-making Terry Melcher.

Their overwhelming popularity to the contrary, playing Beatles songs in Greenwich Village folk clubs required considerable courage and self-confidence in early 1964, when many folkies still thought of the Beatles as a silly, passing phase. McGuinn was urged to stick with what he was doing, though, by some unexpected supporters. "Dion came to see if he wanted to hire me as a sideman, and at the end of the conversation, he said, 'I think you're into something. You ought to go do something with that,'" he laughs. "I said, 'Well, I'm just kind of copying the Beatles.' And he said, 'No man, no, you're doing something different. You ought to go for it.' He was very encouraging." So was another Village "basket house" guitarist, Richie Havens. And at the Troubadour, where McGuinn's Beatle-folk met with initial audience hostility, country-pop humorist Roger Miller "helped me out. He gave me a tip on how to handle the audience better."

There was also Barry McGuire, still largely anonymous to the public, though he'd sung on the New Christy Minstrels' hit "Green, Green." Says McGuire, "Hoyt [Axton] was living in Topanga Canyon, and Roger McGuinn was living in his poolhouse. I went out to Hoyt's one time, and Roger says, 'Hey, come here, let me sing some songs for you.' So he started singing some songs, and he said, 'What do you think about this stuff?' And it just blew me away. 'Can you think of anybody who'd like to hear this?' And I said, 'Roger, that's awesome, just wonderful.' I think Roger had more of a game plan than anybody else had. He calculated and thought, and figured out what he wanted to do before he did it."

"I remember there being a lot of resistance in the folk community to going electric," McGuinn says now. "I don't remember there being a lot of people who wanted to make that move. I remember telling Bob Gibson at the Golden Bear, 'I'm gonna do rock 'n' roll.' He said, 'Oh man, you're selling out!' That was the attitude in the folk community. I was actually trying to give him a tip into the right direction. But he didn't want to go there."

McGuinn did convince one member of his Troubadour audience that there was a lot of validity to what he was doing, setting in motion the improbable formation of the best folk-rock group there ever was. "Gene Clark heard it and he dug it," McGuinn told Ed Ward in a 1970 *Rolling Stone* interview, "and he came over to me and said, 'Do you want to start a duet, like Peter & Gordon or something?'" Some might find it a bit odd that Clark, who had been a Beatles fan from the time he played "She Loves You" repeatedly on a Virginia jukebox when he was still with the New Christy Minstrels, would cite Peter & Gordon as a reference point. That British duo, however, were very much in the minds of Beatles followers at the moment, having just topped the US charts with a Lennon-McCartney composition, "A World Without Love." And McGuinn and Clark, who started to work together right away, were just a duo at this point, not a group.

They were on their way to being a group almost before they knew it, though, when David Crosby approached them at the Troubadour one night. Gene Clark, in an obscure interview with *Omaha Rainbow* in 1977, said Crosby approached the pair as they were playing in the lobby stairway, "where the echo was good," and added his harmonies without asking. McGuinn, in *Rolling Stone*, recalled Crosby getting involved the very same night he and Clark started working together, after friend Paul Potash told McGuinn his duo should get a high harmony singer—such as Crosby, who happened to be standing right next to Potash. "I knew his reputation from back in 1960 when I'd come out with the Limeliters and he was, like, 'Can I play with you guys, huh, huh?'" McGuinn told *Rolling Stone*. "So I didn't know how far to trust him, but we took him anyway, and he sure could sing. He turned out to be a great singer…."

Crosby, like McGuinn and Clark, was a young veteran of the Brillo-scrubbed commercial folk ensembles of the early '60s. An unrecognizably short-haired, tie-and-jacketed Crosby did his time with Les Baxter's Balladeers, one of several folk groups sent out under the auspices of a celebrity nonmember such as easy listening pop bandleader Baxter. He appears with the group on several songs on *Jack Linkletter Presents a Folk Festival*, cheerfully going through the motions on folk boom chestnuts like "Midnight Special" and "Lonesome Traveler." A better clue to his tastes was a different cut from the LP, "Linin' Track"; according to the liner notes, "a traditional Negro work song inspired a young song writer and singer, Freddy Neil, to produce this swinging, pulsating arrangement."

Away from the strictures of the Balladeers, Crosby, under the influence of his friend Neil and others, was developing a more personal style, as unreleased tapes from around 1962 demonstrate, with blues-jazz vocals in the Neil mold and chunky rhythm guitar. "Everybody kept telling me that I sang like a rock 'n' roll singer, and that I played too loud," he recalled on the 1966 promo-only disc "A Special Open-End Interview with the Byrds Talking About Their New LP *Fifth Dimension*." "So when I found out that Jimmy [i.e. Roger McGuinn] was gonna make a rock 'n' roll band, I said, can I sing with you?"

Crosby would have been enough of a find for McGuinn and Clark for his winsome high harmony vocals alone, but he brought another asset to the table that went beyond his own musicianship. For some time, he had been working with record producer and manager Jim Dickson, who had already cut Crosby in the studio with an electric band. (Four of the tracks, including tentative blues-rock covers of Hoyt Axton's "Willie Gene" and Ray Charles's "Come Back Baby" and a strange arrangement of Dino Valenti's "Get Together" with a "Twist and Shout"–styled intro, are on *The Preflyte Sessions*, a compilation of 1964 Byrds rehearsals and demos.) Dickson assumed management of the fledgling trio, and although he wouldn't be able to get his clients a contract right away, he could get them something they needed even more at this point: studio time at World Pacific Studios, where they could work on their sound without immediate pressure to deliver hits.

The trio's first recording, "The Only Girl I Adore" (a track that wouldn't find release until five years later on the *Early L.A.* various-artists compilation), was an embryo of the Beatle-folk crossroads that the Byrds would perfect by 1965. The lyrically lightweight but catchy McGuinn-Crosby tune was almost pure Merseybeat, complete with "yeah yeah" refrains. It was something quite different, however, to hear with nothing but 12-string acoustic guitars, and the soaring harmonies also betraying the group's schooling in folk outfits. The recording set in relief some ingredients of what was to make them special. But it also set in relief what they were at this point lacking: electric guitars and a rhythm section.

For even by mid-1964, many aspiring folkies-turned-rockers lacked the basic equipment, though not the desire, to go fully electric. Money was short for electric guitars and amplifiers, so much more expensive than a sole acoustic axe; the musicians were still unfamiliar with how amplified instruments worked in the first place; and even if they learned their way around them, there was no guarantee they could use them onstage, with so much resistance to electricity on the folk circuit they still haunted. When neophytes lacking the essentials started to make tentative moves toward rock at the New Balladeer, according to Morgan Cavett, they had to resort to putting DeArmond pickups inside their acoustic guitars to simulate rock's volume.

"We were all young and poor, and most of us were trying to be independent, and not depend on our parents to go out and buy new guitars," confirms Roy Marinell. Getting around the problem by inserting pickups into acoustics brought its own headaches. "We all got DeArmond pickups and found we were feeding back, so we started stuffing towels in [our guitars]. And then we decided, okay, it's time we really get into this and get regular ones." The optimal path for doing so would be to find a guitar that managed to combine the volume of electric rock with the timbre of folk. The model for doing so was supplied, again, by the Beatles.

As much of an impact as the Beatles had made with the Ed Sullivan shows and their first raft of hits, it was cranked up yet another notch with the summer release of their film *A Hard Day's Night*. Though they (and especially John Lennon) would stress in later years that their characters in the film were rough caricatures, to a large extent they were playing themselves, running (literally) through an average day in the life. And folkies, already inclined to move toward the Beatles musically, liked what they saw on screen of the group's personalities and lifestyle—thumbing their nose at authority, playing great loud music at every opportunity, and cracking in-jokes among themselves. Plus, of course, being chased and screamed at by young girls all over the place. The life of the folk troubadour couldn't help but start to seem tame in comparison. Tom Campbell, then a young folk songwriter coordinating hootenanny packages in Southern California, remembers Ian Tyson of Ian & Sylvia instructing him to see the film with these words: "[It's] not a fucking Elvis Presley movie."

In 1964, David Freiberg was a folk musician who had once shared a semi-communal pad in L.A. in the bohemian beach community of Venice. The household, which also included fellow incipient folk-rockers Crosby, Paul Kantner, and Sherry Snow, revolved around playing guitars and smoking pot. Money was pooled into a bowl and taken by residents as they needed it. Freiberg and others saw elements of the countercultural ethos they were (if somewhat unwittingly) pioneering mirrored by the Beatles on the big screen, and immediately identified with them. "*A Hard Day's Night* was kind of the way all of us were actually living, the way it was pictured," explains Freiberg, then half of a male-female vocal folk duo, and later to be the most folk-rooted member of the San Francisco psychedelic group Quicksilver Messenger Service. "Even though they *weren't* actually living that way, probably. It pictured them as being a very communal thing. So I said, well, it looks like so much fun."

A Hard Day's Night became not just a cult among the young folk-rock crowd, but an obsession. As Jerry Yester, playing the Troubadour himself with the Modern Folk Quartet in the summer of 1964, tells it: "At the Troubadour, when the bar'd close at two, everybody would go to the Pix, [this] all-night theater in Hollywood, *every night*, to see *A Hard Day's Night*. It was like this instantly formed tradition."

Among those smitten by *A Hard Day's Night* were Roger McGuinn and David Crosby. McGuinn at this point was one of the hapless minions mimicking rock with the wrong equipment, using a pickup on a Gibson acoustic 12-string. When he and his bandmates saw the Beatles film, they took notes on what instruments their heroes were using. McGuinn was especially enamored of George Harrison's electric 12-string Rickenbacker, which the Beatles' lead guitarist had begun to use on the group's records starting in February 1964. The sound of that Rickenbacker would have been unavoidable for anyone listening to the radio or seeing the movie that summer. Harrison opened the song with an anthemic sustained chord whose bell-like chime distilled the essence of the Beatles' call for cultural revolution. For that matter, that same chord opened both the movie itself and the soundtrack album.

McGuinn soon got an electric 12-string Rickenbacker for himself. "He told me one time that when he heard the electric 12-string riff that the Beatles did right at the end of 'Hard Day's Night,'" says McGuire, "Roger went, 'That's it, that's it!' And that's where he got the style for 'Tambourine Man,' '[Eight] Miles High,' and, basically, the Byrds' sound."

Rickenbacker had only developed its electric 12-string the previous year. The one that Harrison bought (within days of the Beatles' arrival in New York in February 1964) was actually one of the very first in circulation, with the first one, strangely enough, having gone to Las Vegas show guitarist Suzi Arden just three months earlier. Harrison wasted no time putting it to use on the Beatles' next recording session later that month, just after their return to England.

Folk musicians such as McGuinn were already well acquainted with acoustic 12-string guitars, which gave their sound a dense texture and power unattainable on standard six-string models. The Rickenbacker increased that power exponentially, while retaining the ringing tone of the folk 12-string. It was especially striking when deployed for circular riffs in which the sustain caused an overlap effect among the notes. The 12-string cascades, particularly when they intermingled with vocal harmonies, created overtones that in turn generated an overlay of whoosh-drone. McGuinn's constant references to a jet-age vibe in the Byrds' early years—most memorably in the liner notes to their first album, where he bragged, "Now we've got the krrrriiiiiissssssshhhhhhhh jet sound"— were not mere horseplay. The sound of an airplane taking off might have been antithetical to folk purists. But for the Byrds, it was just a reflection of the excitement of the times, and not incompatible with their own love of folk music, to which they could and would work in such futuristic technological components.

By the time McGuinn picked up his Rickenbacker, 12-string guitars (or 12-string guitar-like effects) had been used on several 1964 rock records that foreshadowed folk-rock, not just by the Beatles but also by the Searchers, Jackie DeShannon, Peter & Gordon, and others. Even before that, it had been used on some rock records to provide a flourishing touch, as on some Phil Spector sessions with Carol Kaye and Barney Kessel playing electric 12-string. McGuinn, however, would become the electric 12-string's undisputed virtuoso, sculpting it into not just the signature sound of the Byrds, but one of the signature marks of folk-rock as a whole.

In embracing the Rickenbacker, McGuinn was setting a pattern for adventurous risk that would enable the Byrds to push forward, not just in 1964 but for several years, where others mulling over folk-rock possibilities dallied. Others shied at the prospect of doing Beatles folk songs at folk clubs; McGuinn was willing to endure the jeers while he followed the future. Others kept on struggling with their DeArmond pickups and towel-stuffed acoustics for some time yet. McGuinn put everything on the line and threw his lot in with the electronic age. Unlike virtually everyone from his milieu, he saw no reason why electric and acoustic music had to remain separate, instead envisioning the new frontiers opened by the combination of the two.

"I think I'm just a gadget freak," he confesses. "Anything that lights up or whirs fascinates me. The 12-string was my main instrument, even as an acoustic player. So I just crossed over to the electric more. I wouldn't call that a technological change, so much as an improvement of the sound quality of it. I love the Rickenbacker, 'cause especially with compression, it sustains like a wind instrument. You can do things on it you can't really do on other electric guitars." In a 1966 article in *Melody Maker*, he was yet more rhapsodic in his praise of the instrument: "That's got so many sounds, and people just don't seem to know about it. You can do anything on it—Bach organs, harpsichord, jet plane whining turbine engines, air raid sirens, kittens, a baby crying, anything. You know, the whole thing!"

McGuinn, Clark, and Crosby were three singers who probably couldn't have made it on their own as soloists, at least in 1964—McGuinn's voice was too reedy, Clark's too vibrato-laden, and Crosby's too thin. But they already had great harmonies, a developing knack for penning Beatlesque melodies (especially the prolific Clark), and a willingness to experiment. They had a name, the Jet Set, with which no one was too happy. They didn't have the right haircuts, as the earliest photos of the trios demonstrate, the three still looking suitable for a spot on ABC's *Hootenanny* with their swept-back short hair, matching white shirts, and McGuinn's horn-rimmed spectacles.

The right name, hair length, threads, and even spectacles would come soon enough. What they didn't have was a contract, or an electric rhythm section. The Beatles and *A Hard Day's Night* had made it clear that groups were the thing. While the thrown-together partnerships of young guys from all over the US would eventually lead to internecine tensions in the Byrds (which the Beatles wouldn't face until the late '60s), the new trio—to get to where they wanted— would have to become a quintet. They might well have never gotten there without Jim Dickson.

*D*ickson, about a decade older than the trio, had been involved in recording sessions for a few years on projects by comedian Lord Buckley and jazz musicians. Of late he had been working with more folk musicians (sometimes as a freelance A&R man for Elektra), including not just Crosby as a soloist, but also the Modern Folk Quartet (whose self-titled 1963 Warner Brothers album he produced) and the Dillards. In 1963 he became business partners with Eddie Tickner, forming Tickson Music, which published Dino Valenti's future folk-rock anthem "Get Together."

"I was not so much looking for a fusion between folk and rock, but ways to enhance folk music," he reflects. "At first, using jazz musicians Red Mitchell, Jimmy Bond, Bud Shank, Billy Higgins, and Frank Butler, and sometimes cello. I wanted more music: countermelodies from the bass instead of just playing changes. This was followed by Crosby [playing] with [guitarist] Tommy Tedesco, [drummer] Earl Palmer, [and bassist] Ray Pohlman. The above musicians and Glen Campbell were among those I made experiments with, looking for sounds to support folksingers. Working with the Dillards convinced me that better players were possible, as well as [of] the virtues of group singing."

By the time he produced a little-known 1964 single by Dino Valenti for Elektra, he adds, his ambitions to enhance folk arrangements "took on a definite rock flavor." The peripatetic, volatile Valenti had already done some unreleased recordings (including an acoustic demo of "Get Together" for Tom Donahue in San Francisco in early 1964). Cited as an influence by dozens in their leap from folk to rock, Valenti himself never managed to launch a consistent recording career, in part because of an unfortunate mid-'60s stretch in prison on drug-related charges, in part because his own obstinacy made him difficult for labels to record.

His one-off Elektra 45 "Don't Let It Down"/"Birdses," as well as two outtakes from this period that show up on the *Early L.A.* anthology, were awkward and not wholly successful attempts at an early folk-rock marriage, weighed down by inappropriate harpsichord (played by Leon Russell) and pop-soul backup vocals. Actually, reveals Dickson, "Dino wanted a big band with brass, but that was more than I could afford. I had cut some songs with Red Mitchell and Dino, and he was impressed that Red could stay with him without rehearsal. That gave him confidence to proceed with the cuts." The "Black Betty" outtake (on *Early L.A.*) did sound uncannily like the sort of blues-folk-rock that Bob Dylan would venture into in 1965. And for the Byrds, the single served its own little-known purpose, when the Jet Set were searching for a better name later that year, and someone remembered the title of the B-side.

The single was also significant in its indication that Elektra, the hippest American folk label, might be opening its ears to rock music. Elektra president Jac Holzman connects the label's entry into the field with the encroaching staleness of the folk scene in general: "When everybody was thrashing through a repertoire of perhaps 500 songs, it was just too small a pool for so many people. New songs had to be created." Elektra was already active in the distribution of songs by new writers, recording topical songwriters like Phil Ochs and covers of same by Judy Collins, and Holzman was ready to expand its musical palette as well. "There's just so much emphasis you can put by twanging a guitar," he believes. "You need flexibility."

Holzman's interest in rock as a means to expand musical parameters had started sooner than many people realize. As he had announced in *Record Mirror* in 1967, "In 1963 I got turned on to all kinds of rock and roll." (Perhaps he was thinking of an incident mentioned in his autobiography *Follow the Music*, where he remembered hearing the Rolling Stones recording "I'm a King Bee" at an audition for Decca in London in 1963, and being told that a deal with Decca was nearly definite after making inquiries.) In an interesting contrast to McGuinn's recollections, he also cites Elektra artist Bob Gibson as one who "talked about electric instruments from time to time. [He] was resistant in public; I think he was more interested in private. His reputation was one of being a superb instrumentalist, all of which would have translated well to an electrified instrument. Do I think he was gonna go out with 20-stack Marshalls [amps]? No. But I think he definitely would have gotten a small tube Fender and played around with that.

"Electric instruments struck me as an inevitability. I know something *had* to happen somewhere. I just wanted to be in the position to catch hold of it when it did."

Gibson didn't go the folk-rock route in the 1960s, and Holzman was receptive to another one-off Dickson single later in 1964, by his protégés the Jet Set. For the single "Please Let Me Love You"/"Don't Be Long," they were, to their consternation, renamed the Beefeaters. McGuinn, Clark, and Crosby were backed by Ray Pohlman and the ubiquitous Earl Palmer on charming if simplistic tunes, "Please Let Me Love You" sounding very much like a Beatles knockoff. The ingredients for the 1965 Byrds, however, were there in the elementary electric 12-string guitar riffs, full strident folk chording, and glowing harmonies. In fact, "Don't Be Long" would be rerecorded by the Byrds for their second album, where it was retitled "It Won't Be Wrong." But the single, released at the end of 1964, did nothing, and Elektra missed an opportunity to get in on the ground floor of folk-rock's first commercial bloom.

"I don't know why we just got the single, and didn't get the album," muses Holzman. "Jim Dickson really wanted to be on a larger label. He was concerned that singles would be necessary, and Elektra had no track records with singles. I think they wanted to keep the band a little innocent, in case there was an opportunity to make a deal elsewhere. My recollection is that they were asking for far more money than I was willing to pay. Which, in retrospect, was stupid, 'cause I later paid that same amount of money for Love. But they also wanted a ton of stuff that I didn't want to get started with, stuff that was routine in the '80s. They were asking for this stuff back in the mid-'60s." According to Dickson, what they wanted from Holzman was $5,000 to buy instruments, which he would get eventually, though from a far less conventional source than a record company. He also says

The Byrds, shortly after their formation. Left to right: Chris Hillman,
David Crosby, Michael Clarke, Roger McGuinn, Gene Clark

the single was sold to Holzman with the understanding that Holzman pick the name and not reveal who the group was, which in his view was a promise the Elektra president later broke. (Holzman: "That is not my recollection. Besides, it's impossible to keep the names of any group secret, with one famous exception.")

As with many pre-1965 records with various shades of folk-rock, the failure of the Beefeaters single might have been just as well for all parties. Elektra was at this point not ready or able to break a hit single; it had a hard enough time claiming a piece of the LP market. The band had more time to work on its sound and image, not to mention a better name than the Beefeaters, which had been chosen by Holzman "because I was enamored of what was going on with the British Invasion." And most of all, it gave the tenuous trio a chance to solidify its lineup with a permanent drummer and bassist.

They came by the drummer easily enough. Michael Clarke had played congas in folk clubs, and previously met McGuinn and Crosby in Northern California. He had never played drums in a professional band, but no matter. What was more important was his sheepdog haircut, enhancing his physical resemblance to the Rolling Stones' glamour boy Brian Jones. McGuinn recalled that they offered Clarke the position on the spot when they saw him walking on Santa Monica Boulevard near the Troubadour. Recent ex-folkies didn't know many drummers, and it would not be the first time that a major folk-rock band would enlist a drummer with slim-to-nonexistent experience because he looked right, not caring if he could play yet or not. Clarke had played congas; he could learn to play rock drums.

The bass slot was more problematic. Crosby tried to master the electric bass, and was not making satisfactory progress. Dickson thought of Chris Hillman, a 19-year-old musician he had recorded as a mandolinist of the Hillmen, a bluegrass band that also included Alabaman brothers Vern and Rex Gosdin. Hillman of late had resorted to working with yet another of the dying commercial folk ensembles, the Green Grass Group, one of several such acts overseen by Randy Sparks (who was also mastermind of the New Christy Minstrels). He was sticking with the Green Grass Group for the bread only, and eager to get involved with something more creative. He had never played the bass, but at least he had a few years of professional experience, including some recording, to gear him up for the challenge of learning a new instrument.

He also had a coach in Dickson, a man savvy enough to find connective threads between styles that some might see as unrelated. "The last two albums that I did overlapping with the Byrds were [folksinger] Hamilton Camp with [bassist] Red Mitchell, and *Long Gone Miles* with Willie Chambers [of the Chambers Brothers] and Leroy Vinager, which was sort of folk R&B," Dickson points out. "Among the reasons for all this effort was the attempt to create fresh sounds to get airplay, and that started with the strong bass lines that later influenced the Byrds. Chris Hillman listened to Red Mitchell on the Camp album as a start, for instance."

In retrospect, hopes that such a motley lineup of folkies could become the American Beatles were nothing short of incredible. They had barely known each other before getting thrown into the studio, were still learning electric instruments, and in a couple cases had never really even played their assigned instruments at all. Actually, Michael Clarke didn't even have an instrument to start with; on his first rehearsals, and even some recording sessions, he kept time on cardboard boxes. Chris Hillman was little better off, starting off on a cheap Japanese bass. But they had McGuinn's 12-string guitar mastery, sparkling if unpolished vocal harmonies, a growing body of quality original songs, and an indomitable will to somehow morph from folk underlings to rock band. And, not least, they had unlimited studio time to practice and record themselves at night in World Pacific Studios. Dickson had carte blanche there as a reward for his production of the Folkswingers' World Pacific LP *12 String Guitar*, on which Glen Campbell was backed by the Dillards.

As to why Dickson was willing to invest so many hours cultivating unknowns, McGuinn is frank. "I think he saw dollar signs," he chuckles. "I think he saw a Beatles band that he could mold. And he loved to mold things. He was married to an actress. He had found her in summer stock or something, and coached her into getting into the movies. So he was in that sort of eternal developer mode."

The Jet Set spent much of the next few months rehearsing and, just as importantly, taping the rehearsals at World Pacific. Listening to the playbacks immediately afterward was shock treatment that intensified the band's hothouse growth. Unlike most new bands, they had the rare opportunity to hear themselves on studio-quality tapes, enabling them to zero in on their flaws and iron out their kinks. As a result of these hours of tapes, listeners today have the chance, rare when investigating the roots of great artists, to hear the gestation of the Byrds in fine detail. The group, incidentally, *were* finally going by the name the Byrds by Thanksgiving 1964. Inspired in part by the title to Dino Valenti's single "Birdses," it fit in well with McGuinn's love for aeronautics.

Nearly a dozen tracks from the World Pacific sessions would be released five years later on the *Preflyte* compilation (more were unearthed for the *In the Beginning* CD in the late '80s, and yet more for the 2001 CD *The Preflyte Sessions*, which gathers everything previously released from the World Pacific sessions and then some). Far from being mere historical curiosities, these are often gorgeous, moving performances on their own terms. Gene Clark had now emerged as the Byrds' primary composer (often collaborating with McGuinn), with a gift for stringing together unusual sequences of major and minor chords that recalled the Beatles, yet had a bittersweet flavor of their own. The harmonies, likewise, began to move away from the obvious Beatleisms of "Please Let Me Love You," retaining the angelic, almost choral feel that would characterize most of their recordings while Crosby was in the band.

The more minimally arranged pieces, some apparently recorded before Clarke had his full drum kit (such as one version of "You Showed Me," a hit for the Turtles about five years later in a drastically more pop-oriented rearrangement), had something of a beach campfire feel. Yet the more fully produced efforts—some, like "For Me Again," "The Airport Song," and "Tomorrow Is a Long Time," never to be rerecorded for proper Byrds albums—showed McGuinn well on his way to perfecting the sparkling guitar jangle that would become his trademark. The musicians were managing to distill the best of the Beatles' gentler side, while overlaying it with the yearning, direct expressiveness of folk harmonies and the skillful delicacy of acoustic folk guitar strumming and picking. More than any other recordings made before 1965, the Byrds' World Pacific sessions blueprint the sound of folk-rock.

It wouldn't be called folk-rock for some time, and part of its very greatness was the unconscious potpourri of forces that had led the musicians and their mentor to something so new it didn't have a name. "It was not folk-rock as a goal, but to bring a contemporary format to the best of the dying modern folk music," clarifies Dickson. "The Byrds used what skills they had, mostly from folk music, and given the instruments they chose, found a sound compatible with the Beatles."

Had the Byrds continued to rely upon their own songs for most of their material, however, they may have never become the major group that they did. As good as they were, their compositions were still very much in the young adult romantic mold of the early John Lennon and Paul McCartney. It could be reasonably argued that such songs were far more relevant to the everyday experiences of the musicians and their audience, in urban regions in 1964, than were nineteenth-century Appalachian ballads, or maybe even antiwar and antibomb songs.

But that audience was coming of age: civil rights struggles were intensifying, the groundwork was being laid for heavy American involvement in the Vietnam War, sexual promiscuity was rising with widespread use of the pill, and campus rebellion was brewing with the birth of the free speech movement. Songs, whether they directly reflected these issues or not, would need greater lyrical sophistication if they were to mirror listeners' increasingly complex feelings. Though the Byrds couldn't have known it, machinations were at work elsewhere in rock in 1964 to bring the Beatles' unique musicality and Dylan's ambitiously intellectual lyrics closer together.

For one thing, the Beatles themselves were starting to get hip to Dylan, even before they landed in New York. As Lennon told the *New Musical Express* (commonly referred to as *NME* in the UK) in 1965, "We began admiring him during our visit to Paris in January of last year when we cadged a Dylan LP off a DJ who came to interview us. Paul had heard of him before but until we played that record his name did not really mean anything to us. We went potty over the LP—I think it was *Free-wheelin'*—and tried to get more of his records." When the Beatles returned to New York during their second American tour in August 1964, *Saturday Evening Post* journalist Al Aronowitz arranged for Dylan to meet the Beatles in their hotel. Dylan in turn introduced the Beatles to high-grade marijuana—as the now well-known story goes, he had thought the "I can't hide" refrain of "I Want to Hold Your Hand" was "I get high."

The Beatles had already begun using more acoustic, folky guitar changes and melancholy, thoughtful (though still love-minded) lyrics on some *A Hard Day's Night* cuts; songs like "Things We Said Today" and "I'll Be Back" are almost as proto-folk-rock as anything else being recorded in 1964. Their firsthand exposure to Dylan himself intensified the injection of more personal, darker lyrics into their songs, particularly those that were primarily the work of Lennon. "I'm a Loser," from late 1964, was the most blatant of these, with some shrill harmonica soloing in the cast of that heard on Dylan's early albums. Noel Stookey of Peter, Paul & Mary (who, probably unaware of Ringo's putdown of their "Stewball" single, had already been photographed with the Beatles and Ed Sullivan) went as far as to tell *Melody Maker*, "'I'm a Loser' by the Beatles is a protest song. Lennon is saying we are all losers. You can be a loser in life, by not being involved in it."

The Beatles were the group on everyone's minds when you talked about British rock in early 1964. But as bands followed them across the Atlantic, it became evident that other British bands of varying styles were hatching rock-folk cross-pollinations too. Prominent among those were the Searchers, the best Liverpool group other than the Beatles (whose George Harrison named them as his favorite British group in *Melody Maker*). Their clean harmonies and acoustic-electric guitar blends in some ways presaged directions that would be pursued by the Byrds, particularly in the ringing, cyclical guitar riffs of their hits "Needles and Pins" and "When You Walk in the Room." As an indication of the growing interaction between US and UK acts, both were covers of recent singles by L.A. singer-songwriter Jackie DeShannon.

DeShannon, like the Searchers and others dovetailing with folk-rock, has been overlooked by historians documenting the genesis of the folk-rock sound. More successful as a writer, particularly (in collaboration with Sharon Sheeley) of hits by Brenda Lee, than a performer in the early '60s, she nonetheless kept plugging away as a singer on an astonishingly versatile assortment of flop singles, covering everything from rockabilly and country to girl-group pop. One of those singles, "Needles and Pins" (released in April 1963), marked what was probably the first appearance of the "classic" repeated, ringing folk-rock guitar riff on record, played by well-traveled session man Glen Campbell. The single was cowritten by two composers who would later play their own quirky

Jackie DeShannon in her folkie persona

roles in folk-rock, Jack Nitzsche (who also did the arrangement) and Sonny Bono.

"Needles and Pins" made only #84. It took the Searchers (who actually first came across it not from the single, but by hearing it played live in Hamburg by the British band Cliff Bennett and the Rebel Rousers) to come up with an arrangement that truly announced the arrival of the electric 12-string folk-rock guitar riff. Or a 12-string-sounding riff, at any rate, because it turns out that electric 12-strings actually weren't used on the record, in spite of the many references among musicians and writers to it as the first appearance of a Byrds-like guitar flourish. Searchers guitarists John McNally and Mike Pender both had six-string guitars at the session, clarifies McNally, "but we just played the rhythm. Ray Prickett, the engineer, put some reverb on one of the guitars, and suddenly it sounded like an octave, like 12-string guitars. Tony Hatch, our producer at the time, said, 'This sounds like 12-string guitars, doesn't it?' And we all went, 'Oh yeah, Tony, that's right, yeah.' We didn't even know! It was a complete accident, actually, that we stumbled on this 12-string guitar sound. I must say, the Beatles took it one step further, and so did the Byrds." When "Needles and Pins" became a big UK hit in January 1964 (rising to the Top 20 in the US two months later), the group actually had to buy its first electric 12-strings to recreate the effect live.

The electric 12-string became a staple of the Searchers' sound the rest of 1964, and was heard on another cover of a folk riff-driven DeShannon song (this one written by Jackie herself) that had barely reached the Top 100 in late 1963, "When You Walk in the Room." Once again the Searchers had the big international hit with the tune, putting the resonant electric 12-string even more to the fore. DeShannon's songs, though anchored to romantic angst, were clearly something more personal than the usual Top 40 trivia. Informed by her infatuation with Bob Dylan's early work, they were colored by an adult sensuality in both the words and the fetching-yet-earthy delivery. As one who absorbed folk sensibilities into rock rather than going the more usual route of leaping from folk *to* rock, she was a pioneer.

DeShannon made some other forward-thinking moves to bring folk and rock closer. She worked briefly in clubs with unknown L.A. guitarist Ry Cooder (then still in his mid-teens) in a folk duo. She recorded "Don't Turn Your Back on Me,"—another gutsy rocker with 12-strings aplenty that was folk-rock in all but name—in London in October 1964 with young session guitarist Jimmy Page (with whom she also wrote some material). And perhaps a little of her adventurousness rubbed off on the Beatles, for whom she opened on their second American tour in 1964. That's when John Lennon, she revealed in (believe it or not) a 2000 *National Enquirer* article, "sang me a new song he was working on, 'I'm a Loser.' He asked my advice and I raved about it. A few months later it turned up on a Beatles album."

Much like Dusty Springfield (another genre-jumper who sang folk music early in her career, though—unlike DeShannon—she didn't write many of her own songs), DeShannon would not, for all her early groundbreaking, make folk-rock the focus of an unnervingly eclectic career. A hit cover of the Burt Bacharach–Hal David anthem "What the World Needs Now Is Love" in the summer of '65 cast her in the public eye as a singer of orchestrated pop songs, rather than as a rock singer. Much of the work on her ensuing 1960s albums followed that mold, with some peeps here and there of white soul music, although she did join a folk-rock spin-off by becoming an album-oriented singer-songwriter as the '60s turned to the '70s.

There does exist a rare LP, recorded for her publisher Metric Music, of 12 demos on which she's accompanied only by echoing acoustic guitar. (This is dated as May 1965 in the liner notes to the anthology *What the World Needs Now Is . . . Jackie DeShannon, The Definitive Collection*, though it sounds as if it might have been recorded earlier.) Boasting internal rhyme schemes that seem influenced by many nights of listening to *Another Side of Bob Dylan*, it contains heartrendingly sung, slightly raw, and wonderfully haunting compositions. Reflecting the doubt, confusion, and excitement of finding one's adult identity, these include versions of "Don't Doubt Yourself, Babe," recorded by the Byrds on their first album; "Splendor in the Grass," a delicate love song hinting at the loss of virginity; and the stunning minor-keyed "With You in Mind," covered by Marianne Faithfull. It is the only glimmer of what might have been, had DeShannon taken her folk-rock leanings to a higher level.

In addition to cutting DeShannon songs, the Searchers made some little-noticed rock versions of American folk songs, though admittedly only about once per album. In 1963 they recorded Pete Seeger's "Where Have All the Flowers Gone" and Limeliter Glenn Yarborough's arrangement of "All

My Sorrows" (a variation of the song Paul McCartney heard as "All My Trials" when done by Joan Baez). And in late 1964, they made the daring move of putting Malvina Reynolds's "What Have They Done to the Rain" on a single—and having a hit with it—almost a year before protest folk-rock songs came into vogue. The sentimental strings diluted the impact a little, but it was still a remarkable achievement to get such lyrics into the Top 40 in any context.

"We didn't look at it as folk," contends McNally of the Searchers' Seeger and Reynolds covers. "We just looked at it as great tunes, great melodies. Things like 'What Have They Done to the Rain,' we just loved the tune and loved the lyrics. Because it was about nuclear fallout; at that point, the mid-'60s was 'Ban the Bomb' and all that kind of thing. Our record company hated it. We had to fight to have that one released." In a 1998 interview with Spencer Leigh in *Record Collector*, Searchers drummer Chris Curtis might have pointed out more contradictions entailed by the commercial success of such songs than he intended by noting, "It had a very profound message and considering people didn't know what they were listening to, it did very well. It was the first green, ecological hit record and the most money Malvina Reynolds ever earned was from us."

Fellow British Invaders with underestimated traces of folk were Peter & Gordon, usually thought of as a commercial duo riding Paul McCartney's coattails to their (primarily American) success. As the sister of McCartney's girlfriend Jane Asher, Peter had an inside track to Lennon-McCartney songs not used by the Beatles, particularly since McCartney was living in the Asher family's Central London town house at the time. It was not for nothing that Gene Clark had suggested to Roger McGuinn that they should form a Peter & Gordon-type act, though. There was a genuine folky Everly Brothers feel to the harmonies on early P&G hits like "A World Without Love," along with a good deal of acoustic 12-string guitars throughout their early work. Plus, for those who cared to dig into their early albums and B-sides, there were covers of folk tunes like "Barbara Allen," "All My Trials," and Hedy West's "500 Miles," as well as a few respectable originals in a similar getting-toward-folk-rock vein. It's not well known that the teenaged Asher would go to hootenannies on Saturday nights to mix with the likes of Ewan MacColl and Peggy Seeger (MacColl's wife, Pete Seeger's half-sister, and a noted topical songwriter herself). Before he and Gordon Waller recorded, he also performed with Andy Irvine, who though born in London would later become (and to this day remains) one of Ireland's foremost folk performers.

And it turned out that the Everly Brothers' album of traditional folk songs, pretty much ignored as a sidestep in their careers by most listeners and historians, would not be without its influence after all. Waller, who remembers "mucking around with Buddy Holly songs and Everly Brothers songs" with McCartney for hours at the Asher household, confirms that Peter & Gordon's "repertoire in the early days, when we were playing these little clubs, were things like 'All My Trials,' '500 Miles,' 'Guess Things Happen That Way,' 'Big River,' 'Roving Rambler,' 'Barbara Allen,' 'Willow Garden,' 'Long Time Gone.' Those were sort of remnants off *Songs Our Daddy Taught Us*, by the Everly Brothers. That was one of my favorite albums; the Joan Baez album was one of my favorite albums. Basically things that I could learn that had very, very simple chords." He little knew that in the mid-'60s, Baez herself would sing "500 Miles" with the duo at one show.

Those songs are not represented on the Peter & Gordon singles, says Waller, "'cause they were going for hits. We didn't want to release recent cover versions. In those days, there was a lot of people in England covering American hits. We sort of turned the tables on that, and so did the Beatles." Or, as he told *NME* in May 1964, "We'd certainly be very happy if the public would accept us primarily as folk artists, but we have no intention of ramming it down their throats." Countered Asher the following year in *Record Mirror*, "Gordon was basically a rocker—Gene Vincent, the Everlys and Presley were his idols. I was going through a rather 'pseud' stage, listening to Woody Guthrie and being narrow-minded about pop. I liked some pop but didn't like pop versions of folk songs. Playing together our style began to evolve—somewhere between folk and pop. I like to think our voices today still have a folky sound."

The gap between folk and pop-rock was also being mined by some other British singers. The Mojos, a Liverpool band who never made the slightest impression in the States, did a slow, dramatic version of a song by the Weavers' Lee Hays, "Seven Daffodils," though they had actually learned it via Lonnie Donegan's rendition. The Plebs did a decent, commercially ignored beat group treatment of the trad folk warhorse "Babe I'm Gonna Leave You." Rolling Stones producer and manager Andrew Loog Oldham, influenced by his hero Phil Spector, put walls of acoustic 12-string guitar reverb on the doleful yet hypnotic singles he recorded with the Poets, the best Scottish rock group of the 1960s (and one of the world's most underrated rock bands of the decade).

Another Oldham client, Marianne Faithfull, bridged the folk and pop-rock worlds on orchestral arrangements that accentuated her restrained, virginal vocals (a territory explored with greater skill and sexiness by French star Françoise Hardy). Oldham pooh-poohs notions that he was throwing his spices into the folk-rock stew, with his customary colorful tact: "I never had any real affinity for folk music, only acoustic guitars. Folk didn't really affect my life. To my snob-ridden agenda, folkies were a bunch of Gauloise pretentious middle class peons with torn sweaters and no idea of footwear."

He qualifies, "The wonder of the 12-string acoustic guitar when making records, in particular those of the Poets, was that the chang of the chord let you hear all the possibilities as to the tones and placement possible in your arrangement. It was really the palette, the audio color chart, your storyboard, a wonderful sonic brush." As for the wispy folkiness of the early Faithfull discs, he observes, "The range of her voice at the time demanded that sound. She'd have drowned with an electric guitar." Violins, rather than acoustic guitars, carried the arrangements on her flop October 1964 single "Blowin' in the Wind"/"House of the Rising Sun." The results pleased no one, least of all Faithfull, who dismissed the single as a "bad mistake" in *NME*. These were nonetheless daring songs to choose at a time when artists with even tenuous connections to rock, such as Faithfull, had rarely attempted covers of contemporary Dylan tunes or old traditional folk standards. However, her version of "House of the Rising Sun," complete with ostentatious gladiator-of-doom choral backup vocals, couldn't help but pass unnoticed in the wake of a far more successful interpretation of the tune just months earlier, by the Animals.

The Animals were among the best of the British Invasion bands that, more so than the Beatles and Merseybeat groups, ingested blues and R&B as their chief diet. Groups like the Animals, the Rolling Stones, the Yardbirds, and (at least some of the time) Manfred Mann and the Kinks covered many blues-based songs on their early records. As blues were an important strand of folk music itself, it could be said that such artists were doing folk-rock of a sort. That must be qualified by noting that they were usually covering electric, citified post–World War II blues, not the rural acoustic kind that most of the folk audience viewed as the authentic brand.

Still, the Rolling Stones were already starting to write songs that sounded very much like Mississippi Delta blues, such as the early B-side "Good Times, Bad Times." In doing so they were acting as a modern continuation of the British tradition established by bandleader Alexis Korner. Korner, and others like Cyril Davies, had spearheaded the British blues scene back in the 1950s with covers of folkier blues by the likes of Big Bill Broonzy, also helping out visiting American bluesmen like Broonzy, Sonny Terry, and Brownie McGhee during their UK tours. He acted as a mentor to members of the Stones, Manfred Mann, Kinks, John Mayall's Bluesbreakers, and Cream who either played with or received valuable tutelage from him.

It was thus natural that some blues-minded British Invaders sometimes dipped way down into pre-electric folk-blues standards for cover material. Budding producer Joe Boyd, in England in the spring of 1964 as the tour manager for the American Folk Blues and Gospel Caravan, still remembers hearing the Spencer Davis Group (with a teenaged Stevie Winwood on vocals) playing Leadbelly songs. Indeed he cites that as an inspiration for his ambitions to try and put a folk-rock group together with Paul Rothchild upon his return to New York.

It was a song that had been done by Leadbelly and many others that would, in the hands of the Animals, show just how exciting a traditional folk tune could be, given the right electric rock treatment. "House of the Rising Sun," the sorrowful tale of a whorehouse in New Orleans, has taken various forms since it was collected by Alan Lomax, who recorded a version by 16-year-old Georgia Turner in 1937 and subsequently put it into a songbook. By the early '60s it was one of the most oft-covered numbers of folk sets and, increasingly, folk albums. Carolyn Hester and Joan Baez recorded timorous, high-pitched versions, and Bob Dylan put a bluesier one on his first album. Dave Van Ronk later said that Dylan lifted the arrangement from him, before Van Ronk had the chance to record it himself.

Among those listening closely to Dylan's first album were the Animals. "We were never considered to be really involved in the folk world," admits Animals drummer John Steel. "But we did have that background pre– rock 'n' roll of jazz and folk. When I met Eric [Burdon] and we were 15 years old, we formed a jazz band first before we got into rock. And we had a knowledge of mostly black blues and folk, but also of American white folk as well. So we were influenced *before* rock 'n' roll, as much as *with* rock 'n' roll.

"That first album by Bob Dylan just caught a lot of people's fancy," says Steel, who thinks that he and Animals singer Eric Burdon first heard a friend's copy in 1962 or 1963. "To certain kinds of people, it just really rocked everybody back. Obviously there were just such strong similarities to Woody Guthrie, who we knew about then. We were sort of instant converts, instant fans. We took it around to everybody we knew and said, 'You gotta listen to this.'"

The gritty combo from Newcastle had already covered a folk standard from that LP, "Baby Let Me Follow You Down," to good effect on their first British single, Alan Price's punchy organ and Hilton Valentine's biting guitar jelling well around Eric Burdon's soul-soaked vocals. Ironically, the idea to do the song came not from the band but from their hits-minded producer, itself a sign that lines between folk and commercial rock were thinning. Mickie Most, according to Steel, "used to go on these little trips hunting for new material and stuff that bands could cover." Although "Baby Let Me Follow You Down" was a common standby of folk gigs, particularly among the Cambridge crowd, the version that Most found was an extremely obscure one by Hoagy Lands that had been retitled for the commercial market, remembered by Hilton Valentine in Sean Egan's *Animal Tracks* biography as "Baby Let Me Hold Your Hand."

"He came back with that version of 'Baby Let Me Take You Home'"—the title having changed to an even more cautiously innocuous phrase for the Animals' recording—"which we immediately recognized from the song that Dylan had recorded on his first album. Which made it kind of credible for us," Steel laughs. "That was an okay song to do, 'cause Bob Dylan had done it. We were just young guys, and influences like that mattered to us. So we recorded it, and it was our first break," with the Animals' "Baby Let Me Take You Home" peaking at a respectable #21 in the British charts.

"House of the Rising Sun," like "Baby Let Me Take You Home/Follow You Down," may have reached the Animals' ears via more than one version, though again Dylan's was the most important. It's sometimes been written that members of the Animals actually heard Josh White's rendition before Dylan's, and disputes over exactly what happened reveal that elitist reverence of authenticity might not have been limited to Greenwich Village folkies. "Eric would have always claimed that he'd heard it long before, by Josh White," says Steel. "There was a lot of stuff said to sort of improve your credibility. Rather than say somebody had just found this song and told us to record it, you had to pretend to be cool and say, 'Well, we heard it way before anybody else heard it.' The same was said about 'House of the Rising Sun,' that we knew a version by Leadbelly and Josh White. But I think that's wishful thinking. I think Bob Dylan's was the first time we ever heard it."

The controversies over the Animals' brilliant rock arrangement of "House of the Rising Sun" linger to this day. Steele: "The version that all the four of us remember, Alan apart, is that we were rehearsing the number in the Club A-Go-Go in Newcastle, which was our sort of home base. Alan normally was regarded as the arranger for the band, but only in the sense that he would lift chords off whatever number we were gonna cover, and run it through for everybody. When we were trying it, Hilton came up with that arpeggio intro on the guitar, and we liked that a lot. Alan tried to insist on it being an acoustic strumming thing a la Bob Dylan's version. We had a big row about it. Alan stormed off in a huff, and we carried on running the number through. I nicked the drum part off of 'Walk on the Wild Side' by Jimmy Smith, which had that nice feel. When Alan came back and calmed down, all he had to do was drop in with the organ solo, basically. We were all very shocked when the thing finally came out with 'traditional, arrangement Alan Price' on the label.

Our manager at the time said, 'Don't worry, it'll be credited equally with everybody.' But it never was, and Alan['s] been reaping the royalties ever since."

The Animals put "House of the Rising Sun" into their set while opening for a Chuck Berry tour, "because everybody on the bill was going to be playing a lot of rock 'n' roll, [and] it would be good to have a standout number in contrast to that. And it worked. We were on the tour, and the reaction to the song was absolutely…you couldn't ignore it, you know. But Mickie wasn't convinced of the song. He took us into the studio in mid-tour primarily to record a credit title piece for [the] TV show *Ready Steady Go.* We insisted that we record 'Sun' at the same time, because we could tell that it was happening. And he said okay."

The Animals had transformed a folk lament into a powerhouse rock song. Valentine's unforgettable arpeggio guitar line (still one of the most-played licks in the world) was matched by Burdon's wrenching vocals, a wail so loud that he probably didn't need a record to be heard across the ocean. Price, despite his reservations, contributed an incendiary organ solo. "We went in after a gig, we drove back to London about 100 miles and went into the studio sometime after midnight," recalls Steel. "It was a mono track studio, so essentially it was just a live recording. We set it up, and we played halfway through it to get a balance for the engineer, and then we did a take. And that was it. Mickie said, 'We've got a hit here.' And that's when the engineer pointed out that it was four-and-a-half minutes long. Mickie, to his credit, said, 'Well, what the hell, we'll go with it on its full length.' That was a brave choice by Mickie, not to send us back into the studio and do a shortened version of it.

"Consequently, when it was released in America, the record company chopped a big lump out of it, because they said it wouldn't get airplay at that length. It was a shock to us, but that was the only way the record company could see that it would get airplay. If memory serves me right, they just hacked out the organ solo, which is one of the high spots of the number." That wasn't the only compromise in order. Even before it was recorded, the band had changed the lyrics to refer to a gambling house, rather than a house of prostitution. Integrity would only take you so far on AM radio in mid-1964, and it would hardly be the last time folk-rock lyrics would be modified to secure more airplay. Nonetheless, putting out a demonic four-minutes-plus rock cover of a traditional folk-blues tune was courageous enough.

And it certainly got its airplay, reaching #1 in both Britain and America. Not all the punters were happy to see a rock group get hold of the song, laying some kindle for a debate between purists and rockers that would rise to an uproar in 1965. "As an ardent Bob Dylan fan, I urge the Animals to leave his material well alone," wrote Michael Crowther in *Melody Maker*'s letter section. "'Baby Let Me Follow You Down' was fantastic until the Animals got hold of it. Now they've done 'House of the Rising Sun.' What next?" To which Alan Price retorted: "I'd like to give all those people a list of the other people who have recorded 'House of the Rising Sun.' Who's to say we can't record it if we want to? It's a fantastic, ridiculous criticism."

ne of the guys we first wanted to meet when we first went over to America was Bob Dylan," continues Steel. "We met up with Bob and went out for some drinks around Greenwich Village. He told us that we had planted the idea of going electric via 'House of the Rising Sun.' He said he'd been driving along listening to the car radio and suddenly that came on, and he just stopped the car and went, 'Ding!' The light bulb went off in his head." In early 1965 in *NME*, Animals bassist (and future Jimi Hendrix co-manager) Chas Chandler went as far as to say, "Bob bought our record of 'House of the Rising Sun' and was so impressed with it that he bought an electric guitar so that he could include our version in his stage act."

There's no evidence that Dylan played a live electric version of the song in the mid-'60s. There *is* evidence that the Animals hit might have made the light bulb go off in the head of his producer, Tom Wilson. For on December 8, 1964, Wilson overdubbed electric instruments on Dylan's original November 1961 version of "House of the Rising Sun," as well as a couple of the outtakes from *The Freewheelin' Bob Dylan* ("Mixed Up Confusion" and "Rocks and Gravel"). This "House of the Rising Sun" was released on the 1995 CD-ROM *Highway 61 Revisited* and misleadingly (at least initially) billed as having been recorded two years before the Animals' cover.

The strong similarity of the electric instruments (by unknown musicians) on the Wilson-doctored take suggests that he was using the familiar Animals hit as the model, however. A passage in fellow Wilson client Dion's autobiography *The Wanderer* supports this: "Wilson played some of the tracks Bob had been putting down in the studio, and, as usual, they were awesome. Maybe I had my ear on top of the charts too long, but it suddenly occurred to me that, with some players jamming behind some of those songs, Dylan had a chance on Top 40 radio. Tom Wilson thought it was worth a try, so he rounded up a bunch of session cats and took the tapes down to the old Columbia studios. For the next couple of hours, Tom and I worked out some rock 'n' roll arrangements for Dylan's folk stuff, and let the musicians rip. I was right, it was totally in the pocket. Tom agreed, and took the doctored songs back to Bob Dylan."

With Wilson having died in the late '70s, it's impossible to confirm, but the overdubs may have been the final steps to push Dylan into electric rock. Dylan had hardly been inactive as the Beatles conquered America, but had remained for the time being resolutely planted in acoustic folk. His third album, *The Times They Are A-Changin'*, was his most protest-oriented collection, and made the Top 20 shortly after its release at the kickoff of American Beatlemania. *Another Side of Bob Dylan*, released that summer, had not done as well, but had not lost any folk fans due to sell-out additions of rock instruments.

The big controversy among much of his constituency was his abandonment of social protest anthems for personal songs, often romantic ones, though lyrically far more oblique and ingenious than those on the hit parade. As Paul Wolfe wrote in *Broadside* after the 1964 Newport Folk Festival, "His new songs, as performed at Newport, surprised everyone, leaving the majority of the audience annoyed, some even disgusted, and, in general, scratching its collective head in disbelief. The art that had, in the past, produced towering works of power and importance, had, seemingly, degenerated into confusion and innocuousness." Wolfe might have been even more upset had he known that in an informal private jam away from the stage, Dylan and his friends Tony Glover and Bobby Neuwirth were working out the harmonies to "Tell Me," the Rolling Stones' first American Top 40 hit.

Some critics feel that at this point Dylan was writing rock songs that just happened to only use solo acoustic guitar. It's true that he was at last melodically moving largely away from the traditional folk melodies he had set words to for his own purposes on his previous albums. Also true was that some of *Another Side of Bob Dylan*'s songs, like "It Ain't Me Babe" and "All I Really Want to Do," would be adopted by rock bands in 1965 for hit singles. Another, "My Back Pages," could in hindsight be interpreted as a farewell to the medium of the protest song itself (and was also covered for a hit rock single, though not until 1967). Yet, like Peter Stampfel's belief that Dylan was singing folk songs in a rock 'n' roll manner way back in 1961, all this didn't mean that *Another Side of Bob Dylan* was rock. If it was, it would have caused far more hostility within the folk community than it did.

As it was, Dylan had enough to contend with from pundits unhappy with his new lyrical direction. The most notorious attack came from *Sing Out!* editor Irwin Silber, who wrote in his November 1964 "open letter to Bob Dylan": "You said you weren't a writer of 'protest' songs —or any other category, for that matter—but you just wrote songs. Well, okay, call it anything you want. But any songwriter who tries to deal honestly with reality in this world is bound to write 'protest' songs. How can he help himself? Your new songs seem to be all inner-directed now, inner-probing, self-conscious—maybe even a little maudlin or a little cruel on occasion. And it's happening on stage, too. You seem to be relating to a handful of cronies behind the scenes now—rather than to the rest of us out front. Now, that's all okay—if that's the way you want it, Bob. But then you're a different Bob Dylan from the one we knew. The old one never wasted our precious time."

In large part due to that open letter, Silber, and to some extent *Sing Out!*, have been cast as villains in some accounts of the strife within the folk community over Dylan's change of direction in the mid-'60s. "Dylan was moving away from his political songs," says Silber today. "In fact, even saying he just used that for a while in order to get a break. That's what distressed me more than anything else. I mean, here was a guy who'd come along after I'd spent close to 20 years doing this stuff. He was the most exciting person I'd heard since Woody Guthrie, and he combined a great artistic feel with a political sense that was poetic, that moved people. And now, to find him turning his back on it, at a time when. . . .

"Remember, I wrote that open letter in '64. This is when the civil rights movement is at its height, the beginnings of the protest against the Vietnam War, and so on. Politics, after the '50s, was *really* resurging in a big way. [With] the New Left and people who were not stuck in the framework of the Communist Party and Trotskyism and so on, there was a whole new sense of politics. And to have Dylan deliberately, consciously, moving away from it at that time—well, I really felt bad about that."

Silber, like many who were unprepared for Dylan's shift, would come to soften his position within a few years. In 1968, he wrote in *The Guardian*, "Dylan is our poet—not our leader. Poets touch us where we want to be touched. . . . And if he fails to touch, the failure may be ours, not his." As Silber explains now, "Three years later, I was ready to deal with the Bob Dylan that existed, and not the Bob Dylan that I remembered from those first years."

Back in the mid-'60s, however, the immediate sense of shock would be compounded by Dylan's shift not just to non-topical tunes, but also from acoustic folk to electric folk-rock. Dylan's artistic motivations for going with this flow are no secret. He was vocal in his enthusiasms for the new British groups; he had, like many of his generation, grown up with rock; and he had even tinkered briefly with rock 'n' roll as a Columbia recording artist in 1962. But as someone with aspirations to stardom on the level of Elvis Presley, there might have been more calculated reasoning as well.

For the fact was, in late 1964, if Dylan was mulling over a jump into the electric foray, he was in danger of being beaten to the punch from several directions and left behind. His friendly rival Richard Fariña, now a folksinger in a duo with Joan Baez's sister Mimi, was signed to Vanguard, where the pair were by autumn recording their debut album. Though not released until spring 1965, *Celebrations for a Grey Day* gave rhythm and instrumental depth to lyrics not far below the standard of Dylan's, including a couple of songs that went into all-out rock 'n' roll. (Dulcimer maker Terry Hennessy told *Dulcimer Player News* in 1999 that Richard Fariña had asked Hennessy to make him an electric dulcimer before Dylan went electric, although that dulcimer was never made.) Fred Neil, Tim Hardin, and Dino Valenti were groping toward their own matches of serious lyrics with blues-folk-pop melodies and electric rock, both live and in the recording studio.

On the other side of the country, the Byrds were also in danger of getting beaten to the market by other artists that were hitting upon, whether by intent or accident, a form of folk-rock. There were an increasing number of folk-pop records that were using mild but noticeable electric backing. Gale Garnett, yet another low-voiced sensuous female folksinger, is thought of as a one-shot artist for her Top Five hit "We'll Sing in the Sunshine," but actually did some respectable rockish arrangements of traditional folk tunes and folk-based originals on her album of the same name. The Simon Sisters, with a young Carly Simon, sounded like a very lightly folk-rockified Ian & Sylvia or Peter, Paul & Mary on some of their obscure 1964 Kapp recordings. Hoyt Axton, the folksinger who had used McGuinn as an accompanist on his 1962 album *The Balladeer*, made a clumsy rock LP in 1964 that was not so much folk-rock as an awkward intersection of blues-rock and go-go rhythms, like a weird cross between Johnny Rivers and John Hammond, Jr. Even weirder, on the other side of the globe in Sydney, Australia, a benefit concert for the underground magazine *Oz* on November 15 was, according to Francis Evers in *The Australian*, to be an event where "rock & rollers will sing folk songs and folksingers will spoof rock & roll."

Garnett and the Simon Sisters might have been inching toward folk-rock at the rate of a caterpillar, but the Beau Brummels, based up the California coast in San Francisco, represented a far more serious threat. By late 1964, they were recording material that in many ways made innovations similar to those heard in the Byrds' early studio efforts: strong Beatlesque original songs, captivating sweet-sour harmonies and chord progressions, and an overall earnest sincerity that seemed almost as grounded in folk as in rock, given a rock coating by full electric band arrangements. With their first hit single on release and poised to enter the charts in December 1964, the Beau Brummels had a leg up on the Byrds, who had just the one flop single to their name, under a different name no less.

et the Byrds also had good reason to be optimistic as the year drew to a close. They had finally secured state-of-the-art equipment, including a full drum kit for Clarke and a Fender bass for Hillman, in a most unusual deal. Art collector, artist, and theater producer Naomi Hirshhorn, a client of Jim Dickson's partner Eddie Tickner, had invested $5,000 for a 5 percent stake in the group: an extremely risky proposition for an unknown band, and a virtually unheard-of transaction in 1964, when rock wasn't nearly as much of a money-spinning or culturally respected institution as it was by the end of the century. Even more crucially, the Byrds had been signed to Columbia, Bob Dylan's label.

The route to the contract, like the one to their new instruments, was as unconventional as they come. McGuinn, Crosby, and Clark had sung along with a tape of some demos in the living room of entertainment entrepreneur Benny Shapiro (later to help organize the Monterey Pop Festival before being bought out in its early stages), greatly impressing Shapiro's young daughter. The great jazz trumpeter Miles Davis, recalls Dickson, "came to Benny's for breakfast the next day and Benny told him about it. Miles got on the phone to Townsend"—Irving Townsend, head of the West Coast office for Columbia Records—"and arranged a meeting for me with Allen Stanton," CBS's West Coast A&R man (who would also produce the Byrds' third album, *Fifth Dimension*). On November 10, the group was signed to Columbia Records.

The Byrds were still under the gun to return Columbia's investment. Only McGuinn, Crosby, and Clark were signed to the contract, and the label was only required to record four songs before deciding to take up the option for a full five-year deal. What they needed was a song that would be a hit, fast. If the song could take their synthesis of folk and rock to a higher level, so much the better.

Actually, the song that would act as the medium for the best of the Beatles, folk music, and the sophisticated imagery of the newly emerging singer-songwriters to converge was already written. Its strange, laborious transformation from an acoustic folk dirge to a #1 single would prove that the medium was as important as the message.

the mr. tambourine men

n February 1964, as the Beatles were winning over the country with their first visit to the United States, Bob Dylan was making an offbeat American tour of his own. His three-week cross-country trip from New York to California was indeed punctuated by a few concerts. But it was mostly a chance to do his own 1960s version of Jack Kerouac's *On the Road*, accompanied by three hipster friends and much booze and marijuana. There were visits to miners in Kentucky, poet and song collector Carl Sandburg in North Carolina, and the site where Kennedy had been shot less than three months before in Dallas. For light relief, there were also a couple of days of revelry at Mardi Gras in New Orleans. It was in New Orleans, Dylan later remembered, that he did some work on "Mr. Tambourine Man." It was one of several songs he started composing on the trip, using a typewriter in the back of the station wagon.

"Mr. Tambourine Man," like the other material Dylan was developing in early 1964, was emblematic of his escape from the shackles of topical songwriting into more abstract imagery, often suggesting a search for liberation from both external and internal prisons. That quest was quite apparent in another of the songs he worked on during his journey, "Chimes of Freedom," its call for the abolition of repression not tethered to any specific political or social movement. "Mr. Tambourine Man" went yet further, evoking not just escape from bondage but an altered state of perception, with its plea for transportation through mystical ships and corridors of time to a land of diamond-studded skies. It was not, on the face of it, the stuff of which Top 40 hits were made. It was not the kind of thing which the author himself could replicate. "I tried to write another 'Mr. Tambourine Man,'" he admitted to *NME* in 1969, years after the song had become an acknowledged classic. "It was the first and last time I tried to write a song in the same vein as another. I worked on it, but it didn't happen, so I left it."

Dylan cut both "Chimes of Freedom" and "Mr. Tambourine Man" at the marathon one-day session on June 9, 1964 that yielded the entire *Another Side of Bob Dylan* album. "Chimes of

Freedom" was a highlight of the LP, yet "Mr. Tambourine Man," for some reason, was excluded. Dylan told writer Martin Bronstein in March 1966 that he "felt too close to it to put it on." It also may be that the one take he attempted in the studio was simply not judged appropriate or good enough to do justice to the song. For this performance, Dylan enlisted help from his old Village buddy Ramblin' Jack Elliott, who contributed rather wayward vocal harmonies to Bob's first attempt to use backup singing on an official session.

Elliott has said that his timing was erratic in part because, in keeping with Dylan's usual seat-of-the-pants approach to recording, Jack wasn't fully conversant with the lyrics by the time the tape rolled. "I said, 'Do you have the words, Bob?'" he told *Acoustic Guitar Magazine* in 1995. "He said, 'No, I know this one.' So I harmonized on the chorus, because I didn't know the song all the way through." In the *San Francisco Examiner* the following year, he judged the end product harshly: "They made a tape of Dylan and me, 'Hey, Tambourine Man' [sic]. I listened to it once, and I never want to hear it again. It was real bad singing. Amazingly bad."

Elliott's judgement was unreasonably severe, but certainly there was room for improvement before a final track could be put in the can. Running nearly seven minutes, the pace was lugubrious, the accompaniment limited to basic guitar chords, the phrasing and timing awkward in places. That's not to say it was terrible; certainly the song's strength was abundantly evident. Not much more work would have been needed for it to comfortably meet the standards of the rest of *Another Side of Bob Dylan*, but for the time being, it was shelved.

It was too good a song to disappear, and Dylan incorporated it into his live set in mid-1964, suggesting he hadn't entirely abandoned intentions to eventually record it. He played it at, ironically, the topical song workshop at the 1964 Newport Folk Festival, and at a Halloween concert at the New York Philharmonic Hall that was recorded for a possible live album (which didn't come out, though it has often been bootlegged). It also turned out that the Dylan-Elliott attempt at recording the tune hadn't been entirely banished to the closet, as a promotions man named Jack Mass passed on an acetate to Jim Dickson.

ickson had already been an active champion of Dylan's material before working with the Byrds, suggesting Dylan songs to several artists in his stable. The Dillards had done a then-unreleased Dylan tune, "Walkin' Down the Line," on their 1964 live album. Dickson and Hamilton Camp took the strategy of unearthing obscure Dylan tunes to new heights on Camp's 1964 Elektra *Paths of Victory* LP, which had no less than seven Dylan songs, six of which had yet to be released on Dylan's own Columbia records (and a couple of which have *still* not been released on Dylan's official albums). Camp, interestingly, says this mini-archeological exercise in Dylanology was not Dickson's idea, but Jac Holzman's: "Dylan was hot, so Jac thought it was very smart to put more Dylan tunes on there. Much to my regret," he adds, as he would have rather had a more diverse selection of material. (Dickson has a different recollection: "Camp already was as into Dylan as I was and sang what he wanted on that album.")

Dickson had also recorded a couple of songs off Dylan's *The Times They Are A-Changin'* album in 1964 with the Hillmen, the bluegrass band with Chris Hillmen, Vern Gosdin, and Rex

Gosdin. Recording Dylan tunes with bluegrass bands was still a radical idea for the time (though the Dillards had done so), and the Hillmen material lay unissued for five years until it was dusted off for an archival release in 1969. Vern Gosdin, who by the late '70s would be a mainstream country star, reflects, "I got as much respect for Bob Dylan as anybody. I think he's a great artist. But at that particular time, I just didn't see it. Jim Dickson gave my brother and I a Bob Dylan album to listen to, and I couldn't get into it. Tried everything, but couldn't, and gave it back to him. Next thing I know, the Byrds came up and started doing it."

As Dickson emphasizes, in his experiments with crossing folk with other kinds of styles, "the biggest problem was the songs and the search for new stuff. I was very enamored with what Dylan was writing, as well as Dino [Valenti], Tim Hardin, etc. While recording the Camp album, I worked out a good relation with Witmark, the publisher for Dylan. I heard that Dylan had done a session and was not including 'Tambourine Man,' as he had tried it as a duet with Jack Elliott and was not happy with the result. The west coast rep for Witmark, Jack Mass, was able to get me an acetate from that session, and I became a little obsessed with it. I did think everyone should sing Dylan at the time. I once made a demo with Eartha Kitt with Dylan's 'Oxford Town.'"

In the "Mr. Tambourine Man" acetate, he had a hidden jewel: a song as yet unreleased not only by Dylan but by anyone, and a song as good as any Dylan had written. Dickson had approached Clarence White (of the Kentucky Colonels) about doing the song before introducing it to a young group for which it seemed a natural fit, considering they were well on their way to mixing the Beatles and folk music anyway. There was a considerable problem to contend with before he could pass it on to the Byrds, however. At first, the group balked at doing the song.

Roger McGuinn elaborates: "I'd seen Dylan in the Village, and I wasn't really a big fan of his, you know? He was basically a Woody Guthrie imitator when I saw him, in like '61, '62, whenever he first got there." On *Entertainment Tonight* in 1987, David Crosby was blunter, sharing a reaction that was common among many, as late as 1964, to Dylan's uncompromisingly keening vocals: "I was totally resistant to the idea. It's Dylan?! All that scratchy weer-neer-neer-neer... I didn't like it at all." (Even ultra-fan John Lennon described Dylan as a "neigher" in *Melody Maker* in early 1965.)

"I was already into mixing folk and rock, so we probably would have gone in that direction," speculates McGuinn. "We would have done 'Turn! Turn! Turn!' and 'Bells of Rhymney' and other songs that I knew as folk songs. But I'm sure we would not have gone into 'Tambourine Man,' because I didn't know about the song. Dickson was very helpful in that respect."

"Nobody was really keen on 'Tambourine Man' as I recall when we first heard it," says Hillman. "Maybe McGuinn, but I don't know if anybody else was. But Dickson pounded it into our head, literally, to go for a little more depth in the lyric, and really craft the song, and make something you can be proud of ten to fifteen years down the road. He was absolutely right. We were wise-guy little punk kids, and he was our big brother/father figure, but he had a tremendous influence on the Byrds. He pushed for 'Tambourine Man,' and put himself out on the line for that one. And he was right."

He had to push hard. Initially it was sung by Gene Clark, but it was dropped from their rehearsal set, such was the limpness of their enthusiasm. Crosby, says Dickson, was particularly resistant to the song, and "talked Gene out of 'Tambourine Man.' McGuinn said he would like to try it. I watched it grow and McGuinn find a new voice that would serve him quite well." Dickson then played his ultimate ace, getting Dylan himself involved. Dickson already knew Dylan and his assistants/buddies Bobby Neuwirth and Victor Maymudes, and all three of them dropped by World Pacific to check out the Byrds during an L.A. visit (an event Dickson places in mid-1964). The young band's manager "knew they were coming and had the Byrds rehearse 'Tambourine Man' again. They hung out for hours, played, and made friends." As a member of the group told *Record Mirror* in August 1965: "Bob [Dylan] turned up to hear us go through it maybe a dozen times. So Bob eventually said: 'They do it well.' Which is like a million-word work of praise coming from him."

The magnificent harmonies that did much to enable the song's choruses to seize the world's hearts were also hard earned. Dean Webb of the Dillards has an anecdote to illustrate not just the work that went into the polish of those harmonies, but also the little-discussed connection between bluegrass and the birth of folk-rock. "I was driving by World Pacific Studios, and I happened to see Dickson's old Volkswagen siting there," he remembers. "I stopped by to see what was going on. I go in there, and they're working on 'Mr. Tambourine Man,' and they couldn't seem to get anything going, as far as the harmony that they were trying. And they started getting into it, more or less, over trying to do this. So Dickson asked me what *I* would do with it, as far as harmony was concerned.

"I said, 'Okay. Leave the lead singer in there,' which happened to be McGuinn. The other guys go out of the room. I sang the first part of harmony, or the tenor part, and then they played the tape back, and I put the baritone part on the tape, and then they learned the parts from what I did, triad harmonies, the way possibly *we* would have done it. And it worked for 'em." Adds Dickson: "Dean Webb did put a harmony part on a Byrd demo tape in order for me to show Crosby what I wanted on 'Tambourine Man,' as he stubbornly clung to a more modern harmony that didn't fit."

A take of "Mr. Tambourine Man" that surfaced on the *Preflyte* collection of rehearsal tapes indicates the group's problems in coming to grips with the song. Although the skeleton of the arrangement heard on the famous hit version is there, there's an awkward stiffness, particularly in Michael Clarke's elementary drumming, which is far more suited for a high school marching band than a rock one. (The *In the Beginning* CD unearthed a yet more primitive version from their rehearsals that lacked a drum set, leaving actual tambourine rattles to carry the shaky rhythm.) Knowing how unlikely a seven-minute song would be to get airplay of any sort in early 1965, they had already made a severe compromise, cutting out all but one of the four verses, instead centering their interpretation upon the insinuating chorus, which opened and closed the tune. When it finally came time to record the song for an official Columbia single on January 20, 1965, an even tougher compromise would be in order.

I n 1965, as in many if not all other eras of popular music, it was common for session musicians to play some or all of the parts on records credited to groups that, as far as the public knew, played their instruments both in the studio and on stage. Even when the Byrds did their single for Elektra as the Beefeaters, they'd used a couple of session vets. And that was Elektra, still a relatively scrappy if well-respected indie. Columbia was one of the biggest record labels in the world. It was not going to leave anything to chance, especially considering that the Byrds had barely any experience on record, with the marginal exception of McGuinn. Session players were going to be used. Had they objected, the Byrds had virtually no leverage. Not only had they never recorded for Columbia before (or for anyone under their new name), only three of the five—McGuinn, Clark, and Crosby, all of whom did sing on the final track—were actually signed to a Columbia contract. Hillman and Clarke did not sing or play on the cut at all.

Overseeing the session was Terry Melcher. The young Columbia staff producer, like several who played a strong part in folk-rock's evolution on record, was at first glance an odd choice to take the helm. His background was California pop-rock, both as a producer and as a performer, in which capacity he'd recorded with future Beach Boy Bruce Johnston as half of the surf music duo Bruce & Terry. His quick climb up Columbia's ladder was no doubt aided by being the son of Doris Day, one of Columbia's biggest pop stars since the 1940s. During the time he handled the early Byrds (producing their first two albums), the other chief hitmakers under his charge were Paul Revere & the Raiders, the mainstream (if sometimes very tough) pop-rock band that had a residency on Dick Clark's television show *Where the Action Is*.

But if the Byrds' choices were limited to Columbia's staff, Melcher was nonetheless the *best* option. It didn't hurt that he had already played on a single with McGuinn, on the already-forgotten "Beach Ball" single by the City Surfers a couple of years back. As Doris Day's son, he was unlikely to be messed with too much by company fat cats. His very presence in the producer's booth signaled a loosening of corporate restraints. Since the mid-'50s, Columbia had been the slowest of the major labels in embracing rock 'n' roll, hindered by head A&R man (and easy listening star) Mitch Miller's well-publicized hatred for the music. With the Beatles rewriting the rules of the record industry, Columbia now had no choice but to try and catch up, directing many of its efforts through its Los Angeles branch. Melcher was virtually the only producer there who was roughly the same age as rock musicians and, just as importantly, loved rock itself.

As such he was an important advocate for the Byrds and similar groups within the starched-shirt ranks of Columbia. "Bruce Johnston and Terry Melcher were the first pals I had in my life who loved rock 'n' roll, who were *in* rock 'n' roll," explains Billy James, who had done publicity for Dylan in New York and had recently taken the position as manager of information services for Columbia's L.A. office. "Through my friendship with them and my respect for them, I began to develop an appreciation for rock 'n' roll." Though the appreciation was not always reciprocated by less open-minded Columbia personnel than James, who elaborates: "The West Coast A&R department was something of a thorn in the side of the home office in New York. Terry and Bruce were not typical corporate record company producers. There was a lack of comprehension and appreciation for the changes that were going on in popular music in general, and for what Bruce and Terry were doing in particular, at Columbia."

The logs for the "Mr. Tambourine Man" session list a number of A-level L.A. studio hands as players on the track: Jerry Cole on rhythm guitar, Larry Knechtel on bass, Leon Russell (then several years away from beginning a successful solo career) on electric piano, and Hal Blaine, famous as drummer on many Phil Spector and Beach Boys hits. With McGuinn on electric 12-string, this is the lineup that's generally considered to have performed on the single, though, interestingly, bassist Gary Marker (soon to be in another Columbia folk-rock group, the Rising Sons) believes it wasn't the only one that tried.

"I was called in as a kind of 'floater' when the Byrds were recording what I believe was one of many versions of the basic track for Dylan's 'Tambourine Man'," he remembers. "I wasn't even called by Melcher, it may have been some A&R mucky-muck above him—because the sessions weren't going well, or so I understood. I was supposed to stand by with my acoustic bass. I think there was a possibility that someone might step in and hijack the session from Terry, if he didn't get results this time. Lurking in the control booth, I recall looking out into studio A (aka 'The Basketball Court' because of its size) and seeing McGuinn on 12-string, Crosby [who had taken the rhythm guitar slot in the band after Hillman took over the bass] on six-string, Leon Russell on harpsichord (I think), Hal Blaine on drums. I recollect Joe Osborn as being the bassist on that session, not Knechtel. What absolutely stunned me was seeing Barney Kessel, a mainstay of the L.A. jazz scene, also on rhythm guitar."

There was even some thought of using Glen Campbell as lead guitarist. That might seem peculiar to those who know him primarily as a middle-of-the-road pop star, but if a session musician was to be used at all, he would have been a logical choice. He played on many rock dates before his solo career really got off the ground in 1967. He had also played the kind of 12-string guitar lines that would be central to the Byrds' records before, on Jackie DeShannon's seminal "Needles and Pins," and (with Dickson producing) the Folkswingers' *12 String Guitar* album. Fortunately for everyone concerned, McGuinn played the 12-string in the end, which was crucial to establishing his Rickenbacker ring as a signature to the Byrds' identity right out of the gate on their Columbia releases.

Hillman, relegated to the sidelines, nonetheless understands and even defends the use of session men on the single. "Sometimes I wonder, would it have been interesting for us to have cut a version. It might have taken away a bit of that slick pop sound. It's almost too slick. But it's okay. At the time, we weren't ready to cut that song.

"In those days, we got a singles deal: you know, 'If you guys do good with a single, we'll see if we can let you do an album.' I think, in hindsight, those were the right moves to make. Roger had more time on the battlefield as a backup player. He had good time. He could be out there with session guys and do it. We weren't disciplined enough in that area. I had done lots of sessions on mandolin, but bass, it was another animal. It was a brand-new deal. For me to be next to Hal Blaine on that song, yeah, I probably could have pulled it off. But not as well as Larry Knechtel.

"And it does stand up 37 years later. You hear it on the radio, it's a good piece of music. Regardless of if there's session players on that song, or if we'd have cut it. It's a great song."

McGuinn's 12-string guitar was the very first sound heard on what was indeed a great single. It was, by far, a more dramatic rearrangement of a Dylan song than any that had ever been attempted. Inspired by Bach as much as by folk and rock, McGuinn's opening and closing riffs were seductive, hypnotic, and joyous. Knechtel's bass zoomed up in counterpoint to McGuinn's lead almost imme-

Bob Dylan onstage with the Byrds at Ciro's in Hollywood, March 1965. Left to right: David Crosby, Gene Clark, Bob Dylan, Michael Clarke, Roger McGuinn (Byrds bassist Chris Hillman misses the frame)

diately after McGuinn's unaccompanied intro. The choruses and verses were changed from the lugging 2/4 beats of Dylan's acetate to the more standard 4/4 of rock music, and the rhythm guitar on the Byrds' version was specifically inspired by the kind that had recently anchored the Beach Boys' classic "Don't Worry Baby." The singers' harmonies, especially in conjunction with McGuinn's 12-string bed, created an entrancing haze that heightened the mystical tenor of the lyrics. McGuinn himself took the solo vocal on the one verse that had been lifted of the original four from Dylan's demo. His quavering, likable, yet enigmatic voice, as he has repeatedly said since, was an attempt, and a very successful one, to hit an exact midpoint between Bob Dylan and John Lennon.

The result was that elusive treasure in the evolution of popular music: a new sound, albeit one that wouldn't get tagged with a name for a few months yet. Quite apart from the innovative brilliance of the music, never had lyrics of such literary quality and ambiguous meaning been used on a rock record. This is not to say that there had not been brilliant lyrics—some not even tied to conventional romantic scenarios—since rock had started. There had been Chuck Berry's ironic stories of traveling guitarists and young kids growing awkwardly into adults, and Jerry Leiber and Mike Stoller's comic vignettes of everyday teenage frustrations as sung by the Coasters, along with numerous other examples. "Mr. Tambourine Man" took pop song language, however, to a different level. It also supplied an entirely different tributary of material to the Byrds themselves. As good as Gene Clark's songs were, had they had to rely primarily upon those, it's quite possible that they would have been something like a Searchers or Beau Brummels with somewhat greater depth and nuance.

Some would argue that much of "Mr. Tambourine Man"'s impact had been lost by the Byrds' decision to chop out most of the verses and concentrate on the choruses, but what remained was plenty enough to sustain intellectual curiosity. It was not a message song, unless the message was to provoke similar thoughts of exploration and cerebral ecstasy in its listeners. Its free-associative imagery have led some to peg it as one of the first drug-inspired songs, though Dylan denied this. In the liner notes to his *Biograph* box set, he cited guitarist Bruce Langhorne—a session guitarist who had worked with him as far back as the early '60s, and would play on key folk-rock recordings by Dylan

and many others—as the inspiration: "On one session, Tom Wilson had asked him to play tambourine. And he had this gigantic tambourine. It was like, really big. It was as big as a wagon
wheel. He was playing, and this vision of him playing this tambourine just stuck in my mind."
("He's the tambourine king, lest you doubt!" exclaimed Richard Fariña when he introduced Langhorne from the stage as one of his accompanists during Richard & Mimi Fariña's set at the 1965
Newport Folk Festival.)

Though the Byrds were interpreters and not the composers, they did have their own thoughts
about what the song might be reflecting. In Mike Jahn's book *Rock*, McGuinn told the author that
it was "a head trip. It takes you into some area that you really can't put your finger on. You're not
exactly sure what it's about. I don't think Dylan was exactly sure what it's about. It's an impres-
sionistic song." He further speculated that it could deal with "the depersonalization of cities" and
"some sort of spiritual release which says 'wait a minute, man, there's a way out . . . some other approach to life.'"

It remains a source of controversy, and even consternation, that what is roundly acknowledged as the first classic folk-rock recording could have been subject to so many commercial considerations. The use of session men in particular rankles purists, and not just folk ones. It can
be hard for them to accept the song, largely played by L.A. musicians not in the band credited on
the label, as an authentic expression of all the forces that had been working to bring folk and rock
closer together. The group to this day has to fend off accusations that it did not play on its records,
though in fact after this debut single, the Byrds *were* allowed to play their own instruments on
all of their subsequent recordings. The recording that same day of an excellent Gene Clark original, his characteristically moody love song "I Knew I'd Want You," for the B-side might have molli-
fied any queasiness about whether the group was just a front for a studio creation. And even with
only the participation of the front trio's vocals and McGuinn's 12-string, both sides of the single
are amazingly close in feel and sound to almost everything else the Byrds would record as a proper
band throughout the next three years, right down to the hum-drone of the bass lines.

"Mr. Tambourine Man"'s year-long journey from the back of Dylan's station wagon to a rock
hit-single-in-the-waiting *was* an extraordinary confluence of business and artistic interests, many
of them initiated by people other than the Byrds. There was Dylan to thank for writing the song
in the first place, naturally; Dickson for forcing it into their repertoire; and Melcher and the Los
Angeles session aces for knocking it into shape. There were also those unlikely behind-the-scenes
figures who had little to do with rock or folk and yet, directly or inadvertently, eased the way for
the Byrds to make it into Columbia's studio at all: Miles Davis, Doris Day, Naomi Hirshhorn.

But none of them, and not even Bob Dylan himself, could have made the song into a hit single
that spawned an entirely new style of rock music. More than anything else, it was the Byrds themselves who did it. And more than anything else, it was McGuinn's yearning, knowing vocal, and unique
12-string guitar playing, that made that happen. It was the culmination of his own year-long journey,
begun when he dared to put a Beatle beat to folk songs in Greenwich Village folk clubs.

Any celebration, though, would have to be put off for some time. Columbia did not immediately
release the single, though a February 20, 1965 news item in *Billboard* headlined "Melcher Back with

Columbia" intimated it was on its way, announcing that "among the artists working under Melcher's direction are the Birds [sic], a five-man vocal group who just cut a previously unreleased Bob Dylan tune for their first single." The Byrds could do nothing but wait, hope, and try to keep themselves together in the meantime. They may have felt just a little bit better if they had known that a fellow Columbia artist, just days before the recording of "Mr. Tambourine Man," had made his own major contribution to awakening the label to the commercial potential of electrified Bob Dylan songs.

The artist was none other than Dylan himself. Over the course of three sessions on consecutive days from January 13 to January 15, he had recorded all of the songs for his fifth album, *Bringing It All Back Home*. Seven of its eleven tracks featured a full electric rock band. It's still unclear, however, just how committed he was to taking the plunge into rock music.

It's been fashionable for decades in some circles to portray Dylan as a brave lone warrior who yanked folk music into the rock age almost single-handedly. But it should be remembered that he was, like any recording artist, subject to commercial forces and pressures that also shaped his work, perhaps even for the better. Just as the Byrds' flight had been guided by a number of supporters from unlikely directions, so was Dylan abetted in his transition by a colleague with little rock or folk on his resume, producer Tom Wilson. Wilson, as an African-American who had graduated from Harvard with a degree in economics, already boasted an uncommon background for someone involved with major label record production. Before he took over from John Hammond as Dylan's producer in early 1963, his specialty had been progressive jazz, working on albums by artists like John Coltrane and Cecil Taylor.

In an interview he gave while he was still alive (quoted in the notes to Dylan's *Biograph* box set), Wilson took credit for steering Dylan to rock: "I didn't even particularly like folk music. I'd been recording Sun Ra and Coltrane and I thought folk music was for the dumb guys. This guy played like the dumb guys but then these words came out. I was flabbergasted. I said to Albert Grossman, who was there in the studio...'if you put some background to this, you might have a white Ray Charles with a message.' But it wasn't until a year later that everyone agreed that we should put a band behind him. I had to find a band. But it was a very gradual process."

Dylan's prior attempts at recording with a band in late 1962 had not gone too well. The sessions in January 1965 would yield a classic album, but there are no indications that the process was any less haphazard than it had been for his misbegotten "Mixed Up Confusion" single. "The Dylan sessions were *not* arranged," laughs guitarist Bruce Langhorne, one of the musicians selected to accompany the singer. His main memories of Wilson from the Dylan dates are of the producer "hanging out in the control, [saying] 'Oh, we got a take.' 'Oh, that's really cool.'" Langhorne hastens to add that he views the hands-off attitude as an asset, not a hindrance: "Some producers felt that they had a job to do, that the universe would not do the job, but *they* had to do it. And other producers felt that you put the right people together in the right circumstance, and it will evolve. That's the kind of producer Tom was."

Among the shifting cast of supporting musicians those three days was John Sebastian, then still picking up session work as the Lovin' Spoonful tried to get itself a contract. "I had borrowed a bass, and had tried to learn what I could do with it, because Bob had said 'come in and play the session with me, and play bass'," he recalls. "I was kind of awed by how unfocused his recording process was. 'Cause, as completely amateur as we were, Erik [Jacobsen] and I had already been screwing around with, 'Well, what if you run this guitar back through the room and, well, this just sounds regular, let's do something to make it irregular.' All these things to try to keep up with the new pot-smoking attempt at hearing things differently, and carrying through on some of these perception differences that came out of smoking grass," he laughs.

"We were a little surprised that Bob was still just kind of"—here Sebastian adopts a nasal Bob Dylanesque voice—"'Okay, run the tape! Play the song! Okay, that wasn't good!' And he wouldn't repeat songs. Like, the Spoonful would get in there and play it 28 times in a row. Here was this other way of approaching it completely. I just felt like, the guy's a god when he picks up his pen, but he doesn't know necessarily what he's doing in this setting."

Just by asking Sebastian, an accomplished multi-instrumentalist but not an expert bassist, to play bass on the session, Dylan was already employing the off-the-cuff, anything-goes approach to recording he's been known for since he started working with musicians. Another member of the Lovin' Spoonful got involved in the sessions not so much for his qualifications as for his good fortune to happen to be there at the moment. Bassist Steve Boone had just joined the Lovin' Spoonful, who were rehearsing in Long Island at a hotel that was closed for the winter. "When the call came from New York for John to come in and play bass and the call was from Bob Dylan, I was pretty impressed," says Boone. "I was one of the two people that had a car and a driver's license. So I offered to drive him into the city, and we took my bass along with us.

"John tried the part. John's not a bass player, and I'm sure he'd be the first to say that. He was frustrated with it and said, 'Why don't you try my bass player? We just started a band.' And I was, like, flabbergasted. It didn't really intimidate me, because *I'm* a bass player. So I got up there, and basically he gave me a sort of idea of what the style or what he wanted the music to sound, and we went through the songs a couple of times. They weren't really hard songs to learn, so it went pretty smoothly for me, at least from my point of view. I thought I did a good job. I wasn't intimidated, I was like totally stoned to be actually playing with Bob Dylan on a session. Just a month before that, I had been just a rock 'n' roll bass player from Long Island." (Although Boone is not listed as having played on the album sessions in Clinton Heylin's *Bob Dylan: The Recording Sessions [1960-1994]*, Sebastian confirms that "Steve Boone showed up, and if Boone showed up, I think my instinct would have been to hand the instrument to him.")

If half of the Lovin' Spoonful seemed to have gotten involved through friendship and happenstance, it does seem apparent that Wilson and Dylan made some effort to also bring in New York session musicians with substantial experience. Among them were Bill Lee, already a seasoned veteran of New York folk dates; John Hammond's son (then billed as John Hammond, Jr.), the blues singer and guitarist who was already making his own albums for Vanguard; guitarist Kenny Rankin, to become better known as a jazz-pop singer; and drummer Bobby Gregg and pianist Paul Griffin, both to play on numerous folk-rock sessions in the next few years.

The most valuable addition was guitarist Bruce Langhorne, the purported actual Mr. Tambourine Man, who had already played with Dylan in the past, dating back to the 1961 Carolyn Hester session. Partially as a result of a childhood accident that cost him parts of some fingers, he'd developed a distinctive style as an accompanist, compensating for his lack of standard velocity with trilling, responsive triplets. By putting a pickup on his acoustic guitar, he'd arrived at a style that was almost half-electric, half-acoustic in color, an ideal vehicle for Dylan (and others Langhorne would accompany) as they made the tentative turnover from folk to rock. He'd already played in much the same style on the sessions for Richard and Mimi Fariña's debut album, then awaiting spring release.

"I had been experimenting with just putting a pickup on my Martin for a while, before that," says Langhorne. "It was just amplified and sustained acoustic playing, really. I played the same sort of lines that I would play with somebody like Odetta, who would provide the same sort of thing that Dylan provided, which was like a really inevitable rhythmic structure. The people that I most enjoyed playing with were the people who had an unstoppable thread to their music; it couldn't be diverted easily. The root, the core was gonna be there. And my job was really, essentially, icing; I put icing on the cake. But in order for me to do my job, that basic thread had to be there."

His lines were especially beguiling when he devised a tremolo effect by borrowing a twin reverb Fender amp from Sandy Bull, the multi-instrumentalist who fused all kinds of folk and world music on acoustic and electric guitars, banjo, and oud on his underrated, visionary mid-'60s Vanguard albums. In finding a tremolo compatible with the rhythm of the song, Langhorne was following the lead of Roebuck Staples of the Staple Singers. The Staples had made their own small, overlooked contribution to folk-rock by using electric guitar and drums on their gospel-folk recordings between 1962 and 1964, including covers of Dylan's "Masters of War" and "Blowin' in the Wind."

If some would see Dylan's method as more disorganized than spontaneous, Langhorne didn't view it as a drawback. "I was forced to play very much in the moment, because I did not have a great deal of sophistication in classical or jazz technique. I had to rely on communication and empathy to get me to play the next note, the right note, the right phrase or something. Which is why I liked working with somebody like Dylan, because they were able to communicate what the next note or section was gonna be. Some of the Dylan tunes on *Bringing It All Back Home* were done without rehearsal. Everybody was able to tune into what he was going to do next. Not that he was predictable, but he was inevitable."

What matters in records is not so much the process as the outcome, and what Dylan had when he finished was of a very high standard. Seven electric rock songs would comprise side one of the LP, largely devoted to basic blues workouts that the musicians worked over with a clamorous yet purposeful intensity. Dylan's words were becoming more frustrated, angry, humorous, and surreal all at once, adding up to a complaint against straight society, yet delivered with a sardonic, self-amused air. It was most effective on "Maggie's Farm" and the track selected as a single, "Subterranean Homesick Blues."

The latter song's catalog of stream-of-consciousness conformist slogans bore a close relationship in structure to Chuck Berry's series of complaints almost ten years before in his classic "Too Much Monkey Business." The language had been retooled, however, for the mid-'60s, in verbiage both more absurd and blatantly contemptuous of authority. (An alternative interpretation was offered prior to its release by Animal Chas Chandler, who told *NME* in February after talking about the upcoming single with Dylan in the Village: "It's called 'Those Old Subterranean Blues' [sic] and is a story about people living after the Bomb exploded.") Such tracks, however, were balanced by a couple of delicate, more melodic tunes, "Love Minus Zero/No Limit" and "She Belongs to Me," that nonetheless portrayed the objects of his affections in terms both reverential and nebulous.

If Dylan, someone who's always been reluctant to be categorized, was not consciously thinking in terms of combining folk and rock, his producer might have been. "In my opinion (some people differ) Bob's 'Subterranean Homesick Blues' was the second folk-rock record," Wilson would tell *Melody Maker* in 1967. "Because the Animals' 'House of the Rising Sun' was the original folk-rock record, and I consider 'Subterranean' to be the second—the first American-made one.

"My contribution to the Dylan group things was to find good musicians who had the skill of session musicians and the outlook of young rock-and-rollers. Men who sympathized with what he was doing. Of course, Dylan was always entirely open. He listened to everything—Ozark music, Gregorian chants, blues and rock-and-roll and also Coltrane. He plays some nice blues piano himself, you know.

"All I did was to think, and say: 'If you record this guy with a group that knows what's happening you'll have a superstar on your hands.'"

Dylan let slip his own rationale for working with a band in *Newsweek* in September, though his typically whimsical-to-the-point-of-absurdity interview response should be taken with a grain of salt: "I had this thing called 'Subterranean Homesick Blues.' It just didn't sound right by myself. I tried the piano, the harpsichord. I tried it as blues. I tried it on the pipe organ, the kazoo. But it fit right in with the band. I haven't changed a bit. I just got tired of playing guitar by myself."

Yet the way *Bringing It All Back Home* was sequenced suggested that Dylan might not have been quite ready to fully reinvent himself as a rock 'n' roller. The four songs on side two were drumless and primarily acoustic in feel, although some backup by Langhorne on "Mr. Tambourine Man" (finally committed to a release, in a substantially improved version) and bassist Lee on "It's All Over Now, Baby Blue" kept these from being as dry as the solo arrangements that typified Dylan's earlier albums. The songs were more serious and, the jubilant "Mr. Tambourine Man" aside, apocalyptic than those on side one. "It's All Over Now, Baby Blue" was often interpreted, as several Dylan songs from the period were, as bitter farewells to not just old friends, but to the narrow-minded views of the folk community. Perhaps Dylan felt that the relative heaviness of the mood on these songs didn't lend itself as well to rock backing. Or, possibly, he wasn't prepared to totally abandon his folk audience just yet, leaving at least half an album to placate its expectations.

Certainly those who saw his brief East Coast tour in February and March would have had little reason to suspect that Dylan had a rock album, about half of one anyway, ready for release. He played acoustic, as he always had since he had given concerts as a recording artist. He was co-billed with Joan Baez, with whom he did a few duets, as he often had over the past couple of years, though their romance was coming to an end. After the tour ended, he went to Los Angeles, where a release party for *Bringing It All Back Home* was scheduled for March 26. That visit to Los Angeles would also give him a chance to check in on the Byrds, who were still awaiting the release of their version of the song he had seen them rehearsing on an earlier visit.

It had not been easy for the Byrds or their manager to sit tight while "Mr. Tambourine Man" awaited release. There had already been several shake-ups that had threatened to break up the group even before they entered Columbia's studios. At one point, the temperamental Crosby was fired by the others; McGuinn and Clark only relented when Dickson threatened to leave as well if Crosby wasn't immediately reinstated. Crosby, after finding himself without an instrument when Hillman took over on bass, did his bit to shake the reticent Clark's confidence. David carped about Gene's timing on guitar and eventually took over the rhythm guitar duties himself. While he proved quite effective in that role, that in turn left Clark without anything to play except, ironically, the tambourine (though Clark continued to sporadically play some guitar with the others, as some early TV footage proves). Even McGuinn, despite his image as the level-headed, unflappable mainstay of the band, was tempted to form a band with Dino Valenti while waiting out "Mr. Tambourine Man"'s appearance.

The best way to keep a young, already fractious group together was to secure it steady work. An early gig at a bowling alley, where the Byrds had to compete with the sounds of smashing pins, had exactly the opposite effect, doing nothing to raise their spirits. Fortunately, Eddie Tickner was able to get the band a residency at Ciro's, a supper club on Sunset Strip that held about 400 customers. "I remember Ciro's the first night," Gene Clark would tell a sparse crowd of a few dozen people at the Hollywood Cinegrill, only a mile from the spot of that distant past triumph, at one of his last shows in 1991, just a month or so before his death. "The Byrds walked out on stage and there were about ten people, and they all left. But two weeks later, there were lines down the street."

The stint at Ciro's was the Byrds' equivalent to the Beatles' baptism-by-fire at the Cavern in Liverpool, or the Rolling Stones' slow cultivation of a devoted following at the Crawdaddy in London, or the Doors' brief reign as house band just down the road at the Whiskey A-Go-Go, not long after the Byrds had flown the Strip for international stardom. It tightened them as a band immeasurably, simultaneously forming a bond with the audience so intimate that it could never be replicated after they graduated to tours and larger venues. Well before their first hit record, it did much to not only launch them as a cult within Los Angeles, and popularize the mix of folk and rock that had yet to be named, but also to herald the rise of an entire new counterculture.

The Byrds by this point had far more quality original material and imaginative cover interpretations than most veteran bands of the time, let alone ones that had never put out an album. As a club band they were conscious of playing songs that could be danced to, and for those familiar with the group only through their ensuing records, it may come as a surprise to learn that the Byrds' set included popular tunes of the day with little relationship to the folk-rock songs that were their forte. They covered Rolling Stones numbers (they would even cover Buddy Holly's "Not Fade Away" on an early TV appearance, using the arrangement from the Stones' hit version), Chuck Berry's

"Roll Over Beethoven," Jimmy Reed's "Baby What You Want Me to Do," the Beatles' "Things We Said Today," and the early soul standard "Money." But what was generating the true buzz were the radical reworkings of songs by Dylan, including not just "Mr. Tambourine Man," but other recent Dylan tunes like "All I Really Want to Do."

There was even Dylan material that the group never got around to recording. "I think I sang 'Maggie's Farm,' which was a real coup, 'cause I was *so* shy," reveals Hillman, already noted as the least animated Byrd in a live setting. "I mean, I just didn't know what the heck this stuff was yet. It took me a year to figure it all out. I just sort of stayed back there and played." There was also Pete Seeger's "The Bells of Rhymney," by now a huge favorite with the Ciro's crowd. Seeger had used words by Welsh poet Idris Davies as the basis for the song after coming across them in a book by Dylan Thomas; McGuinn had remembered it from those already long-ago days as an arranger for Judy Collins.

For young Angelenos barely out of the twist era, dancing to songs with thought-provoking lyrics by the likes of Dylan and Seeger was an entirely new and thrilling sensation. "They weren't just singing about moon and June anymore," says Billy James, who would do publicity for the Byrds in 1965 as part of his job at Columbia. "The paradox for me was exemplified in 'The Bells of Rhymney,' which is a song about a Welsh mining disaster. And here we all were dancing to this song, which for the time was extraordinary! You didn't associate social dancing with songs about oppressed mine workers going under as a result of the greed of the mine owner. The breaking down of conventional creative choices made what the Byrds were doing so fascinating.

"Dancing to the Byrds was, as our teenage son once put it, R.O.M.—Random Outdoor Movement. It was extraordinarily uninhibited. There were hardcore fans who followed them around, every night." And not just any old hardcore fans, James takes pains to point out, but arty, bohemian ones at the leading edge of California's about-to-blossom colony of hippies.

"The use of Dylan lyrics . . . here was a group using songs written by the guy who changed the face of American popular music. So who are the first people to react to that? Of course it's gonna be fellow musicians, artists, writers, poets, and painters. They are always most sensitive to change. Lots of painters, actors, dancers, people from other pockets of the Los Angeles art community, screenwriters, became part of the audience." Not just struggling ones, either. Among those sighted at Ciro's were Jack Nicholson and Sal Mineo, rock 'n' soul greats Little Richard and Major Lance, and established folksingers Mary Travers, Buffy Sainte-Marie, Judy Henske, and Odetta. Even Dickson, who hadn't danced in 15 years, got out on the floor to move to the music.

Memories of Ciro's scene still excite awe among those fortunate to have been there and caught the Byrds at what most agree was their peak as a live band. "I got to see the Byrds before their first record came out at Ciro's, and they were unbelievable," enthuses Kenny Edwards. "It was so powerful and huge-sounding. They had seriously brought the best qualities of the haunting English folk music, like 'The Bells of Rhymney'—a Welsh folk song—into a rock thing. It made it seem like, 'Oh, that music always *should* have had bass and drums on it.' They were like the Led Zeppelin of their time."

If that comparison seems bizarre to those who think of the Byrds as sensitive jingle-janglers, it should be emphasized that they were, by early 1965 standards, very loud, even groundbreakingly loud. That quality of live excitement never did fully translate to the records, where the wide dynamic range of their vocals and acoustic-electric guitar blends yielded a more pristine clarity. "They *were* loud," contends Edwards. "I remember going into Ciro's and it was, like, deafening in there. But it was so good that it wasn't irritating.

"I remember being disappointed when I heard their records, actually. The production sound...they'd sound more like the Lettermen or the Beach Boys. It was all very air conditioner-smooth. It didn't have nearly the grinding sort of Zeppelin-esque power that they had really displayed when I heard 'em live. There was more of the heavy-metal quality to what they were doing than probably anybody thought at the time, than you might think by listening to the records. 'Turn! Turn! Turn!,' you crank it up loud, and you get a sense of some of that. Their first record was a lot smoother sounding than their subsequent records."

McGuinn views the virtues of their volume with greater caution. "We were undisciplined. Most bands, I think, could probably play more harmoniously than we did. We would all turn it up to 11 and kind of blast each other out. It was a matter of, 'I can't hear myself, man. I gotta turn it up more,' just wanting to hear your own instrument. We played Jane Fonda's birthday party, and Henry [Fonda] kept saying, 'Turn that down!' And Peter [Fonda] kept going, 'C'mon, Dad!' And he'd come up to us and say, 'Don't pay any attention to him, he's an old man. He doesn't know what he's talking about.'"

It wasn't only Hollywood artists, folkies, freaks, and starlets that were becoming converts, either. Jim Pons, guitarist for the Leaves, was one of the college-aged kids who made the trek to Ciro's from the suburbs. They would soon become a folk-rock band of some note themselves, but were in early 1965 still grinding out old rock and blues songs they had learned from records. "We had grown up in the San Fernando Valley, where the hot clubs were places like the Cinnamon Cinder, and the bands choreographed combos with matching suits and processed, Jay Sebring-style hairdos like the Pastel Six," says Pons. "It was good stuff, and inspirational in its own right for young kids just learning how to play their instruments. But the dynamic was typically a band and an audience...two separate entities.

"When we arrived in Hollywood and saw and heard the scene that the Byrds were into, it was a completely new and revolutionary thing. It appeared to be a giant party with no lines drawn between the show on the stage and the show on the dance floor. We had left the *Animal House*–type fraternity music and were entering into an exciting new adventure with real beatniks and hippies. It seemed to be a secret community of serious artists and freaks that lived in Hollywood and were drawn together by their mutual love for something we hadn't experienced before...Bob Dylan songs, psychedelic drugs, social protest, all with a kind of dangerous edge which added to its appeal. Vito [Paulekas, a sculptor in whose basement the Byrds rehearsed], Suzy Creamcheese, Carl Franzoni, and all these characters out of some fantasy world dancing and whirling and singing and being part of the music.

"And the music was loud. Ciro's was a large club, the amplifiers were a very visible and integral part of the experience, and they were turned up all the way. The Byrds weren't always musically precise with the playing of their songs, but they generated a wall of noise which seemed to kind of envelop you and add to the experience. And Roger (Jim) McGuinn had an irresistible vocal style.

"Whatever folk-rock really was, it did seem to start with the folk musicians who had gotten hold of electric guitars and sang stories about traditional values and times when people had moral principles. At least that's the way it looked to me at the Troubadour in Hollywood with McGuinn and Clark and Hillman. It had a newness and a relevance about it, and an 'importance' at a time when the musical community was a directionless combination of novelty songs, teen idols from Philadelphia, and a wave of British skiffle groups."

Even at the time, when rock criticism barely existed, the transportive qualities of the Byrds' music were hailed in the local media, albeit the local underground media. In spring 1965 Paul Jay Robbins gave them gushing, purple praise in the *Los Angeles Free Press*, one of the first alternative papers in the US. He made the band seem not just like saviors of rock 'n' roll, but portals to nirvana: "What the Byrds signify . . . is a concept deeply applied to unification and empathy and a rich joy of life—together with a positive recognition of the bulbous clusters of sickness around us. It represents a passing through negative apathy and an approach into involvement. . . . Dancing with the Byrds becomes a mystic loss of ego and tangibility, you become pure energy some place between sound and notion, and the involvement is total." (Columbia would soon exploit this underground cred for its own purposes, using the quote in Billy James's liner notes for the Byrds' first album.)

It helped that the Byrds looked the part as well as they played the part. The matching white shirts and New Christy Minstrels haircuts long gone, they were starting to look as different as they sounded. "They looked great," says Edwards. "They had that Edwardian thing down, you'd think they were from England for sure if you saw them." They not only had hair as shaggy as any English band's, but would emerge as a true *group* with striking complementary images. There was Michael Clarke, the sex symbol Brian Jones–look-alike drummer; Gene Clark, the group's own "Mr. Tambourine Man," and at this point its true sensitive muse; and Chris Hillman, a stock-still stoic bassist in the John Entwistle school, so poker-faced and rooted to the spot that he doesn't even make the frame in several of the band's earliest TV spots. None were as flamboyant, though, as David Crosby, with his flowing suede cape and dangerously outspoken mouth, and McGuinn, whose tinted Ben Franklin glasses were as much the group's visual trademark as his 12-string Rickenbacker was its audio equivalent. One of the proto-hippies dancing in the audience, Michelle Kerr, would later take the credit for wearing the rectangular glasses that inspired McGuinn to get his own pair.

As a consequence the Byrds looked as exotic as the Beatles had when they first came to the United States—an important feat at a time when America was despairing of grooming its own homegrown equivalent to the British Invasion. Chris Darrow, soon to play folk-rock of unsurpassed eclecticism in Kaleidoscope, remembers the first time he saw McGuinn: "He was wearing Beatle boots, he had those same glasses, he had the hair, and he looked like a freak. None of us had seen a longhaired guy, yet. None of us had any of that kind of stuff. This guy looked like a guy from Mars."

If the Byrds needed any final hip seal of approval, they got it when Dylan dropped into Ciro's in March to jam with the band, singing "All I Really Want to Do" with them onstage. That gave the Byrds a great photo op, a picture of Dylan playing harmonica with the group appearing on the back sleeve of their first LP. Dylan's enthusiasm for the band was genuine, but seeing the Byrds in their native habitat might have also heightened his awareness of their potential for getting his songs to more listeners, and increasing his royalty flow. It also might have helped seal his own determination to cast his lot with rock 'n' roll. For as McGuinn noted in *Rock*, what the Byrds had done with Dylan's songs was benefiting their creator as much as their interpreters: "I think he got his inspiration from us. We had taken one of his songs and done it without sacrificing too much of the aesthetic value, and this confirmed his suspicions that rock was possible for him." That's not idle boasting, since Mike Bloomfield gave firsthand evidence of the Byrds' direct influence on Dylan. In a recollection of his work as a session guitarist on Dylan's 1965 album *Highway 61 Revisited* (as quoted in *Michael Bloomfield: If You Love These Blues*), he claimed that Dylan "had heard records by the Byrds that knocked him out. He wanted me to play like McGuinn. That's what he was shooting for. It was even discussed . . . the Byrds' sound was what he wanted to get in his sessions."

Dylan also made sure to invite the group to an L.A. party that Columbia was putting on in his honor, and to include them in another famous photo taken at that event. All of which could not have hurt the Byrds' tenuous standing with Columbia, which did finally issue the group's cover of "Mr. Tambourine Man" on April 12. With Dylan's new single, "Subterranean Homesick Blues," also on release, that made two risky ventures the company was making into the singles market that spring. Now it was Columbia's turn to join the waiting game, with little firm idea as to whether the public would take to the new music.

ther labels were making their own moves into electrified folk music of sorts around early 1965, though usually with little hopes of attracting a hit single, instead targeting album buyers. All three of the major New York folk imprints—Elektra, Vanguard, and Folkways—put out seminal recordings in the field. Folkways's contribution would be a one-shot, while Elektra and Vanguard's releases heralded a shift from folk to rock and pop that would become more pronounced within each company as the decade progressed.

Although Elektra would ultimately prove more adaptable to the rock era, Vanguard lived up to its name with the spring appearance of Richard and Mimi Fariña's *Celebrations for a Grey Day*. The Fariñas had until that time been secondary figures in the folk movement. Richard was better known as a writer than as a musician, and even so had yet to publish a full-length work, though his *Been Down So Long It Looks Like Up to Me* (published right before his death in 1966) would be acclaimed as a major novel. Mimi, not yet 20, was in the shadow of her older sister Joan Baez, and though she was a better guitar player than Joan, she never would become a noted lead vocalist. During his brief marriage to Carolyn Hester, Richard had learned the dulcimer and done some time on the folk circuit, recording an obscure, unremarkable straight folk album with Eric von Schmidt in England in early 1963 (with some help from Dylan, who contributed under his Blind Boy Grunt pseudonym). After marrying, the Fariñas had done some time on the Cambridge scene, but as a couple were again overshadowed by their friends and sometime companions Bob Dylan and Joan Baez, then in the midst of their own romance.

Richard Fariña was becoming a formidable composer and instrumentalist, though. Some of his earliest songs were tied to the topical-protest tradition; "Michael, Andrew and James" and "Birmingham Sunday" both dealt with tragic casualties of the civil rights movement. And throughout his brief mid-'60s career, he would borrow freely from a variety of traditional folk songs: for example, deriving the tune of "Children of Darkness" from "A Maid That's Deep in Love"; basing "The Falcon" in part on "The Cuckoo"; and taking the melody of "A Swallow Song" from the Ladino tune "Los Bibilicos," which Carolyn Hester had recorded in 1961 for her first Columbia album. Yet like Dylan, he was moving into lyrics that celebrated the breaking of constraints against personal freedom. The compositions themselves broke constraints of popular song in their allegorical use of language, sometimes mixing the personal and political within the same song. As a dulcimer player he was also a rulebreaker, using it in a fiercely rhythmic fashion, rather than the prim manner in which it was usually employed in folk. The duo's arrangements mixed Appalachian music, blues, Asiatic drones, and even hints of Latin rhythms and Mose Allison jazz. Richard was aware of rock 'n' roll too, having played Buddy Holly's "Oh, Boy!" onstage with his dulcimer back in 1963.

Mimi's contributions have been sometimes regarded as peripheral since she did virtually none of the songwriting or lead singing. Yet four unreleased Music Publishers Holding Corporation Reference Recording demos by Richard Fariña (Mimi's presence on these seems limited to occasional, barely audible harmonies) inadvertently demonstrate that she was absolutely essential to injecting the buoyancy necessary to put their music over to a pop audience. In demo form, with no embellishment other than acoustic guitar and harmonica, standout Richard Fariña compositions like "Reno Nevada" and "Joy 'Round My Brain" that were rerecorded for official release are plaintive, repetitive, and almost lugubrious. Mimi's imaginative, winding counterpoint harmonies were necessary to transform them from near-dirges to uplifting, joyous, and melodious manifestos.

The Fariñas' debut LP would have been innovative enough with their stew of world and folk music influences. But they went a step further than progressive folkies such as, for instance, labelmates Ian & Sylvia in adding some electrified guitar by Bruce Langhorne. Though they lacked drums, "One-Way Ticket" and "Reno Nevada" were in every other respect rock songs. "Reno Nevada," which Mimi Fariña said was recorded in hopes that Mose Allison would cover it, was especially good, with its arresting downbeat melody, lacerating guitar and piano riffs, and a lyric of a gambling town where there's nothing left to lose. It would have been a worthy hit single, but Vanguard, despite its one-shot success with the Rooftop Singers' "Walk Right In," was ill-equipped to get the 45 on AM radio.

The use of electric guitars on sessions by the Fariñas and Dylan was going to miff folk purists, but Langhorne was a staunch advocate of their new direction. "Folk music is the music of the people," he observes. "If you look at folk music in any country in the world from any era, the instruments that are used are the instruments available to the indigenous people. For us in America at that time, it happened to be the electric guitar. It was like everyone had electric guitars; there were electric guitars everywhere, and all the records you heard featured electric guitar. It was a perfectly natural evolution, and young, forward-thinking people like Dick and Mimi, and like Bob Dylan, had no choice but to move forward, because it was right there in their face, and they were contemporary artists. They were not traditional artists. It was sort of inevitable, and of course the resistance was also inevitable, because people don't like their icons to change."

Elektra, after a couple of false starts with the Dino Valenti and Beefeaters singles, was making a fuller commitment to electric music as a result of signing a band that had some affiliations with the folk community, but really wasn't coming out of either rock or folk. The Paul Butterfield Blues Band, certainly at its outset, differed little from the electric Chicago blues bands that had proliferated in the windy city since the beginning of the 1950s. Perhaps there was something of a rockish slash to the work of its guitarists, Michael Bloomfield and Elvin Bishop. It was also, unlike virtually every other Chicago blues band, mostly white, though its black rhythm section had played with Howlin' Wolf. Bloomfield, unlike most middle-to-upper-class whites involved in the folk and blues revival, made no secret of his affluent origins. "Hell man, I'm not Son House," he revealed with an almost gleeful fervor in the *Festival* documentary. "I haven't been pissed on and stepped on and shitted on like he has.... Man, my father's a multimillionaire. I've had a rich, fat, happy life. I had a big Bar Mitzvah!"

What truly separated the band from artists like Howlin' Wolf, though, was its audience. Whether it was attributable to its youth and skin color or not, the group made inroads into the folk club and coffeehouse circuit, sometimes presenting some of the first electric music ever to be heard in those venues. In this respect, Butterfield was similar to Vanguard's John Hammond, Jr., another white bluesman, who recorded electric blues covers in late 1964 with Bloomfield and future members of the Band. Bloomfield had recorded some electric band tracks on his own for Columbia in late 1964 and early 1965 (not issued until 1995), mostly produced by John Hammond, Jr.'s father, before taking a permanent place in Butterfield's ensemble. Butterfield and Hammond's backup musicians would both play a role in Dylan's early electric rock music, both live and in the studio.

Butterfield's band had been scouted for Elektra by Paul Rothchild, who had worked at Club 47 in Cambridge, and then become producer for Prestige, where he worked with future Elektra artists like Tom Rush and the Holy Modal Rounders. After getting hired away from Prestige by Jac Holzman, he began to get to know some folk-rockers in the making with his first Elektra project, the Even Dozen Jug Band. Perhaps that group stood for the way he saw music going in early 1964. David Freiberg, then half of a male-female folk duo, remembers that when his act was being eyed for Elektra by Rothchild, "we went and talked to him, and he said, 'You know, I don't think the folk thing is going to last much longer. I don't think I can really use this group as a duo. But would you be interested in being in one of these big groups, like the New Christy Minstrels or whatever,' [that] he was thinking about forming. And we said, 'Well, I don't know. Check with us later.' That was where he made that remark that I'll always remember: 'Folk music isn't going to last any longer, and these new guys, the Beatles, are gonna fade right out!'"

If Paul Rothchild really felt that way, he had certainly changed his mind by the end of the year. The way the Beatles had changed the business would necessitate a change in his thinking anyway, if he wanted to keep his own position in the industry. "Paul could say one thing, and get off his position in a minute if he saw he was wrong," says Holzman. "But Paul felt that electric music was tough to record, and he didn't know how to do it. He felt that way about the first Butterfield album." In fact, Rothchild, dissatisfied with his first attempt, convinced Holzman to rerecord the LP from scratch to get it right.

The Butterfield record's true importance to folk-rock was its role in making Elektra electric. One of the cuts from the Butterfield sessions, "Born in Chicago" (actually a different version from the one that ended up on their first LP), was placed on the Elektra promotional sampler *Folk Song '65*. To the surprise of Holzman, the record sold 60,000 copies, more than twice what he expected. The surge, he learned from stores, was due mostly to that Butterfield track. Though it would take another year or so for Elektra to fully tap into the rock market, in the interim it recorded one of the first crucial albums by a folksinger-songwriter to use electric instruments. Fred Neil's *Bleecker & MacDougal*, produced by Rothchild, came out in May 1965, its front cover photo of Neil at the famous intersection serving as a valentine to and epitaph for the golden age of Village folk.

With top session men John Sebastian on harmonica, Felix Pappalardi and Douglas Hatelid on bass, and Peter Childs (who had been in the Knob Lick Upper 10,000 with Erik Jacobsen) on second guitar and dobro, its effect was something like a full rock band, though one still lacking a drummer. "Our instruments went well together," Sebastian says of his work with Pappalardi. "The harmonica and the guitar could kind of sandwich a folk performer in a very flattering way. Paul Rothchild also heard this, and we began to get work as a kind of team that would rock a little harder on something that was basically a folk arrangement."

Neil had been an admired figure in the Village since the early '60s. Dylan had backed him on harmonica shortly after moving to New York, and his rich, bluesy vocals—no one was more adept at lower-than-low singing than Neil—have been cited as inspirations by Sebastian, David Crosby, Stephen Stills, Paul Kantner, and even Barry McGuire, who calls him a "folksinger's singer. We all wanted to be like him." Despite building up a strong batch of originals that mixed folk with blues, country, and a benign, world-weary philosophical air, he had not yet had a proper showcase for his talents on vinyl.

In part this was because he lacked the ruthless, single-minded ambition of many of his peers, never pushing himself too hard within the business, spending much of his time in Coconut Grove in southern Florida, far away from the nerve center of the entertainment industry. His moody perfectionism could make him difficult to work with. Joe Marra, who booked Neil at the Night Owl Cafe in the Village, remembers Fred stopping a show after getting distracted by someone playing a radio on the street. Cyrus Faryar relished Neil's battles with uncooperative 12-string guitars: "He would be tuning the guitar to the guitar, but also he would be tuning the guitar to other things. Once he was sitting in a club near Coconut Grove, and while he was tuning, an airliner came overhead that was going to land in some major airport some miles away. With his ears, he picked up the sound of this plane, and kind of tuned the plane all the way to the ground."

Neil had already recorded *Tear Down the Walls*, a strong folk album on Elektra, as half of a duo with Vince Martin. While that record was just a couple of steps away from folk-rock, he'd need some heroic assistance in the studio to narrow the distance. Although electric guitar is heard

Fred Neil, the singer-songwriter's singer-songwriter

on *Bleecker & MacDougal*, it's sporadic and subdued. "Whatever we were calling it, it definitely had the qualities of rock 'n' roll," says Sebastian. "But the styles were always just this side of rock 'n' roll. He was a great rhythm guitarist, but he had very little inclination to use an electric. I think that was a wise choice, because that 12-string [had] a certain kind of a propulsion you probably couldn't get out of an electric instrument.

"He was a 'oh, we'll just feel it and it'll work out' kind of a guy. It was Felix's [Pappalardi's] and my particular lot for those [Elektra] years to get Fred in the studio and nail it down a little bit, actually plan where a solo would be so that the guy would be ready when the solo happened. Peter Childs became another member of this 'keep Fred in line' team. Felix and I were in some degree or another baby-sitting these recordings a little bit to help Paul [Rothchild], who we could see had an enormous job to produce these projects." If the rock in *Bleecker & MacDougal* is more implied than realized, the album was still an important source point for many in its eclectic combination of influences. The sound was rootsy but melodic and rhythmically forceful. The attitude was relaxed yet emotional, and the material grounded in folk, yet wholly contemporary in its bemused worldview. Several of the songs, including "Little Bit of Rain" and particularly "Other Side of This Life," were covered by others during the next few years in much harder-rocking arrangements that amplified Neil's pop-rock sensibilities.

While Neil was bound to be a cult singer-songwriter whose most devoted fans were musicians rather than record-buyers, there were even more way-underground moves afoot on the Village warpath from folk to rock. Although Ed Sanders's folk experience was largely limited to singing during civil rights demonstrations, and Tuli Kupferberg, already in his forties, couldn't play anything but the radio, the two Lower Manhattan poets were determined to form a band in early 1965. The backbone of their instrumental support would be Peter Stampfel and Steve Weber, who had epitomized the most irreverent face of the folk revival in their sardonic yet loving takes on old-timey music with the Holy Modal Rounders. "I think one of the seminal influences pushing people to rock, but it was in a really roundabout way, were the Holy Modal Rounders," says Banana of the Youngbloods. "Although they weren't really playing rock, it was so sort of hard-edged."

What Stampfel and Weber had joined, however, was something of a proto-punk-rock jug band, the taboo-breaking starting with their name, the Fugs. There were songs about raw sex, drugs, and left-wing political satire, delivered with a savage and sometimes profane wit, in addition to adaptations of William Blake poems. "I thought of what they were doing as smut rock," says Stampfel. "It was basically sex and drugs and counterculture. Setting classical nineteenth century poems to music, which I think is a very nice foil to things like 'Coca Cola Douche.' The Fugs were covering all sorts of ground that was, music-wise, virgin territory."

Kupferberg, however, points out that songs of lust are, like the songs that had comprised the core of the folk revival, linked to conventions far predating the twentieth century. "There's a long tradition of radical poetry and music, and there are also hidden traditions of free sexual expression in English literature. I have a collection of eighteenth century bawdy songs. Some of them are British, and some are by well-known songwriters of the period, or people who wrote classical songs. There was even a tradition of bars or taverns that men would go to, and sing bawdy songs to each other and get drunk. That was [the] eighteenth century in London. I'm sure those songs existed in America too." In the spring of 1965, Kupferberg and Sanders managed to combine folk music and discussion of contemporary sexual mores outside of the studio when they helped conduct panel discussions on the sexual revolution at Izzy Young's Folklore Center.

Songs about Coca Cola douches and CIA men, and merciless satires of "The Ten Commandments," were going to be hard to place even on open-minded independent labels in 1965. Ironically, the label that did put out *The Fugs First Album* that year was the most established of the New York folk companies, though certainly not the most commercially viable. Sanders's friend Harry Smith, who had done his part to get the folk revival on its way by assembling the *Anthology of American Folk Music* volumes in the early '50s, helped the Fugs get a deal with Moe Asch and Folkways. "Harry and I figured out the best way to float this past Mr. Asch was to call it a jug band," says Sanders. "The first session, we didn't even know that you were supposed to face the microphones. Moe did let us do what we want, and let Harry and I put whatever we wanted on the record."

The Fugs could have just about passed for a jug band when they did their first session for the album in the spring of 1965. But when they did their second and final one (which, like the first, lasted a single afternoon) for the LP in the summer, Stampfel and Weber were gone, an electric guitarist and electric bassist were in, and Ken Weaver had graduated from buffalo hide drums and congas to a full drum kit. By the time folk-rock had become a popular term, the Fugs were part of it, though at the most out-there and subterranean level.

"When we formed, folk-rock had not become a hyphenated word," continues Sanders. "Nor had beat turned to hippies; we were in the pre-folk-rock, pre-hippie beat era. We evolved in a gallery performance space milieu as much as the folk club milieu. I had originally thought we could just get by with buffalo hide drums, maracas, and a couple Weberesque, weirdly tuned, space-tuned guitars. But it didn't happen." Had Stampfel stayed on, "I think we might have evolved into more of what our original intention was: more of a string- and fiddle-based, Incredible String Band–type [group]. We could have done some of these longer suites we did acoustically. We could have gone proto-klezmer. We could have added Cajun, we could have had an accordion player. Probably should have. Didn't, though. And there ain't no time machine." By the next year, the Fugs would be off Folkways and into the *Billboard* Top 100, though on another independent label that if anything made Folkways seem conservative.

Major labels were also issuing albums by the foot soldiers of folk-rock by early 1965. Jesse Colin Young, like Roger McGuinn, had been mentored to a surprising extent by Bobby Darin, who helped Young get signed to Capitol. Young made a nice if derivative solo folk album for the label in 1964, *Soul of a City Boy*, which placed him somewhat in Fred Neil and Tim Hardin's territory. Although working, nominally, in a folk framework, there were simply too many expressive blues, soul, country, and pop tinges to his voice to confine him to the folk circle for long. Young came more into his own, and closer to pop-rock, on his Mercury follow-up *Youngblood*, from March 1965. Original compositions such as "Summer Rain," "Green Hill Mountain Home," and "Lullabye" were wistful and introspective in the manner of Fred Neil and Tim Hardin, yet with a lighter, sunnier touch as opposed to Neil and Hardin's brooding reclusion. "Nobody's Business" had actual drums, and the Neil similarities were bolstered by contributions from two session men who had also worked on *Bleecker & MacDougal*, Peter Childs and the omnipresent John Sebastian. But Young would not take the full leap into folk-rock until forming the Youngbloods, a band that would not start making a national impact until 1967.

Sebastian, while keeping his foot in the scene as an accompanist and session musician (he and Richard Fariña also played on Judy Collins's *Fifth Album* around this time), had not been idle in his aspirations for a career of his own. In late 1964, he and Zal Yanovsky had started plotting a band that would put the good-time eclecticism of ensembles like Cambridge's Jim Kweskin Jug Band into a more contemporary context. It's a measure of how much the New York folk and rock scenes were blurring into each other that the remaining two members of the Lovin' Spoonful were not folkies, but hard-core rock 'n' rollers.

"When I met John and Zally in December of '64, I didn't know anything about either of them," says Steve Boone, who had played bass with drummer Joe Butler in Long Island rock bands since 1962, though he had done some folk gigs with his brother Skip. "They were just two cool guys who

I liked playing music with, and we agreed to get together in January and start this band." While Sebastian and Yanovsky were fired-up folkies itching to go electric, Boone was one of the first noted folk-rockers for whom the folk component would actually be the brave new world. "Right after I first met John and Zally, John invited me to the Night Owl Cafe to hear him. He said it would be him and Fred Neil performing at the Night Owl. I'd never heard of Fred Neil, but I took John up on his offer.

"And I have to tell you, that was maybe one of the most significant nights in my musical life. Because not only was Fred Neil and John playing, but Buzzy Linhart, Felix Pappalardi and Timmy Hardin also were all on the stage together. Obviously they weren't a group, they'd just got thrown together in sort of a hootenanny kind of deal. They did some classic folk covers, some of Freddie's tunes, managed to keep the 12-strings in tune. I was stunned. I had never heard such power in a folk group before. So I was quite determined to follow through after hearing John, and playing with John and Zally a few days before that, with all the connections that [John] obviously had in the Greenwich Village scene."

"When we were looking for the rhythm section," says Erik Jacobsen, who was heavily involved with the group as its producer-in-waiting, "Joe Butler was playing drums in the Sellouts, who were managed by Herbie Cohen [also manager of the Modern Folk Quartet, Judy Henske, and Fred Neil]. We had a drummer that we jammed [with], and he was good, but we were I guess [going through] the same kind of thing as when they got Ringo in the Beatles. You know, 'We need a guy, a little more energy, a little more extroverted, a little more appealing, who could sing as well.' Because we wanted to do harmony. So they went over to see Joe, and I think they were not that hot on him, generally speaking. Zally and Joe almost never got along."

But Butler soon convinced them both how badly he wanted to be in the group, and—quite literally—just how much rock 'n' roll blood he was willing to spill for his chance. Continues Jacobsen, "We had Joe come over to the Albert Hotel, set up in the upstairs ballroom for the rehearsal, and he came in. They were playing some kind of hard-hitting tune. He broke the drumstick, right toward the end of the song. He was playing on a cracked cymbal, a big cymbal with all the little holes and metal rivets for them, which are very sharp on the top. He started hitting it with his hand, keeping beat, and the final chorus, his rivets were just slicing into his hand. Blood started to fly. The guys were like, 'Whoa-oa? Stop, stop!' He had proved his mettle big-time by continuing under such painful circumstances. I guess they decided, 'This guy's okay.'"

Taking its name from lyrics in a song by bluesman Mississippi John Hurt (whom Sebastian had worked with in the Village), the Lovin' Spoonful spent much of early 1965 playing at the Night Owl Cafe. The Night Owl, a narrow room of about 75 by 20 feet with a stage so small that Butler had to play on the floor, was the Spoonful's equivalent to the Byrds' residency at Ciro's, giving the musicians time to refine their sound and develop material as they lobbied labels for a recording contract. When they weren't at the Night Owl, they were rehearsing at the Albert Hotel, where they lived in a single room that also included all their instruments, dodging the rent by having their friend Denny Doherty sweet-talk the female bookkeeper. The great producer Phil Spector even expressed some interest in working with them, but, Sebastian would tell *NME* in 1966, "We turned down Spector's offers because we didn't want to be swallowed up under his name." As Sebastian had played on sessions for Neil, Collins, and the Even Dozen Jug Band, and developed a close rapport with Paul Rothchild and Jac Holzman, Elektra seemed like a natural home for the group.

The band got as far as cutting sessions for the company in early 1965, four of the songs appearing on the Elektra compilation *What's Shakin'* in 1966. As with the Mugwumps' LP, some of the songs were surprisingly ordinary covers of oldies, including the Coasters' "Searchin'" and Chuck Berry's "Almost Grown." A fresh identity, and Sebastian's emergence as a songwriter, only came through on "Good Time Music," a sort of manifesto of the group's optimism in its jaunty rhythms and celebration of the return of good time music to the radio—an obvious tribute to the Beatles and the British Invasion. Elektra seemed set to sign a great vehicle for landing its first rock hits, but it wouldn't happen. After nearly signing with Elektra, the Spoonful would go instead with Kama Sutra in the spring of 1965. "I think the reason we did the four songs for him was because we felt a little bit guilty," confesses Jacobsen. "We had kind of hung [Holzman] out to dry just a little bit on that somehow, and allowed him to have those sides."

"Jac Holzman, obviously, was a friend of John's and Zally's and Eric's, and they were all known to each other as folkies," says Boone. "I had a lot of respect for the Elektra label, just because of the artists that I knew to be on it at the time. But we as a group, and our management and production, all agreed that going with Jac Holzman and Elektra was risky in that we wanted to be clearly identified as a rock band. We wanted the benefits of being on Dick Clark, we wanted to be in *Teen Beat* magazine, we wanted to ride around in limousines and act like rock stars. We really felt that Elektra would be a label that would deliver the quality that we were looking for, [but] couldn't deliver the oomph in the rock 'n' roll department."

"If we had only gone with Jac, what a different world it would have been," sighs Sebastian. "I don't know if the music would have been that different. I think that part of our decision was that we didn't want to change horses in midstream. All of our little practice runs had been with Erik Jacobsen." As Holzman adds, "Nothing would have been different with the Lovin' Spoonful, except insofar as Rothchild might have produced. I'm not sure whether Rothchild would not have been a bit too strong for them. I don't know whether Paul would have let John do what John did without there being some blood on the studio."

What *would* have been different? According to Holzman: "I ran into John Sebastian, he was performing at Central Park many, many years after I had left the business, probably the mid-'80s. I went backstage to see him, and he gave me a big hug, and said, 'What a mistake we made. We would have sold no fewer records on Elektra, and we would have been paid.'" Jacobsen has the not-so-funny punchline on the consequences of choosing the MGM-distributed Kama Sutra over Elektra: "We were taken to the cleaners, like very few people were in the subsequent era."

Kama Sutra *would* deliver hit singles for the band, and even in spring 1965—before the Byrds or Lovin' Spoonful were on AM radio—one American group had demonstrated that it might be possible to make the charts with folk-rockish songs. When the Beau Brummels made #15 in early 1965 with "Laugh, Laugh" on the small local Autumn label, many assumed that the San Francisco musicians were actually from Britain, due both to their name and to their uncannily Beatlesque quasi-British Invasion sound. Yet in some respects, their early records were also a close approximation of what the Byrds and others would present as folk-rock. You can hear it now in the heavy reliance on minor chords, the exceptionally haunting harmonies, Sal Valentino's resonant and forlorn vocals, guitarist Ron Elliott's pensive songs, the occasional harmonica solos, and above all the mix of folky acoustic guitars with electric ones. They would do even better with another original of similar high quality, "Just a Little," which made the Top Ten in the spring. Their sweet-sour flavor also helped set the model for many San Francisco folk-rock and even psychedelic bands that followed.

Remarkably, however, they had little folk in their background, and any folk-rock in their approach seems to have been unintentional. Elliott's major loves were country and theater music, and he didn't even listen to much pop at all until the Beau Brummels formed. "Laugh, Laugh," he says, was specifically inspired not even by the Beatles, but by a Four Seasons song he heard on the radio. "We were a group, but not professional musicians," he surmises. "I had to de-complicate my music and get it simpler and simpler, so that we could play it and make it sound like a popular thing. They weren't top-of-the-line musicians. They were good musicians, just solid and simple stuff to get the point across. Whenever you have a format like that, it sounds folky, because it's not glitzed over with anything. If it had been a group of different players, it would have had a whole totally different thing.

"We only had acoustic and electric guitars," Elliott continues, "so every chance we got, we'd try to add some variety. We couldn't do it much with playing or style differences, because everybody had limited chops, including myself. We weren't professionals in that sense, where people could jump from style to style or do a flashy thing. The only way you could get variety was to go to a harmonica during this song, or get an acoustic in this space; get different moods that way."

Says Valentino of bands like the Byrds, "I think for the most part those guys were from that [folk-rock] idiom, and we weren't really. They knew the folk thing much more than we did. I don't know that Elliott knew it that well." Interestingly, the Byrds did see the Beau Brummels in L.A., and later gave them mixed appraisals. Chris Hillman was mightily impressed: "They're up there and Sal's got his tambourine going and I'm going, 'Wow! I'll never be able to do that!' I was the shyest guy in the band. But they were exceptionally good when I saw them. I remember them doing the hit they had, 'Laugh, Laugh.' They really sort of answered the Beatles before we did, in that sense. Unfortunately, they didn't ever carry it on beyond that song or one other one." (However, the Beau Brummels actually would record a wealth of good original material over the next few years, on albums suffering from weak distribution.) McGuinn was more blasé in a *Rolling Stone* interview, claiming they "had a little trouble singing in tune."

Though not nearly as successful as the Beau Brummels in the singles charts, Bob Dylan also managed his first hit single that spring, even if it was a small one. "Subterranean Homesick Blues" slipped just inside the Top 40 for one week only in mid-May, the same week *Bringing It All Back Home* entered the Top 20. Though these records have since come to symbolize Dylan's break with his folkie past, it's curious to note that, at the time, there was not the firestorm of controversial comment one might expect in the media. *Billboard* and *Variety*, the two leading sources of American music industry coverage, astonishingly made no mention of the use of rock instruments on the first side; nor did *NME*, ambiguously noting, "backing group is good."

The Beau Brummels, at the beginning of their recording career.
Left to right: Ron Meagher, Sal Valentino, Ron Elliott, John Petersen, Dec Mulligan

In part this nonreaction was attributable to the absence of widely circulated monthlies or week-lies for serious and/or adult rock fans in the mid-'60s. Little analysis or depth could be expected from the average *Billboard* review, which for the Dylan LP read in total: "Dylan followers are becoming more and more numerous while his folk fans become even more loyal. His single record 'Subterranean Homesick Blues' is climbing the pop charts and is included on this LP. There's plenty of musical excitement herein for both the swingin' pop music fan as well as the devoted folknik. Guitar and moanin' harmonica accompany his earthy vocals."

Far more prescient, if now likewise dated in its hipster lingo, was Ed Freeman's column in *Boston Broadside*: "The Beatles and the Rolling Stones . . . have shown us that there is yet another music to revive in our own inimitable, folky way: rock 'n' roll. This month marks a major turning point in the history of the folk revival: nestled in amongst the Jean Ritchie records at Briggs & Briggs's folk-oriented record counter is a stack of Robert Dylan's latest record—'Subterranean Homesick Blues,' and, on the flip side, 'She Belongs to Me.' It's a 45, complete with electric guitars, drums, the works. Bob Dylan, the kid who sang blues, the kid who came to New York to visit Woody Guthrie, Dylan, the kid who wrote 'With God on Our Side,' this kid has grown up: now he sings pop music.

"And man, what a gassy record. First of all, it points up one important fact about old man Dylan: he can sing. Secondly, it is fascinating to see how well Dylanism fits pop music. 'Subterranean Homesick Blues' is about as far out as the title would suggest, a natural progression from all his other weirdo songs. 'She Belongs to Me' is even further out than the title would suggest. . . . I would venture to say that in this record, Dylan as an individual has finally found his natural medium. And folk music as a whole has found another step forward that can be taken."

"Subterranean Homesick Blues" was a much bigger hit in England, where it made the Top Ten and *Bringing It All Back Home* went all the way to the top spot. By the time these entered the charts Dylan was undertaking his spring tour of England, where he was, to a much greater degree than in the States, becoming a genuine pop star. His album sales had been strong there since 1964, when a review of a British appearance rated just one paragraph on the last page of *NME*. John Lennon and George Harrison had spent much of an early '65 *Melody Maker* feature praising his work, with Harrison declaring, "I like his whole attitude. The way he dresses, the way he doesn't give a damn. The way he sings discords and plays discords. The way he sends up everything—I mean some of the words are just marvelous, y'know." He still saw some discord between the fans of Dylan and fans of the Beatles: "There must be a lot of staunch folk fans who like Dylan but who don't like the Beatles. I do know he likes our work, and that knocks us out."

Now his cult of UK admirers had expanded way beyond the Beatles and the Animals. Three of his albums made the British Top Ten in the spring, and "The Times They Are A-Changin'" had preceded "Subterranean Homesick Blues" as a Top Ten single. Still, as he had in his just-completed American swing through the East Coast, Dylan toured alone, with an acoustic guitar. The visit was recorded in detail by D.A. Pennebaker's famous documentary *Don't Look Back*, in which Dylan at least acted the rock star, dressing down both nosy and timid newspaper reporters, and ignoring a cowed Joan Baez, who left the entourage after it became clear Dylan wasn't going to invite her onto the stage at his gigs. "I think he was getting bored, musically, with the old songs," says Pennebaker. "You could feel it in his detachment from Joan. Although he liked the songs, he wanted something more adventurous on stage, something more exciting."

Dylan seemed to prefer rock musicians in the company he kept, with Alan Price of the Animals, John Mayall, Marianne Faithfull, and Brian Pendleton of the Pretty Things all making substantial or super-brief cameo appearances in the film. In one sequence, he eyed electric guitars in a music shop window with what seemed like envious longing; in another, he encouraged an unknown local band, the Freewheelers, who seemed almost apologetic for devising rock treatments of his songs. To a young girl disappointed with the rock 'n' roll of "Subterranean Homesick Blues"—"it's not *you*," she whined—he offered conciliatory consolation: "I have to give some work to my friends. . . . Don't you like me to have a good old laugh?"

There was also a memorable battle-of-the-songs with Donovan, the new British star who was the first of a parade of singers that the press, ever since the mid-'60s, have dubbed "the new Dylan." At the end of 1964, Donovan Leitch was an unknown beatnik folksinger playing clubs in Hertfordshire, not far from London. In early February, however, his demos helped secure a spot on the British pop-rock TV show *Ready, Steady, Go*, a rarity for an artist without a record. He was invited back for two consecutive shows, and was a nationally known figure even before his first single, "Catch the Wind," entered the charts at the end of March. By April 11, a month shy of his nineteenth birthday, he was playing before thousands of screaming teens at the *New Musical Express* Pollwinners Concert in Wembley Stadium. Ads for an "authentic Donovan cap," exploiting his early standard ruffian sweater-and-peaked-cap garb, appeared in *NME* for months.

Dylan had apparently never heard of him until he arrived for his spring British tour, where stories comparing the two singers in the British music press made Donovan's emergence unavoidable. The visiting superstar traded songs with the newcomer in a hotel room for one of the most memorable scenes in *Don't Look Back*, Donovan performing "To Sing for You," and Dylan responding with "It's All Over Now, Baby Blue." The sequence fueled mythology, perpetuated over decades, that Donovan was nothing more than a Dylan imitator. That was a debate that had started to fill the letters pages of the British music weeklies even prior to Donovan's first 45, with Dave Larkham denouncing him in *Melody Maker* as "the worst kind of commercialism since the commercialization of Christmas," an *NME* reader pointing out "Catch the Wind"'s similarity to Dylan's "Chimes of Freedom," and producer Tony Meehan telling *Record Mirror* that "Donovan seems to be Dylan without the depth."

In fact, on his early recordings Donovan was already becoming his own man, espousing a gentler and more melodic and romantic vision than Dylan, particularly on his early hits "Catch the Wind" and "Colours." There were still remnants of the topical protest movement on his cover of Buffy Sainte-Marie's "Universal Soldier" and his friend Mick Softley's memorably biting "The War Drags On" and "Goldwatch Blues." He was also already starting to use light backup from accompanying musicians, though without stepping into rock quite yet. If his 1965 recordings sound immature in comparison to Dylan's, it's worth remembering that he was a full five years younger than the American, who at the age of 19 was still singing traditional folk songs in Minneapolis coffeehouses.

"Donovan and Dylan are as different as chalk and cheese, with the exception that we both were weaned on Woody Guthrie and Kerouac," says Donovan now. (In fact, when Donovan burst on the scene in early 1965, his guitar bore the legend "This machine kills," an approximation of the "This machine kills fascists" slogan on Guthrie's guitar.) "Bob sounded like Guthrie for five minutes and I sounded like Bob for the same five minutes. We emulate our heroes, then find our own style. The poor audience were led by the media, who saw only similarities and were ignorant of the roots." Pennebaker dismisses any supposed condescending rivalry between Dylan and Donovan as "bullshit. They kind of went along with it as a joke. I know that Dylan used to sneak in and listen to [Donovan's] record when he didn't think I was watching." Donovan in turn helped make the signs for the famous opening sequence of *Don't Look Back*, in which Dylan held up placards with lyrics from "Subterranean Homesick Blues" as the single blared on the soundtrack.

Donovan goes on to emphasize that other major artists of the time could be extremely imitative of their heroes as they were finding their own style. "I said at the time, 'Dylan has literally taken complete Woody Guthrie tunes and rewritten lyrics, yet no one says a thing. Also every British R&B band, from Stones to Animals, take word for word, nuance for nuance, riff for riff from all the great black blues artists, and not one reporter accuses them of copying. Now that is prejudice.'" He also stresses that his peers certainly did not regard him as a Dylan clone: "In *Don't Look Back*, Alan Price says to Dylan, 'He's [Donovan] not a fake. He's a very good guitar player. He's better than you.' Dylan did comment that I played more like Jack Elliott than I played like Dylan. And there were many private times Dylan and I spent in the Savoy Hotel on friendly terms, away from the glare of publicity."

Donovan may not have been recording rock yet, but he was already thought of in the UK as being just as much a pop singer as a folk one, if not more so. This was not at odds with some goals he'd harbored for a couple of years, goals that were instigated in much the same manner as the Beatles had awakened pop-rock ambitions among folk musicians in America. One difference was that Donovan had the advantage of being able to hear the Beatles earlier than anyone in the States, from the time the Liverpudlians released their first British single.

"When I left home at 16 I was already immersed in bohemian art and culture and wishing to be part of the folk-protest movement, which I had heard from Woody Guthrie, Joan Baez and Pete Seeger, thinking I had left pop music behind," he elucidates. "Then on one trip back home at 17, I was alone in my Mum's council house in Hatfield, and the radio was playing. As I walked up the stairs a song came on the radio which froze me where I stood. I sat down on the stair and listened to acoustic guitars, a harmonica, drums, bass, and vocal harmonies. The band sang 'love, love me do.' I did not know who they were, but I knew in an instant that this was what I would do—merge the acoustic guitars with pop music form, and present new conscious lyrics to an unsuspecting pop audience. The DJ said the band were the Beatles."

There were a growing number of British artists moving pop and folk together in early 1965, though usually without the "conscious" lyrics of Donovan. The Seekers, newly arrived from Australia, had stormed the UK charts with the #1 single "I'll Never Find Another You," which though indebted to Peter, Paul & Mary had a greater sense of pop swing. Unit 4 + 2, who had a mild hit in 1964 with the folk tune "Greenfields," added some pop beats and constant cowbells for their peculiar "Concrete and Clay," another British #1. *Melody Maker* reported in April that the to-remain-unknown trio Peter, Jan and Jon were mixing folk and electricity. Marianne Faithfull recorded an entire album of folk songs, *Come My Way*, and did some live performances accompanied only by 12-string guitarist Jon Mark. Around this time the British magazine *Folk Scene*, which classified Donovan as a "pop-folksinger," viewed him and Faithfull important enough to include in a survey of folkies' thoughts on upcoming trends; declared Faithfull, "The major influence will be white urban blues singers, such urban blues singers as 'Spider' John Koerner."

None of this may have been folk-rock, but some British acts were nudging it along that path, perhaps unconsciously. The Beatles, in addition to putting folky material like "I'm a Loser" and "I'll Follow the Sun" on their *Beatles for Sale* album in late 1964, built their spring single "Ticket to Ride" around a 12-string riff that sounded remarkably close to the riffs about to be popularized by the Byrds. On his televised April 11 *NME* concert, Donovan ran through "Catch the Wind" and the bluesy "You're Gonna Need Somebody on Your Bond" with a full electric band, more than three months before Dylan did his first show with a rock group at the Newport Folk Festival.

Dylan's pop notoriety and dabbling with rock on record was already upsetting some of his British audience, though the resentment was mild in comparison to what he would endure when he returned to tour in 1966. "If they attack me just because I have some success with records, then they're entitled to," he told Ray Coleman in *Melody Maker* in May of 1965. "But I am equally entitled to disagree with them. Popular music—a lot of it is fantastically great music. Are these people trying to hate pop music, or what? I don't hate pop music. Oh man, somebody's got to be a little bit whacky to say: 'I don't like amplified guitar.' What's wrong with electrified guitar? And drums? I was playing with drums before I ever got anywhere. People say how can it be folk music if you've got electrified guitar and drums! Ha!

"These instruments are real. I like them. Aren't they the things everybody uses when they start out? You don't start singing by yourself—you sometimes have drums."

"Subterranean Homesick Blues," Dylan admitted, wasn't "recorded as good as it ought to have been recorded. . . . You could call it an unconscious poem set to music. I'm not going to write anything or sing anything I don't want to do. That song's not a put-on, like somebody said." Then came an odd comment that betrayed some lingering reservations: "Nobody is going to push me into writing rock and roll songs. That's something I don't want to do."

The reluctance of both Dylan and the folk audience to shift allegiance to rock might have been partly attributable to a perception that pop was for teenagers, and folk for adults. As Tom Wilson told *Melody Maker* a couple of years after the smoke had cleared, "What Dylan did was to liberate the whole field of lyric writing from the world of adult fantasy and start talking about real things. He showed everybody that the teenage audience was more adult and receptive to ideas than anyone had ever imagined before." The teen audience was in need of a bigger beat and hook-laden riffs than even the electric side of *Bringing It All Back Home* could supply.

In retrospect, an outtake from *Bringing It All Back Home*, "If You Gotta Go, Go Now" (ultimately released as a rare European single in 1967), seems like it might have been an attempt to reach that audience, though he had actually started playing it live in a solo acoustic version in late 1964. With its dynamic blues-pop riffs and catchy choruses, it seemed like an obvious hit single, its failure to appear at the time unfathomable. Maybe the inscrutable Dylan was dissatisfied with the track, as he made an aborted attempt to cut it again during his visit to England, using John Mayall's Bluesbreakers (with Eric Clapton) as the backup band. The available fragment from the session on bootleg suggests that the idea was a nonstarter, with Dylan making it through just one shambling verse before the take collapses, one of the Bluesbreakers wryly remarking at the outset, "You haven't worked much with bands, have you?"

I n his airplane ride back to the States on June 2, 1965, Dylan began writing "Like a Rolling Stone," the song that would prove to be his ideal marriage of lyrical intrigue and powerful rock, delivered with enough elemental riffs and hooks to hammer its message home to listeners of any age. The song would run for six minutes, though, and it seemed inconceivable that it could secure AM airplay in unaltered form. The Byrds had already whittled a Dylan song of similar duration down to less than half its length only a few months before, as part of that necessary compromise. But "Like a Rolling Stone" would have a far easier time of it on the charts than could have been reasonably expected before he left for England. For, in just the few weeks that Dylan had been gone, everything back home had changed.

The Byrds' "Mr. Tambourine Man" single had been released on April 12. David Crosby had flown up to San Francisco to give an acetate to Tom Donahue, DJ at the city's powerhouse pop radio station KYA. Donahue—ironically, a partner in Autumn Records, the same label that had recently released just-about-folk-rock hits by the Beau Brummels—aired it immediately. The record took off in San Francisco and then other cities throughout California. By May 8, it was noted as a regional breakout single in *Billboard*. Three days later, the Byrds made their national television debut on *Hullaballoo*. Even before that, they'd completed a week-long West Coast tour opening for the Rolling Stones.

By June 12, the record had crashed into the Top Ten. Two weeks later, it was sitting at #1. As poetic justice of sorts that could have never been planned in any screenplay, "Mr. Tambourine Man" had both its genesis and ultimate vindication in the back of major folk revivalists' station wagons. For the Byrds knew they had made it when—while riding in a 1956 Ford station wagon that had belonged to Odetta—the song came on KRLA, the big pop radio station in Los Angeles. Not just once, or twice, but three times. In a row.

It was a triumph not just for the Byrds, but for an entire musical and cultural movement that, largely because of "Mr. Tambourine Man," was about to finally get its name.

4

the folk-rock boom

o one seems to remember exactly who coined the term "folk-rock." But if one piece of media coverage was responsible for popularizing the enduring label on music that has mixed ingredients of folk and rock since mid-1965, it was probably *Billboard*'s cover story on June 12, 1965—the week the Byrds' "Mr. Tambourine Man" entered the Top Ten.

As the house organ of the music industry, *Billboard* had, along with other trade magazines, been partially or mostly responsible for making sure that names given to emerging trends became labels in common usage. The very division of its charts into separate listings for pop, country, rhythm & blues, and other specialized sub-genres helped reinforce such categorization. On occasion *Billboard* itself had even helped name a style of music. The most well-known instance was probably when a staff member named Jerry Wexler coined the term "rhythm and blues" as a less demeaning handle for the African-American segment of what had been called "the race market." By the 1950s rhythm and blues was the standard term for black popular music (as it remains today), and Wexler was well on his way to capitalizing on it as an executive at one of the greatest and most profitable R&B and rock labels, Atlantic Records.

Such terms were not so much for the benefit of the reader or consumer as they were for the benefit of the music business. They made it easier for radio stations, retailers, promoters, and magazines to start trends and, more importantly, sell them. The Byrds' "Mr. Tambourine Man" was clearly something different from other records that had been on the charts. It was also becoming evident that they weren't the only musicians working along those lines, and that a classification of all these newcomers might come in handy.

If *Billboard* didn't come up with the term "folk-rock" on its own to describe the Byrds and others of a similar feather, all hands seem to point to that June 12, 1965 article as the first prominent use of the word in the media. "Folk-rock" had not been used at all in the magazine prior to that date, whether to describe Dylan's early-1965 recordings or any others in a similar vein. Now, under the headline "Folkswinging Wave On—Courtesy of Rock Groups," it was being used by writer Elliot Tiegel no less than six times (and, for good measure, once more in Tiegel's brief review of a Rising Sons show elsewhere in the issue).

Though Tiegel, the head of *Billboard*'s West Coast News editorial office in Hollywood, might have liberally pasted the term into his story as a flag of convenience, his coverage of the emerging movement was fairly astute. "With Bob Dylan as the stimulus, and the Byrds as disciples, a wave of folk-rock is developing in contemporary music," announced the first paragraph. "British groups—such as the Animals and the Nashville Teens [who had a one-shot hit in 1964 with idiosyncratic country-folk-pop songwriter John D. Loudermilk's "Tobacco Road"]—have on occasion used pure country-folk material. But their identity has been really in the Beatles vein. The Byrds, on the other hand—with a similar driving sound—are the first American rock group to obtain the majority of its material from the folk field and make a success out of it."

"The Byrds' sound," Tiegel added, "combines falsetto voicings with blaring guitar chords and a rock bottom drum beat, all applicable for dancing." As the story incongruously jumped pages to continue underneath an article about Bobby Vinton's Copacabana debut, Tiegel continued, "Their repertoire is heavily Dylan, espousing his causes just above the din of their own playing. Their new LP has four Dylan tunes and [material] by Pete Seeger. To some tradesters the blending of folk lyrics with a rock beat is a natural extension for folk music. To the Byrds it's their hoped-for key to success."

Tiegel also observed that singers such as Jackie DeShannon, Sonny & Cher, and Billy J. Kramer had begun using folk-oriented material on their singles as well; that another Los Angeles group, the Rising Sons, was playing folk-rock at the Ash Grove; that Joe & Eddie, a commercial folk duo, were now reported to be moving into folk-rock; and that there was word that a New York band called the Lovin' Spoonful was making folk-rock its calling card. As evidence of the industry's hunger for getting on the folk-rock train, it was also reported that several "diskmen" were even bringing portable recorders to Ciro's to tape the Byrds from the audience.

"If the folk-rock movement takes hold, a song's lyrical content could become as respected as the dominating beat," Tiegel concluded. "With the Beatles in the mainstream as one rock 'n' roll school, the Rolling Stones and Righteous Brothers dominating white R&B, the Byrds are in flight toward a new plateau combining the imagery of folk lyrics with a granitelike beat." As if to reinforce the sense of the Byrds as the vanguard of a folk-rock flock, an ad to the right of the article captioned a picture of Bob Dylan with boasts of his recent triumphs in both British concert halls and British charts.

It would take quite a while for the word "folk-rock" to catch on for good. Even *Billboard* seemed undecided as to what phrase to use, describing the Byrds as a "folk-pop" group the week "Mr. Tambourine Man" reached #1, calling their follow-up single, "All I Really Want to Do," "another hot pop-folk-flavored Bob Dylan tune," and reviewing their *Mr. Tambourine Man* LP as a successful combination of "folk material with pop-dance beat arrangements." Cher's simultaneous cover of "All I Really Want to Do" was described simply as folk with a "powerful, driving dance beat throughout." When the We Five covered Ian & Sylvia's "You Were on My Mind" in June as well, they were viewed to "have taken Sylvia [Tyson's] ballad and given it an exciting dance beat arrangement." But *Billboard* reporters such as Tiegel and Aaron Sternfield persevered in their use of the folk-rock tag, and within a few months it was being used in the nation's biggest general-interest magazines and newspapers, not to mention *Sing Out!*, *Broadside*, and radio DJs interviewing Richard Fariña.

It was a term that was not to the liking of many musicians at the time, and still causes some disgruntled sighs today. For one thing, they didn't want to be categorized as anything, necessarily. And they certainly didn't welcome a manufactured industry label that was going to be used to both hype them and lump others who weren't necessarily doing exactly the same thing under the same unwieldy umbrella. Dylan flatly declared "I don't play folk-rock" at a December 1965 press conference in San Francisco. Not long before, as reported in Nat Hentoff's "American Airmail" column in *NME*, he'd griped, "These people call it folk-rock—if they want to call it that, something that simple, it's good for selling records. I can't call it folk-rock."

Later Paul Simon would tell *NME*, "We certainly don't want to be called folk-rock. Dylan started something beautiful, but some guys came along and destroyed it by writing commercial songs without meaning." Admits Roger McGuinn, "We never liked the term, but it's sort of appropriate. I mean, we *did* blend folk and rock." But, he cautions, "The consensus among people who did that kind of music was that they didn't like the brand, or any other label for that matter. We kept changing musical genres specifically to avoid being labeled like that."

John Sebastian, too, emphasizes that the Lovin' Spoonful weren't just folk, and rock, but also "R&B, the blues, bluegrass, and styles of music that are more demanding than this lowly title we have to work with of folk-rock. And I really had to work with it for a long time," he chuckles. "It is a title that the Spoonful immediately hated. It's a title that we understood: we just have to shut up and smile, because they're not gonna give us a new one. They're not gonna say, 'Hey, 'folk-rock,' but these guys actually listen to Elmore James and care about Bill Monroe and other styles.'"

hatever "Mr. Tambourine Man" was called by the press or others, there's no question that the impact of the single, and of the Byrds, was immediate. It was not, incidentally, the only time a rock or pop act had tried to make a hit out of Dylan songs, even if one discounts Peter, Paul & Mary's covers as folk, not pop. Unknown singer Linda Mason had recorded an equally unknown, and mediocre, album of Dylan's songs way back in May 1964, with all-but-inaudible drums and two session musicians that would play on many folk-rock records, bassist Russ Savakus and (again!) John Sebastian. The same month as "Mr. Tambourine Man" was released, British teen idol Heinz did a jolly version of "Don't Think Twice, It's All Right," which had already been given an equally undistinguished interpretation the prior year by British R&B band the Fairies. Also in April, Solomon Burke, the Atlantic Records singer best known for pop-soul ballads with gospel overtones like "Cry to Me," took a left-field shot at "Maggie's Farm," though the attempt to turn it into an uptempo soul dance tune with brass and slashing guitar wasn't convincing.

The original Dylan version of "Mr. Tambourine Man" had been released at almost exactly the same time, and as one of his most singable tunes to date, it was inevitable that others would have tried to make a hit out of the song as well if the Byrds hadn't gotten there first. Judy Collins put it on her *Fifth Album*, released in the summer of 1965, with Bill Lee (who had played on some of Dylan's *Bringing It All Back Home*) on bass. Marianne Faithfull, apparently under the impression Dylan was about to put out a 45 of the song himself, told *NME* in May that she had decided to put the tune into her live show "some time ago." The New Journeymen, now on the verge of electrifying with a lineup featuring John Phillips, his new wife Michelle, and Denny Doherty, did a pleasant, innocuous version on a 1965 demo that was not released for another 30 years.

The Byrds, however, were the musicians to get the song over to the masses, a feat due at least as much to *how* they did it as to the song itself and its composer. Summarizes manager/producer Jim Dickson, for whom "Mr. Tambourine Man" would kick off a particularly stormy year or two as he struggled to keep the Byrds on course: "I think we collectively expanded the type of songs that could be part of Top 40 radio."

Amplifies Gordon Waller of Peter & Gordon, "I thought, 'What an interesting way to handle a Dylan song!' In those days, it was fairly unheard of to take somebody's song and completely and utterly change it. That specific song was the first one that I can remember where they'd taken the song and completely changed the whole concept of it, which I was thought was great."

As Denny Doherty tells it, hearing the Byrds' version convinced the New Journeymen, then working in isolation on the Virgin Islands, to get on the stick with *real* electric rock. "We were doing 'Mr. Tambourine Man' with a folk arrangement. Duffy, the man that had befriended us down there, says, 'I got some new 45s from New York.' Throws them on the jukebox, plugs it in, and starts playing…" Doherty pauses to mimic the opening bass line. "It was the Byrds, doing 'Mr. Tambourine Man.' We didn't know who the hell it was. 'The Byrds?! What are the Byrds?' And we all went—'Aaah! Yeah! We can't play *everything* through this bass amp, can we? It's not gonna sound too good, no matter *what* we do.'" Thus enlightened, the New Journeymen were already one step further on the bumpy road to becoming the Mamas & the Papas.

The week "Mr. Tambourine Man" reached #1, the Byrds delivered conclusive proof that they were no one-hit wonder with their *Mr. Tambourine Man* album. If the session logs enclosed in their 1987 archive release *Never Before* are to be trusted, Columbia must have had some faith that the band would be around longer than a single or two even before "Mr. Tambourine Man" came out, as the first recordings for the LP took place on March 8. Finished with a couple more sessions in April, the record was a tour de force manifesto of the new folk-rock, and indeed one of the greatest debut full-lengths ever. The Beatles had proved that rock albums didn't have to be a single or two surrounded by filler or pale copies of the hits. The Byrds were the first American band to rise to the challenge of making an album of uniformly strong songs that didn't grind the same formula into the ground.

As "Mr. Tambourine Man" had put them on the map, it came as no surprise that the album featured three additional Dylan songs, all taken from *Another Side of Bob Dylan*. If Dylan diehards maintain to this day that the only true versions were the original ones, and that the Byrds prettified and watered them down for mass consumption, it nonetheless remains true that Dylan could have never made "Chimes of Freedom," "All I Really Want to Do," and "Spanish Harlem Incident" as gorgeous a listening experience. The Byrds were not copyists, and somehow transformed the sluggish pound of Dylan's acoustic guitars into danceable tempos. McGuinn introduced declarative, spellbinding 12-string riffs, particularly at the opening and closing of the arrangements, that were wholly of his own invention, while the Byrds' harmonies imbued the songs with an uplifting joy largely missing from Dylan's own work.

McGuinn took lead vocals on all of these, reinforcing his stature as leader of the band, and as a singer unmatched in his aptitude for crafting vocals that were Dylanesque, yet far more pleasing to the pop ear than Dylan's own. The ex-Jet Set member was still fond of using electronic space age allegories for the music he was making, both in his (by 1965 standards) far-out quotes on the LP's liner notes, and in *Melody Maker*, where he pronounced: "We simply like the sort of music that Bob Dylan writes. Music that is associated with the jet age. All Dylan's material can have the jet age applied to it." As for "Mr. Tambourine Man" itself, he allowed, "I think we were lucky with a combination of circumstances. Perhaps there was a gap between the pop music that was currently going on, and between the folk and rock fields, that needed filling. Maybe we filled it."

Elsewhere on the LP, the Byrds unveiled their willingness for blending original and outside material of unparalleled eclecticism. "The Bells of Rhymney" was an exceptionally strong cover of Pete Seeger's ode to struggling Welsh miners, its wordless gothic harmonies to inspire even more imitations than those heard on the Byrds' famous hit singles. Jackie DeShannon, an early Byrds supporter who had even used them as a backing band for an uncharacteristically sloppy arrangement of her "Splendor in the Grass" in April, gave them "Don't Doubt Yourself, Babe." The band managed to brighten it with both buoyant folk-rock harmonies and a Bo Diddley beat.

Gene Clark's storehouse of original songs became to some degree a casualty of the Byrds' imaginative cover versions. Still, he proved himself a strong composer of romantic Beatlesque folk-rock material with the anthemic "I'll Feel a Whole Lot Better" and the gothic "Here Without You." A collaboration with McGuinn, "It's No Use," was as tough a rocker as any British Invader had managed, the jagged 12-string solo foreshadowing their excursions into psychedelia. The whole thing was topped off with what became a Byrds tradition of tongue-in-cheek closing tracks, "We'll Meet Again," a World War II–era pop standard by Vera Lynn that the group learned from the song's appearance at the end of the *Dr. Strangelove* soundtrack. The eerie burst of distorted guitar at the very end, which seemed to reverberate into infinity, gave the interpretation a disquieting irony. It also signaled an appetite for electronic futurism that the group would immerse themselves in deeper and deeper over their next few albums.

Mr. Tambourine Man set the prototype for the Byrds' first five LPs, which were unsurpassed balancing acts between updates of traditional folk songs, folk-rock covers of contemporary folk and pop songwriters, and an ever-widening scope of quality original songs and stylistic influences. "We did want to be balanced," acknowledges McGuinn. "I used to regard the Byrds' albums as kind of electronic magazines. You wanted a little bit of this, a little bit of that." All created, it must be stressed, by the Byrds themselves. Chris Hillman and Michael Clarke had signed on to the Columbia contract as full members in March, and the Byrds played all of the instruments on *Mr. Tambourine Man*, excepting the two songs that had already been released on the "Mr. Tambourine Man" single.

"I love it to this day when somebody says, yeah, you guys didn't play on the first album," Hillman chortles. "If those are session players, then we must have had the C-level group of 'em. You know it's us, because it's all kinds of weird stuff going on." Several flubbed bass notes on "Spanish Harlem Incident" prove his point, though Hillman would rapidly become one of the best rock bassists around. The rest of the album, he concedes, "doesn't stand up to the 'Tambourine Man' track, as far as that preciseness. [But] it's okay. Because I tend to like the raw edge of the band, as opposed to the slickness of the session date."

Like the single of the same name, *Mr. Tambourine Man* was a big seller, getting to #6 that summer and solidifying their new crown as America's answer to the Beatles. Their mastery of the LP format helped extend the Byrds' immediate bombshell impact beyond the teenage girls that still comprised the great majority of singles-buyers. In the summer of 1965, Richie Furay, after the collapse of the Au Go-Go Singers (which had also included Stephen Stills), had lost out to John Denver in the audition to replace Chad Mitchell in the Chad Mitchell Trio. Putting his folk music ambitions on hold, he was working for Pratt & Whitney Aircraft in New England, "staying with the family of one of the Au Go-Go members," he remembers. "I would go back and forth to New York City to audition for different things and would stay at the apartment that some of the band rented. Gram Parsons lived across the street and we became friends.

"Sometimes he would come up to visit me in Massachusetts, and one time he brought the Byrds' first album. When he played it for me—that was it. Enough of handing out tools in the tool crib. I had to get back to playing music and pursuing my dreams. I had never heard anything like their album. As far as music went, for me at that time it was them, the Beach Boys, and the Beatles. Folk music had long gone. It was now electric with harmony." Within a year Furay had reteamed with Stills and would be singing and playing guitar with the Byrds' most serious Hollywood rivals, Buffalo Springfield.

Some established folksingers were also getting the message. "When we first heard about the Byrds, we did think that that was a good idea," says Sylvia Tyson. "And we felt, certainly, that it was the next logical step towards a more popular music than, say, Peter Paul & Mary. I'm getting into touchy territory here," she acknowledges with a laugh, "but Peter, Paul & Mary was a manufactured group. I mean, those people never had sung together before Albert Grossman and Milt Okun put them together. Although Milt certainly did a great job with their arrangements and they were deservedly very popular, the next step [in covering] the contemporary songwriters of that day would be some group that did it with perhaps a little more abandon."

As people and performers, the Byrds were also breaking with the established order, setting new standards for hip, detached cool and refusing to cheerily jump onto the all-around entertainment merry-go-round that was still par for the course for hitmakers. In 1965, Ian Whitcomb was a one-shot British Invader, touring the States on the back of his campy falsetto rock-soul hit "You Turn Me On." "Amongst the acts lip-synching with me on a show called *Hollywood A Go-Go* was a group called the Byrds," he wrote in *After the Ball: Pop Music from Rag to Rock*. "Now, whilst everyone else and me was clapping along to the beat, smiling and showing teeth, these Byrds stood like ice-cold tombstones. They didn't wear band-suits; they wore buckskin with fringes, and soiled polo-necked sweaters and jeans. No velour in sight. They only half-heartedly lip-synched and I could have sworn they were having a chat whilst they were supposed to be singing on the air. But the main surprise was: *they didn't smile.*

"They sang 'Hey Mr. Tambourine Man' to the accompaniment of drums, and electric guitars (notably a 12-string affair that sounded Elizabethan). Afterwards I went up to their rostrum and, flashing a smile, asked them who wrote the song (just for polite conversation). The 12-string guitarist, wearing National Health type glasses and a wry look said softly so I could hardly hear: 'Dylan, man, like don't you know?' I said no but I do know the other song you sang, 'We'll Meet Again,' originally made famous by Vera Lynn, the Forces Sweetheart. 'We think it's kinda funny and old,' said their spokesman. I said that the song meant an awful lot to those who had fought in the Second World War. 'I trust everything will turn out right,' replied the spokesman mysteriously."

The resulting effect on lingering folkies was much the same as that of the Beatles just over a year earlier. Chris Darrow had met Chris Hillman around 1964, when both Chrises had taken stints in bluegrass bands at Disneyland. They ran into each other at the Ash Grove later that year, at which time, according to Darrow, Hillman seemed about as embarrassed at admitting to playing rock 'n' roll as he would have been admitting to playing Disneyland. "I said, 'Hi Chris, how're you doing?' And he kind of held his head down and says, 'I just joined a rock 'n' roll band.' I said, 'Oh.' He said, 'Yeah, I'm playing bass. I need the money.'

"So I'm watching TV, it was I think the first *Hullabaloo* show [the Byrds] did. All of a sudden"—he breaks off for a moment to sing the opening 12-string riff to "Mr. Tambourine Man"—"I said [to] my ex-wife, 'Donna, see that guy right there? I met that guy! Don't you remember? He was backstage. That's Hillman!!' The last time I'd seen him, he was wearing T-shirts and Levis and tennis shoes and had short hair. All of a sudden he's got long hair, he's got Beatle boots, he's got tight pants. Then, [I recognized] David Crosby, 'cause Crosby had been in a group called the Les Baxter Balladeers who used to play around the Ice House and stuff. McGuinn stuck out like a sore thumb. 'God, I know all these guys!' I was just stunned by it all. It wasn't so surprising to have these guys be doing this material so much as it was surprising to see who it was. CHUNK! The door open[ed] right then."

That door to instant emulation was far more accessible now than it had been in February 1964, when folk musicians had been just as stunned by the Beatles, but had no real means of going out and playing like the Beatles the next day. Now they were 15 months older, more acclimated to rock music (and often more experienced on electric instruments), and had seen one of their own make the transition to full-fledged rock 'n' roll band, with the attendant hit records and screaming teenage girls chasing them in public. (And they *did* scream for the Byrds like they did for the Beatles, as shown in their live appearance on the rarely seen rockumentary *The Big T.N.T. Show*, where hysterical teenagers almost drown out their performances of "Mr. Tambourine Man," "Turn! Turn! Turn!," and "The Bells of Rhymney.")

John McEuen of the Nitty Gritty Dirt Band's reaction was instantaneous: "I was driving to college one day the year before the Dirt Band started. I was starting to play music and playing in the clubs at night. And I hear the Byrds' first record on the radio, and I knew that guy was a mandolin player that was playing bass. And it's like, if *he* can do it, maybe I can." He also appreciated how the new folk-rock was different from the rest of rock 'n' roll: "It's more message-oriented, delivering some form of either social or personal message. It's not 'Mustang Sally,' it's not party music. One guy can sit with a guitar and sing the song, whereas it's hard to do 'Foxy Lady' by yourself, or 'Sunshine of Your Love.' But you can sit and play 'Tambourine Man,' and a bunch of people will sing along. It's a recognizable melody, and a delivery of a lyric, that brings a message or story that's memorable."

Gary Marker was just starting to play folk-rock when "Mr. Tambourine Man" hit, as bassist in the Rising Sons, one of the first Los Angeles groups to adopt the style in the wake of the Byrds. He goes as far as to claim that "a massive paradigm shift occurred in 1965 with the advent of one group: the Byrds. Until then, outside of R&B, American rock was essentially moribund. The Byrds changed all that, at least in L.A. They were a rough assemblage of local ex-folkies and wannabe rockers struggling with the peculiarities of electrified guitars. The Byrds produced a mutant popular form, fusing several random musical elements: American non-blues white folk music with tight vocal harmonies, the music of a folk cult singer named Bob Dylan—and electric guitars. It also gave a lot of other L.A. folk and jazz musicians the idea that if the Byrds could make a dent in the commercial market, maybe they had a chance as well—just maybe all those skinny, pale English guys didn't rule the roost after all."

The Byrds gave fledgling songwriters hope as well. Pamela Polland, who had played acoustic blues as half of a teenage duo with future Rising Sons guitarist Ry Cooder, was in early 1965 having a hard time either recording her material or placing it with other artists. She had left Los Angeles to try and work some of her songs into the New York publishing/recording machine, but continued to be told she was either too rock to be folk, or too folk to be rock. "When I left for New York, I was still in the 'no bin' situation," she remembers. "But when I came back, the Byrds had just taken off, and it was a whole new ballgame. I came back to an L.A. that was abuzz with this 'folk-rock' concept, and suddenly, everything I did musically made sense to the business climate. I'll never forget hearing the Byrds for the first time and feeling like—AT LAST!!! Somebody gave this style a chance, and the public loves it." And within a couple years, Polland would be recording folk-rock for the producer of "Mr. Tambourine Man," Terry Melcher, as part of the Gentle Soul.

The first wave of Los Angeles folk-rockers was filled out by many who had, like most of the Byrds, served time in commercial folk ensembles. They might have been enticed as much by the prospect of release from the boot camp of commercial folk's wholesome, restricted lifestyles as they were by the chance to play electric instruments. A surprising number of them had even served apprenticeships at Disneyland, where future Kaleidoscope multi-instrumentalists Darrow and David Lindley played as part of the Dry City Scat Band, and McEuen worked for a concessionaire in the Magic Castle.

Tom Campbell, the entertainment director who'd arranged the folkies' gigs in the amusement park, is still referred to as "the mayor of Disneyland" by Roy Marinell. The mayor, however, wasn't some old bureaucrat. He hooked up Marinell, Steve Gillette, and Polland into a trio in hopes that

The Rising Sons. Left to right: Ry Cooder, Taj Mahal, Kevin Kelley, Jesse Kincaid, Gary Marker

they would play Disneyland; though Marinell doesn't remember if they ever did, all three became noted if somewhat behind-the-scenes songwriters in the L.A. folk-rock community. Campbell himself wrote songs with Gillette and Linda Albertano that would later get recorded by the likes of Linda Ronstadt and Ian & Sylvia. But for the time being the six-foot-plus Albertano (now a respected performance artist) had to suffer the ignominy of working as part of a duo of "Space Girls" in Disneyland with Shannon Lee. "They wore these incredibly garish space costumes, with big bubble headpieces and high heels, so they were close to seven-feet tall," says Gillette. "It was very humiliating for Linda."

The inherent uncoolness of playing in and in front of Disneyland rides, or even dressing up in spacesuits for families to gawk at, was alleviated by midnight jam sessions in the park's Golden Horseshoe, after the rides had shut down. The young hootenanniers were too hip to last far into the Beatles era in such an anodyne environment; Campbell left in 1964 after "they told me that they weren't gonna continue allowing me to produce shows. I was a bad boy. My hair was getting way too long." He subsequently organized a Pepsi-Cola Hootenanny Hoot tour around Southern California that included the Dry City Scat Band and Gillette. Hootenanny tours too, of course, were soon to become a thing of the past, and Campbell recalls one visitor delivering an advance warning: "My first knowledge of interaction between McGuinn and Darrow and Lindley and all those people was in the dressing room on one of those ill-fated Hootenanny Hoot shows. He was playing the rock 'n' roll stuff that would later become the Byrds."

The clean-cut, apple-cheeked image of the folk ensembles put together by entrepreneurs like Randy Sparks—including the New Christy Minstrels and the Back Porch Majority—was likewise starting to seem as anachronistically stifling as Disneyland by mid-1965. Marinell, who had played with Hillman and Larry Murray (later of the folk-rock-country group Hearts & Flowers) in a Sparks outfit called the Green Grass Group, sets the scene: "Randy had a calendar where he had the dates marked where every Stephen Foster song came up public domain, so he could rewrite a lyric and copyright it. One of the most popular songs we did was called 'Billy's Mule'—'Billy's mule can tote a wagon, he can pull a plow.' That kind of stuff. It was the corniest shit you ever, ever heard of! And we all knew it. We'd all roll our eyes at it and laugh and snicker.

"But at the same time, we were making a living. A bunch of us were all living in the same house and having a bonding experience. We were playing six nights a week at Ledbetter's, and there were UCLA girls coming in there, young college girls. And we were in heaven! More than the idea of what Randy was offering in terms of musical outlet, it was really the ability to be able to perform and have a place to live and food in your stomach that was driving that train."

It was a train that was coming to the end of the line: the Byrds' success was instrumental in kidnapping many of its passengers. Larry Murray: "Chris hated playing that kind of music, and so did I. We were playing and looking to get another group together. Chris was playing with McGuinn, and I was, off and on, jamming at everything. They started going in one direction, like electric instruments. I respected electric instruments, but they were doing Dylanish-type songs. And my attitude towards them was, 'Well, I'm wasting my time with them, because people aren't going to take folk music with a full electric band. You know, you're going to have to play something else.' My first mistake!," he laughs. "It was almost like a garage band. And I was going, 'Noooo way! You guys'll become a delivery job, I'll get a real job.'

"And sure enough, they started working. They just kind of clammed up, they went into hibernation. And I actually didn't see Chris or any of those guys for a long time, and I kind of forgot about 'em. Then I heard they had a group and it was making a record, and I said, great, good luck. Then all of a sudden, [it was] all I heard on the radio. I was really surprised—'Well, it's a fluke, you know.' But then it became so big, I finally admitted that that's where it's at. And I immediately, in my own stuff, started performing music in that kind of style, [which] I knew anyway. It was instant influence."

As in any revolution, there were those who didn't get it, like John Denver. "When John came to L.A., he came with a Fender guitar and amplifier, [and] did not know how to fingerpick," says Marinell. "All I wanted to do at that point was play rock 'n' roll. All he wanted to do was play folk music. I taught him to fingerpick, he taught me to flat pick. We traded an acoustic guitar for an electric guitar." It would take a few years for the tide to swing back in Denver's favor.

Randy Sparks saw how much of a danger the Byrds and their ilk were to his livelihood, as according to Hillman, "Randy was incensed that Columbia had even signed us, and called up [Columbia president] Goddard Lieberson and was demanding that we be thrown off the label. We represented new things happening. Randy was a little envious and didn't quite understand how to make that transition. It was a threat to him."

Sales speak louder than threats, though, and in June Columbia signed another of the upstart new L.A. folk-rock bands, the Rising Sons, who were assigned to the Byrds' producer, Terry Melcher. A supergroup before its time, the lineup boasted ace guitarists Ry Cooder and Taj Mahal, as well as future Spirit drummer Ed Cassidy (who would soon be replaced by Chris Hillman's cousin, and future Byrd, Kevin Kelley). In the same issue as his cover story announcing the arrival of folk-rock, *Billboard*'s Elliot Tiegel had given their Ash Grove performance a remarkably positive review considering they had yet to release a record: "The Rising Sons also feature lyrics of the rural South, but with amplified guitars and a heavy drum beat. Taj Mahal is the group's strength, possessing a Ray Charles soulful quality." Unfortunately, due to a business/management impasse that's still difficult to fathom, the prodigiously talented band would barely manage to put out one single. It would really take a year or two for the rootsiest Los Angeles folk-rockers, like Darrow, Murray, Kenny Edwards, and Pamela Polland, to start to make their mark on records by bands like Kaleidoscope, Hearts and Flowers, the Stone Poneys, and the Gentle Soul.

The first opportunists in Los Angeles to ride the Byrds' wings onto the charts would not be schooled in the authentic roots folk-blues of the Ash Grove, nor even the more commercial folk of the Troubadour. Sonny & Cher paid their dues not in coffeehouses, but in Hollywood studios. Sonny Bono had been clawing for a foothold in the record business since the late '50s, when he did writing and production for the great L.A. rock and R&B label Specialty, even penning material for '50s rock star Larry Williams. After Specialty folded, he did some odds and ends for Phil Spector, ranging from gofering to playing percussion and singing. He did his bit for proto-folk-rock by cowriting "Needles and Pins" with another Spector protégé, Jack Nitzsche. By 1965 he was married to a teenager more than a decade younger than he was, Cher, with whom he'd already recorded a few flop singles, the first of those under the name Caesar & Cleo.

Bono was one of those "diskmen" taping the Byrds at Ciro's. He fashioned Cher's cover version of Dylan's "All I Really Want to Do" after the group's arrangement, with the addition of some Spectoresque touches. When Columbia got wind of Cher's release, they put out the Byrds' own— and immensely superior—rendition in head-to-head competition, though "Mr. Tambourine Man" was still at the top of the charts. As a consequence, both Cher and the Byrds entered the Top 100 with the same song the first week of July, splitting sales and hurting both releases. Cher's version eventually pulled away and became the big American hit, though both singles made the Top Ten in Britain, where "Mr. Tambourine Man" had just repeated its US success.

Chasing Cher's "All I Really Want to Do" up the charts was Sonny & Cher's "I Got You Babe," which adeptly deployed the dragging beat, tambourine clomps, and (on Sonny's part) Dylanesque whine that were becoming commercial folk-rock's stocks in trade. Session guitarist Carol Kaye sees the folk-rock trimmings as a conscious decision on Bono's part: "Sonny was a brilliant producer and understood the importance of the 'identification' in sounds like Spector's 'wall of sound' for their hit records. Sonny & Cher used me for electric 12-string fills as they kept wanting that as their identification. It helped them sell a lot of records."

In the twenty-first century, it can be difficult to comprehend or acknowledge that Sonny & Cher, for just a few brief months in the summer of 1965, were considered folk-rockers. The images of Sonny & Cher that have burned themselves most strongly into our consciousness are those of the banal comedian/hosts on their 1970s variety show, rather than those of the furry-vested, bell-bottomed couple they were in the early days of their marriage. Reconciliation of Cher's subsequent mega-film stardom, and the late Bono's reign as conservative Republican mayor of Palm Springs and congressman, with their earlier incarnation as hippie rebels, is not easy. Yet that is how they were perceived when "I Got You Babe" swamped the airwaves in the summer of 1965, even if it was at heart a conventional sentimental pop love song, its glockenspiels, bassoon, and throbbing percussion marking it as a son-of-Phil-Spector production job. As *Record Mirror* reader Ron Turnbull cruelly and concisely summarized, "Its melody is a combination of Donovan's 'Catch the Wind' and Dylan's 'It Ain't Me Babe' and 'Chimes of Freedom.' Its backing is nicked from Phil Spector. Cher sings flat."

So folk-rock was already in the process of being commercialized, though Bono wasn't doing anything he hadn't done for ten years as a Hollywood also-ran looking for an opening into a cutthroat business. It so happened that folk-rock gave him and his teenage bride their shot. In Sonny's case, it was probably his last shot. He'd just turned 30, and had an adenoidal, atonal voice that made Dylan's sound relatively conventional. There was little ground for him to compete on a level playing field with the younger, more angelic looks and voices of most emerging pop stars, the Byrds included. But Dylan, and folk-rock, had made it possible for someone with his voice to get a hearing. That's what he got on his sole solo hit, "Laugh at Me," a "why-does-everyone-have-to-criticize-me-for-the-way-I-act-and-look" diatribe that made the Top Ten at the end of the summer, and would never have gotten onto playlists just a few months earlier. It may have sounded like a sub-Dylanesque protest song, but the backing track still sounded a lot like a Phil Spector session.

Sonny & Cher's musical limitations didn't mean that they weren't hip in some ways. They had befriended and helped the Rolling Stones when that band made its first visit to California in 1964, well before the Stones became Stateside stars. And it did take some courage for Bono to attempt to enter restaurants with Ringo Starr–length hair in mid-'60s America; his ejection from one after a ruckus that started over the way he looked was the specific inspiration for "Laugh at Me." Yet for him and Cher, folk-rock was not a calling, but a stepping stone toward becoming pop stars and all-around entertainers, with few of their post-1965 recordings (or even some of the sides they did in 1965) bearing much relationship to the form.

Sonny & Cher's part in folk-rock may have been fleeting, but before their exit they caused more problems for the movement's true leaders. McGuinn told *Sounds* in 1971 that the always-unpredictable Dylan was peeved at Cher's triumph with "All I Really Want to Do," inferring that the songwriter even somehow held the Byrds accountable: "What really got to me most was Dylan coming up to me and saying, 'They beat you man,' and he lost faith in me. He was shattered. His material had been bastardized. There we were, the defenders and protectors of his music, and we'd let Sonny & Cher get away with it." Then Sonny & Cher stole some of the thunder from the Byrds on the group's first British tour, which had anticlimactic, mixed results at best after the band was built up to the British public as the American response to the Beatles.

*The Lovin' Spoonful with Sonny Bono. Left to right: Joe Butler,
Sonny Bono, John Sebastian, Steve Boone, Zal Yanovsky*

In many respects, the Byrds *were* the American response to the Beatles: a group who looked great, played great, and were avatars of the future. The Beatles, however, had been playing together since they were teenagers in the 1950s. The Byrds, their status as lords of the manor at Ciro's notwithstanding, had only been playing regularly before live audiences for about half a year. Where Sunset Strippers had found their laconic stage presence and reckless amplification cool, many British punters complained about the extreme volume and lack of friendly banter with the audience. Two of their shows were canceled due to poor box office support. They were even served with a writ for improper use of their own name by the British band the Birds, whose lead guitarist was a young Ron Wood.

Several of the Byrds fell ill on the tour, and though McGuinn's quotes from the period certainly find him an articulate spokesman for the group, the musicians were not nearly as loquacious or forthcoming as the Beatles, the band to which they were being incessantly compared. That left room for the more media-savvy Sonny Bono, visiting the UK hot on the heels of the Byrds with Cher, to charm the press. Time may have venerated the Byrds' music as far more significant and artistic than Sonny & Cher's, yet the fickle 1965 British public, often as concerned with image as substance, found the husband-and-wife pair more interesting copy. Sonny Bono even made a game attempt to rename folk-rock itself, proclaiming in *Melody Maker*, "What do we sing? We call it folk-n-roll— a sort of folk music with a rocking beat. But with a smile. Ours is happy music—we haven't any message to impart." The Byrds' management did fight back successfully on that score. "I avoided the term 'folk-rock' as long as I could," says Jim Dickson. "[Byrds publicist] Derek Taylor wanted to use it and I prevented it until Sonny Bono coined 'Folk & Roll' and I was forced to relent."

The Byrds would never regain the momentum that their "Mr. Tambourine Man" and "All I Really Want to Do" had given them in the UK. They never made the Top 20 there again in the 1960s, not even with "Turn! Turn! Turn!" later in the year. The British tour, however, was good for one thing that would last far longer than any bitter aftertaste from indifferent audiences and journalists. The three Byrds who had founded the Jet Set would use the experience as grist for the lyrics of "Eight Miles High," the song that took folk-rock into the psychedelic stratosphere (and that takes this book into its sequel of the same name).

Before folk-rock could ascend to the heavens, however, it was in danger of becoming assimilated into the mainstream as just another trend. In their quest to inject meaning into the hit parade, the Byrds would soon have the most important ally they could have imagined. For just as Dylan had returned from his spring British tour to find the pop landscape altered with the rise of the Byrds' "Mr. Tambourine Man," so did the Byrds return from their summer British tour to a different world. Bob Dylan himself now had a huge hit single.

A couple weeks after his return to the States at the beginning of June, Dylan was recording the song he'd started writing on the airplane home, "Like a Rolling Stone." Although he was using some of the same musicians that had been contributors to the *Bringing It All Back Home* sessions, a couple of new boys would give the song a piercing blues-rock edge. One was Michael Bloomfield, the hotshot guitarist with the Paul Butterfield Blues Band. The other, in keeping with Dylan's readiness to go with the flow, was an organist who had not even been booked for the date, had never before met the singer, and had barely played the organ before.

Al Kooper was another of the several figures entering folk-rock who was more in his element writing in a Brill Building cubicle, or playing on rock and pop sessions, than he was at a coffeehouse. The cowriter of Gary Lewis & the Playboys' massive hit "This Diamond Ring," he'd recently become a Dylan fan and started to do open mikes at a Forest Hills folk club. He'd become friendly enough with Tom Wilson to get invited to watch a Dylan session. Kooper was not planning to stay glued to his seat in the control booth, although his scheme to brag his way into the session as a guitarist was scuttled after he heard Bloomfield warming up. When it was decided to move Paul Griffin from organ to piano, Kooper saw his window of opportunity.

He's told the story often over the last few decades, and best in his autobiography, *Backstage Passes & Backstabbing Bastards*: how he snuck over to the organ uninvited after unsuccessfully pestering Wilson for a chance to take Griffin's place at the instrument; how Wilson had the good grace not to kick him out after seeing Kooper in place and ready to go for the next take; and how Al, not even knowing the song, followed the changes as best he could, like "a little kid fumbling in the dark for the light switch," as he wrote in his memoir. Dylan liked the organ part enough to ask Wilson to turn it up, despite the producer's objections that Kooper wasn't even an organist. The rich, swelling tone of Kooper's organ would become an integral asset to Dylan's other 1965–66 recordings, and as a consequence Kooper was booked by several other newly anointed folk-rockers looking for session men who could emulate the Dylan sound.

He was but one important factor in the creation of a record that communicated Dylan's poetic expression of freedom, doubt, cynicism, and alienation with more power than anything he had done previously (and, arguably, anything he's done since). The arrangement was denser and fuller than anything on *Bringing It All Back Home*. Its elementary chord progression, during much of the verses and all of the choruses, was not dissimilar to three-chord rock classics like "Louie, Louie" and Ritchie Valens's "La Bamba." Everything worked, though, to augment Dylan's searing and sneering vocal, the lyric mixing invective against a mysterious lost soul with his by-now habitually enigmatic images of diplomats with Siamese cats and the like.

As with many of his early electric songs, it could be taken as a vicious putdown of a poor un-with-it ex-lover or flunkie (or folkie). On its broadest terms, however, it reflected the doubt and excitement of anyone cast into unfamiliar realms, whether they were entering or leaving relationships, moving from folk to pop, or kids leaving home to be on their own. *Billboard*'s review— "lyric aimed at the teen market, with a dance beat to boot"—seemed to hint at a suspicion that Dylan had tailored the song to the adolescents and young adults that comprised the overwhelming majority of his listeners. "Like a Rolling Stone" has endured as an ageless classic, however, because in truth you didn't have to be a college student just out of the house to identify with the lyric. Its message of uncertainty and drifting impermanence may have been accusatory in his singularly venomous fashion. But it was also universal, applicable to almost anyone, not least of all Dylan himself.

The six-minute length of the track would probably have presented an insurmountable barrier for any other artist hoping for his first big American single. Not so Dylan. MGM might have hacked parts of the Animals' "House of the Rising Sun" out of their 45 for the American market, and the Byrds might have done little more than an excerpt of "Mr. Tambourine Man," but "Like a Rolling Stone" was going out unedited. Columbia tried to turn the length to its advantage with a bold two-page ad in *Billboard* that asked, "A six-minute single? Why not! When you have six minutes of Bob Dylan singing his great new song 'Like a Rolling Stone.'"

Melody Maker's Bob Dawbarn, in a piece headlined "thank goodness we won't get this six-minute Bob Dylan single in Britain," was dubious. Laboring under the mistaken impression that Columbia would not issue the single in the UK, he sourly rated it as "the six longest minutes since the invention of time," predicting that it would "offend the folk purists with its strings [though no strings were used on the record] and electric guitars. It is unlikely to appeal to pop fans because of its length, monotony and uncommercial lyric."

Pop fans did not agree. By early September, "Like a Rolling Stone" was #2 in America, kept out of the top position only by the Beatles' own Dylan-influenced single, "Help!" In the UK it made #4, and still remains his biggest hit single there. Dylan was now a superstar. Why with "Like a Rolling Stone," and not with his acoustic folk protest songs? As Paul Cable wrote in *Bob Dylan: His Unreleased Recordings*, "Like a Rolling Stone" had the sort of "thump that makes you not only want to stamp your feet but throw your whole body into the thing and celebrate being human. You could not do *that* to '[With] God on Our Side.'"

Dylan made his controversial debut with an electric band on July 25, 1965 at the Newport Folk Festival, and despite his mixed reception remained on the rock 'n' roll track. He began sessions for *Highway 61 Revisited* a few days later, and then started to tour in earnest with less ad hoc lineups than the one that had been thrown together at Newport, though he split his program into acoustic and electric halves. The Byrds' mass exposure of the Dylan songbook had boosted Dylan's album sales considerably—*Bringing It All Back Home* had become his first Top Ten LP, without the benefit of a major hit single—and *Highway 61 Revisited*, released at the end of August, did even better, getting to #3.

The inclusion of "Like a Rolling Stone" as its opening cut no doubt helped, but the main reason Dylan was selling better than ever was that *Highway 61 Revisited* was wall-to-wall rock 'n' roll, with the exception of the marathon acoustic closer "Desolation Row." The sound was crunchy and full, anchored by Bloomfield's blistering blues guitar and Kooper, now comfortably installed as Dylan's organist of choice. If the lyrics were often despairing in their portraits of confused losers ("Ballad of a Thin Man," "Desolation Row," "Just Like Tom Thumb's Blues") and the surreal hyperchaotic pace of American life, they were leavened by a certain gleeful energy and gallows humor, particularly on "Tombstone Blues," which pounds away at a furious pace akin to punk rock in spirit. At the same time, he continued to expand his musical range, borrowing from the descending minor chords of Ray Charles in "Ballad of a Thin Man," conjuring a melodic quirky love song that could have been a hit under its own steam with "Queen Jane Approximately." The front cover photo was no less a shock wave than the music, Dylan having in less than two years transformed from Woody Guthrie's son to flashy mod rocker in florid colors with a motorcycle T-shirt.

Except for "Like a Rolling Stone," the entire album was produced by Bob Johnston, whose entrance into Dylan's world was about as will o' the wisp as most decisions having to do with the singer's career at Columbia. Johnston had done some minor songwriting and production for artists ranging from rockabilly singer Mac Curtis to fading easy listening star Patti Page, as well as doing A&R for Kapp Records. The reasons for replacing Tom Wilson, who had done much to ease Dylan's changeover from folk to rock, are not entirely clear, though Kooper thinks "Wilson's departure was precipitated by Albert Grossman. Albert didn't like him. Johnston was the total opposite of the Harvard-educated, well-mannered African-American—he was a wild redneck from Tennessee. He patted Bob on the back quite a bit more than Wilson ever did. Maybe that's what was needed, I don't really know." Johnston did make his voice heard, however, in getting his Nashville session virtuoso friend Charlie McCoy to play on some takes, foreshadowing a direction that Dylan would follow on his next album.

Outside the studio, Dylan continued to move at a lightning speed. When he gave his first post-Newport show at Forest Hills Stadium in New York in late August, his band included two musicians who had recently recorded with him on the yet-to-be-released *Highway 61 Revisited* album, Al Kooper (on organ) and Harvey Brooks (on bass). Filling out the lineup were two of the musicians from the little-known Toronto band the Hawks, guitarist Robbie Robertson and drummer Levon Helm, both of whom had worked on John Hammond, Jr.'s *So Many Roads*.

Dylan's decision to split the show into acoustic and electric sets didn't mollify everyone. "At Forest Hills, which is quite a big open place, the minute he started going electric, everybody was rather upset about it," says Paul Nelson, who was in attendance. "Some kid a few rows down said, 'Joan Baez would never do that.' I was about the only one clapping. I truly felt scared." The kid who upheld Baez as a guardian of the flame was doubly behind the curve. Joan was already quite a rock fan, having met the Beatles in Denver during their second American tour ("a sort of female Dylan as far as the words of her songs go, but more polished" is how George Harrison described her to *Melody Maker*), and had preceded "House of the Rising Sun" with a plug for the Animals at one of her 1965 British concerts.

The reception got generally warmer, though never unanimously positive, as Dylan played in various venues throughout the country and audiences assimilated his new persona. After Kooper dropped out of the live band to pursue both session work and a new slot as keyboardist of the Blues Project, Dylan roped in the rest of the Hawks to serve as his backing unit, shoring up the rock halves of his sets (though Levon Helm dropped out in November, the drum chair subsequently filled by Bobby Gregg, Sandy Konikoff, and Mickey Jones over the following months). In more demand than ever by the media, Dylan turned interviews and press conferences into theaters of the absurd. When the questions struck him as sophomoric, which was most of the time, he responded in kind with juvenile non sequiturs, listing "frozen tabbacco [sic]" as his favorite drink in an *NME* "Lifelines" feature, adding that his personal ambition was "to be a waitress," his professional ambition "to be a stewardess." The pleasure he took in dispensing vicious cruelty to rival Village songwriters lapping at his coattails was legendary. In one particularly infamous incident, he kicked Phil Ochs out of his cab (or limo) after Ochs had the temerity to suggest that Dylan's latest single (variously reported as "Can You Please Crawl Out Your Window?" or "One of Us Most Know (Sooner or Later)" wasn't going to be a hit.

Whichever song of the two it was, neither *was* a significant hit. However, a non-LP single from the *Highway 61 Revisited* sessions, "Positively 4th Street," *was* a Top Ten hit in late 1965. It remains the ultimate snide putdown in a year when Dylan was full of them. This one in particular was often interpreted as a blast against sycophants and two-faced friends from the Village, where 4th Street ran along Washington Square Park. Not far from 4th Street, Dylan would still meet with folk songwriters—some on the verge of wading into folk-rock themselves—in the Kettle of Fish, the upstairs bar in the same building as the Gaslight folk club. Legend would have it that Dylan would hold court and turn these into cutting sessions, arrogantly criticizing the work of friends and cohorts like Eric Andersen, Phil Ochs, Tom Paxton, and David Cohen (aka David Blue). Paxton, who fondly recalls Dylan singing him the newly penned "Gates of Eden" at one of these gatherings, puts the kibosh on those tales: "Bob was not a take-over-the-room kind of guy. He didn't demand that the table fall silent while he sang a new song or anything. What you *would* hear would be Dylan and Ochs going at it. Bob could be very mean to Phil, because Phil would be a little excitable, shall we say."

N ow that Dylan was fully aboard the folk-rock boom, its tentacles began to infiltrate deeper layers of pop, folk, and the music industry. The most obvious manifestation of Dylan and folk-rock's exploding popularity was the sudden proliferation of rock and pop artists rushing to cover his songs. For just a brief period, the Dylan catalog would be eyed in the same way as Lennon-McCartney's as a potential goldmine for publishers, producers, and musicians looking for a quick hit.

One of the first major bands off the mark was England's Manfred Mann. Though the musicians in that group had established themselves as British Invasion stars with covers of songs by American Brill Building songwriters, like "Doo Wah Diddy Diddy" and "Sha La La," they were among the most intellectual pop stars of the day. Bandleader Manfred Mann had originally aspired to be a serious jazz keyboardist before pragmatically switching his focus to pop-rock. Singer Paul Jones had studied at Oxford before throwing his lot in with the Manfreds, and was renowned for his (by pop star standards, at any rate) radical politics, wearing ban-the-bomb badges and putting the symbol for the Campaign for Nuclear Disarmament under his autographs. Dylan had given a thumbs-up to the band after seeing them in London's Marquee club on a 1964 visit, and the Manfreds were attracted to his material as they looked for ways to expand their repertoire in a more serious direction.

The first Dylan song they covered was "With God on Our Side," for a mid-1965 EP. It was quite adventurous to translate an acoustic lament on warring self-righteousness, complete with a reference to six million Jews frying in ovens, into an arrangement suitable for their pop-rock audience. To their credit they did so very effectively, and in a manner quite different than the Byrds applied in their Dylan covers, building to a crescendo with ominous orchestral drums, Jones's resonant vocal, and Mann's thundering quasi-classical piano. The BBC found it too hot to handle, banning it from its "Saturday Swings" program, and raising Mann's ire in *Melody Maker*: "Groups are frequently accused of performing meaningless numbers. We decided to do 'With God on Our Side,' a Bob Dylan protest song, mainly for this reason." Chimed in Paul Jones in *NME*: "With the possible exception of 'Masters of War,' another Dylan number, it is the finest antiwar song ever written."

Predictably, Manfred Mann found itself attacked from the Left as well as the Right, with Colin Rushing complaining in the same paper's letters section, "I am sure all Bob Dylan fans will join me in condemning the Manfred Mann group for singing 'With God on Our Side,' not only on television but now on record. The Manfreds are only musically equipped for playing ordinary beat music, and not Bob Dylan's style of folk music."

For its next crack at the Dylan oeuvre, Manfred Mann opted for a far more chipper and pop-friendly tune, "If You Gotta Go, Go Now," the same song Dylan had inexplicably failed to release (as a single or otherwise) earlier in the year. With a more ethical form of ingenuity than Sonny & Cher had employed to procure "All I Really Want to Do," Mann seized the opportunity to cut it after watching Dylan do the song live on British TV. Manfred Mann's upbeat rendition, with organ, harmonica, and insistent repetitions of the insinuating chorus, rose to #2 on the British charts, though it flopped in America.

Though the lyrics' hints at spending the night together sound tame now, these again got the group in some hot water with the guardians of British morals. Manfred Mann's voice "shook with anger," reported *NME*, as he came to the song's defense: "Let's be honest. The words of this song mean exactly what most people think they mean. I don't deny it. It's about sex—what else? But the only thing I can say is that the message is open, clear and healthy... isn't it far better to say what you mean instead of turning it into something, you know, 'not quite nice'? It disgusts me when parents tell a child he or she was brought by the stork, or came from under a gooseberry bush, when they should come right out and be honest about the whole thing." All this after a coy denial from Paul Jones, who insisted the song was merely about a guy who was tired and asking a girl to leave so he could catch some sleep. As with "With God on Our Side," Manfred Mann couldn't wholly escape censorship with their new Dylan cover: when they performed "If You Gotta Go, Go Now" live at the Richmond Jazz Festival on *Shindig*, the line "or else you gotta stay all night" was edited out of the soundtrack.

Manfred Mann never made folk-rock its focus, but returned to Dylan periodically over the next few years when the group was in need of a hit. It landed a big British single with "Just Like a Woman" (though Dylan's own version was the one that made the Top 40 in the States), and in 1968 did a delightful top-to-bottom reworking of his then-unreleased "The Mighty Quinn," with its unerasably memorable recorder trills. Far from taking umbrage at the Manfreds' retooling of his songs for pop listeners, Dylan named them as his favorite interpreters at his December 1965 San Francisco press conference, when surely almost everyone expected him to cite the Byrds. "Each one of [Manfred Mann's Dylan covers] has been right in context with what the song was all about," he pronounced.

Mann sees the strengths of his group's Dylan covers as "the ability to change it, because it always seemed as if the original version was very personal to him. It didn't seem like a definitive version, in some funny way. I don't mean that in any way as an insult, 'cause I absolutely loved the original versions. But it just seemed that there was space there to do something, and make it different. Which you couldn't do with Elton John—he seems to have done it in the standard way. Dylan did it in a very idiosyncratic way. And therefore, there was the space to do it in a different way. I almost feel that I straightened them out in a way.

"We approached it without any respect for the original. That's absolutely essential. You can't go around with so much respect for the original that you can't function. It was quite simply, 'What can we do with this?' And my general thing was to have it in music form, in front of me in paper, and just play it and play it and play it until in the end I *wouldn't* refer to the original record, after I knew it. If you play it long enough, you find you're playing it your way." His way would extend to taking liberties that some Dylanologists would see as heresy, though they ruffled Mann not at all: "I would cut sections out if I needed to. In 'Just Like a Woman,' I cut out the whole middle bridge. We didn't want to do it, and we just didn't do it."

Mann also views their seizure of unreleased Dylan songs for British hits as intelligent, tasteful expediency: "We had the songs that everybody else had missed, where the original versions were sometimes quite idiosyncratic and a bit left-field. But I could use it. I was simply a bit of a predator, looking for material." As for Dylan's endorsement, Mann laughs, "Hey look—I wasn't depressed to read it, was I? I was obviously pleased."

In the United States, the first group other than the Byrds to rock up a Dylan song for a big hit was the Turtles, also from Los Angeles. They took "It Ain't Me Babe" into the Top Ten with an arrangement that, like Manfred Mann's "If You Gotta Go, Go Now," had drained away virtually all remaining vestiges of its folk origins, turning it into an upbeat pop-rock love song. It might have sounded like many other rock love songs of the day when the merry chorus came over the radio, but like "If You Gotta Go, Go Now," it did offer unusual lyrical depth for those who bothered to dig under the surface and puzzle over the words. The Turtles have been derided for neutering the anguish of Dylan's original, and as bandwagon-jumpers who had, only about a year earlier, been the Crossfires, a just-out-of-high school instrumental surf combo in the L.A. suburb of Westchester. But like Manfred Mann, they're not apologetic about daring to stand a Dylan song on its head for reinterpretation.

"I think that we proved that 'folk rock' was not such an elitist form of expression," claims the Turtles' Howard Kaylan. "This was not the pin-striped folk music of the Newport Festival, and it wasn't as claustrophobic as Joan Baez. We were just kids singing songs with a different interpretation. For instance, because I was a huge fan of the Zombies, I arranged 'It Ain't Me Babe' like 'She's Not There.' I sing really softly in the verses and then we all blast into a straight-four chorus, and I sing Dylan's words angrily, not mournfully. [It was] teenaged angst, and a lack of experience. Others did the same.

"It was only a record, man. We didn't know that you were supposed to be pure, else we would have ridden the rails like Woody Guthrie or at least have sung in the Village. There wasn't, nor is there now—to my knowledge—any animosity from anybody about having a hit record. Believe me, Dylan has been bastardized by bigger artists than us. This, to purists, may have been a dilution of folk music. All folk-rock, by nature, is. But it was in no way a commercialization of folk-rock. That genre is self-described as a hybrid."

The Turtles, though they would put additional covers by Dylan and other folk-rock composers like P.F. Sloan, Bob Lind, and the young Warren Zevon on their early records, would soon find their true metier in happy-go-lucky pop-rock. Their path from quick-off-the-mark-Dylan cover to the mainstream was also followed, with a different starting point, by the Association. Those who remember being inundated by "Windy" and "Never My Love" in 1967 may be a little taken aback to find that the band had evolved from a 13-part folk group called the Men that played the Troubadour. "It was early folk-rock, but it was unbearable," laughs Chris Darrow. "It was pompous, it was really bad. It was"—he breaks off to sing a snatch of "Sinner Man" in stentorian voice as illustration—"pathos folk-rock of a heavy order. You wouldn't find *that* at the Ash Grove."

When the Men trimmed down into an altered lineup as the Association, they actually made a couple of pretty fair stabs at folk-rock in late 1965, one of them a cover of Dylan's "One Too Many Mornings," though it got no more than local action. That had been preceded by an effectively moody, if only lightly electrified, adaptation of the well-traveled trad folk number "Babe I'm Gonna Leave You." Soon the Association's harmonies and arrangements took a decidedly slick pop turn, with "Along Comes Mary" beginning a series of hits that made the group one of the most popular staples of AM radio of the late '60s.

Darrow's mocking comments on the Men aside, the Association's Jim Yester (brother of Jerry) says the members suffered little backlash for their switch to rock: "I think most of the feedback we got from our fellow 'folkies' was support, and glad to see we were making it. We considered them friends as we knew most of them from hanging out at the Troubadour. Later on, after we had a great deal of success, I think the bands that were rock per se considered us as part of the establishment. This mainly, I think, was due to our image, Mom and Apple pie and all that, as opposed to being 'Bad Boys' and fostering an anarchistic image. Of course none of those groups copped to the fact that we opened a lot of doors for all the other rock bands by breaking the barrier at venues that had refused to use self-contained rock bands, which we couldn't have done with a bad boy image." As for similar gripes that the Turtles were just bending whichever way the wind blew, Kaylan points out that the Turtles' awareness of folk was not negligible. He'd bought Kingston Trio albums at the age of 12, seen Hoyt Axton at the Ice House in Pasadena as junior high schooler, and had a high school vocal group called the Crosswind Singers that did folky Kaylan originals. "But we didn't think that this stuff had a lot to do with commercial music."

Now, Dylan had a *lot* to do with commercial music. In the first week of September, *Billboard* reported that 48 Dylan covers had been cut within the last month, most on the West Coast. "In all my years as a publisher, I've never seen such activity for one writer," Music Publishers Holding Corporation's Jack Mass (who had passed Dylan's acetate of "Mr. Tambourine Man" to Jim Dickson) enthused to the magazine. "I've got people calling me for his material." The mini-trend was indirectly noted by Columbia in its ad for Dylan's single "Positively 4th Street," which spread the famous slogan "Nobody sings Dylan like Dylan." Seven Dylan tunes were on the charts, and a host of unlikely Dylan covers that never got anywhere would quickly appear.

Link Wray, the 1950s wildman known for growling distorted guitar instrumentals like "Rumble," put a rare, wracked vocal on a punky reading of "Girl from the North Country"; Christopher & the Chaps, with a pre-Left Banke Michael Brown on keyboards, did a garage take on "It's All Over Now, Baby Blue"; and country star Leroy Van Dyke did a peculiar version of that same song. The Grass Roots, prior to lineup changes that transmogrified them into a happy-go-lucky pop group, bubbled under the Top 100 with a grungy reading of "Ballad of a Thin Man." Gordon Lightfoot, in 1965 barely known as a songwriter let alone a recording artist, did a clumsy 45-only cover of "Just Like Tom Thumb's Blues" with overbearing mise-en-scène brass.

The Wonder Who?, actually the Four Seasons under a pseudonym, went all the way to #12 with a tongue-in-cheek treatment of "Don't Think Twice, It's Alright," featuring castrato vocals that were gratingly exaggerated even by Frankie Valli's matchless standards. Under their own name, the Four Seasons paid one of the most clueless tributes to the songwriter with an album that teamed one LP side of Dylan covers with another LP side of Bacharach-David tunes. In England, black American actor Ben Carruthers, best known for his role as the troubled younger brother in John Cassavetes's groundbreaking 1959 independent film *Shadows*, set to music part of a Dylan poem from the back cover of *Another Side of Bob Dylan*. Backed by a British group called the Deep, the resulting single, "Jack o' Diamonds," actually wasn't bad; it was produced by Shel Talmy, another expatriate American, more famous for his work on early classics by the Kinks and the Who. Duane Eddy, the king of instrumental rock guitar twang, smothered Dylan songs in reverb for *Duane Does Dylan*, which tossed in a cover of "Eve of Destruction" for good measure. There was even an album on Epic of, as a full-page ad in *Billboard* disclosed, a "Bob Dylan Song Book played by the Golden Gate Strings."

Tin Pin Alley's gold rush on Dylan songs actually yielded more tin than gold. The Byrds, Cher, the Turtles, and the Wonder Who? (whose effort was really more a fluke novelty release than a serious recording) were the only acts to score really big American hits by covering his material in 1965. It did, perhaps, awaken broader general interest in the possibilities of reworking the compositions of folksinger-songwriters for the pop-rock market. The We Five, a San Francisco group produced by Kingston Trio manager Frank Werber, got one of the first monster folk-rock hits in the summer of 1965 with "You Were on My Mind," a cover of the first song ever written by Sylvia Tyson. As heard on Ian & Sylvia's 1964 *Northern Journey* album, it was a lovely tune with a driving if drumless beat, a blues-gospel gutsiness, and a pop palatability in both the irresistible melody and Sylvia's own flourishes of autoharp.

The We Five washed some of the grit out of the song, not to mention some of the earthier images of the lyrics, which in the original version had the singer getting drunk and sick to ease her pain. On the other hand, they added real drums and sparkling electric guitars, as well as rounded male-female harmonies that foreshadowed those to be used in the near future by Jefferson Airplane and the Mamas & the Papas. "We worked it over a lot in the studio to get what I thought would be public attention," says Werber. "It was a distinct folk song, and I thought their rendition still left it in that bag. Some of the drum licks, and that solo guitar pick thing, I think, that ends it, were added post-recording by me, with their tacit approval." Ian & Sylvia, remembers a bemused Sylvia Tyson, were unaware that a rock group was covering the song until they "were driving down Highway 101, and turned on the radio, and there it was, by god. I wasn't that thrilled with how they changed the lyrics. But I certainly knew the limitations of pop radio in those days, and that the lyrics 'I got drunk and I got sick' probably wouldn't pass muster."

It did add up to a memorable and worthy hit record, though the We Five's first lineup (with Mike Stewart, brother of the Kingston Trio's John Stewart) never could match it with their other recordings. Their albums were inconsistent mish-mashes of alternately solid and twee early folk-rock, covers of pop standards like "My Favorite Things," and selections from *West Side Story*. Whether intentional or not, the impression was that they, like many of the New Christy Minstrels–type ensembles, might still have been thinking of being all-around entertainers suitable for all age groups. They did have the foresight to cover Dino Valenti's brotherly love hymn "Let's Get Together," which made a fleeting appearance in the Top 40 in late 1965 as the first of many folk-rock versions of the song.

Also on the agenda for pop conversion was Buffy Sainte-Marie's "The Universal Soldier," her moving paean to the universal waste of war. Donovan, not yet recording with a full electric band in the studio, went head-to-head with a competing version by the not-so-young but still relatively unknown Glen Campbell. Sainte-Marie and Donovan's folk versions are the ones that are remembered, yet at the time Campbell's Hollywood pop rendition of the tune, with the requisite Phil Spector–like glockenspiels, was the one that (barely) triumphed on the charts, reaching #45 while Donovan's single stalled at #53. To the surprise of many, perhaps, Sainte-Marie actually prefers Campbell's rendition, in part because "I wished that Donovan had gotten the words right. Glen's version was a real compliment to the songwriter part of me, as he recorded several of my songs, each real unique."

Donovan notes that when Sainte-Marie later met him while he was recording in Nashville, she told him that she loved his version and that it was her bad pronunciation of the word "Dachau" that led him to get "only one word wrong."

ot everyone was as magnanimous as Sainte-Marie in their reactions to the incursion of folk-rock into the hit parade. That might have surprised some who surmised that folkies might appreciate the introduction of thought-provoking lyrics and arrangements indebted to folk music into the mainstream consciousness in any form. Yet it should be remembered that the folk community was often elitist and resistant to commercialization of any sort. This attitude predated the emergence of rock in the 1950s, and even post-dated the commercial triumph of folk-rock in the 1960s. "There were the folk Nazis out there," maintains Roger McGuinn. "They were not only upset about rock and electric instruments, they were upset even when it was all just folk, and there was the ethnic-versus-commercial camps in folk. I mean, they'd be upset at anybody. Even Seeger crossed the line for them.

"But they would like the New Lost City Ramblers 'cause their records never sold. They'd like Malvina Reynolds or Bascom Lamar Lunsford or somebody like that. But anyone who sold any records, then they'd be commercial, and they wouldn't like that. So, naturally, these people are going to be resistant to rock when the folksingers start strapping on Stratocasters. There were those people, and they're *still* out there. But the *real* folksingers—I would regard Pete as one of them—didn't really have that problem." Asked about the pros and cons of electric folk-rock today, Seeger is diplomatic: "There's a tendency for the words to get lost when the music is too loud, and I'm a word man. I love Nat King Cole, whose words were so clear. 'Nature Boy' and the rest, you could understand every syllable. And Woody Guthrie, he pronounced things pretty clearly. On the other hand, I have to confess, a lot of truly great musicians you can't understand clearly. Leadbelly, or Odetta, or Bob [Dylan], and so on. So I'm ambivalent, as usual."

Purist protests that music should remain acoustic, and that electric amplification was the ultimate tool for sullying the authenticity of folk, was running out of steam, if it was even that much of a locomotive in the first place. The whole notion of using electricity as a measure for authenticity could seem arbitrary, to say the least, when the brilliant guitarist Doc Watson was "discovered" in the early '60s and championed as a leading exponent of Appalachian music. It was conveniently ignored that Watson had actually often played electric guitar in rock and country bands before starting his career as an acoustic folk guitarist for Folkways. Similarly, bluesmen John Lee Hooker and Snooks Eaglin managed to maintain wholly different careers for electric blues and acoustic folk audiences, cutting folky acoustic albums for companies such as Prestige while continuing to make full-band commercial R&B singles for labels like Vee-Jay and Imperial.

"I think the essence of a kind of simplicity and grass-roots spirit of the way in which folk music was conveyed by the oral tradition was, for many people, violated by the inclusion of electronic instruments," offers Peter Yarrow. "And I think that was due to the fact that they cared so much about keeping that spirit in their own lives in a very precious place. They didn't *want* the mediazation, or commercialization, of songs like 'If I Had a Hammer,' 'We Shall Overcome,' 'Blowin' in the Wind.' To them, [doing] 'We Shall Overcome' in a folk-rock fashion, by incorporating electronic instruments, would have been destructive to the very essence of the dignity of a song that was, for instance, sung by us at the graveside of Andrew Goodman [the civil rights activist who was slain in Mississippi in 1964], or in the basement of churches where people consoled each other and got their courage back after having been set upon by dogs and high-pressure water hoses, beaten, put in jail, and sometimes killed. All of a sudden, [folk-rockers were] turning this into something which had, as its form, a kind of style that spoke to commercialization or entertainment, [and] seemed incompatible and an insult. It was, in a way, sacrilegious."

"Electricity wasn't the thing, except for the super-purists," insists Irwin Silber. "There were many people who were certainly very important to the folk scene, mostly black but not all—Brownie McGhee and others—who amplified their guitar." Many folk musicians who had been, and would remain, almost wholly acoustic nevertheless not only had no moral objection to others using electric instruments if they so chose, but even advocated electric music if the spirit moved them. One was Dave Van Ronk, who according to *Sing Out!* tried to convince Ralph Rinzler to book Tommy Tucker (famous for his blues-rock hit "Hi-Heel Sneakers") for the Newport Folk Festival in 1964, a year before the whole folk-rock furor had exploded.

Another was Happy Traum, who was briefly in the Children of Paradise, a New York rock band that did one single for Columbia. "One of the reasons I left the group was that I was really feeling like I wasn't contributing," he says. "'Cause it just wasn't the kind of music that interested me. I *thought* it was going to be. It seemed like it was exciting and new, and I liked listening to a lot of this music. But as an electric player, I never kind of caught on to the nuances of getting good sounds and really knowing how to work the amps and all that stuff. [Confirms Children of Paradise bassist Marc Silber, "Happy never was into playing electric and I could never get him to change any settings on his amp!"] I wanted to finger-pick and play blues more.

"What we [Traum and his brother Artie, who was also in the Children of Paradise] eventually ended up doing after I left the Children of Paradise was sort of shaping that experience into what became our own acoustic-based sound, but still using a lot of the more rock 'n' roll and country sensibilities. So when we made our albums for Capitol, we did use drums and some electric instruments. Eric Kaz [of the Children of Paradise] stayed on, he played harmonica for us and a little piano, and that kind of became something else. And it became much more simpatico with what I personally was tuned into.

"I think people were feeling their way a lot with this electric stuff, and you did have the groups like the New Lost City Ramblers that were stuck in the '20s. I mean, I love them, but they definitely were not going to go electric. It was not even a question for them. Or some of the blues players who were into rediscovery of Skip James or Son House and those kinds of people. They were also very kind of hardcore that the only kind of good music was from the Mississippi Delta between 1927 and 1929, or something."

Traum, like several others sitting on the folk-rock fence at the time, feels the whole purist-rocker feud has been overblown. "That type of person who was really into ethnic acoustic music, they wouldn't have liked Bob [Dylan] *anyway*. They wouldn't have cared one way or another, because they wouldn't have even liked him acoustic. They would have stayed in their world, and it wouldn't have affected them one way or the other that Bob went electric."

Still Dylan, far more than any other figure, was the target of rage among folkies who were incensed, threatened, or both by the folk-rock onslaught. True, groups like the Byrds and newly emerging ones such as the Lovin' Spoonful had members with years of folk experience, and some hardcore folkies even knew exactly who McGuinn and John Sebastian were before those groups popped up on prime-time TV shows. However, as musicians who hadn't even released records except as accompanists prior to joining their electric groups, they didn't carry nearly as much baggage in the way of high expectations from a devoted audience. If they wanted to sell out to a teenybopper audience, as the perception sometimes was, they weren't about to be high-fived by the folk establishment at a special ceremony on the corner of Bleecker and Macdougal. But they would at least pretty much be ignored by the world they'd grown out of, except for the odd passing putdown in small-circulation periodicals. "I was on the fringe of folk," says McGuinn. "I was always in the commercial camp, and even at that, I was only an accompanist. So I was never a name artist in folk, and didn't have anything to lose, really, with [the purists]."

Dylan was another matter. He'd already been a star before going electric, and some saw his flight into loud rock 'n' roll, coming on top of his farewell to topical songwriting, as nothing less than a betrayal. Eric Andersen feels that "Bob had the biggest problem, because he went an outrageous way—he went to a folk festival [Newport] and did this. He pulled a stunt, it was a big impulse, and he got a reaction. He went up in a polka dot shirt and said, 'I'm not standing for this anymore. I *can't* stand this anymore.' And he did something else he wanted to do. But I mean, it wasn't that far from what he was starting with."

"People took Bob very much to heart," elaborates Paxton. "In many, many ways, they identified strongly with Bob. And when Bob changed, it was like a betrayal of themselves. So a lot of people couldn't make that shift with him, and *they* felt betrayed. They shouldn't have felt betrayed. He had a right to do what he wanted to do. But that's the way a lot of them felt. So they tended to take it very, very seriously, very, very personally."

If Dylan was truly worried about a backlash or getting tarred as a mercenary, he didn't make it easier on himself by making his feelings on the matter clear in an October 17, 1965 article in the *Long Island Press*, headlined "Dylan Disowns His Protest Songs." "I never wanted to write topical songs," he told reporter Frances Taylor. "That was my chance. In the Village there was a little publication called *Broadside* and with a topical song you could get in there. I wasn't getting far with the things I was doing, songs like I'm writing now, but *Broadside* gave me a start."

T he stage was set for the conflict that some see to be at the heart of the folk-rock revolution: a standoff between fuddy-duddy purists on one side, and cool, knowing prophets of the future on the other. It makes a good hook to the story, if nothing else, and one in which the good guys win— mobilizing an entire generation with deathless rock anthems while the stuffed shirts retreated wimpering to their outdated, corny "We Shall Overcome" sing-alongs and Trotskyite newsletters. Viewing history in such black-and-white terms, however, is misleading and problematic. The fact is that upon closer inspection, this schism was simply not as bitter and divisive as it's often made out to have been.

It might be reasonably expected that *Sing Out!* and *Broadside*, the two most influential American folk magazines of the era, would be the prime vehicles for attacks on folk-rock's defilement of the folk tradition. There are indeed some assaults of that nature in those pages. *Sing Out!* wrote at the outset of the folk-rock explosion that "the 'folk-rock' movement is pretty much a dither cooked up in a vacuum by a bunch of hip city kids. It can't last long because it does not have its feet on the ground. It is a product mostly of the recording studio and the musicians who skipped from 'folk' to 'blues' to 'folk-rock' as the times dictated. . . .The quickness of the movement caught *Sing Out!* completely off guard as it all seemed to happen between issues."

Sing Out! associate editor Izzy Young took some especially pointed jabs at Dylan in his "Frets and Frails" column: "Some of the new Bob Dylan songs are beginning to rhyme just like the old fashioned moon-June-spoon stuff we were all against just a few years ago. . . . Bob Dylan has become a pawn in his own game. He has ceased his Quest for a Universal Sound and has settled for a liaison with the music trade's Top 40 Hit Parade. . . . Next year, he'll be writing rhythm-and-blues songs when they get high on the charts. The following year, the Polish polka will make it, and then he'll write them, too. By then, he'll be so mired in the popularity charts that he'll be safe enough for the State Department to have them send him to entertain troops at whatever battlefront we're on at the time."

"When Dylan went electric, I didn't want to be at *Sing Out!*, 'cause I knew what they were gonna do," says Paul Nelson. "[When] I wrote the defense of Dylan at Newport, I didn't trust Irwin [Silber] to print the damn thing as I wrote it. But I trusted Moe Asch"—Silber's partner in Oak Publications, which published the magazine—"and said, 'This is my last piece, and I'd like you to print it like I wrote it.' And he said, 'Yeah, don't worry about it.'"

Yet *Sing Out!*, and *Broadside*, actually presented a surprisingly diverse range of opinions on both Dylan and folk-rock. Nelson may have quit as managing editor in anticipation of the furor over Dylan, but the magazine gave him plenty of space to write at length about his favorite rock records in some subsequent issues, including ecstatic reviews of albums by the Byrds, the Lovin' Spoonful, the Beatles, Love, and even the Rolling Stones. As for Nelson's contention that he had to slip his review of Dylan at Newport into the magazine, Silber chuckles, "I knew his opinion. It wouldn't have gone in if I didn't say okay. I think Paul said he wanted to write an alternate opinion. I was always for controversy, and it didn't make any difference if it was directed against me or not. I don't think he had any problem getting it into *Sing Out!*."

By the same token, Young may have blown raspberries at Dylan, yet even before "Mr. Tambourine Man" he was singing the praises of the Beatles, the Rolling Stones, and the Animals. "The Beatles have gone further than all the contemporary folk song writers in that they are not so obvious in their philosophy," he wrote. "Their enjoyment of life now is a strong protest and alternative to world preparation for war and the strong bureaucratic governments that surround us all. Their lyrics don't guarantee that we'll live 'happy ever after' and that is as it should be. . . . If American folk music can be eclipsed by the Beatles, then it deserves to be eclipsed." Far from fitting the purist stereotype, Young also took time to call Smokey Robinson "one of the best vocalists and songwriters in the US today," and passed on a tip from a young David Grisman, "who found the Warlocks to be the best rock-and-roll group he heard in California. He especially liked a song written by their lead guitarist, Jerry Garcia, titled 'Bending Your Mind.'" The Warlocks, of course, would soon rename themselves the Grateful Dead.

Silber admits he was not a big folk-rock fan: "The biggest problem I had with it was that the heavy emphasis on the rock side of it all interfered with the communication. There was certainly an audience, but in my view it wasn't related to the politics. If you could actually break down the lyrics and hear them clearly, there were pretty good things, in many cases. But I don't think they had the same kinds of impact on political struggles or movements, which to me was the function of *Sing Out!* in the first place. Now, that's an old-fashioned way of looking at it, at the time. But that's why I got into it in the first place. I wanted to promote songs as a way of building up the enthusiasm of political activists, and of reaching out to new audiences who would be attracted. I didn't feel that folk-rock was doing that. Even the anti-war stuff, most of it didn't come through the folk-rock artists that I could tell. It was lacking that political focus that I thought was important."

Yet even Silber judged folk-rock musicians on a case-by-case basis and found ones to like and admire, interviewing Country Joe McDonald at length for a *Sing Out!* feature in June 1968. Nor was *Sing Out!* above accepting advertising for folk-rock records on Vanguard, Elektra, and Verve/Folkways, the fledgling rock magazine *Crawdaddy*, or even electric guitars hawking "the free ridin' beat of folk-rock." There were also many passionate advocates of, and attacks against, folk-rock in the volatile letters section, which sometimes resembled trench warfare in its hurtle of back-and-forth missives. Dan Fisher called the Animals "a group of greasy, long-haired, electric guitar–flailing English delinquents who rose to success with a bastardized version of 'House of the Risin' [sic] Sun.'" Signing her letter "Disillusioned Dylan fan," Bonnie Wright wrote, "Concerning Bob Dylan's new album, *Bringing It All Back Home*, he can take it to hell back home and keep it there." Countered Nancy Snell, "Our generation is moving and they [the musicians] are too. We have Dylan when we want to think and the Beatles when we want to have fun. They're completely compatible." Others attempted to make light of the whole Beatles-Dylan symbiosis with a silly ongoing debate-joke about whether Dylan and John Lennon were the same person.

Far from viewing the furor with distaste, Silber took on the turmoil with gleeful relish. "I love that stuff!," he says now. "To me, that was one of the big weaknesses of the old Communist movement. Everything had to be just so, and the debates were so sterile. This was live stuff. I'm a journalist. That's really what I set out to be before I got all wrapped up in this folk music stuff. And controversy is the heart of it. Letters to the editor that people read and get agitated about? I can't think of a better circulation builder."

Looking back it might seem like much sound and fury signifying nothing, but at the time, the ascendance of folk-rock was treated as a very serious matter indeed. The Berkeley Folk Festival held a panel discussion on "The Beatle Mystique" that may have been as valuable as a study concluding mice were drawn to cheese, judging from the *Livermore Independent*'s report. This announced, to the surprise of no one who had listened to the radio over the past year, that "one of the inescapable conclusions drawn from the panel [was that] 'folk music is linking up with rock and roll.'" At the Big Sur Hot Springs Folk Music Festival, esteemed music critic Ralph Gleason reported in the *San Francisco Chronicle*, "Joan Baez was asked the question directly: 'Is rock and roll folk music?' And she answered with a flat unequivocal 'Yes!'"

At that same event, Gleason moderated a panel on the British Invasion that, according to folksinger Mark Spoelstra's jaded report in *Boston Broadside*, "centered mostly around Joan Baez's following Bob Dylan in going R&R [rock 'n' roll]. The panel was in agreement that we should all do so…except for me. Actually, the whole discussion was of no use and pretty boring, and the audience was quite confused on what the hell we were talking about." Later in 1965, the Village Gate held yet another "folk-rock" panel featuring Silber, countercultural commentator Paul Krassner, famed New York DJ Murray the K, *New York Times* critic Robert Shelton, and Tom Paxton. Shelton and other journalists like Gleason were about a generation older than the age group at which folk-rock was primarily aimed, and some might question whether they were entitled to be pontificating at such events at all. But their praise for the music was an underestimated factor in validating it for the general public.

Still, such panels may have been well advised to quote a plaintive letter to *Sing Out!* from Barbara Nathanson of West Orange, New Jersey, who probably summarized what was happening more succinctly and accurately than any tribunal of scholars could have. "People may criticize folk-rock, but I think it's great," she stated. "Most kids listen solely to 'rock 'n' roll' and what they hear on their 'rock 'n' roll' stations and those are the records they buy. I was one of those. In rock 'n' roll, the song must have a good beat…the words mean nothing. But when folk-rock came along, I had to listen to the words. Whether I agreed with them or not didn't matter, but the fact that they meant something *does* matter.

"Folk-rock introduced me to folk music, *Sing Out!*, guitar (which I love to play), and good music to dance to and listen to. Folk music is great, but how much true folk music actually reaches the average teen? Folk-rock hits us all and makes us think. An adult friend of mine said it all in a sentence: 'It seems that this is the only form of protest around these days.'"

Perhaps inadvertently, Nathanson was pointing out something that many folkies, and many adults in general, could have been overlooking. The audience for folk, and for pop music in general, was changing, just as musicians like McGuinn, Dylan, and Sebastian were. Part of that change was a simple matter of demographics. As a result of the baby boom, 17-year-olds in 1964 became the single largest age group in the United States. That was the same year *Seventeen* magazine estimated that 11 million teenage girls spent $321 million a year on records. Post-war babies had seized dominance of the record market, and would retain it for the rest of the 1960s.

But there was more going on than simple economics. The year 1965 was precisely when most of those at the leading edge of the baby boom were entering college, leaving home, and thinking at length (and without direct parental guidance and authority) for the first time about more serious issues than sports and going steady. Exposure to free speech debates on campus heightened awareness of politics and civil rights. The war in Vietnam was escalating rapidly, with Lyndon

Johnson announcing on July 28 that call-ups would double to 35,000 a month. By the end of 1966, there would be almost 400,000 American troops in Vietnam. For the male half of the population, vulnerability to the draft made consideration of politics and the morality of imperialistic intervention an urgent necessity, even for those who were apolitical by nature.

Antiwar songs, whether directed at war in general or American involvement in Vietnam specifically, would only be one aspect of folk-rock throughout the rest of the decade, and not a few folk-rockers entirely avoided such issues. But fear of death in Vietnam, and death by nuclear obliteration, cannot be overestimated as factors that made both listeners and musicians grow up faster, and with a live-for-the-moment perspective they might not have had in calmer times. Most folk-rockers (if they were male), like their audience, were of draft age. Very, very few had their careers interrupted by the draft; as entertainers with advisers from record labels and managers, they often had access to far greater legal assistance in attaining deferment and exemptions. As guys with an antiauthoritarian outlook to begin with, they were also more willing to pull outrageous stunts at the draft board to gain those exemptions, whether it was Michael Clarke pretending to be a homosexual, or Al Kooper loading himself up with 40 joints and speed the night before his physical.

Others didn't have to go to such lengths: McGuinn was classified as 4-F purely on the basis of bad attitude (a couple of years before the Army got more desperate for warm bodies). Most famously, Arlo Guthrie was declared unfit for service due to a conviction for littering, a labyrinthine tale put to music on his 18-minute "Alice's Restaurant Massacree." There were others who were exempt because they had actually already served in the Armed Forces, including some surprising names, like Country Joe McDonald, Jerry Garcia, Tom Paxton, Tim Hardin, Tim Rose, Mike Nesmith, and the Lovin' Spoonful's Joe Butler. Whatever their reasons for not being eligible for military service, folk-rockers were singing and talking about considering the option of not fighting more than almost any others in the media eye. The knowledge that the high life could end for them and their listeners at the whim of a draft board, or at the touch of a detonation button that had nothing to do with Vietnam, made it imperative to do what they could in a short period of time.

The heated politics of 1965, the pressing need to find alternate ways of survival and peaceful coexistence as the war disrupted or ended uncounted young lives, and the entry of the oldest baby boomers into college meant that folk-rock's arrival coincided exactly with the flowering of intellectual curiosity within pop music's core audience. The adolescents and college students of the mid-'60s rarely had ingrained resistance to rock 'n' roll, having listened to it since elementary school. They embraced folk-rock as pop music with lyrical substance, in not too different a manner as those of a similar age had embraced folk music in the late '50s.

If it seemed crass that AM radio (and sometimes prime-time network television) would act as a primary conduit for this countercultural expression, it must be understood that it was the most readily accessible avenue for both the musicians and their audience. While magazines like *Sing Out!* and *Broadside* linked music with social consciousness, and published lyrics and music to new songs extending that venerable tradition, their impact was, in all reality, limited. *Sing Out!*'s circulation was 25,000 at its peak, and *Broadside*'s was just one-tenth of that. For those seeking wider exposure, the channels of mainstream media were, for the most part, closed to those under 25, or at least did not take them terribly seriously. Those under 21 couldn't even vote, though males between the ages of 18 and 21 could, in contrast, be sent to Vietnam. Even if much folk-rock was recorded and issued by huge corporations, and broadcast over radio and television stations owned for the most part by the same or similar pillars of the establishment, they nonetheless were among the few means available to young adults and teenagers for getting their voice heard.

In 1965, Arlo Guthrie was one of those baby boomers, though the 18-year-old folksinger was a couple of years away from beginning his recording career. "That volatile combination of what we called folk-rock was about the only means of communication open to people who were otherwise powerless around the world," he observes. "The corporations, the businessmen and women who were controlling the entertainment business, did not understand the lyrics of the songs that they were selling. The guys on the radio didn't get it. The guys that owned the radio had no connection with the music, in terms of understanding it. For the first time, there was an explosion of all different kinds of music being played. And the lyrics were unintelligible. Not just the lyrics—the philosophy, the heart of it, was unreadable, unknowable, to the people who controlled the industry.

"So all of a sudden, all around the world, for a very short time . . . imagine a world where everybody's got a radio, and all of a sudden everybody's saying what they really think, in words that you could understand, but that your parents couldn't. *That's* what folk-rock was all about. It communicated and expressed all of the stuff we were talking about [and] thinking about. Whether it was sex, whether it was drugs, whether it was rock 'n' roll, whether it was end of the war, clean the air, fix this, do that. All of it combined. The whole thing all of a sudden was open. A floodgate had opened, because we were using a language that couldn't be understood over whose system we were using to communicate it. And it was so wonderful. People were walking down the street plain laughing, just having a great time, because all of a sudden, it was free."

Joni Mitchell voiced the peculiar conundrum of slipping such messages into the media at a January 1968 appearance at Club 47 in Cambridge, in her introduction to an unreleased song she wrote for a Canadian public affairs program, "The Way It Is": "I thought it would be a good time to write a song that I could say some things that were on my mind then, and I had to say it in a very quiet way so as not to upset people, you know. And I thought, well, it's gotta be subtle enough that they [the program's producers] won't try to understand what I'm trying to get across. It's gotta be *simple* enough that a lot of people can understand what I'm trying to say!"

Donovan takes a holistic view of the social changes that brought folk-rock into being, the intermingling of the personal and the political in songwriters such as himself, and the social changes that folk-rock itself would facilitate: "The lyrics introduced into pop charts called to a generation who were not able to read the important works of the twentieth century. This created an appetite to absorb new ideas and improve one's awareness of our fathers' war-torn world and our own youthful inner angst. We would explore the human condition through love songs, which are the essence of youth. But also we would rediscover the social cause, the rights of man. Once forcefully suppressed secret teachings of the East and the West would become tools again to break the conditioning which had driven Western mankind to the brink of self-destruction. The bonds of Christian dogma and racial hatred were being loosened.

"Never before had such knowledge been available to so many youths. Nations had controlled what their people read and saw. Now, with the advent of records, television, and liberal thought, the institutions and bigoted opinions were being shown for what they truly are. It was with full consciousness that myself and certain others introduced these ideas into popular music, film, and literature."

"It didn't last really long," resumes Guthrie. "They figured it out pretty quick, and a lot of it was shut down, and a lot of the guys just plain died, 'cause some of it was self-destructive. But for a little while, it was pretty cool. You've experienced this in the first days of the Internet, when everything was free, when you could say anything you wanted to, and you could talk to anybody you wanted to. The only difference is that when the Internet exploded, not everybody had computers." But virtually everybody had a radio, even in 1965.

The flipside of the voice, albeit one with many strings attached, that Columbia Records and commercial radio could offer to youth was its potential to drown out some other voices that deserved to be heard. Those voices were not always, like most folk-rock listeners, young, white, and middle-class, and in the views of some had stronger links to the folk tradition than groups like the Byrds did. Folklorist Alan Lomax, says his daughter Anna Chairetakis, "believed that folk music represented the important strains of culture from all over the world, and that it was important to keep alive these many forms of creative expression in all their richness and subtlety. Because they give us a pool of distinctive and highly crystallized aesthetic, emotional, and stylistic traditions to which we can return for inspiration; because they literally represent and reaffirm the struggles and basic achievements of human beings across history. He saw that mass media was eroding these even as it was opening up the channels of communication." Lomax may have entertained hopes for the likes of Hobart Smith and the Georgia Sea Island Singers to gain wide national audiences. But in the context of the hit parade and AM radio, there was no way such artists could compete against young, long-haired folk-rock groups, either in volume, teen-ready marketable images, or construction of recordings around easy-to-assimilate hooks.

rucially, it wasn't just suburban New Jersey rock 'n' rollers who were being seduced by the folk-rock beat, but also young folk fans who were approaching the hybrid from a different direction. Writer Paul Williams (not to be confused with Paul Williams the pop singer), 17 years of age in 1965, was already an habitué of Club 47 in Cambridge, Massachusetts, but immediately took to the new electric music. "Club 47 was a folk music place, and in those days, conceptually, you didn't think of the two mixing," he says. "Folk music people would constantly show their affection for rock 'n' roll, bring it into what they were doing. If you take a Dick and Mimi Fariña, what they were doing, like what most people were doing, was reaching from folk music in the direction of the new, eclectic, even slightly Beatles-influenced rock 'n' roll. But you wouldn't think of something that was identifiably being a band playing at Club 47, unless—and even that was a stretch—it was a blues band.

"That song 'that Good Time Music, now it's back on the radio' [i.e. the Lovin' Spoonful's "Good Time Music"] really spoke to a sincere feeling that there was a kind of good music that, if you were open-minded enough, went beyond a purist definition of folk music. There was good music that you could identify amongst your friends and your community that was not limited by whether or not it was folk music in a pure sense." Though still a teenager, Williams was inspired enough by the new sounds to found *Crawdaddy*, the first American magazine devoted to serious adult appreciation of rock music, the following year. Nor was he the only nascent rock critic, or just plain fan, with a grounding in folk to get sucked into the folk-rock vortex. As future *Rolling Stone* editor Paul Nelson confesses, "My innocence about rock 'n' roll was pretty complete. I don't think I knew any people into rock 'n' roll at that point. Dylan dragged me into it somehow. It was so powerful. I was quite blown away by it."

What's more, actual rock bands were starting to play folk venues like Club 47, not only blurring the lines between the musics further, but also taking some listeners with lingering purist sympathies unawares. Williams, like many musicians and listeners from the period, cites the Paul Butterfield Blues Band as groundbreakers in opening the coffeehouse circuit to full electric ensembles, and praises their shows at Club 47 in particular as landmarks in that respect. But Club 47 was also starting to book folk-rock groups that could not even be tenuously linked to ethnic folk via a solid blues repertoire. A watershed in that respect was an early appearance by the Lovin' Spoonful. As Williams says, "For a band like that to come to Club 47 was revolutionary, in terms of Cambridge['s] holier-than-thou purist attitude about folk music."

Not everyone was instantly converted. If there were unsuspecting prudes in the audience for the Spoonful's Cambridge debut, though, the group would fight back with a mixture of humor and aggression. "I remember this hilarious moment when we start off, and by about the third tune, there's a real kind of Joanie lookalike in the third row, the long ironed hair," says John Sebastian. "And she very carefully gets me and [guitarist] Zally's attention, points out toward the amplifier, and puts her fingers in her ears. And Zally gave her his broadest and most affectionate smile, and turned his amplifier up as loud as he could. That was a real transition."

Those who reacted to amplified folk-rock with such horror might logically be expected to turn to the remaining acoustic topical songwriters as saviors in the battle against the new upstarts. That movement had not died with the arrival of the Beatles, with Dylan's renunciation of the protest song, or even with the rise of folk-rock. The years 1964 and 1965 saw the important first, and sometimes first and second, albums by a posse of talented folksinger-songwriters. Buffy Sainte-Marie, a Canadian of Native American descent with a unique vibrato voice, had attracted considerable praise for songs detailing discrimination against indigenous peoples and the futility of war, though she'd already written and recorded a genuine romantic pop standard, "Until It's Time for You to Go." Eric Andersen was on his way to becoming one of the first of the American "new Dylans" with his maiden Vanguard release. Tom Paxton (who had recorded his debut album in 1962 for the tiny Gaslight label before issuing his first Elektra LP in 1964) was attacking war, media brainwashing, the exploitation of miners, and other social ills, though his more romantic and melodic tales of rambling, like "The Last Thing on My Mind" and "I Can't Help But Wonder Where I'm Bound," would prove more enduring.

In England, Donovan had announced a forthcoming EP of antiwar songs in unassailably politically correct wording in *NME*: "This is what I've always wanted. To try and use my position to do good. As I get better known, I'd like to try and make my songs a kinda force for a better world. There are so many wrong things on the earth. An' I want to try and right those wrongs." Back in the Village, Phil Ochs's first two albums established him as the wittiest, most right-on champion of civil rights, draft dodgers, and organized labor. When Dylan abdicated his throne as king of the soapbox, Ochs was tapped as the most likely successor. Viewed cynically, the vacuum created in acoustic folk music by the sprint toward electric rock created an opportunity for Ochs, and others, upon which to capitalize.

Remarkably, not only did few troubadours take the bait, but most would end up going electric themselves, and sooner rather than later. Even before they went electric, they would not only vociferously advocate the right of Dylan and others to go electric, but joyously praise their favorite folk-rock in the widest public forums available to them. Ochs, never one to shirk from iconoclastic controversy even if it meant upsetting the Left rather than the Right, rubbed salt in folkies' wounds by using their favorite magazines to yank their chains. He fiercely defended Dylan's rock albums in *Broadside*, both in open letters and lengthy interviews, as well as gushing over the Beatles and the Rolling Stones. As early as April 1965, he'd informed *Broadside* readers, "It is an easy error to get the parochial view that protest is the most exciting movement going on in American music. I believe there is an equally important revolution being generated by the Beatles and several other groups in the popular area. For example, I would highly recommend [that] all people interested in songwriting and real communication through music tune in to a record produced by Phil Spector called 'You've Lost That Lovin' Feeling,' sung by the Righteous Brothers."

In the September 1965 issue of *Sing Out!* Ochs went on, "There are two major revolutions going on in music today: one is the revolution in songwriting, adding perceptive protest and valid poetry; the other is the solidifying of the pop revolution of the '50s started by Hank Williams, Elvis Presley, Buddy Holly, and Chuck Berry and now being carried on by the Beatles, the Rolling Stones, the Righteous Brothers, and the Lovin' Spoonful; that is, the firm entrenchment of rhythm-and-blues slightly flavored by country-and-western that led to the sudden and final destruction of the big band sound. Both of them are extremely important because they manage to communicate reality with such an abundance of beauty, soul, and entertainment that they plant themselves in your mind, never to leave.... The only thing that counts about Dylan's writing in the end is how good it is, not what it's about." Ochs's own foray into rock was some way off in the future, though he had performed a jokey take on the Beatles' "I Should Have Known Better" with Eric Andersen at a fall 1964 *Broadside* hoot at the Village Gate (eventually issued on Ochs's *The Broadside Tapes* album).

As for the Dylan-Donovan rivalry that had been played up in the British press, Donovan was having none of it. "Electric guitars and folk? Do they mix?," he asked *NME*. "Sure, if you want them to. Why not. Dylan uses electric guitars because he likes it that way. He doesn't care what people think.

"Dylan does what he wants, man. Not what convention says he's gotta do. I feel the same. All young rebels are like this. People say I'm a folk singer, but I sing anything I want. Beatles songs, everything. You have to smash down convention. Joan Baez sings Beatles songs, too. They're beautiful." Baez, he added in *Melody Maker* in July, "has recorded my 'Colours' with her being backed by bass and drums."

Folk-rock, and the territory it opened for topical songwriters in the pop field, also helped some of the performers bust out of a protest pigeonhole in which they might not have been entirely comfortable. Yes, many folk musicians were social activists. It was not unusual to read in *Sing Out!* in 1964, for instance, that Paxton, Ochs, Andersen, Carolyn Hester, and Danny Kalb (who accompanied Phil Ochs on early acoustic sessions and later went electric with the Blues Project) had just attended a three-day conference on unemployment in Hazard, Kentucky. As the civil rights movement gained important victories, however—and blacks justifiably demanded a greater voice on its administrative and leadership end—traveling to the South for activist work became less of a focus among folkies. The escalating war in Vietnam was of course still of grave concern to many folk artists (and a growing number of rock ones), and indeed many folkies turned folk-rockers would maintain some, or much, visible involvement in political causes.

But they were artists as well, for whom freedom was not just the liberty to write about hot political issues, but the freedom to write about anything. For the most part they wanted to be known not as folk songwriters, or political songwriters, but as songwriters, period. By way of illustration, Buffy Sainte-Marie, at that point still thought of as a topical songsmith, was at the same time recording "Until It's Time for You to Go," later covered by Elvis Presley, Barbra Streisand, Sonny & Cher, Neil Diamond, and Roberta Flack. "They all thought I was a pop writer!" she emphasizes. "Bobby Bare, Chet Atkins, Dottie West and lots of other country artists were recording [Sainte-Marie's] 'Piney Wood Hills' and 'I'm Gonna Be a Country Girl Again.' They thought I was a country writer. David Crosby of the Byrds, Bob Dylan, [future Monkee] Michael Nesmith, and lots of other acoustic singer-songwriters like me were listening and writing across all the categories."

If the battle between purists and folk-rockers was shaping up as a tug of war, the ensuing struggle was as much of a mismatch as lining up the sixth-graders on one side and the third-graders on the other. "It was a six-day war," Bruce Langhorne hoots with roaring laughter. "There's just so much more happening when you have music that you can dance to. It speaks to a whole other center. And that's what folk-rock was. It was danceable folk music. You didn't have to *just* listen. Listening was an option. You didn't have to hear the words." Plus, points out Sylvia Tyson, "A lot of the so-called folk fans were not traditional music fans. They were fans of the Limeliters and the Kingston Trio. It was a form of pop music for them. That transition [to folk-rock], I think, wasn't as hard for them as it was for the real purists."

Speaking as a fan, rather than the artist manager he would shortly become, Michael Ochs surmises, "I think folk would have become too boring for all of us anyway. It had to grow somehow, and you just can't keep doing acoustic stuff. We all would have been looking for some other form of music, some other form of excitement. That's what I love about the mid-'60s, it's got to be the most exciting time for pop music ever. You had everything to the fore, from Motown to Stax to folk-rock to psychedelia to garage band to killer pure pop. Every form of music was hitting a new zenith, and it was coming from *everywhere*. Did I see folk-rock coming? Not per se. [But] I don't think folk would have survived that anyway."

The verdict on the virtues of folk-rock was not unanimous. Tom Paxton responded with an infamous article in *Sing Out!*, headlined "Folk Rot," in which he ranted, "It isn't folk, and if Bob Dylan hadn't led, fed and bred it no one would ever have dreamed of confusing it with folk music. . . . One group claims that if just one line of 'Mr. Tambourine Man' gets through to the teenies it will all have been worth it. They are doomed to a disappointment which I trust they'll survive. For the sad fact is that although rock versions of 'Blowin' in the Wind' have by now been danced to in nearly every lily-white frat house in the South, no great rush to sign up Negro 'brothers' seems to have resulted." (In the spirit of the day, *Boston Broadside* soon ran a rebuttal to the "Folk Rot" tirade by Dave Wilson.) In *Broadside*, Paxton was somewhat calmer: "I don't think that the audience that's buying the folk-rock protest knows what's happening or cares . . . the protest songs that are in the mass media aren't any damn good. They're either simple-minded or they're atrociously written, or they miss the point altogether."

In time Paxton's opinion mellowed, and indeed by the end of the decade he was using some electric accompaniment on his own records, though he admits, "I just never felt the pull for it." It was true that Paxton songs like "Last Train to Auschwitz" or even "Lyndon Johnson Told the Nation" were simply too hot to handle for artists looking for potential hit singles (said Paxton of the latter tune in *Broadside*, "I don't care if the Beatles recorded it—would it be played?"). Yet even Paxton was being pulled into the folk-rock slipstream as artists began to cover his less controversial love songs. A San Francisco group, the Vejtables, had a minor hit with his "Last Thing on My Mind." Dion, now moving into folk-rock with Dylan producer Tom Wilson at the controls, tried his hand at "I Can't Help But Wonder Where I'm Bound." Concedes Paxton, "I was tickled to death with Dion's record-ing when I finally heard it, because I thought that he absolutely understood the song and read the lyric the way I would like to hear it read. I thought it was one of the best recordings of that song I've heard."

latant social protest, nonetheless, was about to crack the charts with the most successful, and no-torious, folk-rock-protest single of all time. This had its origination not in the cafes of Greenwich Village, but, like so much of the folk-rock selling like mad as summer turned to autumn, from mu-sicians frequenting the audience at Ciro's and the lapsed-wholesome-folk-veteran community of Los Angeles. Barry McGuire, late of the New Christy Minstrels, had feet in both camps. "When I left the Christys," he chuckles, "Roger McGuinn wanted to get in, and we were full and wouldn't let him in. David Crosby was all pissed off because he couldn't get in the Christys, and Hoyt Axton couldn't get in, and all the guys that were loose in the streets, a lot of them, wanted to get in."

By 1965, the tables had turned. "I was out of a job, and I'd been to every producer in Holly-wood trying to get a job singing. But nobody wanted to know me. So Roger says, 'Well, we're open-ing up at Ciro's.' The press was saying that everybody was going to be there. I'm like, 'Sure.' Bob [Dylan] was there, P.F. Sloan, and Lou"—producer Lou Adler—"was there. I was just dancing on the floor. Adler came in and said, 'Hey, you're Barry McGuire?' 'Yeah.' 'Well, what are you doing these days?' 'Nothing.' He said, 'Well, come over to my house next week.' So he sent a car to get me, I went over, I heard Phil's songs, and I really liked them."

Phil was P.F. Sloan, a young veteran of the West Coast equivalent to the Brill Building factory. He'd already written and played on dozens of L.A. pop-rock records, sometimes as part of the Jan

& Dean soundalike group the Fantastic Baggys. As well-crafted as some of his songs were, they were usually teen piffle, made to order for surf and hot rod singers, girl groups, teen idols, and British Invasion imitators. There was nothing in his background to suggest a writer particularly concerned with social decay, or especially eager to lay his innermost feelings on the line for the world to hear. That changed in 1965, after Byrds' producer Terry Melcher gave Adler *Bringing It All Back Home*. Adler remembers passing it on to Sloan with the recommendation, "'This is something that I think is happening.' In that transformation, he changed his writing style, in good deal due to exposure to the music of Bob Dylan." In the bedroom of his parents' house, five songs gushed forth in one night that metamorphosed Sloan from pop-rock lightweight to angst-ridden troubadour, venting his determination to be his own man and his doubts about the very fate of the world. One of the songs was "Eve of Destruction."

"When I originally wrote the song I must admit that I never visualized it sounding as it does on the record," Sloan told *NME*. "But I don't mind what they do to my songs. I just want a lot of people to hear them. If somebody comes along and dresses up honesty with a beat then that's fine by me. The more people hear it the better."

Although "Eve of Destruction" was blunt in its delineation of civil rights clashes, war, and nuclear proliferation leading society to the brink of apocalypse, it was nonetheless remarkable to bring even the faintest discussion of such issues to commercial radio in 1965. McGuire delivered the lyrics in a gravel-growl that—as with the vocals of Dylan, Sonny Bono, even Roger McGuinn—might have stood little chance of getting a hearing a year or two earlier. Sloan gave the song a pop color that someone like Dylan might have been unable or unwilling to conjure, particularly in the chorus, and Lou Adler's production coated it with enough ghostly background voices and ominous drums to ease its way onto playlists. It wasn't *that* easy to get radio stations to touch a lyric like "Eve of Destruction," but once the record was broken on WCFL in Chicago, it stormed to #1 in the nation.

"I left the Christys really in search of some answers," reflects McGuire, who would go on to record numerous other Sloan songs, most of them less anguished than "Eve of Destruction." "If something is real for me, then I can do it. But I can't really pretend I can do it if it's not. That's why I had to quit the Christys, 'cause it wasn't real for me anymore. I thought, 'Well, the only way I'm going to find the truth is if I speak the truth.' I really tried to be a truth speaker, and the songs that I heard, if it wasn't true for me, I couldn't sing it anymore. I wrote [the New Christy Minstrels' hit] 'Green, Green,' but I've never been much of a songwriter. Phil wrote those songs that were just tailor-made for me. To have a songwriter that wrote so specifically what I felt to be true...I discovered a lot of truth in those songs."

"Eve of Destruction" is sometimes dismissed as protest pop at its most exploitative today, but at the time, controversy over its impact was simply enormous. Even as crosstown rival radio station WCLF was making it into a hit, WIND's program director Jack Williams called the record "sick" in *Billboard*. Los Angeles DJ (and future *Newlywed Game* host) Bob Eubanks told *Time*, "How do you think the enemy will feel with a tune like that no. 1 in America?" (Exactly who "the enemy" was wasn't specified.) Rabbi Richard Rubenstein of Beth Shalom synagogue in Pittsburgh, reported

Barry McGuire

Variety, chided Dylan and McGuire in a Yom Kippur sermon, deploring "the attitude of youngsters who feel that destruction is tomorrow and 'we might just as well fold our arms and wait.'"

Back at the ranch McGuire had abandoned, New Christy Minstrels spokesman Bill Teague, under the headline "Christy Minstrels Bar 'Protest' Songs, Find No Entertainment in Messages," gave "Eve of Destruction" the limpest of dispensations. As *Variety* noted, "He considers that the underlying message of 'Eve of Destruction' was not strong enough to blow down a house of cards, much less society." The Spokesmen group issued an "answer" record, "The Dawn of Correction," a combination of self-righteous counterrevolutionary attack and unfunny satire, replete with twanging Jew's harp and clanging bells. It nonetheless squeezed inside the Top 40 in October. KCLV in Clovis, New Mexico, perhaps confused and trying to cover fallouts from every direction, banned both "Eve of Destruction" *and* "Dawn of Correction."

Predictably, there was some flak from fellow musicians as well as from the media, with some attacking the song as too obvious and commercial. Said Paul Jones of Manfred Mann in *NME*, "I think that Barry McGuire must have been paid by the State Department. 'The Eve of Destruction' protests about nothing. It is simply a 'Thy Doom at Hand Song' with no point. Sweeping generalizations like 'Look at all the hate in Red China' don't strike me as the observations of someone out to promote peace. That kind of comment deserves to get the record banned. Donovan's record

'Universal Soldier' is a sincere anti-war song which has value—I bought it myself." Huffed Pete Seeger in *Sing Out!*, "I only heard the song 'Eve of Destruction' once. On a neighbor's car radio. It was interesting to listen to, but after it was over, I got the feeling that to say there is no hope in anything, not in anything at all in the world, is next to saying therefore that you might as well just look out for yourself, Let's you and me have a ball, baby. That's what pop music has been saying about as long as I can remember."

Paul McCartney weighed in with his view in *Melody Maker*: "I don't like 'Eve of Destruction' very much. It seems to be cashing in on a trend. Somebody like Bob Dylan comes up and people say 'Let's copy him, he's good,' and then the whole market gets saturated." Noel Stookey added in the same paper, "I think 'Eve of Destruction' is a terribly depressing song and it doesn't point the way. Maybe it just stirs things up, but it doesn't offer a solution." John Lennon concurred: "The 'protest' label in particular means absolutely nothing—it's just something that the press has latched on to, and as usual is flogged to death! Some of the songs which appear under this heading are simply good songs—some are not. But personally I have no time for the 'Eve of Destruction' songs."

Yet there were also murmurs of approval, some from unexpected corners. Malvina Reynolds defended the song in *Broadside*, seeing it, "Universal Soldier," and "a hundred more" as "contributing each some thrust to the movement for peace, integration, conservation—the pro-life movement." Six months after its release, Judy Collins, then just expanding into folk-rock herself, commented to *Melody Maker*, "The reason young people identify so readily with folk music may be the world situation. You can't ignore the world—everything in it is so complex, everyone must ask questions and ponder what is going on. That's why I think we need songs like 'Eve of Destruction.' It's a frightening song, but I think it would have been far more frightening if the song hadn't been written." Insisted Sloan himself in *Billboard*: "The message of the song has been misunderstood. It is a love song: stop hating, start loving."

For McGuire, the surprise success of "Eve of Destruction" turned out to be a double-edged sword. "There was a report that used to come out back in those days, I don't know if it was the *Gavin Report* or something like that. And they said, 'No matter what McGuire comes out with next, we're not gonna play it.' Because their feeling was that I was like a loose cannon in the record industry, and they wanted to get me back in line. Rather than a career maker, 'Eve of Destruction' turned into a career-breaker." McGuire had turned out to be a prophet of his own doom. Despite numerous attempts at folk-rock follow-ups, including quality Sloan compositions like "The Sins of a Family" that demonstrated there was much more to the songwriter than sloganeering, McGuire never had another Top 40 single.

Howard Kaylan of the Turtles, in fact, says that the band turned down "Eve of Destruction" in recognition of its potential to wreak long-term damage. "Sloan was introduced to us while we were backstage during a run at the Sunset Strip club the Crescendo [later The Trip]. Our producer, Bones Howe, brings this guy in with a potential follow-up to our first single. Sloan proceeds to sing 'Eve of Destruction' and our jaws hit the ground. We all knew that it would be a monster hit, it was that powerful. But we also knew that whoever recorded this song was doomed to have only one record in their/his career. You just couldn't make a statement like that and ever work again.

"We explained to him that we were young, white, middle-class kids from the suburbs and had very little to protest, actually. Then we asked if he had anything else, and he played 'Let Me Be' for us. Ah, just the perfect level of rebellion . . . haircuts and non-conformity. That was as far as we were willing to go. Even then we knew that we wouldn't be singing protest songs much longer." The Turtles had a decent-sized hit with "Let Me Be," which, like many Sloan tunes of the time, eschewed direct social protest in favor of a more general assertion of the right to be an individual of one's choosing.

While Sloan would continue to write hits for another year or two, "Eve of Destruction" turned out to be as much of a millstone around his neck as it was for Barry McGuire. Underneath the snarl of "Eve of Destruction" was a more sophisticated, personal songwriter, given to introspections that were something of a more self-pitying, adolescent counterpart to Dylan and the like. Yet these were also possessed of sharp hooks and honesty that made his pop-flecked folk-rock more accessible than work by slightly older, more worldly singer-songwriters. Sloan was also a vastly underrated singer, producing two albums of his own interpretations of his more serious works for Dunhill that got lost in the shuffle before he virtually disappeared from the industry after 1967. Before that tragedy played itself out, though, he'd continue to play a role as one of the best, most sought-after songwriters during folk-rock's loudest commercial boom.

Protest songs like "Eve of Destruction," sometimes labeled with the broader, less inflammatory designation "message songs," were what the media usually singled out in its coverage of folk-rock. That coverage reached its most frenzied peak as students went back to high school and college in September 1965, the same month *Time* and *Newsweek* ran virtually simultaneous stories on the folk-rock craze. "West Coast recording companies are rushing to cut Bob Dylan songs, with the message-protest material all but killing surfing, hot rod, and other teen types this summer," announced Elliot Tiegel in *Billboard*'s September 4 issue. "Teenagers are listening to the lyrics. Despite the heavy commercial rock 'n' roll beat and the blasting overamplified guitars, tradesters state that the lyrical content of a song is getting through to young people. The rock background helped get the singles on Top 40 stations. There are some skeptics, however, who feel the kids aren't listening to the words, only the beat."

Tiegel's latest folk-rock bulletin went on to claim, "All the Beach Boys–type groups have been washed out to sea by the Dylan-influenced groups who have begun imitating Dylan's droning, monotonous vocal style. Dylan's overwhelming emergence as the chief of the meaningful protest songwriters has all but obliterated other young folk-oriented writers also creating in this vein (Phil Ochs, Fariñas, Pamela Polland, Paul [sic] Sloan). The current message trend has all but eliminated Caucasian groups from singing 'Let's go to the hop'–type songs."

Respected music critic and social commentator Nat Hentoff added in the same publication, "The kind of world Jerome Kerr and Cole Porter wrote about was insular, and quite unlike the world we live in today. McGuire and Bob Dylan are spokesmen for a new generation. A whole range of social evils are being protested in their songs—and I think it's about time!" That same month, even the *New York Post*'s "Teen Talk" columnist Susan Szekely offered an astute observation of how the new "message" songs differed from those of the past: "The music is being accepted by the broad segment of the population represented by the hit parade rather than a group which espouses a special cause."

In Britain, the September 11 *Melody Maker* made "Pop Protest Songs Soar" its front-page feature, also devoting a large spread to polling both readers and pop stars on the matter. To the loaded question "Sincere or Insincere?," Paul McCartney responded, "The songs are all getting a bit silly, aren't they? Sonny's even on about protests on the length of his hair. If you think about it 'Don't Stand [sic] on My Blue Suede Shoes' was a protest song! Protest songs make me concentrate too much on the lyric which I don't like." A couple of columns over Paul Simon, then still a fairly obscure visiting American folksinger, brought the argument back round to "Eve of Destruction": "I have not yet heard one pop protest song that has been sincere. 'Eve of Destruction' is the most ludicrous thing I've ever heard—an insult to one's intelligence. I don't agree with the sentiments of pop protest songs at all. If you are not convinced with the absurdity of war then no song will change you. They are insincere and degrading in what they're trying to say."

While the era may have gone down in history as one in which social dissent began to bubble over, particularly among the young, it was inaccurate to suggest that protest was taking over the charts or even becoming the primary focus of folk-rock composers. Take a look at most *Billboard* Top 100 charts in 1965, and you'll see far less folk-rock than you will soul, conventional British Invasion love songs, easy listening ballads, exuberant mindless dance tunes like Sam the Sham & the Pharaohs' "Wooly Bully," and novelty tripe like TV comedian Soupy Sales's "The Mouse." The very week that the Byrds' "Mr. Tambourine Man" had debuted at #87, it was nestled just above a reading of "Chim, Chim, Cheree" from *Mary Poppins* at #88 by none other than the New Christy Minstrels, whose nest so many budding folk-rockers had fled.

Too, the press's definition of folk-rock protest could be so flexible as to encompass songs whose links to folk or folk-rock were negligible. Minor country-pop singer Jody Miller's sole prior hit had been "Queen of the House," an answer record to the unrelated Roger Miller's "King of the Road." Yet she found herself lumped into the folk-rock bag with the orchestral pop-rock production "Home of the Brave," a tender plea on behalf of a boy expelled from school over the length of his hair (a *big* issue among teens in those days, as trivial as it might seem now). The song was written by Brill Building stalwarts Barry Mann and Cynthia Weil, who also penned another 1965 hit, "We Gotta Get Out of This Place," that was given the "protest" tag after it became a big hit via a simmering rock treatment by the Animals. The husband-and-wife team was described, without much justification, as "the East Coast extension of folk rock" in *Time* magazine's feature on the folk-rock trend in September.

Perhaps there was some validity to that protest appellation after all, as "We Gotta Get Out of This Place" unexpectedly became an unofficial anthem of sorts among American soldiers serving in Vietnam; it even merited a story in *The New York Times* in June 1967, headlined "Rock 'n' roll Song Becoming Vietnam's Tipperary." It did testify to folk-rock's widening influence throughout pop itself, as Barry Mann told *Billboard*, "There is no doubt that Bob Dylan is leader of the present movement. He's affected so many people with what he's writing and singing."

Most importantly, few folk-rock musicians were eager to cast themselves as protest singers, whether or not some of their songs decried social injustice. It is strange that Tiegel's *Billboard* article hailed Dylan as the "chief of the meaningful protest songwriters" when the singer had stopped referring to specific social problems in his writing a year and a half before, though perhaps his more ranting numbers could be seen as catch-all protests against everything. While most folk-rock performers held left-of-center beliefs, they were determined to explore new lyrics and sounds, and the "protest" label was just as confining as the "folk" one had been.

Sometimes they didn't even hold beliefs that jibed with what they were singing. Glen Campbell may have had a reasonable-sized hit with "Universal Soldier," but in October he let *Variety* know "that he thinks people who burn their draft cards 'should be hung.... If you don't have enough guts to fight for your country, you're not a man.' He said the 'Universal Soldier' disk resulted in his receipt of several anonymous complaint letters from fans, but that he really didn't think protest songs do much in shaping or changing opinions. Campbell, however, emphasized that if he records any more protest songs, they will be of the 'red-blooded American variety.'" Any reservations he might have felt about being classified as a folk-rocker, however, had not kept him from milking the folk-rock craze by participating in the Seattle Folk Rock and All Cause Music Festival on October 1, sharing the bill with McGuire, the Grassroot Singers, Jody Miller, P.F. Sloan, and others.

The doom-and-gloom of "Eve of Destruction" and the ensuing, if brief, press swarm over earnest protest and message songs threatened to paint folk-rock as a one-dimensional music. But there was an optimistic, sunny side to the movement that was also causing big waves on the charts at the exact same time, largely due to the Lovin' Spoonful. By the standards of the lightning shifts that characterized mid-'60s popular music, it had seemed like eons since John Sebastian and Erik Jacobsen had began fooling around with electrified jug band sounds. In fact it had only been a year and a half, and the Lovin' Spoonful had been going for less than a year. But it still seemed like an endless waiting game after the group recorded "Do You Believe in Magic" in early 1965 and, according to Steve Boone, shopped it around to "almost every label of significance without success" before Kama Sutra finally released it.

In a sense, the delay had been fortuitous, as by that time the Byrds had already paved the way for another long-haired, casually dressed folk-rock band to hit it big. "Do You Believe in Magic," the best celebration of rock 'n' roll itself ever sung, made the Top Ten in the autumn, establishing the Lovin' Spoonful as the premier feel-good group of its generation. If the song, as John Sebastian has since revealed, owed much of its inspiration to Motown, the links to jug band and folk music were there to hear, particularly in Sebastian's use of the autoharp. By putting a ukulele contact mike on the back of it and plugging the mike into an amplifier, he'd made the autoharp into a rock instrument—an innovation used by surprisingly few folk-rockers. (The autoharp did, however, crop up in some folk-rock recordings by Ian & Sylvia, the Charlatans, Hearts and Flowers, Fairport Convention, and others, and the Stone Poneys worked with electric autoharp player Kit Alderson in their early days before they recorded.) "It just suddenly fit for one of the things I was writing, and we had something that was a little different. Nobody else could play the damn thing!" laughs Sebastian.

Putting a jug band–like arsenal of instruments to use in a rock context would be the trademark of the Spoonful's original lineup over the next two years. Sebastian and his bandmates lacked the Byrds' brazen adventurousness of diving into free jazz, raga, and heavily distorted amplification. Their albums were maddeningly inconsistent, with the average track far below the quality of their best half-dozen or so hits, and too many forgettable outings into straight blues or old-timey tunes. But, emphasizes producer Jacobsen, "John and Zal [Yanovsky] had a tremendous desire to explore everything that came up. When they went to the music stores, Zal got every new gizmo. John had a big collection of great old vintage instruments, and vintage electric guitars." That relatively exotic, for rock certainly, collection of instruments insured that no one could shove aside the band for session cats, even on a debut single. "The Spoonful were adamantly against using studio musicians," says Sebastian. "The one thing we didn't ever do was just sit back and let it be the Wrecking Crew that played the records or something. That was the only thing that distinguished us from five or six very powerful bands."

"I think that if I were to say what one thing did the Spoonful add to the folk-rock genre, it would be that we incorporated a lot of unusual instruments," agrees Boone with pride. "Our earliest influences—predominantly John's, and to some lesser degree Zally's, but I quickly became a convert to it—were the jug band, Jim Kweskin most notably. The element that they brought that was different from other folk influences was that they tended to not only put a lighthearted spin on their music, but they also adapted really odd instruments to use in the studio. We were one of the few folk-rock bands that played on all our records. We did all the playing, there was no studio musicians involved. Our producer gave us a lot of latitude to experiment in that fashion. So we got to bring in all these offbeat instruments and play them on records and incorporate them into the arrangements. Like the autoharp, most specifically and most obviously, but a lot of other things. There was the giant marimbas that are hardly ever seen any more, we played them on a record. On the *Hums of the Lovin' Spoonful* album, man, we just went nuts with all sorts of crazy instruments."

On the creative end, there was no doubt that Sebastian was the chief visionary as the group's primary songwriter. "The thing that was really amazing about the guy is all the different things he reached for," says Jacobsen. "It was like an all-American potpourri of pop and rock and folk, drawing from a tremendously wide palette of American musical types." As for the Spoonful's image, time has obscured the contribution of Zal Yanovsky, who, contrary to the band's rather easygoing music, "was like one of the original wild and crazy-type guys," in Jacobsen's estimation. "I think Zally invented the hole-y jeans, falling apart T-shirts, crazy rock guitar antics on stage, the whole subsequent thing of rock 'n' roll guitar[ists] being wild, crazy individualists." Judy Henske, who knew the band well (and would marry Yanovsky's replacement, Jerry Yester), doesn't beat about the bush in her appraisal of the group's dynamic: "The Lovin' Spoonful without Zalman was nothing. 'Cause you know what he was? The *juice*. Nobody else had the juice."

The Spoonful's contribution to folk-rock was, as Boone puts it, to "put a lighthearted spin" on the style. Hit songs about daydreams ("Daydream"), the power of rock 'n' roll ("Do You Believe in Magic"), falling in love with two sisters at once ("Did You Ever Have to Make Up Your Mind"), and "Rain on the Roof" might have seemed frivolous next to pleas for peace and Dylan's mind games. But they were still vital affirmations of the right to enjoy oneself in a society that had frowned on spontaneous love and celebration throughout the Cold War era. The Beatles had done that as well, but the Lovin' Spoonful plugged that current into the folk lineage, through both their jug band sensibilities and their benignly philosophical songs.

Sebastian is quick to cop to some key inspirations on both counts: "The Spoonful listened very carefully to the Kweskin Jug Band, and redid several of their tunes with only a minimal electric difference." And as a songwriter, an important role model was his old buddy Fred Neil, whose songs were "a real lesson in how to let a lyric sound like it just fell out of your mouth, like you hadn't really labored over it. I was certainly taking note of how effortless those songs sounded."

The only group to rival the Lovin' Spoonful as happy, romantic consistent folk-rock hitmakers had crossed paths with Sebastian and Co. many times over the past two years. Ironically, that group was given its big break by Barry McGuire, the singer of the ultimate morose protest folk-rock smash.

Since fending off the Spoonful's bill collection at the Albert Hotel, Denny Doherty had decamped to the Virgin Islands with John and Michelle Phillips. Hearing "Mr. Tambourine Man" had fired their ambitions to go electric, but at first the quest seemed hopeless. The story was told well in the Mamas & the Papas' subsequent hit, "Creeque Alley," but Doherty's happy to go through the basics yet again: "It was sort of like we were thrashing around with what was left of the Mugwumps' thrust, with John and Michelle and I trying to salvage what was left of the Journeymen as the New Journeymen. Eric Hord, our guitar player, was with us. We scoured the islands picking up old Sears Silvertone guitars and a bass. I didn't even know what the hell the name of the bass was. And to get a set of drums?! And there were no amplifiers! Duffy, the man that had befriended us down there, got us an amplifier that we plugged everything into—the bass, the guitars. I don't know what the fuck it was. It was sorta folk-fuck. It wasn't folk-rock. It was just a mess. It didn't work, and Duffy's was closed anyway. We were all thrown off the island.

"So we all came back to New York. Everybody was gone! David Crosby, Stephen Stills, Roger McGuinn, Barry McGuire—they're all in L.A. There was *nothing* in New York. Michelle, being a Los Angeleno, said [adopts whining tone], 'I'm going back home.' So we got a U-drive and drove to L.A. Cass [Elliot] was already out there. She was staying with her friend Jim Hendricks of the Big Three in a crash pad, and we all wound up living together. And Cass just started singing with us, with John and Michelle and I.

"Cass had come down to the islands. She and John butted heads, it didn't work. [But] John couldn't deny his frigging ears when he started working with Cass. I saw his eyes light up. We'd do an arrangement, and John would go, 'Oh! Well, Cass, if you sing that, and Michelle, you can sing that octave! Sing the octave unison!' And Michelle goes, 'What's an octave unison?' 'Well, sing what Cass is singing, only sing it up contralto, can you sing it really high? Sing as high as you can!' So Cass and Michelle would be getting up into their registers, and then John, you could see him going, 'Now, Den, can you sing this?' And I'd sing this, and instead of having three parts, he had four parts, so he could double. He could do octave unisons, and get his arrangement happening a little more.

"And once the arrangements got interesting, shit, man, throw a backbeat on it! Every song that had any kind of feel for it, John's 12-string was driving it along. Chunga-chunga...that's where we got chunga's revenge. We were a quartet with a 12-string guitar when we walked into Western Recorders Studio Three at Barry McGuire's session one night. Cass called McGuire, McGuire came over to the apartment and [heard] us singing 'California Dreamin',' and went, 'Oh, shit, why don't you come down to the studio tonight and sing for Adler?' We sang him 'Monday Monday' and 'California Dreamin',' all the songs that we had on the first album, but just with a 12-string.

"He's heard all this stuff as McGuire's next album material. 'California Dreamin'' was gonna be McGuire's next single. So we go in, and we do all the tracks and we do all the backgrounds for McGuire to come in and put the lead on. And when he put the lead on, Lou goes, 'Mmm...no. Uh, Denny, go in with the lead on.' So I put the lead on, and that was 'California Dreamin'.' It was in the can and finished." Released in November, it went to #4 by early 1966.

McGuire confirms the story, with minor variations, and bears no resentment for losing out on another potential hit single: "It was going to be my next single release. They did the backup vocals on [my] album. And when they were doing my backup vocals, they started doing a counterpoint with 'all the leaves are brown, and the sky was gray'; that all came together on my recording session. They heard it and thought, 'That's the sound. That's what we want, that counterpoint thing.' Then John asked me if they could release 'California Dreamin'' as their first single, and I said, 'Hey, you wrote the tune. Do whatever you want.' So they did. They took my voice off, and put Denny's voice on, and they had that flute player guy come in and [he] did a toodle-toodle in the middle of the song. And it was a monster hit for them. If you get *The Best of the Mamas and Papas*, you listen to the left track, you can still hear a little bit of my voice."

It has all the trappings of an overnight success story, but as for most folk-rockers, it had only come after many years in the trenches, particularly in Phillips's case. The main songwriter of the Mamas & the Papas had labored in several commercial folk groups, and recorded in the early '60s with Scott McKenzie as part of the Smoothies and the Journeymen, without coming anywhere close to stardom. Those records had shown barely any more hints of his future greatness than those of the New Christy Minstrels, Les Baxter's Balladeers, Chad Mitchell Trio, and such had for the members that would form the Byrds. These discs did show Phillips's flair for combining folk with the sophisticated pop harmonies of acts such as the Four Freshmen and the Hi-Lo's.

Flashes of a more adventurous songwriter with a knack for haunting melodies and striking storytelling were not absent. Judy Collins, with her unequaled eye for emerging tunesmiths, had recorded Phillips's "Me and My Uncle" on her 1964 concert album. "California Dreamin'" itself was based on a walk John and Michelle Phillips had taken back in Greenwich Village, years before meeting Lou Adler, pining for some sunshine in the midst of a snowstorm. Doherty believes Phillips held back from taking too many risks as folk-rock got off the ground, however, for fear of losing what little commercial ground the Journeymen had gained. "John just didn't want to hear it, until he could hear something that *he* could work with. The Journeymen died hard. He didn't want to hear anybody *else*'s successes. He didn't want to hear anybody else's ideas about how to arrange music. He had his own ideas, but he was stuck in something that was successful.

"John could write as strange as anybody. It just took him a year to find the freedom to say, 'No one's gonna look at you weird if you write a song about a day of the week.' Except," adds Doherty with typical contrarian wit, "everybody in the group going, 'This is a stupid fucking song. It's about a day in a week.'" That song was "Monday, Monday," but as to its subsequent future as a #1 single, "Who knew? No one knew."

Not Frank Werber, who had once managed Phillips in the Journeymen, and was now coasting on the folk-rock wave with the We Five. He was given a tape of the Mamas & the Papas by John Stewart of the Kingston Trio, and admits, "I tossed John Phillips out of my office. He had the tape with 'Monday, Monday' and 'California Dreamin'' in his hand, their demo. I said, 'John, I gotta tell you, I haven't even listened to this. I'm sure it's great, 'cause you do great work. But you're also a major pain in the ass. And I really don't want to work with you.' He went down and found Lou Adler, and the next thing I knew, I was hearing it in my ear." As it had for Sonny Bono and Barry McGuire—both, like Phillips, already 30 years old—folk-rock had opened the door to overnight success after five to ten years of clinging to the underside of the record business. Phillips, by far the most talented songwriter of the trio, would make the Mamas & the Papas the biggest-selling act of folk-rock's golden age.

Paul Simon had only just turned 24 in the fall of 1965, but he too may never have climbed those golden stairs had not folk-rock allowed him to reinvent himself. By the early '60s, he'd spent five years vainly trying to follow up the success of "Hey Schoolgirl," the Everly Brothers–inspired hit he'd recorded with Art Garfunkel as half of Tom & Jerry in 1957. He briefly wrote songs with Carole King before she hooked up with Gerry Goffin to become one of the Brill Building's top teams, and spun out a series of crummy novelty, teen idol, and light pop-rock singles, sometimes under pseudonyms such as Jerry Landis and True Taylor. "By the age of 19 I was very depressed," he confessed to *Record Mirror* in 1966. "I thought I was over the hill, washed up already. I'd peaked at 15."

Immersion in the Village folk scene, with some mentorship from Tom Paxton and Dave Van Ronk, helped rejuvenate his muse, and in 1964 he'd rejoined Art Garfunkel to record a folk album for Columbia, *Wednesday Morning 3 A.M.* The album flopped, Simon & Garfunkel split, and Simon split for England, where he enjoyed considerable cult acclaim as an expatriate American folksinger. A rare UK-only solo folk album from 1965, *The Paul Simon Songbook*, testifies to his enormous promise as a literate composer with a gift for pop melodicism, including several songs that were also recorded by Simon & Garfunkel, such as "The Sound of Silence."

He may have remained in England much longer if not for the ingenuity of a man who had already done a lot to pioneer folk-rock production, Tom Wilson. Wilson's days at Columbia were numbered after his ouster from Dylan's sessions in mid-1965, but he had continued to make some interesting folk-rock recordings with Dion. The Bronx-bred teen idol was one of the very few 1950s rock stars to evolve in progressive artistic directions in the subsequent decade. He had gotten turned on to acoustic folk-blues after Columbia exec John Hammond played him an album by the long-dead Delta bluesman Robert Johnson, then a cult artist known only to aficionados. By 1965, he was suddenly covering Dylan's "It's All Over Now, Baby Blue" and Paxton's "I Can't Help But

Wonder Where I'm Bound," and starting to write respectable introspective material with a folk influence.

Some Dion sessions overseen by Wilson in the fall were close in arrangement to Dylan's 1965 recordings, including a dynamite cover of the little-known Dylan blues song "Baby, I'm in the Mood for You" that wouldn't be issued for 25 years. Dion was by this time struggling with heroin addiction, and his mid-'60s experiments would unfortunately be largely ignored or unissued until their inclusion on archival CD compilations. Wilson was virtually out Columbia's door by the time of those Dion recordings, about to accept a position as East Coast A&R director of Verve Records. Before he left, however, he had one last trick up his sleeve.

Wilson had produced Simon & Garfunkel's debut album, a largely green, callow mating of the Everly Brothers with the dying embers of the folk revival (even including a cover of "The Times They Are A-Changin'"). Far and away the best cut was an acoustic version of "The Sound of Silence," Simon's eerie evocation of contemporary loneliness, complemented by an unforgettable and equally eerie melody. About six months after the album, and the duo, had been abandoned as dead in the water, a DJ on WBZ in Boston began playing the song, which found an avid audience among the region's large college population. Wilson had a brainstorm that, if crude in execution, had already served a purpose in opening the gates for Dylan to go rock, when the producer had overdubbed electric instruments on "House of the Rising Sun." He used the same technique to polish off another folk-rock classic, overdubbing electric guitar, bass, and drums onto "The Sound of Silence."

The result was the most freakish folk-rock success story of them all, in a year jammed with unimaginably rapid alchemizations of also-ran folkies and rockers into folk-rock icons. "The Sound of Silence"'s transformation into folk-rock may have been contrived; Wilson had not even asked the duo for permission to tamper with its work. But, as with the use of session men on "Mr. Tambourine Man," did that matter so much when the end product was undisputedly one of the all-time folk-rock classics? The jangling guitar and crashing drums gave the song exponentially greater gravity and weight.

Simon, still in Europe and oblivious to the goings-on at Columbia's studios, was in Denmark when he picked up an American trade paper to learn that "The Sound of Silence" was in the national charts. Simon was back in New York to reunite with Garfunkel even before the single made #1, just as 1965 turned to 1966. "Those electric instruments were added when Paul wasn't even in the country," laughs Roy Halee, the duo's recording engineer and, starting with 1968's *Bookends*, coproducer (sharing production credit with both Simon and Garfunkel). "But he was very, very glad to have a hit."

It had all the earmarks of a fluke one-shot smash, yet "The Sound of Silence" inaugurated the reign of what would turn out to be folk-rock's greatest duo, and one whose fame and influence would persist well beyond folk-rock's heyday. It would take some culture shock for Simon to fully acclimate to his sudden status as rock star, however. Vinnie Bell, the session guitarist who had created an electric 12-string-like tone on "The Sound of Silence" with his self-invented Bellzouki, was privy to an especially embarrassing incident. Bell happened to find himself assigned to back Simon & Garfunkel when they performed their hit on *Hullabaloo*, where an unwary Simon,

Simon & Garfunkel, as they appeared the cover of their Sounds of Silence *album*

Bell revealed to Bob Shannon and John Javna in *Behind the Hits*, "talked to the musical conductor, who was Peter Matz. He said, 'I'd like to show the guitar player how to play this thing.' So Peter Matz knew I did the record. He said, 'I think he knows.' But Paul Simon insisted. He said, 'No, I did a special thing on the record that I want him to do with the sound.' And Peter Matz looks at me and he says, 'All right, go ahead.'

"So Simon walked through the orchestra and he gets to me, and he said, 'Hi, I'm Paul Simon.' I said, 'Hi, I'm Vinnie Bell.' He said, 'I'd like to show you, if you don't mind, how I did this thing on the record. We have a record out, I don't know if you know it, it's a big hit, 'Sound of Silence.' So I said to him, 'Yes, I know the record. To tell you the truth, I know just what to play.' He said, 'No, here, just watch my fingers,' and he showed me with his guitar. 'Paul,' I said, 'I did the record.' And of course there was silence. And he said, 'Well…okay…are you sure you did the record?' I said, 'Yeah. It's *this*, right?' And I played [sings part]. And he said, 'Yeah, that's it.' And I said, 'Okay, you'll get that. Don't worry.'"

here were additional, more pleasant surprises as folk-rock rang out its maiden year. As "The Sound of Silence" scaled the charts in December, the Beatles' *Rubber Soul* was released, many of its songs bearing an unmistakable stamp of folk-rock's influence. In a way, this was folk-rock's ultimate validation. It was only two years before that the Beatles had spurred folk musicians to lay down their weary tunes. Now Dylan, the Byrds, and others could lay fair claim to having pushed the Beatles themselves to a new level. The Transatlantic crossfire is not mere conjuncture. The Beatles' own personal meetings with Dylan are well-documented, and they had also hung with the Byrds in Beverly Hills in August during the California leg of their 1965 American tour. There the groups jammed on 12-string guitars while flying on acid, McGuinn and Crosby giving their new friends their first taste of Ravi Shankar.

On September 1, George Harrison and Paul McCartney watched the Byrds record "The Times They Are A-Changin'" at Columbia's studios on Sunset Boulevard. As the man whose 12-string had indirectly led to McGuinn's Rickenbacker, Harrison could have been expected to feel a special affinity for the Byrds' sound. One of his songs on *Rubber Soul*, "If I Needed Someone," was as explicit a Byrds homage as any, both in the ringing 12-string guitar riffs and the "Bells of Rhymney"–derived harmonies. When an advance copy of the album was delivered to the Byrds care of publicist Derek Taylor (who had worked for the Beatles before relocating to Hollywood), it was accompanied by a note from Harrison that made this clear: "Tell Jim [McGuinn] and David [Crosby] that 'If I Needed Someone' is the riff from 'The Bells of Rhymney' and the drumming from [the Byrds B-side] 'She Don't Care About Time,' or my impression of it."

If Harrison was under the spell of the Byrds for the moment, Lennon's main man was Dylan. He'd already displayed his debt in "I'm a Loser" and, more explicitly, "You've Got to Hide Your Love Away," from the soundtrack of the Beatles' summer 1965 movie, *Help!* "Help!" itself was an illustration par excellence of Lennon taking cues from Dylan's verbose, cathartic writing, although the Beatle put a more confessional, self-doubting tilt on the style, as well as melodies that Dylan couldn't hope to match. Lennon's words grew yet more ambitious and more personal by *Rubber Soul*, and sometimes quite folky as well, particularly in "Girl," where he worked religious commentary into his romantic torments; "In My Life," a loving autobiography of lifetime friendships; and "Norwegian Wood," a cleverly worded recount of an extramarital affair. (Dylan, famously, returned the favor with "Fourth Time Around" in 1966, widely regarded as a "Norwegian Wood" satire.) Lennon was also the Beatle responsible for "Nowhere Man," a sympathetic ode to a man adrift without purpose, marking the first Beatles original to venture into lyrical territory with no ties to man/woman romance whatsoever.

Although *Rubber Soul*'s mature, reflective tone, melodies, and arrangements owed much to folk-rock, it would not be quite accurate to classify it as an entirely folk-rock album. (Though at least a few listeners thought it was more folk than rock. After Sylvia Tyson gave it to her teenaged rock drummer brother, she told the Canadian folk magazine *Hoot* that "the basic feeling between him and his friends that play in the group around Chatham [in Canada] is that this is a folk record and not a rock record.") The Beatles were too eclectic to allow themselves to be wedded to any one or two styles, and *Rubber Soul* also contained its share of great songs whose links to folk were tenuous or nonexistent, like "Drive My Car" and "Michelle." Paul McCartney, though the equal of Lennon as songwriter, never seemed to absorb or advocate Dylan and folk-rock nearly as avidly as Lennon and Harrison did. Even he, however, supplied a song, "I'm Looking Through You" (based on real-life difficulties with girlfriend Jane Asher), that was as thoroughbred folk-rock as anything recorded by anyone in 1965. A few months earlier, he'd come up with "I've Just Seen a Face" (issued on *Help!* in the UK and saved for *Rubber Soul* in the States), probably the most bluegrass-soaked rock song of the 1960s.

The Beatles would never make another album as folk-rockish in flavor as *Rubber Soul*. For the Beatles and many leading British groups, folk-rock was a pool into which to dip on occasion. The true significance of the Beatles' folk-rock phase was to enlighten the group to infinitely greater possibilities in the subjects and the sophistication of their lyrics, and to some extent broader musical and melodic textures as well. As with other British groups whose songs grew more lyrically complex throughout the rest of the 1960s, those advancements can be specifically attributed to folk-rock, and by extension a folk tradition in which a song's words could carry as much import as the music.

"When the rock 'n' roll music of the Beatles evidenced itself, it was mainly bubblegum music in the beginning," feels Peter Yarrow. "It had a spirit that was wonderfully energetic and very appealing. But it didn't *have* the sense of those roots of consideration that related to folk music, and related to an intent to use music as a platform for galvanizing community, and asserting a different perspective vis a vis the possibilities for a fairer and more just society. But as the years progressed, in the era following the alteration of their perspective, they were writing songs with great mystery, content, and poetry, and vision that was directly evolved from folk music, via the contemporary singer-songwriters. Particularly Bob Dylan. I think that he was *the* most pervasive influence in terms of converting to another perspective."

When the Beatles had watched the Byrds record "The Times They Are A-Changin'," the hope had been to make it the California group's next single. That didn't work out, although a version did appear on the Byrds' second album. Although it had only been a few months since "Mr. Tambourine Man" had peaked, choosing a suitable follow-up was crucial, in a time when just a few hitless months could see you dismissed as has-beens. Perhaps they were wary of riding the backs of yet another Dylan song. "All I Really Want to Do" had failed to rise above #40 despite its excellence (mostly due to getting scooped by Cher), and the group already had to fend off criticism for relying too heavily on Dylan material. The song they did select for their autumn single was not by Dylan, and would be the only recording to challenge "Mr. Tambourine Man" as the ultimate folk-rock statement. The evolution of the song, "Turn! Turn! Turn!," from plaintive acoustic sing-along to rock anthem was also the greatest instance of the folk process bridging not only the acoustic and electronic ages, but also Biblical times with the twentieth century.

The Pete Seeger composition may have been first written and recorded as a standard folk arrangement, but even at its conception was shaped in part by commercial considerations. As Seeger wrote in his songbook *Where Have All the Flowers Gone*, "About 1959 I got a letter from my publisher complaining, 'Pete, can't you write another song like "Goodnight Irene?" I can't sell or promote these protest songs.'

"I angrily tore off a note to him, 'You better find another songwriter. This is the only kind of song I know how to write.' I leafed through my pocket notebook to some verses I'd copied down a year before, verses by a bearded fellow with sandals, a tough minded fellow called Ecclesiastes who lived in Judea, like 3,000 years ago. I added one line ('a time of peace, I swear it's not too late'), omitted a few lines, and repeated the first two lines as a chorus, plus one new word repeated three times. Taped it. Mailed it next morning. Got a letter from the publisher two days later, 'Wonderful; just what I hoped for'. . . .

"A day or so after writing the melody... I worried that I was getting into a rut with my melodies—it was so similar to the melody I'd found for 'Bells of Rhymney,' which I'd worked out less than a year before. And a couple others. And on closer examination I realized that both tunes owed more than a little to that ancient mother-of-tunes, 'Twinkle, Twinkle, Little Star,' starting on the first note of the scale, going up to the fifth note and working their way back down to the first note again. . . . Both the melodies 'Rhymney' and 'Turn, Turn' are fairly conventional, one might even say 'cautious,' except that they are more rhythmically adventurous. Some singers have tried to even out the irregularities. I've urged them not to."

Seeger's original version, recorded live in the Village at the Bitter End in May 1962, was released on his *The Bitter and the Sweet* LP in January 1963. Its arrangement was bare and dry, leaving, as many Seeger tunes did, plenty of space for the audience to sing along. Judy Collins's version, recorded in late 1963 for her #3 album, did much to make his adaptation of words from the Book of Ecclesiastes more musically appealing, with its delicately pretty, roving accompanying guitar lines from Roger McGuinn. McGuinn had already been well acquainted with the song before playing and arranging it for Collins: "I'd heard 'Bells of Rhymney' and 'Turn! Turn! Turn!' before I worked with Judy. I was a big fan of Pete Seeger's, and I used to go to all his concerts, so I was into those songs before that." It was second nature for him to play it on request when his girlfriend asked if he knew the song, on a bus during a grueling Byrds tour of the midwest in 1965.

"It was a standard folk song by that time, so I played it and it came out rock 'n' roll, 'cause that's what I was programmed to, like a computer," McGuinn told John Cohen in *Sing Out!* three years later. "I couldn't do it as it was done traditionally. It came out with that samba beat, and we thought it would be a good single. It had everything; a good message, a good melody, and the beat was there. It fit right into the commercial formula of the time."

When they'd finished with it in the studio, however, the Byrds had changed "Turn! Turn! Turn!" just as dramatically and effectively as they'd altered "Mr. Tambourine Man." McGuinn and Crosby devised another arresting opening riff, the plangent 12-string guitar weaving circles around fat counterpoint walking bass. The vocal harmonies were equally brilliant, Crosby widening the melodic frame with high descending repetitions of the title phrase. While recognizably Seeger's song, it had, within five years, gone through an equivalent to the changeovers that had shaped folk tunes over the course of centuries.

"I would agree that was a good example of the folk process," says McGuinn. "I changed the chord structure to be more, like, kind of Beatley, and we changed the beat. Pete's version was arrhythmical, really. Judy was more rhythmical; I believe it was in 4/4 style. But it was more of a flowing kind of arpeggio. We put a kick, that Phil Spector beat, basically, to it. And some neat Rickenbacker stuff."

And how did Seeger, the folk institution who's suffered accusations of threatening to pull the plug on Dylan at Newport for years, react? While he claims to have "only heard it once or twice," he adds, "I was *delighted* with what they did with 'Turn! Turn! Turn!,' even though they changed my melody. When I sing it now, I have to laugh, because half the audience is singing their melody, and half the audience is singing mine, and they clash." For the third edition of his songbook, "I decided I'd print the Byrds version with their harmony as much as I can, as well as my own version, and the chords to go along with each one. In general, I encourage people to sing it their own way, make up their own minds."

"He wrote me a letter, and I was thrilled," pitches in McGuinn. "He said, 'Dear Byrds, I really liked the way you did 'Turn! Turn! Turn!' I love those chiming guitars. They sound like bells. My only musical query is why you didn't do the last chorus.' The answer was, we were already running overtime. It was three minutes and thirty seconds, which was a long time for a single. 2:30 was more desirable. We were pushing the envelope." Indeed, Crosby almost got them kicked off *The Ed Sullivan Show* when he staunchly refused to go along with the producer's request to cut a minute out of the song for broadcast. Last-minute pleas from management not only got them reinstated, but allowed them to sing the entire, unabridged "Turn! Turn! Turn!" on America's most popular television variety hour.

The battle to keep folk songs at their true length had already been fought by Judy Collins on *Hootenanny* and the Animals for "House of the Rising Sun." While it was hard to envision much strenuous protest against a song of patience and tolerance for all phases of life—birth, death, and renewal—the Byrds also risked charges of blasphemy for putting Biblical verse to a rock beat. The song was actually banned in South Africa for that reason, said McGuinn in his *Sing Out!* interview. Yet at the same time, he noted, it was also taught by nuns in Catholic schools.

But when it came time to finalize the single, the Byrds did not compromise as much as they had in selecting just one verse of "Mr. Tambourine Man." And "Turn! Turn! Turn!"'s three-minute, forty-nine–second duration did not keep the song from perching at *Billboard*'s #1 slot for three consecutive weeks in December. The addition of that one key line from Seeger pleading for peace while time remained was crucial, turning what could have been interpreted as a song of resignation to a song of hope, optimism, and oh-so-subtle social comment. The late-1965 Dylan would have never allowed such positivism to shine forth; the Lovin' Spoonful and the good-time folk-rockers would not have been capable of delivering a message of such seriousness; and Pete Seeger could not have given his song enough musical and rhythmic imagination to bring it to millions of ears, as the Byrds did. The Byrds were still unequaled at striking the ideal balance between folk and rock, realism and wishful thinking, passion and intellect. With "Turn! Turn! Turn," they had concluded the year of folk-rock's triumph on its highest possible grace note.

5

folk-rock

coast-to-coast

If you believed some reports at the start of 1966, folk-rock had ushered in the dawning of a new age for the whole of popular music. Gushed Herm Schoenfeld in his valedictory summary of 1965 for *Variety*: "It was the year of Bob Dylan, folk-rock and 'the message song.' It was the very end of the trail for the 'moon-June-spoon' school of pop songwriters and the beginning of a new epoch when hipsterism, nihilism and the rebellion of youth against their elders became the indispensable passwords to the best-selling charts." Under a *Billboard* headline "1965—Year of Change for Contemporary Music," Aaron Sternfield bubbled: "Probably the most significant development during the course of the year is the form variously called folk-rock, urban blues or protest. Essentially, it's the refinement of the rock instrumentation and the incorporation of meaningful lyrics into a ballad of today."

In fact, folk-rock's heyday as a trend, a craze, or something that DJs and fans would refer to in general conversation was brief. Though still generating headlines and heated debates at the outset of the year, by the end of 1966, folk-rock as a phrase had passed out of wide usage. The *music* was far from dead, continuing to evolve and infiltrate rock, pop, and society at its deepest levels. The media and the public are fickle, however, and there were new bandwagons to create and jump aboard, including new genres that folk-rock itself would spawn.

However, 1966 would see no fewer folk-rock breakthroughs and classic recordings than the prior year, and perhaps more. It was in 1966 that the Lovin' Spoonful and the Mamas & the Papas had their biggest and best hits; that Simon & Garfunkel would cement their position as superstars; that Bob Dylan would record some of his greatest work; and that exciting new California folk-rock bands Love, Buffalo Springfield, and Jefferson Airplane would make their first albums. Major folk-singers like Donovan, Judy Collins, and Tim Hardin made their full transition to electric folk-rock. The Byrds, though never again the superstars they were in 1965, continued to make some of the best music of their career and forge thrilling new directions. Garage bands, British Invasion groups, and even some artists from non-English speaking countries all made interesting-to-classic recordings that borrowed heavily from the idiom.

Folk-rock's disappearance from the front page was not a sign that the form had died, but rather that it was now such an integral part of pop's fabric that its presence did not need to be excitedly commented upon and debated. Of course, the establishment's acceptance of the changes wrought by folk-rock could still be grudging and condescending even when couched in guarded approval. In an October piece headlined "The New Troubadours," *Time* gave its thumbs-up to the coming generation in a fashion that could not conceal a general loathing for rock itself: "In the past, the amplified din was so intense that the singers were wailing away in tongues that sounded like a cross between banshee and Bantu. Now, after the takeover of the folk rockers, the words are understandable and, in some cases, even worth understanding."

aybe it wasn't front-page news by mid-1966, but controversy over what folk-rock was and what it meant was still kicking up a fuss in some quarters early that year. Robert Shelton, the longstanding *New York Times* folk critic and Dylan chum (who had penned early liner notes for Dylan under a pseudonym), had embraced folk-rock wholeheartedly. On January 30, he ran a lengthy, major article in the paper, "On Records: The Folk-Rock Rage," conferring legitimacy on the genre, and, by association, the whole of rock music. Beginning with a summarization of folk-rock's genesis, he reviewed records by the Byrds, Dylan, P.F. Sloan, Judy Collins, the Lovin' Spoonful, Mimi & Richard Fariña, and others, also dragging British bands the Animals and the Yardbirds into the mix, illustrating how nebulous the definition of folk-rock still was in the new year. The article, he noted, was sparked by *Sing Out!*'s narrow-minded coverage of the movement: "Mostly, the *Sing Out!* critics of folk-rock and others who have dwelled on its inadequacies rather than its potential take the naive point of view that hit chart popularity is an evidence of compromise and poor quality. This attitude reveals the critics' alienation from the masses of young American music listeners, not the 'crime of detachment' of Dylan, or others who have the need and the nerve to experiment."

That in turn set off a testy exchange of viewpoints in *The New York Times* a few weeks later. Under the headline "A Symposium: Is Folk Rock Really 'White Rock?'," *Sing Out!* editor Irwin Silber doused Shelton's folk-rock fire with these words: "What could have been a vital musical integration in keeping with the spirit of the civil rights revolution has turned into just another Tin Pan Alley gimmick.... Perhaps the white musician, by and large, is not yet ready for 'grits.' But that is precisely what Folk Rock today is lacking.... Its superficial electronic frenzy cannot cover up its fundamental non-involvement with life." Shelton countered, "This conservative wing of the folk Establishment is becoming aware of its loss of influence on and communication with a new generation of folk listeners.... Were Mr. Silber's view to prevail, we would have a rather dull folk-music community, mired in the monolithism of People's Songs." Nat Hentoff, admitting that "much of folk rock is indeed dross," came to Shelton's defense, accurately predicting that "definitions of Folk Rock will become both broader and deeper." Paul Nelson, now no longer on *Sing Out!*'s editorial staff, castigated Silber ("a man I respect") "for his fantastic and spurious 'connection' of Folk Rock with the civil rights movement," and argued that "the best of folk-rock—Bob Dylan, the Beatles, Love, the Lovin' Spoonful—makes most of the present-day urban folk movement seem remarkably outmoded and spinsterish."

Silber did raise a point that few folk-rock fans pondered at length: there were not many African-Americans involved in the music. Only a few blacks—Arthur Lee of Love and Richie Havens, most notably—would become major folk-rock performer-songwriters, though Tom Wilson and Bruce Langhorne were important figures as a producer and session guitarist respectively. At the same time, Silber's rough equation of folk-rock as another in a line of popular music forms built on white dilution/exploitation of black innovations was simplistic, not taking into full account the broad traditions, white and black (and sometimes non-American), that informed both folk and folk-rock. In a major feature in *Sing Out!* around the same time entitled "Folk Rock: Thunder Without Rain," Josh Dunson ran the idea into the ground, viewing folk-rock primarily as a pale, ineffectual distillation of "race music," largely of the African-American kind. There was no indication that he appreciated or understood the many shades of ethnic and popular styles folk-rockers admired, or what they were adding to their inspirations.

More valuable, and certainly more reflective of a wide spectrum of opinions, was a lengthy symposium of its own that *Sing Out!* devoted to "Folk Songs & the Top 40." Pete Seeger, Earl Scruggs (of Flatt & Scruggs), Ralph J. Gleason, Jac Holzman, John Cohen of the New Lost City Ramblers, Paul Nelson, Mark Spoelstra, and Chris Strachwitz (founder of still-active roots music label Arhoolie Records) all weighed in with their feelings on the matter, generally espousing greater tolerance for diversity than some of the previous pundits on the issue had. In any case, by August, *Sing Out!* seemed to have realized that folk-rock was going to be accepted as a part of America's musical landscape, with little further comment needed about what it meant and whether it should be resisted. As Bruce Jackson wrote of folk-rock in its pages that month, "So many of the arguments and complaints seem, when one considers the advantages, petty and insignificant. Last year there was hysteria when Dylan revealed he turned on [his guitar]; the flap was so great you might have thought he'd announced his songs had been goldwritten by Barry Ghostwater [sic]. Now everybody's digging electric."

Even allowing that much of such symposiums were hot air, their dominance of media discussion of the style highlights a serious gap in cultural documentation of folk-rock's ascension. Quite simply, discourse over folk-rock at the time suffered from a shortage of forums for intelligent writing about rock music in general. *Billboard* and *Variety* were trade publications, concerned far more with how well the music sold (and how to sell it) than what the music was. Although *Sing Out!* and *Broadside* did allot some space for folk-rock, their coverage was slanted toward discussion of its social implications, often by writers with little sympathy for the music or its audience. It's also important to bear in mind that, as blustery as some of the back-and-forth arguments about folk-rock were, they constituted a relatively minor portion of those small-circulation magazines. In the main those periodicals continued to cover straight folk music, publish the words and lyrics to old and new songs, and present regular columns on festivals, musical instrument tips and techniques, and the like. While *Sing Out!* covered Dylan's conversion to electric music in 1965–66, for the most part the rest of the magazine was business as usual, articles ranging from overviews of the folk music of Japan and a feature on the Chambers Brothers, to an interview with Appalachian musician Roscoe Holcomb and a piece on the ins and outs of converting acoustic six-string guitars to 12-string models.

In Britain, the situation was somewhat better. To compensate for antiquated broadcast formats allowing just three national BBC radio stations (plus some pirate stations operating briefly offshore), no regional ones, and only limited amounts of pop music programming, there were several weekly music papers. The most important of these—*Melody Maker, New Musical Express, Record Mirror*, and *Disc & Music Echo*—gave far more detailed coverage of records and interviews with musicians than the trade and teen magazines in the States did. As a bizarre consequence, from 1965 to 1967, it was often far easier to find intelligent discussion about and with American folk-rock musicians in the British music press than it was in US periodicals. Even so, features were usually limited to a few paragraphs, and heavily oriented toward acts with chart singles.

What America needed were regularly published spaces for intelligent writing about rock music by actual rock fans who were of a similar age as the musicians, treating the records and performers with as much respect as that given to other serious art forms. *Crawdaddy*, founded by college-aged folk and rock fan Paul Williams in 1966 (and headquartered right next to Izzy Young's Folklore Center), was an important first step in that direction. Williams even devoted the editorial of his March 1966 issue to criticizing media-imposed definitions of "Folk, Rock, & Other Four-Letter Words." But *Crawdaddy* didn't have the professional design, hard news reporting, and, most of all, wide circulation necessary to make a serious impact, still straining to crack the 20,000-copy barrier at the end of 1967. Not until *Rolling Stone* began publication at the end of 1967 did rock music receive widely read, dedicated critical coverage in the United States.

Nonetheless, some critics with a similar disposition to Williams were starting to write about folk-rock from an inside perspective, rather than as a specimen to be examined through different angles, as through bars in a zoo cage. Peter Stampfel, in and around his stints with the Holy Modal Rounders and the Fugs, made breakthroughs on two fronts with his *Boston Broadside* column "Holy Modal Blither." Here was not just a writer, but also a folk or just-ex-folk musician, fawning over not just the de rigeur Alan Lomax compilations, idiosyncratic Bahamas guitarist Joseph Spence, and delta bluesmen Fred McDowell and Bukka White, but also hardcore British Invasion rock by Them, the Yardbirds, the Rolling Stones, even the Sorrows (who never had an American hit, and whose record Stampfel must have taken some effort to locate). Such enthusiastic catholic taste, insists Ian & Sylvia guitarist Rick Turner, was more typical than rare among folkies his age: "I'd get off the road from Ian & Sylvia and wear out [the Rolling Stones'] '19th Nervous Breakdown' on my record player."

Just as crucially, Stampfel did not use the polite academic over-reverence common to folk publications, stamping his approval in the most colorful of terms. On the Rolling Stones: "If you haven't heard *Out of Our Heads* by the Stones, what are you a dope? Stands at pinnacle of contemporary achievement." On the Yardbirds' "Happenings Ten Years Time Ago": "The record that answers the burning question—is Jeff Beck really the Eggplant that ate Chicago?" In a more serious vein, on the Beatles: "Since the Beatles came along, all the professional failures who said it

Judy Collins

was impossible to be good and sell at the same time have been answered finally." Stampfel, obviously, was not confining his reviews to folk and folk-rock records. If that seems like the only responsible thing to do for a contemporary music critic now, at the time it gave unspoken permission for folkies such as Stampfel to admit enthusiasm for and influences from all kinds of music.

In the same spirit, writers for *The Little Sandy Review*, the palm-sized mimeographed pamphlet founded by folk fans who had known Dylan in his Minneapolis days, were finding their attention irresistibly tugged away from folk to folk-rock. Even in its early days, the publication had a refreshing, if somewhat immature, irreverence toward even progressive folk icons. *The Freewheelin' Bob Dylan* was "a mess"; Judy Collins's debut LP was dismissed with the pan "nowhere in her album is there any evidence that she knows anything about folk music or folk-singing, or that she regards her music as anything better than entertainment for drunks and impressionable adolescents." By July 1966, under the direction of editor/publisher Barry Hansen (now famous as Dr. Demento) and with a staff including future Canned Heat guitarist Al Wilson, *The Little Sandy Review* was reviewing the Byrds, Love, Donovan, the Rolling Stones, the Beatles, the Fugs, the Blues Project, even rock records with no real connection to folk music, such as the maiden voyage of the Mothers of Invention. Wrote the publication's co-editor Jon Pankake in *Sing Out!*, "Young people are having fun and creating with electric guitars and harmonica in a different spirit from those of us who intellectually embraced and 'revived' folk music a few years ago. They are accepting the music as a *form*, not an object, and while the hastily assembled high school Kingston Trio groups of 1959–60 can no longer remember their lyrics and arrangements, these kids may well be able to improvise a rock progression until they're wheeled into the euthanasiums of 2010 A.D."

The readership of *Boston Broadside* was regionally limited and the circulation of *The Little Sandy Review* and *Crawdaddy* were small. However, their readers and writers were mostly college-aged or beyond, and older and more sophisticated than those who devoured the teen magazines that had been the main vehicles for pop music journalism in the States. The migration of such listeners from folk to rock served notice that the demographic of rock's audience was expanding upward. Those minding the store were taking notice and reshaping their product accordingly months before 1966 started. This was particularly true of New York album-oriented companies that had previously specialized almost exclusively in folk. The most prominent—Elektra, Vanguard, and Verve/Folkways—would alter their lines with varying success, in the process recording some of the most enduring releases as folk-rock got more adult-oriented and serious. For the most part, their early signings were also New York–based, or at least East Coasters recording in New York.

In August 1965, *Billboard* reported that Elektra, still known almost exclusively as a folk operation, would branch out from folk into rock, country, pop, and blues. A singles-only label, Bounty, was unveiled as a part of the transition (though that label proved to be short-lived). According to Elektra president Jac Holzman, the magazine noted, "The move is not so much prompted by a desire to cover all musical categories as specialized markets, but as a recognition that musical categories now have little meaning." A couple of weeks later, under the headline "Folk+Rock+Protest=An Erupting New Sound," *Billboard* announced that Verve/Folkways would follow Elektra into the folk-rock battlefield. The MGM-distributed label had been founded in 1963 with the dual purpose of giving MGM a way to break into the folk market, and supplying an outlet for Folkways' more commercially accessible recordings. Verve/Folkways executive Jerry Schoenbaum rationalized his decision, according to the article, on the grounds that "while pure folk was a limited and well-defined market, much of folk borders on rock and country, and the lines of demarcation are blurred."

Elektra, the label that would effect this crossover with the highest degree of artistic integrity and commercial acumen, had already made its ventures into electric rock with the Byrds (on the single credited to the Beefeaters), Lovin' Spoonful demos, and Paul Butterfield Blues Band albums.

To fully understand the label's journey from folk to rock, says Holzman, it's necessary to backpedal to the reason pure folk was withering in the first place: the exhaustion of the folk repertoire, which instigated the search for both new songs and new ways to play music. He stresses, "I have never lost my love for folk music, but I also loved the energy of rock 'n' roll. But I was looking for a different kind of rock. I was looking for music that had something to say."

The label's first serious full-scale effort to invade folk-rock territory was probably Judy Collins's cover of Dylan's "I'll Keep It with Mine," in late 1965. It was a real coup to get an unreleased Dylan composition at a time when he couldn't have been hotter, but it went nowhere. Despite a rave review by Shelton in *The New York Times*, who called it "one of the best folk-rock performances yet recorded," Collins holds a dim opinion of the track: "There's a very good reason that it never made it onto an album. It's not a very good song, particularly. Certainly not a Dylan song that lives up to its name. It doesn't really go anywhere, the lyric's kind of flat, and the singing is very flat." Its real importance was as a calling card for both the artist and company. Elektra's biggest star, one who had not sung rock 'n' roll before, was moving into electric music. The arrangement came complete with Dylanesque organ (no coincidence, as it was played by Al Kooper) and a tinkling harpsichord riff that sounded remarkably similar in places to the one used a couple of years later on Collins's cover of Joni Mitchell's "Both Sides Now," which *did* give both her and Elektra their biggest folk-rock hit.

Collins's shift from folk to rock would involve more planning and deliberation than such commonplace strategy as electrifying a Dylan song. In the summer of 1966, she recorded her breakthrough *In My Life* album in London with elaborate, classical-influenced arrangements by Joshua Rifkin. The ex–Even Dozen Jug Band member had just translated Lennon-McCartney to baroque settings for the critically acclaimed Elektra LP *The Baroque Beatles Book*. Rifkin put the same approach to use on Collins's interpretations of songs by Dylan, the Beatles, Donovan, and the as-yet-barely-known Leonard Cohen and Randy Newman. Collins and Rifkin could occasionally unveil some rock chops; her reading of Richard Fariña's "Hard Lovin' Loser," with its urgent ascending harpsichord riff and barrelhouse piano, sounds like a hit single that never was, and far surpasses Richard & Mimi Fariña's original recording.

For the most part, though, they were bridging not just folk and pop-rock, but folk, rock, and classical music. Collins's expansion of her repertoire into songs by Brecht-Weill and Jacques Brel reinforced the sense of hearing not just a folk-rock or pop singer, but an art-song singer capable of holding her own in classical recital halls. More than any other record, *In My Life* was the album responsible for the folk-rock sub-genre tagged "folk-baroque," a term which was used in numerous reviews at the time without ever catching on with the general public.

Holzman sees *In My Life*, and indeed Collins's subsequent Elektra recordings, as embodiments of "her willingness to explore and to ignore all limits. At the very beginning, Judy was compared to Joan Baez a lot. In fact, I did it myself. But I recognized something about Judy that was different from Joan Baez. Judy had a more interesting musical range, and a more interesting emotional and song-choosing range, than Joan had. We did with Judy what we did with any artist. We tried to figure out what was the most ideal setting for the song, and let the instrumentation follow that. That's why we engaged Josh Rifkin to do arrangements."

The process was easier than might have been expected because Collins, like so many of the important folk-rock artists, had actually first immersed herself in a different kind of music before concentrating on folk. Where Collins differed from most folk-rock pioneers was that her early schooling was in classical piano rather than rock. In a way, says Collins, integrating classical features into her arrangements was a homecoming, "because it brought me back into my own piano playing when I did the Kurt Weill–Berthold Brecht. I was never comfortable on the guitar. I had to start playing the piano again to just get my brains around some of that material."

In the summer of 1966, Elektra proved capable of transiting a folk artist to straightforward rock 'n' roll with Tom Rush's second album for the label, *Take a Little Walk with Me*. The Harvard-educated Cambridge folksinger had already recorded a couple of albums for Prestige before following producer Paul Rothchild to Elektra. His initial outing for the label, 1965's *Tom Rush*, was still very much in the affable interpretive folksinger bag, though it was bolstered by backup from the usual session men suspects (John Sebastian, Felix Pappalardi, and Bill Lee). *Take a Little Walk with Me* was something like Rush's own *Bringing It All Back Home*, divided between one side of flat-out rock and one of acoustic folk-blues. Rush was not much of a songwriter at this point, though, which meant that the rockin' side was primarily devoted to covers of '50s rock and R&B classics by Bo Diddley, Chuck Berry, and Buddy Holly. Al Kooper, in addition to playing piano (under the pseudonym Roosevelt Gook), organized a band that amounted to a variation of Dylan's 1965 studio sessions, as all of the other players—Bruce Langhorne, Harvey Brooks, and Bobby Gregg—had also contributed to Dylan's recordings the previous year.

Rush's route to rock 'n' roll revivalism is something of a capsule history of the forces yanking folkies everywhere off the traditional path. "My formative years, musically, were the late '50s. The late '50s were just marvelous. It was all that wonderfully energetic, rebellious shit on the radio. Chuck Berry and Elvis, the Everly Brothers, Fats Domino, Little Richard. There were a lot of very different sounds. It wasn't like they were all cut from the same cloth. But they all had the same energy. And it was great. I've always had a fondness for that music, and basically, I was running out of folk tunes to do. I couldn't find any more that really excited me. There's a limited number of traditional songs. You can't write a traditional [song]; it has to already be there.

"I felt that I had sort of fished that pond out. So I was looking for something else to do, and said, 'Well, I'll go back and touch base with my roots.' It was kind of halfway in between the original event of the late '50s and the official [rock 'n' roll] revival, which happened somewhat later on. So there's some debate about whether I was prophetic or retarded, 'cause I was kind of halfway in between. But basically, I was just looking for good songs that I had fun playing, and that's where I found 'em."

Rush's conversion to rock was not greeted with anything like the outrage to which Dylan and some others were subjected, due in some measure to Tom having already established a maverick sensibility. "Folk is an umbrella that covers an awful lot of disparate audiences," he observes. "It goes all the way from Celtic to Delta blues to Cajun . . . audiences that wouldn't be caught dead in the same room with each other. Most of the performers around the Cambridge scene were specialists. There was a guy that did mainly Woody Guthrie tunes, and another guy would do Delta blues, and somebody would do Appalachian ballads, and then there were the bluegrass guys. They basically were interested in traditional music.

"There were a few exceptions, and I think I might have been one of them. 'Cause I would slip in a Bo Diddley tune. I was more of a generalist. I graded the songlist, and I'd take a tune from here and a tune from there, and mix 'em up. So my audience wasn't really coming to me for purity. They were coming to me for, I think, good songs done in an enthusiastic way. And diversity." Which may have enabled Tom Rush to cross the bridge from folk to rock with less fuss than most, as "when I extended the diversity another notch, it didn't upset them too much. *My* audience didn't seem to be particularly pissed off [about him going electric], in general. Or at least, I wasn't hearing about [it] if they were." Though at least one critic was piqued: "Well, there goes another virgin in folk music," sighed Ralph Earle in his negative review of the LP in *Boston Broadside*.

In other respects, Elektra's entry into rock was more fitful. Tom Paxton, author of the "Folk Rot" manifesto in *Sing Out!*, was by 1966 making his folk-rock debut with the British single "One Time and One Time Only." Remarkably, he emphatically disowned it in his own liner notes to his 1966 album *Outward Bound*, calling it "a disastrously overarranged version for which I take the blame," and including a different acoustic take for the LP. David Blue's sole Elektra album, 1966's *David Blue*, was an almost grotesque aping of Dylan's *Highway 61 Revisited* and *Blonde on Blonde* phase. Blue, formerly David Cohen, was a bona fide Dylan chum who had played in the Unicorn Jook Band with Eric Andersen in Cambridge. On the sleeve, however, he seemed to be auditioning for the part of Dylan's stunt double, down to the Medusa haircut and sunglasses. The participation of two session men from *Highway 61 Revisited* itself, Harvey Brooks and Paul Harris, ensured that the end product sounded much like a Dylan facsimile. It was an uncommonly imitative misstep by Elektra, usually so devoted to cultivating artists with a distinct musical identity. For lovers of uncanny replications of form without substance, however, *David Blue* has some undeniable charm purely as a curiosity piece.

"I guess that was the sound of the moment that he was looking for," shrugs producer/manager Arthur Gorson when asked about the record's strong resemblance to mid-'60s Dylan. "It was a tough thing for [David], 'cause that's what he knew." It couldn't have been any easier when, according to Gorson, "Dylan would come to the studio and taunt David during the making of the album." An even more obscure Mercury LP, *Dick Campbell Sings Where It's At*, went even further out on the limb with blatant Dylan rip-offs, to the point where it was difficult to determine whether it was homage or parody. And again, it created a sub–*Highway 61 Revisited* aura with the presence of Dylan sidemen in the band, though in this case with members of the Paul Butterfield Band who had played with Dylan in 1965, including Mike Bloomfield. Shortly before his death in 2002, Campbell said he didn't like Dylan's voice and had no intention of doing folk-rock, but a friend "convinced me to write a couple of Dylanlike songs for Mercury to publish before I left [Chicago] for the West Coast. The upshot was Mercury liked the songs, Columbia had Dylan, Mercury didn't, and I was told to come back in two weeks with ten more songs so we could cut an album. Frankly, it was an offer I couldn't refuse. True, I did take a shot at singing like Dylan." As for the musicians in the Butterfield Band, who were hired by producer Lou Reizner, Campbell confesses, "I didn't have the foggiest idea who they were."

Elektra's most notable folk-rock false start was the 1966 "electric" version of Phil Ochs's classic war protest "I Ain't Marching Anymore." If ever there was a successful reworking of a plaintive acoustic song into a dynamic electric one, this Paul Rothchild production was it. With backing by the Blues Project, the newly launched New York rock band featuring Al Kooper and Danny Kalb, it thundered along with ten times the impact of the original recording. Opening and closing with buzzing bagpipes, its piano sounded much like the Rolling Stones' "Street Fighting Man" on the fade. It was even catchy enough to be a hit single. But it wasn't, and not only because the no-doubt-about-it antiwar message might have been too controversial for AM radio. Though it seemed an ideal vehicle for breaking Ochs to a wider audience, it was released only as a British single, and as a flexi-disc in *Sing Out!* (Ochs always was one to try to break down barriers between warring camps.)

It seems odd that this would remain Ochs's sole electric recording for Elektra. The folksinger had been extremely vocal in his support of rock recordings by both Dylan and other performers, even ones with no ties to folk or folk-rock. The "singing journalist," as he'd been dubbed by both positive and negative critics, was also starting to move beyond topical songs, particularly on the abstract love song "Changes," a highlight of his third and final Elektra album *In Concert.* Yet he would record not only no other rock than the "I Ain't Marching Anymore" single for Elektra, but virtually nothing at all throughout much of 1966 and 1967, in part due to his search for a new record deal after deciding to leave the label.

"It was basically to test the waters," says Michael Ochs, Phil's brother and (starting in 1967) manager, of the single. "He wanted to expand his music, and so he thought, 'Wouldn't this be great, to do a rock version.' I'm not sure it that was his decision to be careful and only put it out in England. Phil was very tight with Murray the K, and Murray the K was on [New York's] WOR-FM at that point, doing a very hip show. Every week he'd play like three new releases for major artists, and people would call in and pick their favorite. I know he played Phil's electric 'I Ain't Marching Anymore' against the latest Stones record and one other major one, and the calls that came in all said they loved Phil's record the best." Who singer Roger Daltrey most likely would not have agreed; asked for his reaction to the single in *Melody Maker*'s "Blind Date" column, he spat, "It sounds like a punished protest song. Turn it off, turn it off, turn it off! It's not even good for my grandmother." At any rate, Phil Ochs's best shot at a hit single would never achieve general release in America during the 1960s.

lektra was still figuring out the game plan in its expansion into rock music. But its very willingness to do so, absorbing some blows along the way, can be pinpointed as the exact juncture at which it pulled ahead of its primary rival. Vanguard Records was trying to do pretty much the same thing at the exact same time: move its esteemed folkies into electric band music, take advantage of the growing LP market for folk-rock, and take some stabs at chart singles along the way. Not infrequently, the two labels bid for the same artists; in some cases very early recordings by artists who ended up on Elektra (Paxton, Ochs) were done for Vanguard, and vice versa (in Richard Fariña and Patrick Sky's cases). Simply by virtue of its best-selling LPs by Joan Baez, Vanguard was a more financially successful label than Elektra in 1965. Several of its top folkies—Baez, Ian & Sylvia, Richard

& Mimi Fariña, Buffy Sainte-Marie, Eric Andersen—were exploring folk-rock by 1966 and 1967. Yet Vanguard, whose pop wing was under the direction of Maynard Solomon, could not or would not be nearly as shrewd in spreading its wings into folk-rock as Elektra was, despite contributing several fine recordings to the style.

The Fariñas were the most adept of the early Vanguard folk-rockers, as well as the most pioneering, having made their first electric recordings just prior to Dylan's *Bringing It All Back Home*. Their first album had only contained a couple of full-out rock tracks, but their follow-up, *Reflections in a Crystal Wind* (from the end of 1965), saw them jump into the pool to at least shoulder level. "Sell-Out Agitation Waltz" was certainly their best straight rock song, the characteristic fluttering Bruce Langhorne guitar work backing a tense lyric of social disorder that stands up well to Dylan's similar efforts from the mid-'60s. Richard Fariña distinguished himself more as his own man on compositions that sounded like seafaring narratives in folk-rock settings, like "Raven Girl" and "Bold Marauder," as well as on his gorgeous, sad, romantic ballads, like "Children of Darkness."

"I always enjoyed Richard's love songs," said Mimi Fariña shortly before her death in 2001. "The more political stuff got too angry for me. Sometimes it pushed the corny button, and you can get an audience riled up easily. It's much easier to make people cry than it is to make them laugh, and you can press certain buttons to get their attention. I felt, sometimes with the political material, that that's what he was going for. But they were all good songs. Dick was able to write love songs and political songs, mix those two metaphors together in a song. And I always appreciated that." There was more where that came from, in "Joy 'Round My Brain"'s exuberant images of upside-down hummingbirds and congressmen tearing off their clothes, and the Celtic drone of "The Quiet Joys of Brotherhood." By the time those two songs were released in 1968, however, Richard and Mimi Fariña had not recorded for two years, and their career was over.

Richard Fariña, at least as serious a writer as a musician, had finally published his first novel, *Been Down So Long It Looks Like Up to Me*, when he died in a motorcycle accident on April 30, 1966. It was just a few hours after the publication party, on Mimi's twenty-first birthday. The novel, a semi-autobiographical account of the beatnik era on the cusp of the '60s counterculture, was posthumously acclaimed, overshadowing to a large degree the Fariñas' substantial musical achievements. It's not known whether Richard would have focused more on writing or music had he survived. But as the first major folk-rocker to die, and at the peak of his powers no less, the loss to popular music was far greater than was acknowledged, at the time or since. Perhaps he and his wife would have continued to grow in unforeseen directions, taking their blend of whimsical poetry, Celtic and Appalachian melodies, Latin rhythms, and eastern modes to some new folk-rock-world fusion height. As it stands, his death created the biggest "what if?" question in all of 1960s folk-rock.

Before his death, Richard Fariña had produced a rock album on Vanguard for sister-in-law Joan Baez that was to include songs by Burt Bacharach and Hal David, Lennon-McCartney, and Paul Simon, as well as some of Fariña's tunes. A couple of those tracks, including the magnificent folk-baroque lament "All the World Has Gone By," did appear in 1968 on the posthumous Richard & Mimi Fariña outtakes album *Memories*, and Baez's mild folk-rock version of the Fariñas' famous

"Pack Up Your Sorrows" came out as a single. But the album was scrapped after Richard's death, and, apparently, not wholly because of his passing. Baez, bluntly, was not comfortable or adaptable to rock. As much as she herself loved rock, she was candid enough to realistically assess her strengths and decide not to follow the lead of so many others, such as Judy Collins.

"I listened to all the tapes for two or three months," Baez told *Sunday Ramparts* at the time. "They just didn't make me happy. I read something Gandhi wrote, something I was thinking, about how art should elevate the spirit. That decided me. It's hard to tell what's going to make me feel good. Good rock 'n' roll at its best makes me feel good, but there is a whole other level of being which rock doesn't come close to. That involves eliminating, not adding to, what's in your head." Before she'd laid rest to the album, though, she made a memorable appearance on the obscure rock concert movie *The Big T.N.T Show*, singing a truly odd, gotta-hear-it-to-believe it version of the Righteous Brothers' "You've Lost That Lovin' Feelin'" with Phil Spector on piano.

Baez did not, however, doggedly remain acoustic, and indeed had already used the ever-ready Bruce Langhorne on electric guitar for a few songs on her late-1965 album *Farewell Angelina*. She would, in the 1970s, have a couple of soft rock hits with a cover of the Band's "The Night They Drove Old Dixie Down" and her own "Diamonds and Rust." Back in 1966 she plainly did not have the aptitude to go electric with correspondingly wild results, however. In any case she spent much of the last half of the 1960s more committed to social activism and antiwar protest than record-making, founding an institute for the study of nonviolence (in which Richard & Mimi Fariña had taught and participated). Her near-absence from folk-rock certainly handicapped Vanguard's efforts to effectively build a presence in the pop arena.

Ian & Sylvia, probably Vanguard's most popular folk act other than Baez, were neither as ready to rock as the Fariñas, nor as noncommittal about exploring rock as Baez was. More than almost any other performers, they were caught in the middle, willing to rock themselves up to some extent, but not quite capable of going whole hog. Sylvia Tyson's "You Were on My Mind" had been a huge folk-rock hit in the We Five's hands, and the duo's male-female harmonies undoubtedly influenced groups like the Mamas & the Papas. As Sylvia proudly states, "Michelle Phillips once said to me, 'When I was starting out, every girl in the music business wanted to be Sylvia Tyson.'" Ian & Sylvia's mix of original compositions, interpretations of contemporary songwriters, and traditional songs seems (if by nothing more than accident) to have set the template for the similar balance of material exploited by the Byrds and Fairport Convention on those groups' albums. Fairport's Iain Matthews even named his first post-Fairport band, Matthews' Southern Comfort, after an Ian & Sylvia song. And in Buffalo Springfield's very first interview (in May 1966 with Jennifer Starkey of *TeenSet*), both Stephen Stills and Neil Young immediately and enthusiastically hailed Ian & Sylvia as their favorite folk artists. Stills singled out the duo's "Four Rode By" for special praise, and even Ian & Sylvia's accompanists did not escape the Springfield's notice, Stills extolling the work of John Herald, and Young admiring David Rea.

Yet, despite some good folk-rock recordings between 1966 and 1968, they just never seemed fully comfortable in the new era for which they had laid important groundwork. At times they sounded like folksingers awkwardly trying to fit themselves to rock arrangements; sometimes the addition of orchestration worked well (as on their unexpectedly fine cover of Bacharach-David's "24 Hours from Tulsa"), sometimes it tended to smother their strengths. Plus, as traditional songs became passé and they relied more on their own compositions, their material became far more uneven, even as they continued to champion important new songwriters (they were among the first to cover Joni Mitchell) and pen quality songs like Ian Tyson's "The French Girl" and "Lovin' Sound." When Ian & Sylvia briefly left Vanguard for MGM for the 1967 album *Lovin' Sound*, Sylvia Tyson acknowledges, "There was a little pressure from the record company to do something aimed a little more towards pop music. Although I think there are some good songs on that album, there are some flaws in the arrangements which show that we really were not pop artists."

"There was a sort of cookie-cutter-stamped overlay on top of their music," says Rick Turner, who played guitar on Ian & Sylvia's first album to head in a folk-rock direction, 1966's *So Much for Dreaming*. "I think some of it has to do with the issue of giving up control of the sound of the music to other people. Ian liked to be in charge, and had pretty good instincts with the smaller ensemble stuff. When it got to that point where you're having to hire arrangers, and you've got a studio full of violin players who were playing poker in between takes . . . literally, that was the attitude of the New York studio guys. For them, it was just another call. And that was not the case for Ian nor Sylvia. Ian & Sylvia were not musical lightweights. They were trying to differentiate from Peter, Paul & Mary. Personally, I probably would have preferred to see them add a dobro player, add a mandolin player, something like that. Maybe keep it a little on the acoustic folky side, but expand instrumentation a little bit."

Sylvia Tyson has an observation that might startle those who think of Vanguard as a primarily folk and folk-rock concern, and explains to some degree the inconsistency of its folk-rock efforts in the second half of the 1960s. "I think that Vanguard, despite the folk artists and their success with them, was always primarily a classical label. Their whole approach to recording was really based on how they recorded classical music. There was always a kind of a bottom-line attitude that, 'Well, this is all very well and good, but what we're really about is classical music.' Their idea of a big promotion was to buy an ad in the *Evergreen Review*. When we actually had one of our albums on the national charts at one point, it was not due to any kind of promotion that Vanguard did. It was strictly because we were out in the trenches, working and promoting the record. I think that's true of all Vanguard's artists." (To be fair to Vanguard, full-page ads for the label in the mid-'60s can be seen not only in folk rags like *Broadside*, but in *Billboard* magazine as well, including on more than one occasion for Ian & Sylvia.)

Elaborates Buffy Sainte-Marie, who like Baez and Ian & Sylvia never exactly went the hard rock route: "I believe that [Vanguard] primarily wanted to sell records, which now I understand was their job. On the way to accomplishing that goal, they tried to make good records, but their taste was real limited and came from their own New York background. They did things the way they wanted, in spite of my artistic requests, and it was painful to me to hear each new record include the 'wrong takes' in my opinion. I also had a tough time with very straight photographers, writers, and musicians they would assign me. Looking back on it, I needed a younger, more ethnic team who may have helped me maximize the uniqueness of my songs and what they represented."

In late 1967, Maynard Solomon did tell *Billboard* that Vanguard's output had reached a point where 75 percent of it was pop and 25 percent classical, as opposed to a 50-50 percent split a couple of years before that. Still, Irwin Silber corroborates that "Manny Solomon produced the Weavers and so on, but I always had the sense that the folk music stuff was an adjunct for Vanguard. Both in terms of Manny's sentiments and tastes, but also in terms of where their real market was. It was more a classical label than anything else." As for its promotional budget, Silber thinks "they poured it into Joan Baez," not putting equal effort behind its less proven and profitable acts.

Whether or not it had the inclination to record folk-rock, there's no question that Vanguard wanted a piece of the pie. It didn't neglect the singles market either, even if, like Elektra, it lacked much know-how or experience in the art of getting 45s played on the radio and distributed. As a result, there were some clunky curios as it attempted to get in on the game. Virtually totally unknown folk-rockish singles were pressed by the Hi-Fives and Project X; in early 1966, *Billboard* even announced an upcoming Vanguard single by future TV Kung Fu star David Carradine, the intriguingly titled "Guns of Danang." Patrick Sky, a minor singer-songwriter who vacillated between earnest musings like "Many a Mile" (covered by Buffy Sainte-Marie) and forced comedy, took a shot at electric folk-rock with a single-only cover of Tim Hardin's "Reason to Believe." Jackie Washington, a black folksinger well-liked on the Cambridge circuit but not well known nationally, made a folk-rock album in which he sounded not so much adventurous as disoriented, veering between bad Dylan imitations and labored, uncertain folk-baroque numbers. The sole LP by the slight yet likable male-female duo Jonathan & Leigh sounded, quite literally, rushed through to execution, both in an impatience that didn't leave the teenaged-looking pair more time to develop their songwriting, and erratic rhythms that sometimes gave the impression that the backup band was wholly unfamiliar with either the specific songs or the general requirements of folk-oriented performers.

Probably no one suffered more from Vanguard's shaky grasp of rock than Eric Andersen. While his 1965 debut for the label had been something of a minor counterpoint to *The Freewheelin' Bob Dylan* era, his 1966 *'Bout Changes & Things* showed him growing into a skilled songwriter. Certainly it remained Dylanesque, but in a gentler, more sensitive way than most. The civil rights movement–inspired "Thirsty Boots" was one of the last topical folk songs of the '60s to get wide attention. But introspective romantic, tuneful odes like "Violets of Dawn" were more indicative of his persona, and that song was already attracting folk-rock cover versions by the Blues Project and the Daily Flash.

There was no electric rock on the album, however, save Harvey Brooks's electric bass on a couple of cuts. So Vanguard took the step—either bold or foolhardy, depending on the perspective—of making Andersen's third album an electric version of exactly the same songs, titled *'Bout Changes & Things Take Two*. The hope might have been to break him into the rock market, but it might well have had the ultimate effect of baffling consumers and splitting sales. "The original album hadn't been released in Europe, so they were gonna release this one instead," says Andersen. "Then it got released everywhere, and it got totally confusing. They just got greedy. They thought they could make money."

'Bout Changes & Things Take Two was but one of several attempts to rerecord or overdub acoustic tracks by rising singer-songwriters for rock 'n' roll ears. After Richie Havens began to make a national name for himself with his debut for Verve/Folkways in 1967, producer Alan Douglas took some solo demos, mostly of traditional material, that Havens had done a few years before, and overdubbed the tracks with a full electric band. The results were a couple of unauthorized exploitation albums on his own Douglas label, *Richie Havens Record* and *Electric Havens*, the latter adorned with an illustration of a huge electric plug on the cover, in case anyone missed the point. Actually the records weren't too bad, even if the overdubs sometimes wavered out-of-sync with the original contents. (Douglas, incidentally, went on to endure a deluge of criticism for insensitive posthumous overdubs to numerous Jimi Hendrix recordings.)

Prior to the Havens albums, Verve/Folkways had slapped much sloppier electric rock and string overdubs onto old acoustic Bob Lind demos, in the wake of that singer-songwriter's 1966 folk-rock smash "Elusive Butterfly." Not only were the new parts frequently blatantly out of sync with Lind's voice and acoustic guitar, but the label even had the gall to name the album *The Elusive Bob Lind*, in spite of the absence of "Elusive Butterfly." "It's unconscionable what they did," bristles Lind. "It was just such a piece of shit that I just cringe every time I see it."

Perhaps these releases, which made *'Bout Changes & Things* seem dignified, were inspired by Tom Wilson's phenomenal success in overdubbing Simon & Garfunkel's "The Sound of Silence." But that single's success was not a simple formula that could be exploited. Not everyone was as good a producer as Tom Wilson, and few songs were as good as "The Sound of Silence."

As unethical as such releases were, they were a bellwether of just how hungry industry mavens were to hitch a ride on the folk-rock balloon before it burst. Verve/Folkways, usually a label with more rigorous aesthetic standards than it had applied to the packaging and release of *The Elusive Bob Lind*, had itself been only recently founded. It was originally envisioned as a vehicle for the more commercial folk recordings on Folkways, as its distribution via MGM would allow for far more exposure than Folkways could garner on its own. The first Verve/Folkways releases included albums by Pete Seeger, Woody Guthrie, Leadbelly, and the New Lost City Ramblers.

When folk-rock took off, though, Verve/Folkways (and its imprint Verve/Forecast) got hot on the trail of singer-songwriters and groups working the turf, particularly those from the New York area. This expansion would be helmed not by Moe Asch of Folkways, but by Verve's Jerry Schoenbaum, a more traditional record industry executive. Asch, despite having issued one of the first New York folk-rock albums with the Fugs in 1965, had neither the aptitude nor the resources to exploit the new music. "He couldn't afford it," explains Irwin Silber, who knew Asch well as a business partner. "I mean, Folkways was a cheapo label. Most people who recorded for Folkways did it because they wanted to get the stuff out. They didn't do it for the money. He relied on people who were not gonna make undue demands on him. He was sort of resigned to the fact that if he did get somebody who was a star, they'd probably go somewhere else sooner or later. So I don't think folk-rock was for him. But it was at least as much a market decision as anything else."

One of Verve's mid-'60s signings was the Blues Project, a New York quintet that was one of the first American rock groups to focus primarily on the LP market. It was also among the first to use folk-rock as just one color in a kaleidoscope of influences, though most of the band did have origins in the folk scene. Danny Kalb had played acoustic guitar on many sessions, including dates for Phil Ochs and Judy Collins; Steve Katz was one of several folk-rock alumni of the Even Dozen Jug Band, having replaced Artie Traum in a formative lineup of the Blues Project; and Kooper, of course, had within months of "Like a Rolling Stone" become the most in-demand folk-rock session keyboardist, even if his roots were rock and pop rather than folk and blues. The Blues Project was more blues-rock than anything else, but it was not just a New York version of the Paul Butterfield Band. It threw in occasional folk-rock covers of songs by Eric Andersen, Bob Lind, Donovan, and Patrick Sky, as well as writing a few tunes in the same vein, the arrangements highlighting Kooper's glowing organ. "For the Blues Project, it was just another pond to stick our feet in," says Kooper of their folk-rock excursions. "It was the only correct category for Steve Katz's voice, so he sang most of the folk-rockers."

As for whether Verve's folk-rock roster signified an aesthetic vision for the label, Kooper's skeptical: "Believe me, it was PURELY a capitalistic move. If something looked commercially viable, the sharks came in and the feeding began." Janis Ian, a fellow Verve/Forecast artist, has a more charitable yet realistic view: "The only other company I can recall that offered similar freedom was Elektra, but it wasn't quite as much. I personally suspect Verve/Forecast was begun as a tax loss for MGM. That would explain the huge amounts of money they shoveled into it, and why they were willing to fund something like the three-time release of [Ian's hit] 'Society's Child.'" Howard Solomon, owner of the Cafe Au Go Go in the Village—a key venue for newly electrified folk artists—points out that Schoenbaum *was* in touch with what was going on at the street level: "He came down to the Au Go Go every time I had a new act."

Verve's biggest folk-rock catch was Tim Hardin. The irascible singer-songwriter had kept recording and performing since those mid-1964 demo recordings that had done much to anticipate some folk-rock threads. His drug habit and general unpredictable irresponsibility had made landing a record deal, and then cutting a coherent album, a challenge for his young manager/producer Erik Jacobsen. Actually, Hardin was an impresario's nightmare. According to Jacobsen, the singer once defaulted on a week-long gig in Chicago by slapping the clubowner with a $700 bill for new suits, selling those suits for drugs, and hiding out in his hotel until Jacobsen got his mother to slip Tim $100 so he could take a bus back to New York. Jacobsen is dispassionately frank in his assessment of Hardin's character: "He was very self-destructive, kind of a super-selfish, preoccupied, mean, unethical liar. Merciless with the women, merciless. All the girls liked him. He'd go over, he'd say, 'You're my new wife,' and in a week or ten days, he'd get all her cash from her account, she'd buy him clothes, and then boom!, he's like over on the next case. He was a very charismatic and intense individual. A miserable, miserable guy. But so talented."

Talented enough to make Jacobsen unusually persistent in helping Hardin piece together an album, considering the low ratio of payoff to outlay. "What I did was kind of invent, with those first records, something that didn't even exist [for Tim]," Jacobsen says. "Which was: have a kind of co-

Tim Hardin in the studio

herent and cogent development of songs, an end and a form to 'em. I bought him a tape recorder and said, 'You just write these songs with your guitar, get 'em on demos, and I'll give you 50 bucks for every couple of verses and a chorus. Seventy-five if you get a bridge.' He was bringing tapes over every week for a period there, all those for that first record. And a lot of 'em that were on the second, like the demo on 'If I Were a Carpenter,' 'Lady Came From Baltimore,' and 'Black Sheep Boy'—all those also came during that same period. I think they took my demos with 'em and put strings on 'em and stuff in some cases, on that second record that he put out."

As is the case with numerous tormented artists, Hardin was able to convey far greater sensitivity and vulnerability through his music than he was in real life. *Tim Hardin 1*, released in mid-1966, showed a quantum leap in his songwriting from the blues rewrites of his 1964 demos. His words and vibrato vocals oozed sadness and tenderness. His melodies escaped standard blues progressions to craft a wistful blend of folk, country, blues, jazz, and pop on "Don't Make Promises," "Misty Roses," "How Can We Hang on to a Dream," and the oft-covered "Reason to Believe." "Timmy wrote songs of such simplicity, yet they had so much personal meaning in them," praises Steve Boone of the Lovin' Spoonful, a fan of Hardin's since first seeing him at the Night Owl in late 1964. "As opposed to the flower-dropping type of image you get of a folksinger, singing higher than their range and wailing on with this song of love and passion, Timmy kind of delivered a working man's version of that."

The understated production was as much a matter of practical necessity as conscious design, as Jacobsen points out, "We didn't have too much choice. Because we never knew on any given day when he would show up, whether he was straight enough to sing, or even wanted to sing. If it seems like there's a lack of coherence in some senses, style-wise and arrangement-wise, it's just because there *was* no real coherence. It was pieced together. And I had to do some of it without him there, because he was interested, but [sometimes] not interested." In *Record Mirror*, Hardin summarized his appeal in a fashion that alluded to his drug use: "The way I sound on records is passive, because I'm usually sick at the time. On record, I'm crying with fatigue. The sound that most people know me by is the sound of me, wasted."

If Hardin sounded wizened beyond his years, Verve's other major folk-rock find of 1966, Janis Ian, was the music's youngest prodigy. Ian wasn't even in her teens when her first material was published in *Broadside*, and only 15 when her debut single, "Society's Child," was released in August 1966. If there was any possible topic more controversial than antiwar protest or civil rights advocacy, "Society's Child" managed to find it with its bitter description of a crushed interracial teen romance. "Society's Child" did have its beginnings as an acoustic folk song, as evidenced by the inclusion of a previously unreleased acoustic performance of the tune by Ian on *The Best of Broadside 1962–1988*. Its transformation into a hit rock single was about as much of a long and winding road as that traveled by Simon & Garfunkel's "The Sound of Silence."

Shadow Morton, the eccentrically inventive producer of classic girl-group hits for the Shangri-Las such as "Leader of the Pack," got Atlantic to pay $5,000 for a session to record "Society's Child." The song was completely made over with electric rock backup and sparkling keyboards, abruptly changing tempo when it trailed off into its dreamy, mysterious bridges, ending with a foreboding, stuttering blast of blues organ. It was a testament to folk-rock's impact on all levels of the industry that a Brill Building producer with no folk background could effectively midwife a topical folk songwriter's transition to rock. In Morton's case, his background worked to his and Ian's advantage, as he created a studio ambience of Spectoresque depth that was beyond the imagination of most folkschooled recording technicians. A difference between him and Phil Spector, who treated the recording artist as one cog in the wheel of his arrangements, was that Morton knew that a different sort of empathy and respect would be necessary to get the best out of an artist such as Ian. As Janis observes, Morton "was unusual in that he let me have absolutely free rein in the studio from the first. I directed the band, I did the charts, I wrote the intros and outros."

If folk-rock had the effect of liberalizing the industry, however, it hadn't quite radicalized it. Atlantic passed on "Society's Child," as did more than 20 other companies. "The biggest insult was that I had to try to convince people who are fighting for equal rights to release this recording," fumed Shadow Morton to Robert Shelton in *The New York Times*. Chipped in Ian in *Broadside*, "It seemed all these people who refused to release the record took dubs home for their private collections. H-m-m-m-m."

"Society's Child" did become a Top 20 hit, but not until nearly a year after its release. It took a guest spot on a Leonard Bernstein–hosted CBS television special on pop music to push it onto radio playlists. (On this program, Bernstein praised the "sassy retort of the organ at the end" of "Society's Child," and Ian had to suffer an exceptionally clumsy, nationally televised accolade from her host, who informed her, "You're a great creature.") By that time Ian, like many folk-rock artists who made an initial splash with an issues-related song or two, was diversifying into all sorts of material. The "one-hit wonder teen prodigy" tag, however, would haunt her for nearly a decade, until she, remarkably, persevered and landed much bigger hit albums and singles in the mid-'70s than she ever had at the outset of her career.

Perhaps because her ties with the *Broadside* community were stronger than those of most folk-rock singer-songwriters, Ian continued to get some cold shoulders from the folk crowd even after 1966, when going electric had for the most part ceased to be an issue. African-American folksinger Julius Lester let loose with some surprisingly judgmental, bitter words in *Broadside* in 1967, chiding Ian for changing her name from Janis Fink and noting with dissatisfaction, "Now she's on TV with all sorts of lights and camera angles and I just know she's not protesting anymore. She's making it and it's sad. Like there goes another one chasing that American dream of fame and money and meanwhile the kids on my block make up games using garbage can lids and stop their stickball games to kill a rat crossing the street to the juicy garbage on the other side."

If that's what making pop records cost, Ian has no regrets. "There were a great many people in the folk movement who literally stopped talking to me after 'Society's Child' came out, because it had drums on it. There were articles in folk magazines excoriating me for daring to use a band and 'selling out.' It was all incredibly stupid. I mean, which is better—to cut something with a vocal and guitar that gets heard by 100 people and changes their lives for the better and makes them think, or to cut something with a band that gets heard by a million people and makes them think?"

A far more obscure '66 release on Verve/Forecast, Jim & Jean's *Changes* LP, was an object lesson in how the extended support system of early New York folk-rock—involving songwriters, session musicians, producers, and managers—could help a fairly anonymous duo craft a quite respectable folk-rock album. The husband-and-wife team of Jim Glover and Jean Ray, when left to their own devices, were a pretty minor-league derivation of Ian & Sylvia, as heard on their prior, self-titled album for Philips. They wrote little of their own material. But, as the cliché goes, they had connections. Glover had been a good friend of Phil Ochs since they had roomed together at Ohio State and formed a folk duo, the Sundowners. Ochs's manager, Arthur Gorson, took Jim & Jean onto his client roster. Gorson also happened to be a producer, and roped in New York's top coterie of folk-rock session players for *Changes*, including Harvey Brooks, Bobby Gregg, and Paul Harris (Al Kooper played on the two songs produced by Tom Wilson). And, Gorson happened to manage several other green folk-rock singer-songwriters, including David Blue and Eric Andersen. Jim & Jean thus had clear access to cherry-pick Ochs, Blue, and Andersen songs, some of them yet to be recorded by the composers when the pair made those tunes the backbone of their album.

As a consequence of all these factors, *Changes* was a far more effective, comfortable-sounding folk-rock album than any folk-rock LP Ian & Sylvia did, even though Ian & Sylvia were far more talented than Jim & Jean. Jim & Jean's dramatic reading of Ochs's "Crucifixion," a devastating allegorical commentary on slain heroes, was arguably more effective than the author's version (not released until late 1967), with its mournful close harmonies and tense tick-tock rhythms. The supremely haunting, ethereal "Strangers in a Strange Land" was a true lost folk-rock classic and, unbelievably, a better David Blue song than any that the composer had put on his own Elektra debut. Their cover of Ochs's "Changes," driven by Harris's harpsichord, was sprightly enough to have been a hit single given the right breaks. The ghostly ballad "One Sure Thing," one of the few originals on the record, was strong enough to merit a cover version on Fairport Convention's first album.

Gorson admits that *Changes* was a good example of neophytes winging it in the studio, managing to produce a record that might have sounded as good as it did precisely because of the spontaneity involved in delving into electric music for the first time. "What was going on in the studio was all these people who didn't have a lot of experience coming together to try to make a record. The goal was to make a commercial folk-rock album. Jim & Jean were on the folk circuit, but they were by no means part of the Greenwich Village hard-edged street scene. They were more in the commercial folk realm. They had these brilliant new songs that no one else [had] recorded and no one else could even hear how to record. They had the benefit, and the intelligence, to understand Phil Ochs songs. 'Crucifixion,' on that album, is just brilliant; Phil always thought that was the best performance of the song. The version of 'Changes' is great.

"The Jim & Jean album was the first sort of exercise in how little we knew, or how great the people we knew were. It's a good album; it was a naive album. That was the first album I did. The engineer on that album was Bill Szymczyk, who ended up producing the Eagles. He had come from the midwest and shooting snakes in the celery patch or something. We didn't know anything. That album was designed as it was recorded. When we started mixing it, we said, 'Now, let's talk about the stereo.' And I remember Bill Szymczyk saying, 'I didn't know you wanted stereo.' As a result, when you listen to the album, the only thing that's in stereo is Jim & Jean['s vocals], left and right, and the rest of it was all thrown in the middle because even the recording techniques were naive. Everything happened in a sort of spontaneous way. It was exciting."

The pool of session players that crop up on numerous New York folk-rock records of the mid-'60s—Kooper, Harris, Brooks, Pappalardi (who also worked often as an arranger and a producer, and later produced Cream), Langhorne, Russ Savakus, and some others—is small enough to make one think there was almost an incestuous floating house band of sorts as the city struggled to mix folk and rock in the studio. "We ended up using a very small group of musicians who perhaps played on a Dylan album or something like that," says Gorson, who also produced records by David Blue, Phil Ochs, and Tom Rush during the same era. "Harvey was about as much as we knew about the electric bass. Paul Harris shows up, because Al Kooper wasn't available on the first sessions we were doing. Paul was one of the only other piano players that we knew. We knew the people who played with Dylan, because they were around the same scene. We didn't *know* anyone else. *We* were the only people we knew!"

"There were not a lot of electric instrumentalists who were comfortable with people who came out of the folk genre," agrees Jac Holzman. "Harvey [Brooks], Al Kooper, they were like contract players for motion picture studios. When you saw a whole bunch of other names and people that you liked as contract players playing secondary roles, it made the movie a little bit more enjoyable. And I think there was a certain guarantee of quality there." And efficiency, as well; as Tom Rush says of Langhorne, "Bruce is good enough that he could, the first time through, play the song like he'd been doing it his whole life."

The small print on Dylan albums was the shortlist of hired guns. Asked why he was invited to so many folk-rock sessions, Kooper is candid enough to shoot back, "The fact that I was Dylan's organist. That fact only, believe me." Langhorne uses subtler reasoning, noting how a childhood accident that left him without the use of some of his fingers meant that "since I played basically with three fingers, I couldn't develop technique to the point where I could play the entire repertoire of guitar music. I had to develop a technique based on my own aesthetics. I had pretty good control of three voices on guitar; I could control four-note voicing, but it was only with extra physical effort. I got to be a very good accompanist for that reason. Because I was really forced to *listen*."

It also may have helped, though, that Kooper and Langhorne were more in tune with the vibe of the rock generation, both musically and personally, than some of the hired hands were. Sometimes early folk-rockers, having emerged from a scene where hanging out, jamming, and crashing on friends' floors were the norm, were taken aback by the businesslike attitude of their accompanists. "I was not used to that kind of professionalism," recalled Mimi Fariña. "I'll never forget when we finished our first session, and Russ Savakus wrapped up his bass, said goodnight, and left. And I thought, 'Well! Where is he going? Aren't we all gonna go hang out somewhere? Aren't we gonna party now?' But that's how professional musicians behaved. He was a studio musician, probably on to another gig."

Others were sometimes disappointed with the quality of the sessionaires they were assigned. "None of the young drummers then were any good," says Tim Rose, who was beginning his folk-rock solo career with Columbia in the mid-'60s. "They were just learning to do it." It wasn't until he worked with Bernard Purdie that "finally I found a drummer I could communicate with, who wasn't from the old be-bop school of drumming. Why did I have to record with strangers? That makes a great deal of difference." Rose has an example at the ready of how working with a kindred spirit could make a tangible difference, hailing Felix Pappalardi for devising the piano riff that anchors Tim's effective interpretation of "Morning Dew."

Professionalism, though sometimes of the awkward variety, was usually a hallmark of Elektra, Vanguard, and Verve as they navigated their way through the folk-rock thicket. There was, however, one New York independent label that made important folk-rock waves without sticking to rulebooks of any sort. ESP Records, founded in 1963 by Bernard Stollman, was initially devoted to avant-garde free jazz by the likes of Albert Ayler, Pharoah Sanders, and Sun Ra, recording entire albums in one take, the artists often supplying artwork for the sleeves themselves. A couple of years later, ESP was ready to expand into rock music, with groups that were every bit as underground, uncompromising, and uncommercial as the label was. With the Fugs, ESP met its ideal match. "I was ecstatic," says Stollman, "because I knew I had a group that, culturally at least, had its own statement to make. Sure, they weren't musicians, really, at all. But they were poets, and I was very much taken with their statements; I consider their work very important. They were also, of course, vehemently antiwar, anti-Vietnam. This was our first project as a record company to confront the war, and try to deal with it in the media."

Maybe the Fugs "weren't musicians, really" when they made their 1965 debut for Folkways (subsequently reissued on ESP). But by the time they put out *The Fugs Second Album* in 1966, they were an actual coherent, if still fairly raw, rock band, and had also developed into better, more tuneful songwriters. Smart social satire was still the order of the day for many of the album's songs, particularly "Kill for Peace"; "Dirty Old Man," which lampooned paranoia over left-wing conspirators with a comic sneer instead of an earnest manifesto; and "Frenzy," an orgiastic balls-to-the-walls rocker celebrating free love. Their folk-rock roots, however, were still very much audible on "I Want to Know," which set a Charles Olson poem to gorgeous music, and "Morning Morning," adapted from the folk song "Morgen Morgen." There was even a preview of psychedelia in the 11-minute suite "Virgin Forest." To the shock of everyone involved, *The Fugs Second Album* made the *Billboard* Top 100, without the benefit of any singles (ESP wouldn't even put out any nationwide single releases until mid-1967) or much radio airplay of any kind. The hippie underground was starting to infiltrate the mainstream, with the most controversial and outrageous lyrics imaginable. The bold frankness of the folk tradition was not the only strain the Fugs drew upon for their weltanschauung, but it undoubtedly was a building block of their innovations.

"Until the '60s, except for country and western, American pop music, in the mainstream, was 99 percent courtship music," says the Fugs' Tuli Kupferberg. "We threw politics into the arena of popular song. Some other people did it too; a lot of folksingers did, and still do it. The Beatles did it, the Stones did it, and Billy Bragg does it. But we did it too, and we also were part of making pop music able to sing about *anything*, every aspect of human life. People in the community, work, life, family or lack of family, and sex—we were part of opening up pop music to anything people wanted to write about. I think that was very important for human culture."

For all its unconstricted abandon, even the Fugs' breakthrough had been to some degree spurred by financial considerations. "I needed a way of earning a living," says Fugs leader Ed Sanders of his band's evolution from punky jug band to relatively polished rock one. "I had just graduated from college. We had just had a baby. My bookstore [the Peace Eye on 10th Street in the East Village] made some profit, but not a lot at the time. It was more of a postmodern hangout center than an actual bookstore. I realized that to earn a living from one's art, one needed some sort of gloss of professionalism. We jumped on the electromagnetic steamboat to play clubs."

However, even at their tightest, the Fugs retained a grimy Lower East Side realism that was also heard, with more overdone comic anarchy, on an ESP album by the Holy Modal Rounders, *Indian War Whoop*. More explicit, hard-edged commentary on drugs, sex, and New York street life also found its way into the work of the Velvet Underground, who recorded its debut for Verve in 1966 (though it wasn't issued until the following year). Revisionist historians might find it inconceivable to mention the group, now venerated as punk/new wave progenitors, in a folk-rock history. The influence of folk-rock is nonetheless there to hear in their early work, in Lou Reed's hipster spin on Dylanesque vocals, and in reflective Reed compositions like "Sunday Morning" (which almost could have passed for a Mamas & the Papas song), "Pale Blue Eyes," and "I'll Be Your Mirror." Drumless 1965 demos that showed up on the Velvets' *Peel Slowly and See* box set make their sadomasochistic ode "Venus in Furs" sound like a Celtic folk ballad, with Reed uncharacteristically caricaturing Dylan's early topical songs (complete with shrill harmonica) on the otherwise unreleased "Prominent Men." The Velvet Underground was *not* a folk-rock band, overall. Yet it might not have been possible had folk-rock not opened the door for, as Kupferberg points out, songs about *anything*—even topics considered socially irredeemable—and sing-speak vocalists like Reed who projected far more personality than conventional note-hitting ability.

As ESP continued to work folk-rock with acts like Pearls Before Swine and Bruce MacKay that made the Fugs seem positively commercial, and Elektra, Vanguard, and Verve cornered the market on developing folk-rockers with simultaneous sales potential and artistic integrity, more pop-driven New York companies were also avidly strip-mining the genre. New Voice, run by Four Seasons producer Bob Crewe, bagged a one-shot folk-rock novelty hit in early 1966 with Norma Tanega's "Walkin' My Cat Named Dog." That record actually wasn't too typical of her material, which matched folky picking with New York pop-soul production. Tanega, who'd been discovered while working as a music counselor at camps in New York's Catskill Mountains, was a nearly unnoticed forerunner of the kind of personal, introspective singer-songwriting that Janis Ian and Laura Nyro would also set to savvy pop arrangements. Unlike Ian and Nyro, Tanega was handicapped by a tendency to wander into shaky, off-pitch notes in her otherwise appealing low range.

Among majors, Columbia was the leader of the folk-rock pack, if as much due to the sheer size of its roster as its astute judgement (though Clive Davis made Donovan his first signing, to the subsidiary label Epic, after becoming vice president of Columbia in the mid-'60s). The Byrds and Dylan alone put Columbia far ahead of the field, and in 1966 Simon & Garfunkel would join them as artists that were both idolized as prophets and sold huge numbers of records. "The Sound of Silence" might have seemed like an aberrant accident to some insiders, but the pair immediately followed that up with a series of well-crafted hits in 1966, including "Homeward Bound," "I Am a Rock," and the pounding, underrated "Hazy Shade of Winter." As an album act, they were slower to attain such consistency. But even on their first two rock LPs, *Sounds of Silence* and *Parsley, Sage, Rosemary and Thyme* (both from 1966), there were outstanding, eclectic songs.

Paul Simon could be dour in his hymns to alienation ("I Am a Rock" being the most famous instance), and blunt in his wry attacks on establishment figures (as on "Richard Cory," based on an Edwin Arlington Robinson poem about the suicide of the most well-respected man in town). Yet he also gave New York City one of its most jubilant unofficial anthems in "The 59th Street Bridge Song (Feelin' Groovy)," and wrote about romance with delicate complexity in "April Come She Will" and "For Emily, Whenever I May Find Her." Simon was also on his way to rivaling Dylan as folk-rock's most interpreted songwriter, one publisher telling *NME* in April that 22 of the 29 Simon songs he represented were being recorded (including, intriguingly, a planned cover of "Richard Cory" by the Animals that never was released).

Simon's early work has been criticized for a certain literary, collegiate stiffness, a trait which no doubt immediately made them leading attractions on campuses where students were constantly slaving over their own English papers. Indeed, by the end of 1966, his lyrics were being studied in high school English courses, according to *Time*. The studied craftsmanship was of real substance, however, and coated for mass appeal by Art Garfunkel's angelic voice, whether in harmony with Simon or spotlighted on lead vocals. If the dissent they provoked was more apt to be welcomed by parents in family living rooms than the more abrasive work of Bob Dylan was, that was hardly a breakthrough to be shunned.

Although Simon claimed in *The New York Times* that "I write and perform to entertain, not to teach or preach," he immediately added, "If we make them think, okay—it's an added dimension. We are just creating doubts and raising questions. There are doubts in every area." He was also wise and confident enough in his own abilities to realize he had something to offer that was both as intellectual as Dylan and filling a separate, yet similarly important, need. As he told *Disc & Music Echo* (often referred to simply as *Disc*), "Our philosophies are different—he's always dumping people more than I do. It's really easy to put someone down—it's tougher to love than to hate." This didn't stop Simon & Garfunkel from putting an unbecomingly klutzy, sour Dylan parody, "A Simple Desultory Philippic," on *Parsley, Sage, Rosemary and Thyme*.

If Simon & Garfunkel's instant adaptability to pop-folk-rock came as a surprise, it was less of a shock when their then-obscure past track record was taken into account. (And they *did* try to keep their '50s rocker past in the closet, successfully pressuring Pickwick Records to withdraw a 1966 cash-in album, misleadingly titled *Simon and Garfunkel*, of early sides the pair had recorded as Tom & Jerry.) All of that Brill Building woodshedding had not been in vain. Unlike most early folk-rock singer-songwriters, Simon knew his way around a studio, and both he and Garfunkel were used to recording with other musicians. In addition, very few Americans were aware of Simon's 1965 British LP *The Paul Simon Songbook*. That meant Simon, who was actually not a rapid songwriter, had a sizable back catalog to draw upon when Simon & Garfunkel reformed in the wake of "The Sound of Silence" and needed to come up with some product in a hurry. No less than nine songs from *The Paul Simon Songbook* would be rerecorded for Simon & Garfunkel's 1966 albums.

By this time Tom Wilson, who electrified "The Sound of Silence" into a hit, was gone from Columbia. Simon & Garfunkel's production duties were assumed by Bob Johnston, who'd already produced most of Dylan's *Highway 61 Revisited*. Johnston, a gregarious man who sees his main contribution as giving artists freedom to do their own thing, readily declares that "Paul Simon is a genius. One of the best guitar players in the goddamn world. Paul Simon [wrote] it, he played guitar, he got the musicians. I'm sure I got a few musicians or whatever. But he was the little genius behind everything, and the one that did most of that stuff. He could have done it by himself. Garfunkel sat there and twisted his hair, and did a few little vocal riffs or something in there, background. I'm not going to say [Simon] really didn't need me or [engineer Roy] Halee or anything, because we did an enormous amount of work there for years. But he'd been making records since they were teenyboppers. He should have done his records by himself." Which, as everyone knows, Simon would do with great rewards starting in the early '70s.

Columbia was not always adept at creating an organic framework for new folk-rock singer-songwriters to do their thing. It was a large corporation, used to doing things in a corporate style, and not all of their staff producers were as sympathetic to the new order as Johnston was. One who struggled against the machine was Tim Rose, who had been striving for some kind of folk-rock combination since his days in the Big Three with Cass Elliot. On his self-titled Columbia debut—released in 1967, but at least partially recorded in 1966—he was a far grittier, more soulful singer than he had been with the Big Three. He put door-of-Armageddon gravel into rock readings of "Hey Joe," Bonnie Dobson's cautionary nuclear apocalypse warning "Morning Dew" (with some rewritten lyrics), and the more ominous atom bomb aftermath tale "Come Away, Melinda" (co-written by Fred Hellerman of the Weavers, and recorded by Judy Collins in her folkie days). In incongruous but not unimpressive contrast, there was also a pull-out-the-stops version of the Barry Mann–Cynthia Weil melodrama "I'm Gonna Be Strong," which had been a hit for Gene Pitney. "Hey Joe," the murder ballad of obscure origins that was a hit for the Leaves in 1966, was given a drastically slowed-down arrangement on a Tim Rose single the same year that may have influenced Jimi Hendrix's recording of the same tune on his debut single.

Columbia might have been baffled, however, as to how to market an artist as eclectic and idiosyncratic as Rose. "When I did my first album, I knew exactly what I wanted to do," he says. "I wanted to take that core of bluegrass and country and blues, and not copy it. Not be like Fleetwood Mac, and copy American blues. I didn't want to copy anybody. I wanted to synthesize. We got close. I wasn't a rock 'n' roller, and yet I wasn't folky. That was the problem that CBS had. Clive [Davis] finally told me in 1968. He says, 'Tim, I know what you're not. I don't know what you *are*. And we just don't know how to market [you]. I know you've made some great records, but we haven't been able to sell 'em.'" Rose was also pushed to record the blue-eyed soul of "I'm Gonna Be Strong" against his wishes: "That wasn't my idea. That was, 'Do it or we don't record. We gotta have a single; try this.'" And "when it came time to do that album, [producer] Dave Rubinson didn't have time to mix it. He said, 'If you want to mix it, go in and mix it.' So I did. I mixed my first album, on eight-track. Who the fuck knew what eight-track was? Who knew what stereo was? David didn't even fucking have time to do it, he was that uninterested."

If that sounds like labels and producers might have been feeling their way around the near-virgin territory of folk-rock even more gingerly than the artists were, that's basically correct. Janis Ian confronted a Catch-22 when she was simultaneously given conflicting, inaccurate appraisals from two of the most highly regarded icons of the folk world. She recalls that Jac Holzman wanted to sign her as a writer, but not a singer, and that the same day, Judy Collins's manager Harold Leventhal told Janis she had potential as a singer, but would never make it as a writer. (To Holzman's recollection, "We did talk to her about signing with Elektra; I think we weren't willing to make a commitment to an album, but to four singles.") Says Ian, "That day taught me that no one knew what the fuck they were talking about, so I might as well go with my own instincts anyhow." Which led Ian to make it as *both* a writer and a singer.

"Until the age of 'folk rock' or 'folk music,' only jazz producers and A&R people allowed artists to actively participate in things like band choice, song choice, cover art choice, bio choice and approval, etc.," Ian goes on to note. "Most pop artists (if not all) were pre-fabricated—told what to sing, what to wear, how to move, what their name would be. [Ian, incidentally, did change her name from Janis Fink for professional purposes, but at least it was her own choice.] Folksingers, and producers like Shadow [Morton], changed all that. The studio became a joint effort rather than the bailiwick of war. People like Jerry Schoenbaum were willing to take a chance and sign us. Younger producers allowed the artist to choose their own material (not to mention write that material), and often their own band lineup."

Holzman knew that learning the ropes of electric music was a seat-of-the-pants flight. At the outset, it led to the embarrassment of Paul Butterfield bassist Jerome Arnold complaining to *Crawdaddy*, "When we recorded the first album we were dealing with engineers and A&R people [at Elektra] who had just been working with folk music and they had never done any amplified stuff before, and that put us at sort of a disadvantage." Elektra's Bounty subsidiary, which put out obscurities like Peter Antell's electric version of "The Times They Are A-Changin'" and straight rock by Toronto band Luke & the Apostles, "was a way of experimenting without infecting the Elektra name," clarifies Holzman. "Another reason we did some of the Bounty singles was to get more experience recording electric music. We discovered that nobody knew much more than we knew.

"But at the time, my thing at Elektra was, I ran scared all the time. In other words, I always assumed I knew nothing. But I was willing to learn it quickly." Though not, he says, at the expense of quality: "In many cases, records got stopped in the middle while we figured out what the hell we were doing. The Judy Collins *In My Life* album, which was so important, got stopped halfway through because we couldn't figure out what the hell we were doing. When we had it done, we didn't like it. And then along comes the glue on the Leonard Cohen songs."

Whether or not they knew what they were doing—and in the defense of figures like Holzman and Leventhal, not even the shrewdest entertainment moguls can assess talent and predict outcomes without making many grievous mistakes—the thirst for folk-rock talent was getting insatiable. There was much more money to be made in rock and pop than there had been in folk, for one thing. Managers understood this as well as record labels did. Albert Grossman was building an empire, at various points representing not just Dylan, Peter, Paul & Mary, and Ian & Sylvia, but also rising Canadian singer-songwriter Gordon Lightfoot, Richard & Mimi Fariña, Phil Ochs, Richie Havens, and the Paul Butterfield Blues Band, later expanding into full-bore rock with Janis Joplin and the Band. Harold Leventhal had Judy Collins and Tom Paxton (for a while), and picked up Arlo Guthrie, who would begin his recording career in 1967. On the West Coast, one-time coffeehouse owner Herbie Cohen handled Judy Henske, Fred Neil, Linda Ronstadt & the Stone Poneys, Tim Buckley, and a newly electrified Modern Folk Quartet, while Charlie Greene and Brian Stone snagged Sonny & Cher, Buffalo Springfield, the Daily Flash, and Bob Lind. Pat Boone even came into Ciro's and signed the folk-rock band he saw there, the Leaves, to his production company.

Grossman, Cohen, Greene, and Stone have been criticized by some of their artists for not being as driven by the music as by the dollar, and by not being as free with the dollar as they could have been. At the same time, artists needed such figures to take care of business, particularly young artistic ones without a head for financial matters. "Herbie was absolutely terrifying," says Jerry Yester. "I saw him decimate these big people who thought he was a pushover, and he would clean house on 'em. There was a time the MFQ was working, and they brought us off, like, two songs early. Herbie came up to the stage manager, got his keys out, got the point of a key in the guy's back like it was a knife, and said, 'Get 'em back on stage, motherfucker.' The guy threw the switch and rumbled us back on for two songs." In the estimation of Howard Solomon, later to manage Fred Neil, Cohen "was in it for the publishing. Everybody knocks Herbie, they'd say he didn't pay them. I keep telling 'em, you know, if he didn't do it, where would you be? He went out and *did* it, in a time when things weren't getting done."

Arthur Gorson, younger and less experienced than the likes of Grossman, had almost gotten into folk-rock management inadvertently, his background in political activism leading to a position as Phil Ochs's manager. Gorson was similar in age and background to the folk-rockers; he had done field recording in the hills of North Carolina for the Library of Congress folk archives, organized coal miners and civil rights demonstrations, played banjo and guitar, and produced benefit concerts. This perhaps made it easier for him to relate to folk-rockers than old-school folk managers like Leventhal could, and at various junctures he represented Ochs, Eric Andersen, Tom Rush, Jim & Jean, David Blue, and (briefly, in a publishing capacity) Joni Mitchell, sometimes producing the artists as well. He freely admits that at the same time, he couldn't compete with Grossman, "who was much more experienced in the cut-throat business of business. Harold Leventhal wasn't about big-time commercial success; he was a prince, a fair man who treated his clients as children that he took good care of. Albert Grossman took huge percentages from them. Harold Leventhal and [Joan Baez's manager] Manny Greenhill wanted to present a quality act in a folk environment. The Albert Grossmans of the world wanted to be forces in the music business. Grossman was tough, but also, he was brilliant with words. He was a star in his own right."

Grossman (who died in 1986) is still spoken of by friends, rivals, and clients with an awe that mixes admiration and fear. "I don't know that Albert had a great musical ear," says one of his ex-charges, Sylvia Tyson. "What he did know how to do was to keep his ear to the ground, to hear what other people were listening to. He was very good at picking up trends. He was very laissez-faire with his artists. He really believed that artists should be allowed to develop at their own speed, in their own way. In some ways that was an asset, and in other ways, it was a drawback. Because one line that I never forgot from Albert was that he said that artists should be allowed to self-destruct, if that's the way they're going." In his Folklore Center newsletter, Izzy Young would go as far as to call Grossman a co-conspirator in the self-murder of Janis Joplin.

But you won't get Geoff Muldaur of the Jim Kweskin Jug Band, also represented by Grossman, to say a bad word about his former manager: "He had the Midas touch. Albert Grossman could literally ask you, 'Which label do you want to get on? Is it going to be Capitol, is it gonna be Warner Brothers?' He had so much power, it didn't matter what anybody said, you were going to go where he wanted you to go. That's just unheard of today." Muldaur's also grateful to Grossman for getting the Kweskin Jug Band out of its Vanguard contract: "They didn't just fall off a turnip truck, those two guys [Maynard and Seymour Solomon of Vanguard]. There just happened to be tens of thousands of dollars in unpaid royalties. He audited them. It made it pretty easy to leave."

"Albert absolutely was smitten by music that moved people, wherever it came from," points out Peter Yarrow. "It didn't matter whether it was Richie Havens's amazing voice or the chemistry of Peter, Paul & Mary. He made very powerful suggestions that were very important to us. He wasn't 100 percent right, but he was in retrospect 99 percent right. He was a person of extraordinary integrity in terms of the music and the talent. And he was a vehicle by which music in America was changed. He loved Bobby [Dylan]; he nurtured him, he protected him from the press. Though Bobby and he later were in a lawsuit, there's no way not to acknowledge the extraordinary gift that Albert gave Bobby by protecting him from the forces of the business."

The super-concentration of songwriting talent and industry muscle in New York couldn't prevent the well from the danger of running dry after the flurry of folk-rock signings in 1965 and 1966. Additionally, for whatever reason, there weren't a great number of interesting folk-rock groups in New York, though folk-rock singer-songwriters were choking the Village's sidewalks. Of course there were exceptions. The Lovin' Spoonful enjoyed its greatest year in 1966 with five Top Ten singles, among them "Daydream," the jaunty whistle-while-you-walk tune that would be the most popular folk-rock song with a strong link to the jug band era. The Spoonful also proved there was more to the band than sunshine and light with its #1 hit "Summer in the City" (a collaboration between John Sebastian, Steve Boone, and John's teenage brother Mark), a hard rock celebration of New York life with compulsive descending minor keyboard stutters. For the growing rock underground, there were the Fugs and the Blues Project. The Youngbloods, the Jesse Colin Young–fronted group that was similar to the Lovin' Spoonful in their versatile good-time folk-rock, were just getting off the ground. The freshest impetus for not just folk-rock, but rock itself, was going to come from elsewhere. "I knew it was gonna come out of California," says Jac Holzman. "The east coast was too picked over."

Holzman agrees that California was also a more fertile environment for cultivating groups, rather than the type of solo performers dominating the East Coast scene. "There's a reason for it. California in that period was a hangin'-out place. People would just get together, coagulate into a group. The social scene was extremely flexible and flowing. People were in and out of bands day by day. Everybody was up at everybody's house. It was a very special dynamic that was going on, that New York was not conducive to. You don't sort of lie out under the stars in New York, get loaded, pass the guitar around, smoke a joint, do harmonies. That doesn't happen in New York that easily. But it sure happened in L.A." Though it should be noted that many of the musicians in Los Angeles bands had paid their dues in the Village. Denny Doherty's discovery, after the Mamas & the Papas' sojourn in the Virgin Islands, that most of their folk-singing friends had left New York for L.A. was not a mere aberration, but symptomatic of a large migration.

"Most of the record companies were based in the east, so I think the West Coast was more experimental," feels Michael Ochs. "I think the Byrds wouldn't have been able to record as well as they did as soon if they were on the east. There were no traditions, there were no limitations as far as, 'Well, this is not done.' It was a much more open scene, and definitely slicker, because the West Coast is much more teen-oriented. The East Coast is a little more staid."

The Byrds' impact was greater in L.A. than anywhere else, naturally. From mid-1965 onward there were many bands trying to emulate them, whether blatantly with electric 12-strings and choral harmonies, or in a more careerist sense of electrifying an eclectic mix of folk influences and trying to land hit singles through major labels. In some cases word-of-mouth raves and devoted live followings simply couldn't translate to record sales. No band suffered greater injustice than the Rising Sons, a supergroup-before-its-time featuring both Taj Mahal and Ry Cooder (and, for a while, future Spirit drummer Ed Cassidy, who was replaced by Kevin Kelley). The very way in which they formed signified how crass Hollywood commercialism could push things along faster in Tinseltown than Cambridge, from where Mahal and singer-guitarist Jesse Kincaid had moved in 1964.

"The electric switch happened in one turnaround, in the Hollywood Palladium," recalls an amused Kincaid. "There was this Teenage Fair. There were booths and displays that would appeal to teenagers, and among the booths were bands. Cooder got asked by Martin guitars to demo Martin guitars. Martin was trying to make an inroad to the teenagers and display their goods. So Ry was the guy who suggested that we all go and play at this Teenage Fair. This is L.A. now, all the bands were electric bands with kind of a 'Gloria'-type theme with an organ, bass, and drums. We said, 'Well look, why don't we find a drummer and a bass player,' since that seemed to be the direction in L.A. We just jumped into this rock 'n' roll thing, like, overnight. At the Teenage Fair we were this sensation. We were the only ones who weren't playing 'Gloria.' We were playing the blues, and people dug it. That was the move right there into electric in L.A, and there was no lookin' back."

The Rising Sons conjured an invigorating, if somewhat stylistically inconsistent, blend of blues, folk, hard rock, and Beatlesque pop. Their eclecticism was unmatched on the L.A. scene, with a repertoire including electrified country blues and traditional folk tunes, slightly spacey originals in the same vein, strong interpretations of compositions by rising local writers like Pamela Polland and Linda Albertano, and even Goffin-King's "Take a Giant Step" (which they recorded months before the Monkees released a version). In addition to playing six- and 12-string guitar, Cooder added offbeat color to the standard rock lineup with mandolin, dobro, and slide and bottleneck guitar. They also had a contract at Columbia, where they were produced by Terry Melcher, then flush with kudos for overseeing the Byrds' early hits. But for all that, just one single, with routine run-throughs of Reverend Gary Davis and Skip James blues songs, was issued before they broke up in 1966. Fortunately 20 additional tracks were recorded and, along with the single, retrieved for release on compact disc in 1992.

Both Kincaid and Rising Sons bassist Gary Marker see their Columbia affiliation as an obstacle, rather than an advantage, with record company politics leading to the mysterious cancellation of what would have been their debut album. "Terry came in and we thought he was going to try and do a Beach Boys thing, or a Byrds thing," says Marker. "And he didn't. He kind of wanted us to be a blues band or maybe a pop band. He wasn't sure. *We* weren't sure. The band was so schizophrenic anyway. It was just possibly the worst possible combination to try to put together pop records that ever existed." Chris Hillman, a cousin of Rising Sons drummer Kevin Kelley, is yet blunter: "They didn't really have the goods. There wasn't anything to promote there, in that particular time frame. If it would have been 1972, they probably would have been right on FM rock radio and doing quite well, as an eclectic type of band. But it was about five years ahead of its time in that sense. I just didn't hear it when they were together."

"There were two pulses that were strong in the band," picks up Kincaid. "One was a pop music sensibility, and the other was a blues sensibility. Terry didn't have the power to separate and make two bands out of it. There were these two directions within the band that both seemed to be strong and working pretty well, but he couldn't ever reconcile any of those into any success. Personally, in retrospect, I think Columbia was just a big mistake. Because all they did really was try to make a hit single out of us, which we didn't *have* in us. So consequently nothing got released; they didn't do an album on the band. And they never explored the acoustic textures in the band, in any kind of a way, until the very last session. We'd have been better off with Vanguard or Elektra, somebody who was into the musical style."

Artistic tugs-of-war were just the half of it, the business end of the stick providing a cautionary tale to everyone who thought a major like Columbia was the ticket to easy street. "Terry and Billy [James, Byrds publicist] wanted to manage the band, and in the end basically strong-armed us to become our managers," says Kincaid. "We didn't want them to do it. That soured everything, and Terry just kind of dumped us pretty much, didn't want to work with us anymore. Wanted a piece of the action, I suppose. But we were kind of fighting over nothing, because we never *got* any action. The ending was a little bit unpleasant. We had Terry and Billy saying, 'Well, if you don't sign with us, you're not gonna work again.' Then Taj and Ry kind of drifted off into their own areas." Mahal went far deeper into the blues in his early solo records, while Cooder became one of the most versatile Los Angeles session multi-instrumentalists, not properly starting his solo career until the 1970s.

"There was always the scary part about the biggest labels," says Michael Ochs, soon to be embroiled in the process of weeding through offers for Phil Ochs's expired Elektra contract. "There was just too much product that they were putting out that they couldn't work properly. There's no way in the world a station's going to play ten new Columbia releases at the expense of every other label. If they were pushing Dylan and Simon & Garfunkel, I'm sure Phil would have gotten lost in the shuffle, just as Eric Andersen did [on Andersen's post-Vanguard major-label releases]. Like, I couldn't believe 'Hey Joe' by Tim Rose [on Columbia] didn't sell. That was a groundbreaking single."

Another band that benefited little from big-time label/producer connections was the Modern Folk Quartet, which had electrified at the Night Owl around the same time its friends the Lovin' Spoonful did. (Cyrus Faryar of the MFQ, incidentally, says Roger McGuinn called him to see if Cyrus was interesting in joining a band Roger was forming, which turned out to be the Byrds—"I was a fool, I should have joined them.") Soon the MFQ too had made L.A. its base, with a long-running residency at the Trip. The group had a devoted live following, and stood out from the usual folk-rock horde courtesy of Henry Diltz's electrified banjo and 22-minute versions of "Swing Time." But little of that weirdness or originality translated into its obscure flop Warner Brothers singles, which were ordinary efforts falling well to the pop side of folk-rock. Phil Spector, then being surpassed left and right by new trends in popular music, signed on as the band's producer. But as with the Rising Sons' work with Terry Melcher, virtually no tangible results came of the association, despite much work in the studio. No Spector-produced tracks by the Modern Folk Quartet saw the light of day in the 1960s, unless you count the grandiose Harry Nilsson–penned "This Could Be the Night," which they sang on the soundtrack to the all-star rock concert movie *The Big T.N.T. Show*.

ot all the folk-rock bands heating up Hollywood clubs in 1965 and 1966 were from electrified ex-folkie conglomerations. The best of the first wave of blatantly Byrds-inspired outfits were the Leaves, San Fernando Valley youngsters who had cut their teeth as a standard rock group playing the fraternity house circuit, not the coffeehouse one. By early 1965, they were getting their heads turned around as regulars in the audience for Byrds sets at Ciro's. By mid-1965, they *were* the house band at Ciro's. Sure, occasionally their Byrdsian guitars and harmonies crossed the line from inspiration to imitation, as on their cover of Bob Dylan's "Love Minus Zero," or their "original" "Be With You," which was the Byrds' arrangement of "All I Really Want to Do" with some inversion here and there. And like the Rising Sons, they sometimes sounded in the midst of an identity crisis, not sure as to whether they wanted to be the Beatles, the Byrds, or the Rolling Stones. They certainly tipped hats to the Stones on their debut single, the harmonica-and-slide-powered protest song "Too Many People," a local L.A. hit in mid-1965. All that considered, the Leaves produced some quite enjoyable music, coming closer to the heart of the Byrds' appeal than any other act that would be labeled as a garage band in subsequent decades by rock historians.

"As far as a transition from rock to folk-rock, it was probably nothing more than the discovery of the Byrds," says modest Leaves founder-bassist Jim Pons. "It pleased and delighted me that we were accepted and adopted by this sophisticated musical community in Hollywood. And it also surprised me. I never thought we were anything other than good copycats, playing music in a style that we knew was currently fashionable by other bands we knew and admired."

The Leaves' sole national hit, "Hey Joe," took a song whose evolution through the folk process was a story in itself. The plaintive dirge about a man on the run to Mexico after killing his woman had been making the rounds in sets by folk troubadours for years before someone saw fit to record it. It remains a little-noted irony that one of the most popular and frequently covered songs of the 1960s, often stereotyped as a decade of peace-and-love pop music, was about a gun-wielding killer with bloodthirsty vengeance on his mind.

Although Billy Roberts was credited as author of the ominous folk-blues song, others have tried to claim its copyright over the years, particularly Dino Valenti, who only backed off after Roberts confronted the publishers who had copyrighted it in Valenti's name. Lawyer Martin Cohen (brother of manager Herbie Cohen) of Third Story Music, which administers the rights to the song on Roberts's behalf, told *MOJO* in 1998 that "it's always been difficult for me to believe that this guy [Roberts] could write this phenomenon and then never write another good song."

However, Steve Lalor, who played folk with Roberts in the early '60s with the Driftwood Singers, maintains that "Billy liked to compose. One wonders if young Jimi Hendrix ever heard him sing 'Hey Joe' during that period. When Billy and I played together, he would occasionally play 'Hey Joe' for me, in the same bluesy style that Jimi did it." Lalor's group, the Daily Flash, did a solid folk-rock cover of another respectable Roberts composition, "The Girl from North Alberta."

All this taken into account, it still remains possible the song was in part inspired by a traditional one that had been floating around. Tim Rose, who recorded one of the most famous versions, says he heard it in 1960 at a bluegrass festival. Rose heard it performed a bit later by Fred Neil's one-time duo partner Vince Martin, who told Rose he'd heard it done by "some woman," and said it was fine for Rose to use the number himself. Jesse Colin Young recorded a song with totally different lyrics and a nearly identical melody, "Four in the Morning," in 1964, its authorship credited to George Remaily.

"Hey Joe" was also a favorite of David Crosby, who had learned the song from Dino Valenti before joining the Byrds. In an early 1967 Byrds studio session recorded for broadcast on Swedish radio, David Crosby claimed that he had first arranged it as a rock 'n' roll song four or five years previously, though it seems unlikely he would have done so as early as 1962 or 1963. He further asserted that "since then, a whole lot of people have learned it from me and done it in a number of different versions all over the world." He had been lobbying for the Byrds to record it for some time before it appeared on their mid-1966 *Fifth Dimension* album, fearful that one of their L.A. rivals would beat them to the punch, which is exactly what the Leaves did.

There seems to have been some bickering, both petty and good-natured, as to which band in Los Angeles was entitled to record it first. The Byrds, Leaves, and Love were all doing it live (a little later Buffalo Springfield did it live too, though the group never recorded the tune). "It was the most requested song that Love did, the most requested tune that we did, and one of the most requested tunes that the Byrds did," Leaves singer John Beck told *Ugly Things* fanzine. "Some other bands got

Love. Left to right: Alban "Snoopy" Pfisterer, Arthur Lee, Ken Forssi, Bryan MacLean, John Echols

wise to the song and doing it, and I heard that Cory Wells [later of Three Dog Night] and the Enemys were gonna record the song [which they did, on a non-hit single produced by fellow Three Dog Night founder Danny Hutton], and that really pissed me off because they weren't entitled to it at all—they just copied it from the rest of us. We were smart enough to know that whoever put it out first was gonna have a hit with it." Love played it because one of their singer-songwriters, Bryan MacLean, had learned it during his brief stint as a roadie for the Byrds. "We did it because they did it," Love leader Arthur Lee told Andrew Sandoval in the liner notes to the *Love Story* compilation. "The Leaves asked [Love guitarist] Johnny Echols for the words to the song, and he gave them the wrong words, and it became #1 in L.A." Here was the folk process at work, all right, but in a new, hungry venomous Hollywood rock star fashion.

Any in-fighting over "Hey Joe" was really moot considering that the best version won. The Byrds' recording, with Crosby on lead vocals, was one of their sloppiest, most pedestrian performances; Love's, on its debut LP, was unimaginative. The Leaves added a devastating, screaming fuzz guitar and over-the-edge manic vocals, and certainly put a lot of work into it, placing no less than three different versions onto singles before the final one clicked. "Purists may rightly say that the Leaves weren't true to the traditional arrangement of the song, but that's not so bad," says Pons. "Everybody in Hollywood was playing the song the same way in those days. We added some fuzz guitar, a middle eight that no one else was doing, and a few other things and got lucky. I stole the bass part from an old Larry Williams song called 'Bony Moronie' and put in a couple things which I guess Noel Redding used on the slowed down version that Hendrix did later. [Love's] version of 'Hey Joe' was pretty much the same as the Byrds, interesting and entertaining in person, but without much commercial radio appeal. But there was a spirit of 'love and acceptance' which everyone aspired to in those days, and there was no apparent animosity.

"We got especially close to Arthur Lee and Love because we were similar in style, management and experience. And we always seemed to be in the same places and hanging out together. Despite the commercial success the Leaves achieved at the time, it was Love which developed a lasting legacy, largely because of the original material they contributed. It was a time when bands were becoming respected for making their own personal 'statements,' not something the Leaves were noted for." It was Love, then, that fulfilled Jac Holzman's criteria of "music that had something to say" when he made the group Elektra's first West Coast rock band.

ove, like the Leaves, was (with one exception) formed by musicians from rock backgrounds who'd had their cranial light bulbs exploded by seeing the Byrds in Hollywood. Principal singer-songwriter Arthur Lee had already done some unknown flop soul-rock singles, and produced a Rosa Lee Brooks single that brought him into contact with a then-unknown session guitarist, Jimi Hendrix. Lee subsequently became a standout anomaly on the Sunset Strip scene: an African-American who took his inspiration from the British Invasion and the Byrds, singing in a Mick Jaggerish snarl or a Johnny Mathis croon as the song demanded. "When I went to Ciro's and I saw the Byrds, it was all over with," he said in an electronic press kit promoting Rhino's *Love Story* compilation. "Because those are the kind of songs that I was writing all along. But I didn't know if that would work, or be accepted."

The supporting cast of Love was, like the Byrds, assembled from ragtag parts. Ken Forssi had been bassist in the Surfaris, the surf group famous for "Wipe Out" (although Forssi joined after that hit). Fellow songwriter and Brian Jones look-alike Bryan MacLean, one of the teenagers who'd hung out at the New Balladeer coffeehouse in the already long-ago folkie days of 1964, was the sole member to have come to rock from the folk circuit. His rock ambitions had been stoked by his brief stint as the Byrds' road manager, and his romantic, tremulous voice and songs worked as an effective counterpart to Lee's darker, more ambiguous visions. After serving the usual baptism-by-fire of a Hollywood club residency (at Bido Lito's, just off Sunset Strip), Love was signed to Elektra, its self-titled debut album appearing in the spring of 1966.

Holzman, who co-produced *Love*, contends, "I don't consider them a folk-rock band at all. I just thought they were a rock band. I did not feel it was folk-rock any more than I thought the Doors [whom Love heavily influenced] was folk-rock." Yet the evidence is there to hear: Love *was* a folk-rock band most of the time on its first LP, the arrangements heavily soaked in the chiming, circular guitars of the Byrds. Sometimes the musicians effected a curious Byrds-Rolling Stones fusion. On "My Little Red Book," which became Elektra's first chart hit single, they were just an eccentric rock band, totally transforming a cute Bacharach-David song (originally performed by Manfred Mann) into sullen punk rock. But there was also wistful folk-rock balladry on "A Message to Pretty"; a supreme downer of a first-person junkie folk-blues on "Signed D.C."; and a tearful view of nuclear apocalypse on "Mushroom Clouds." What did set them apart from the Byrds, or the Leaves, was the sheer enigma of Lee's lyrics, posing more questions than answers, alternating between raucous anger and lilting, idealistic surrealism. Bryan MacLean's occasional contributions, just as pretty melodically, were in contrast more straightforward romantic longing, though delivered with an aching fragility suggesting a man too sensitive to endure the real world for long.

Although *Love* made a relatively modest #57 on the charts (though its sales were huge in Southern California), the album was a breakthrough for Elektra on several fronts. "There was no independent record company that was functioning on both coasts," points out Holzman. "That was a leap of faith, and an expensive one for me. It didn't work out when I first tried it in 1962 to 1963. But it worked out in 1964, '65, when I went back and did it again. I just thought that it needed a fresh scene where things could happen that would be exciting, where it was not yet the #1 media center."

That sense of risk and adventure, he believes, was a crucial step in pushing Elektra ahead in its race with rival Vanguard: "Maynard and Seymour were not oriented to do what it was I was willing to do. *They* didn't pick up, go to California. They were just too straight and strange to deal with some of the people that I had to deal with. Now, I dealt with a lot of classical musicians over the years, and they can be as nuts as rock musicians. But they have a common language. Maynard and Seymour [Solomon] did not have a common language with any of these artists. Do you see those guys dealing with Arthur Lee? I don't." Actually not many record execs anywhere in 1966 were prepared to deal with Lee, a guy who would walk around in one moccasin or take the stage with one boot, both as a fashion statement and because those were all the clothes he had.

"It was interesting and very cool that Love was on Elektra," says Paul Williams, who gave *Love* a long, enthusiastic review in the fourth issue of *Crawdaddy*. "That would cause folk music fans at college radio, which I was, actually, to start listening to 'Message to Pretty' and the first Love album, and discover they liked it. But they would listen to it *because* it was on Elektra. 'Message to Pretty,' you couldn't resist that if you were a folk music fan. And it wasn't just like, 'Well, I like Love, but I only like these songs.' Pretty soon you liked the whole thing. It was like you were discovering that the new rock and roll was *your* music."

Another band that Holzman desperately wanted to sign, but ultimately could not, would prove to be the Byrds' most serious challengers for the L.A. folk-rock throne. Buffalo Springfield boasted three singer-songwriters who each, on his own, could have been the focus of his own group. Two of them, Stephen Stills and Richie Furay, had done their sterile folk ensemble boot camp in New York with the Au Go-Go Singers. Their otherwise tepid 1964 album had included a Stills-sung, electric version of "High Flying Bird," and that was the direction he flung himself into when the group fell apart shortly afterward. "At that time in my life I probably didn't have as much foresight as Stephen did," says Furay. "He attempted to put together a band shortly after the Au Go-Gos that would have been modeled after the Lovin' Spoonful, only with a woman also in the band. I was working at Pratt & Whitney aircraft at the time and was asked to come down to maybe be a part of it. I couldn't see the potential and elected to go back to P&W. Steve had a lot of ambition and was certainly not afraid to take chances and try something until it worked."

The trio that would become the nexus of Buffalo Springfield ran across each other at various points in 1965 without ever all being in the same place at once. Stills met Neil Young while touring with the folk group the Company in Fort William, Ontario, where he saw Young's band, the Squires. The Squires, originally from Winnipeg, had been an ordinary rock group when they recorded their rare 1963 single, with two instrumentals crossing surf music and the Shadows. Now they were doing rock versions of "Tom Dooley," "Oh Susannah," and "Cotton Fields." "We tried to, maybe, rock 'n' roll-ize folk songs," says Squires bassist Ken Koblun, later to play briefly in Buffalo Springfield himself, as well as in the Canadian pop-folk-rock group 3's a Crowd. "Take a song like 'Comin' Round the Mountain,' the same words, in more modern fashion."

They weren't the first to think up the concept. In fact, "Tom Dooley" and "Oh Susannah" had been recorded in rocked-up arrangements by the Erik Jacobsen–produced clique of musicians in 1964. Neil Young has recalled that the Squires' "Oh Susannah" cover was based on an arrangement by the Thorns, a group that Tim Rose sang with between his stint in the Big Three and the start of his solo career. But it was still quite a novelty to come across this in April 1965, far from the Village or Sunset Strip. Stills and Young hit it off, but when Stephen tried to get in touch with him later that year to propose forming a rock group in New York, he found that Neil was now trying to make it on his own as an acoustic singer-songwriter. When Young did come down to the Village in late 1965, he discovered Stills had left for L.A. He did find time to record some solo acoustic demos at Elektra spotlighting his wraith-like, shaky voice and compellingly haunting, if inscrutable, compositions like "Sugar Mountain." He also met Richie Furay, to whom he taught another of the numbers he'd demoed at Elektra, "Nowadays Clancy Can't Even Sing."

Stills had been banging his head against the folk-rock door for months in Los Angeles. He auditioned for the Monkees, but didn't make the finals, where a part went to his friend and fellow ex-Village folkie Peter Tork, who played with Stills in a short-lived L.A. trio that also included bassist Ron Long. Plans to put together a group with Van Dyke Parks failed, although they did write a few songs together. Kenny Edwards, later of the Stone Poneys, remembers meeting with Stills at a deli to mull over working together, but nothing came of it. Stills, getting desperate, pulled his ultimate stunt of bravado. "I got in touch with Stephen, who had moved to California by now," remembers Furay. "He assured me, 'Come on out.' He had a band and all he needed was another singer. That's all I needed. I took care of unfinished business, quit my job at P&W, and headed west. I must admit when I got to L.A., I was a little taken back because Steve *didn't* have a band at that time. It was me and him. There were a couple of weeks of real soul-searching whether or not I would stick it out."

Fortunately, Neil Young was just as determined to get a band happening, even if it also meant behaving in a way some would find reckless or foolhardy. He'd endured his own skein of hard knocks in late 1965 and early 1966. A law unto himself even as a 20-year-old, he'd gone against the tide by trading in his electric Gretsch for a 12-string acoustic guitar. Attempts to establish himself as a solo acoustic folksinger in Toronto's hip Yorkville district met with near starvation, and he joined a straight rock group, the Mynah Birds, fronted by singer Ricky James Matthews. A deal with Motown, for whom they actually recorded about an album's worth of unreleased material, went up in smoke when it was discovered that Matthews was AWOL from the US navy (Matthews would later resurface as funk star Rick James). The Mynah Birds broke up, and Young, together with the group's bassist Bruce Palmer, decided to travel to Los Angeles in hopes of finding Stills, for whom they had no address or telephone number. Their arduous journey to L.A., in a Pontiac hearse, was financed by pawning Mynah Birds equipment that did not actually belong to them.

The subsequent meeting of Young, Palmer, Stills, and Furay in Los Angeles in April 1966 might be the most famous, and most serendipitous, of all folk-rock legends. Having searched for Stills for days without success, a dispirited Young and Palmer were heading north for San Francisco in a Sunset Boulevard traffic jam when Stills, Furay, and friend/mentor Barry Friedman passed them in a van going the opposite direction. On a collective hunch that a hearse with Ontario license plates could belong to no one *but* Neil Young, Friedman did a U-turn and managed to catch up with the vehicle and get it to pull over. After reuniting, everyone went back to Friedman's house, where Stills and Furay played the version they'd worked up of "Nowadays Clancy Can't Even Sing." Buffalo Springfield formed, pretty much, then and there. A third Canadian, Dewey Martin, was drafted in on drums, as Michael Clarke had been for the Byrds, because he looked appropriate, or more appropriate than a drummer who had rehearsed with them briefly, Billy Mundi. Martin did bring some substantial experience to the role: he'd played live with the Dillards, Roy Orbison, and the Modern Folk Quartet, as well as fronting and actually recording with his own rock band in the northwest, Sir Raleigh and the Coupons.

Incredibly, within a couple of weeks or so of forming, Buffalo Springfield was opening for the Byrds on a short Californian tour. Right after that the group began a lengthy residency at the Whisky-A-Go-Go, now established as the hottest venue on Sunset Strip. While the group in some respects resembled the Byrds, clearly it was distinct and special. The vocals, whether lead or in harmony, were an exhilarating complementary blend of Furay's clear, winsome tenor, Stills's lived-in bluesy grit, and Young's one-of-a-kind high, cracking whine. No other band, past or present, was as skillful at blending acoustic country-folk guitar runs and strums with screaming, demented electric solos or more delicate reverb-flecked electric picking. The quintet was a more dynamic live act than the Byrds were, and, in Stills and Young, had prodigiously talented songwriters who both offset and drew out the best in each other, much as Lennon and McCartney did. Stills's no-nonsense, won't-take-no-guff approach spilled over from real life to his songs; Young, more influenced by Dylan, took puzzling neurotic wordplay to new heights. Both nonetheless had melodic gifts nearly on par with those of the Beatles.

In time, however, those talents would create ego battles that would keep the group from *becoming* the American Beatles. "One of the criteria for the Buffalo Springfield [was] that each one of the people in it were able to hold an audience on their own, as a single performer on stage," says Barry Friedman (soon to change his name to Frazier Mohawk), who managed the band before getting edged out by Sonny & Cher's handlers, Charlie Greene and Brian Stone. "Which is probably why it blew up. It was just too much." Before they imploded, they made some great music, in a fashion that at least initially made the sum greater than the parts rather than showcasing individuals. "As long as the group was together with the original members, it worked," says Furay. "It didn't matter who wrote what song. We figured out a way to find the blend! Sometimes it would be by unison singing, especially Steve and myself. He would give my voice some edge, and I'd smooth out his, and together it had an awesome blend. Neil, getting involved with [producer-arranger] Jack Nitzsche, found ways to experiment with his songs. Steve and I were more straightahead. Both guys were excellent song-writers and very advanced for as young as we were. Neil combined more of the folk-rock influence while Steve's were more rock- and blues-influenced. I guess I added the country influence."

Buffalo Springfield never had a purer folk-rock blend than on its first album, *Buffalo Spring-field* (issued by Atlantic in late 1966). Stills songs like "Everybody's Wrong," "Pay the Price," and "Go and Say Goodbye" combined effervescent country-folk harmonies with a dynamic rock thrust. Early Young efforts like "Flying on the Ground Is Wrong" and "Out of My Mind" were less folk-oriented and harder to get one's mind around, with their brooding self-doubts and hints of para-noia, yet equally tuneful. Frequent flourishes of hollow-body Gretsch guitar, playing Chet Atkins–like country licks with reverb added by a Bigsby wiggle stick, added the kind of past-future dynamic at which the Byrds also excelled. "Go and Say Goodbye," anchored by a riff learned from a bluegrass instrumental called "Salt Creek" that Chris Hillman had taught Stills, and "Nowadays Clancy Can't Even Sing" were paired for Buffalo Springfield's debut single. But it made little impact beyond L.A., in part because of the then-controversial use of the word "damn" in the latter song. Not until Stills plugged into the zeitgeist of youth unrest on Sunset Strip would the Springfield be rewarded with its sole national smash, "For What It's Worth."

While Buffalo Springfield, Love, and the Byrds were managing to both spearhead the counter-culture and (to maniacally variegated success) sell both albums and singles, there was also a far more blatantly commercial pop dimension to the Los Angeles folk-rock scene. One of the rea-sons that so many figureheads—McGuinn, Stills, Young, Phillips, et al.—had migrated to the coast in the first place was because Hollywood, as much as its glitz was despised by the in-crowd, offered so many more opportunities for quick advancement than anywhere else. Hardheaded self-starters like Stills were one of the crowd in Manhattan, where his ambitions to get into the Lovin' Spoon-ful had been brushed off. People who had a vision and stuck to it, like Stills and Roger McGuinn, found Hollywood more open. Its record labels (whether based solely in L.A. or branches of majors and prominent indies founded in New York) were starting to rival New York in power and influ-ence, and were not nearly as set in their ways.

L.A. was also the base of numerous major national television shows, at a time when prime-time variety hours were much more likely to showcase rock acts than they would be in subsequent decades. New releases by the Byrds were often accompanied by large ads in trade magazines that simultaneously plugged the records and upcoming TV appearances. Naturally it was much more convenient to book slots on Hollywood-based programs if the artists were in town already. When

Buffalo Springfield at their first photo session, 1966. Left to right, leaning against tree: Richie Furay, Dewey Martin, Neil Young, Stephen Stills, Bruce Palmer. In the upper left corner is Dickie Davis, the group's road manager

a couple of L.A. producers decided to manufacture a Beatlesque rock group to star in a TV series of its own, *The Monkees*, they put out the call for vague young hipster types. With so many aspiring folk-rockers pounding the pavement, it was no accident that one of the failed applicants was Stephen Stills, and that two of the winners, Peter Tork and Michael Nesmith, were more folk musicians than actors.

Nesmith had already put out some records (sometimes under the name of Michael Blessing), including a cover of Buffy Sainte-Marie's "Until It's Time for You to Go," and bad satires of both draft dodgers ("The New Recruit") and Bob Dylan-like folksingers ("What's the Trouble, Officer?"). He had some credibility in the folk-rock community, having emceed Monday night hoots at the Troubadour, and written a song, "Mary, Mary," which the Paul Butterfield Blues Band recorded in 1966 (produced, as it happens, by Barry Friedman). Nesmith tended to be the writer of the Monkees' most credible original material, usually in a country-influenced folk-rock style that anticipated his future work in country-rock. The Monkees-folk-rock connection doesn't end there. Jerry Yester of the Modern Folk Quartet says that *Monkees* co-producer Bob Rafelson offered him the position that went to Peter Tork, a plan that fell through when Yester said he wouldn't take part unless the entire MFQ was cast as the group starring in the show. The MFQ's Chip Douglas went on to produce the Monkees and act as a virtual fifth member on what is regarded as their best album, *Headquarters*.

Indeed there was not nearly as much gauche commercialism separating the Monkees and the bold Sunset Strip vanguard as is commonly believed. The Byrds, Buffalo Springfield, and Barry McGuire might have been landing hit records with social protest both gentle and incendiary, but they were tethered to a corporate media establishment in order to deliver those messages. On television's *Where the Action Is* you could see the Byrds lip-synching "The Bells of Rhymney" in front of vacuous, grinning beach bunnies and muscle men cavorting on diving boards and plastic inner tubes. When Buffalo Springfield mimed to "For What It's Worth" on *The Smothers Brothers Show*, they suffered the insertion of a shot of Tom Smothers pointing a gun at the camera during the line "there's a man with a gun over there," to a burst of uproarious canned laughter. When he hosted *Hullaballoo*, Barry McGuire put on his best shit-eating grin for a duet with Brenda Lee on "Gotta Get A-Goin'," a song that could have fit snugly onto a sing-along-with-Mitch Miller LP. Also on *Hullaballoo*, host Michael Landon wiggled through a lounge version of "You Were on My Mind" during a ludicrous medley that also featured the Byrds singing along with a pit-band snatch of "Do You Believe in Magic" with all the enthusiasm of boys forced to rehearse for the Sunday school pageant when they would much rather have been out playing baseball or chasing girls.

Did it affect their art? No, but overhype did cause at least one song by a leading band to get written and recorded that otherwise never would have been even vaguely considered. In August 1967, L.A. radio station KHJ ran a contest in which a listener would write the words for Buffalo Springfield to put to music, for a prize of $1,000 cash and publishing royalties. So it was that Richie Furay of Buffalo Springfield was saddled with the task of writing a melody for teenager Micki Callen's poem "The Hour of Not Quite Rain," which ended up on the group's third album. To his credit he pulled it off, even if it meant devising particularly tortuous phrasing to make the words fit, swamped with orchestration in the absence of anything resembling a standard rock rhythm.

Slick manufactured packaging also spilled over to some L.A. folk-rock records in the frequent use of session musicians. Of course session musicians played just as strong a role in New York folk-rock, but a difference was that those were usually by solo artists, and that the best New York folk-rock groups, from the Lovin' Spoonful to the Fugs, were adamant that they play their own tunes whenever possible. This didn't mean, however, that some records with backup by L.A.'s clique of ace players—often built around first-call instrumentalists such as drummers Hal Blaine and Earl Palmer, bassist and sometime 12-string guitarist Carol Kaye, and keyboardist Leon Russell—weren't good.

Kaye is unembarrassed about her role in covering for groups, or at least members of groups, who did not play on their own records. "You simply did not use musicians who had no idea of how to play and invent inside the studios, let alone have the technique, gear, and the experience one needed to do studio work. There were sometimes a few players who tried it and were glad to get out of the studios. They were so scared and sometimes humiliated they couldn't do it—their technique and inexperience showing and costing the studio time and money with delays etc.... it's not a place for non-studio musicians who don't make their living recording hit records 12–16 hours a day." The best, and certainly most successful, group to rely heavily on session musicians was the Mamas & the Papas. They had six consecutive Top Five hits in 1966 and the first half of 1967: "California Dreamin'," "Monday, Monday," "I Saw Her Again," "Words of Love," "Dedicated to the One I Love," and "Creeque Alley." As live footage of the group from the 1967 Monterey Pop Festival inadvertently demonstrated, they always sounded much better in the studio.

"It was more happening than calculated," says Lou Adler, who used many of the same Hollywood session vets for his productions with the Mamas & the Papas and Barry McGuire. "I was using basically the same rhythm section for whomever I was doing. And that rhythm section, being very accomplished musicians, were able to fit Jan & Dean, Barry McGuire, Johnny Rivers, Mamas & Papas. John [Phillips] was the perfect kind of writer to work with, because he was open to discussions, and open to feels. He was a very accomplished songwriter, able to cross those lines. He wasn't just a folk writer; he was a *songwriter*. So that if he wrote a good song and I was able to bring that rhythm section to it, we could make it work. If you listen to the Mamas and Papas records, it sounds like they're playing, as opposed to some of the other groups of that day, where you hear a track, and you know they're singing over it."

Adler credits Denny Doherty and Michelle Phillips as the key forces pressuring Phillips to move into rock, and Doherty in turn is quick to credit Phillips's innate talents: "It wasn't folk music we took in. They were contemporary songs that John had written when he was a folk musician. All the stuff that had been boiling in the back burner in his brain that he couldn't bring out in folk music because it didn't fit, he couldn't sell it in his head." Folk-rock, in Doherty's estimation, "freed him up. He didn't have to fit a pigeonhole that was folk music, that had to be this English country garden, or American western, or protest, or any of that shit. Rock 'n' roll? Write anything you want. Any thing at all. There are no rules in rock 'n' roll. And away he went. When they said, 'What else you got in the back of your brain?,' out it came; songs that he had in his repertoire, and just put away. He [had] said, it's not gonna work in folk music, and I don't know what the hell this is. It was rock 'n' roll, is what he was into. And eventually *he* got into it."

What Phillips had a special knack for was, rather than commenting directly on issues, capturing internal moods ("Monday, Monday" and "California Dreamin'") and the shifting attitudes of the times toward romantic and sexual promiscuity ("I Saw Her Again," "Go Where You Wanna Go," "Got a Feelin'"). Here real life made its impact on art, though relatively few listeners knew that Phillips's marriage was getting rocked by, among other things, his wife's affairs with Gene Clark and Denny Doherty. "He was going through a situation with Michelle where there were different thoughts coming through his mind, as opposed to what he was writing as a folk writer," says Adler. "He was now experiencing romance and the love affairs, the rollercoaster that she was putting him on." It was all wrapped in such luscious production, with instantly memorable melodies, heavenly strings, and blockbuster vocal harmonies, that any personal traumas motivating the songs came out as joyous-sounding melodrama on record.

Doherty occasionally cowrote with Phillips, as on "I Saw Her Again" and B-side gem "Got a Feelin'," a lovely tune whose hypnotic melody belied an undercurrent of worry over Michelle Phillips's roving eye. "Who knew it was as personal as it turned out to be? At that point, Michelle and I had said hello, that's it. We hadn't done anything else. But maybe John had a feeling about something that she was doing with somebody else. To write a song would take days, because he would go into therapy for three days. He wouldn't come out of the hole, he'd stay in there, he'd get it finished. He'd write the song ten different ways, and you'd take bits and pieces of all ten different ways, and make it again, and keep going."

The Mamas & the Papas' real-life soap opera found its way into one of their biggest hits in a manner that saw the song used as a weapon for cruel and unusual punishment. "'I Saw Her Again' was a song I had the melody and the changes for, but I had no idea for a song," recounts a wry Doherty. "By then, Michelle and I had said more than hello, and John wrote the lyrics—'I saw her again last night, and I know that I shouldn't.' Because he wanted me to sing it onstage every night. 'Here you are—sing about it!' So the writing of those kinds of songs was therapeutic, but not until they were done."

For Phillips was nothing if not, as he wrote in one of his best songs, a "Straight Shooter." "The whole rock and roll thing has expanded enough, at least for a writer, that all you have to do is write about your own experiences," he told *NME*. "That's the greatest thing for a writer—not to have to be phony at all. You just put down exactly how you feel about things and people like it."

The Mamas & the Papas' and McGuire's label, Dunhill, was also home to other artists who espoused a feel-good brand of sunny L.A. folk-rock. Several of them were overseen by the songwriting-production team of P.F. Sloan and Steve Barri. They turned the Grass Roots, originally an actual band from the San Francisco Bay Area, into a front for their pop-folk-rock creations, played in the studio by them and session musicians. Under this guise the Grass Roots had a pleasant if lightweight folk-rock hit, "Where Were You When I Needed You," before evolving into a straight pop act in which Sloan was not involved.

Indeed the Dunhill stable, and particularly the Mamas & the Papas, were instrumental to establishing a whole school of lightweight L.A. rock. Retroactively dubbed "sunshine pop" by rock historians, this emulated the harmonies and lush arrangements of the Mamas & the Papas without the depth of Phillips's or Sloan's songwriting. Even so, numerous sunshine pop artists, such as Spanky and Our Gang, had members with genuine folk roots that still peeked out through the harmonies.

Sloan tended to reserve his more serious statements for his own records. He continued, often in collaboration with Steve Barri, to churn out cheery pop-rock hits for the likes of Herman & the Hermits ("A Must to Avoid"), the Turtles ("You Baby"), and Johnny Rivers ("Secret Agent Man") at the same time he was delving into the dark recesses of his soul on his solo outings. Perhaps because his multiple roles gave him the image of a made-to-order hack, his solo outings were until quite

The Mamas and the Papas. Left to right: Michelle Phillips, Denny Doherty, Cass Elliot, John Phillips

recently almost wholly dismissed by rock critics. Viewed with less prejudice, his two albums endure as the work of an outstanding singer-songwriter. A songwriter that sometimes sounded like a junior version of Dylan, it's true. But one with a far greater grasp of melodic pop dynamics, whether reflecting the confusion of his generation in "The Sins of a Family" and "What Exactly's the Matter with Me," posing as a rebel-on-his-own-terms in "Take Me for What I'm Worth" (a British hit for the Searchers), or tendering guarded, wistful romance in the lost non-LP single "I Can't Help But Wonder, Elizabeth." Sloan's solo work was not properly promoted and encouraged, and ground to a near-halt in 1967, when he moved to New York and gradually disappeared from the industry. Sloan told biographer Stephen J. McParland (in *P.F.—Travelling on a Barefoot Rocky Road*) that Dunhill partner Jay Lasker threatened him and his family with grievous bodily harm unless he left town in 24 hours, although it is not entirely clear why an executive would sabotage the career of one of his most profitable writer-producers.

The most opulent Los Angeles pop-folk-rock hit was Bob Lind's "Elusive Butterfly," arranged by Jack Nitzsche, the gadfly who embellished recordings by everyone from the Rolling Stones to (at the end of the decade) Neil Young. "World Pacific was all jazz before me, and Liberty Records bought the label," says Lind. "Dick Bock, who owned it and started it, treated it as a sort of Ma and Pa kind of label. Liberty forced themselves to watch a closer bottom line. They saw in me an opportunity to compete with Dylan and some of these other guys that were on these other labels, in that genre that we call folk-rock.

"At the time, I hadn't fully formed as a writer. Certainly I wasn't singing very well, and my melodies were tremendously limited. My melodies are bland, my melodies just stand there. Jack Nitzsche found something in my melodies that I didn't know was there, and he enhanced it. He made the songs beautiful." Specifically he gave "Elusive Butterfly" a string arrangement, which enabled it to soar without dripping sentiment. That was crucial to putting Lind's somewhat lugubrious compositions and vocals over, whether they were imagistic romantic songs like "Elusive Butterfly" or portraits of disconnected modern life like "Mr. Zero."

"I had a tremendous amount of passion, a tremendous amount of energy, and a tremendous amount of adolescent or post-adolescent gush," admits Lind. "There was a lot of sap in me, and those songs were wordy. I hadn't learned how to edit myself. But nevertheless, there was some raw enthusiasm, a love of words, although I had not learned how to temper that. So the songs went on and on and on and on. The songs were 20 verses long. 'Elusive Butterfly' itself was originally five verses, and there was only two cut for the single. I never did record those other three verses."

While Lind never had another hit, he quickly became one of folk-rock's more interpreted songwriters, attracting covers by the Turtles ("Down in Suburbia"), the Blues Project ("Cheryl's Goin' Home"), Marianne Faithfull ("Counting"), and Yardbirds lead singer Keith Relf ("Mr. Zero"). His true contribution, though, was widening the parameters of folk-rock's arrangements with "Elusive Butterfly," which helped demonstrate that strings could work to the advantage of a folk-based singer-songwriter. Although Nitzsche hardly limited himself to folk-rock in the studio, he added similar ornaments to barely-known mid-'60s singles by Judy Henske, including a cover of Fred Neil's "The Dolphins" with downright spooky Spectoresque ambience. (Way back in 1961, long before Henske or anyone else was thinking about folk-rock, Nitzsche had also produced a strange gospel-pop-rock single, "That's Enough"/"Oh, Didn't He Ramble," by Judy Hart, who turns out to have been then-folksinger Henske using a pseudonym.) Says an admiring Henske, "He was completely courageous, willing to try anything, and willing to try to get the money anywhere to do whatever his idea was." He also added a graceful touch to some of the songs on the 1966 Elektra debut of Tim Buckley, the label's first venture into young West Coast–based folk-rock singer-songwriters.

By the summer of 1966, Los Angeles folk-rock had diversified in many unforeseen exciting ways since the Byrds kicked it off a couple of long years before. At the beginning of 1966, given all the furious competition, there may have been doubts as to who remained the city's leading lights. The group's second album, *Turn! Turn! Turn!* (released at the end of 1965), would have been considered a major triumph by most other acts, but wasn't quite up to the magnificence of *Mr. Tambourine Man*. Gene Clark's compositions remained compellingly brooding, and he showed signs of developing an abstract Dylanesque lyricism in "Set You Free This Time." But Roger McGuinn and David Crosby were yet to develop into composers of that order, still devising above-average Beatlesque songs, and the LP's Dylan covers weren't nearly as remarkable as those on *Mr. Tambourine Man*.

McGuinn, Clark, and Crosby had an extraordinary collaboration in waiting, however, that would advance not just their own music but all of rock into an unimagined brave new world. Crosby had for some time been feeding McGuinn large doses of both the Indian music of Ravi Shankar and the free-jazz improvisations of John Coltrane, playing their recordings repeatedly in their mobile home during a lengthy tour. "We had a cassette player, and a tape of Ravi Shankar on one side, and John Coltrane on the other," said McGuinn in Mike Jahn's *Rock*. "We played that damn thing 50 or 100 times, through a Fender amplifier that was plugged into an alternator in the car."

The band, and particularly McGuinn, applied those lessons to a new Clark-McGuinn-Crosby composition, "Eight Miles High." The song was by itself an impressive diary of their disoriented sensations during their 1965 tour of England. With all the members making heroic contributions, however, it was turned into something entirely alien when the Byrds had finished with it in the studio. Chris Hillman pushed it into gear with a pulverizing, ominous unaccompanied bass line that remains one of rock's all-time great intros. McGuinn uncorked three mesmerizing solos that put Coltrane's fractured free jazz and Shankar's ragas onto the electric 12-string, with a fury and speed that perfectly complemented the song's flight metaphors. The harmonies were never more ghostly and uplifting than they were during the verses, evoking a mysterious land both seductive and menacing. It all came to a crashing end as the tempos accelerated and the keys rose, easing to a finale much like an airplane cruising onto a landing strip.

Much as they had with folk-rock in late 1964 and early 1965, the Byrds were so far ahead of the curve that they were playing a music that had yet to be named. It was psychedelic rock, and for the song's title alone, many assumed it was drug-inspired. For that reason *Bill Gavin's Record Report* opined in April that the single implied "encouragement and/or approval of the use of marijuana and LSD," and thus could not be recommended for airplay. The Byrds, particularly McGuinn, always denied this. They repeatedly emphasized that the song's title referred to the altitude of an airplane in flight, such as the plane they had flown to England. Six miles high, they admitted, would have been the more aeronautically correct altitude for a jet in flight, but Clark lobbied for "Eight Miles High" as it sounded better and more poetic. The damage was done, though. "Eight Miles High" rose no higher than #14, and the Byrds never had another Top 20 hit.

McGuinn insists that underneath all the psychedelic frenzy, "Eight Miles High" is "a folk song. It tells a story like a folk song. It's the story of the Byrds going to England in '65, of experiencing cultural shock. 'The signs on the street that say where you're going'—street signs in America are always on posts and they're at corners and intersections. In England, they're up on the second or third floor story of a side of a building, and they're big rectangular things. And some of them have fallen off, and you really can't tell where you are a lot. So [there's the line] 'signs on the street that say where you're going are somewhere just being their own.'

"'Rain gray town, known for its sound' is London," he continues. "'In places, small faces unbound' are the audiences we encountered. "Eight miles high, and when you touch down, you'll find that it's stranger than known'—that's the airplane ride to England . . . when you get there, it's different. 'Nowhere is there warmth to be found, among those afraid of losing their ground'—that was the bands and the press and the people who had kind of a chip on their shoulder about, 'What do you mean, you're America's answer to the Beatles?' It's a folk song, there's no question in my mind about that." Furthermore, McGuinn views with approval how the folk process itself has shaped radically different subsequent cover versions of the song by acoustic guitar virtuoso Leo Kottke and 1980s punk band Hüsker Dü, who "did it with a lot of anger and clashing chords."

After "Eight Miles High" there was no weight (not that there ever had been) to detractors' accusations that the group was merely riding on Dylan's coattails. Dylan couldn't have come up with "Eight Miles High," and nor could anyone else. The Byrds were now in a league of their own. They would continue to take folk-rock into the stratosphere throughout 1966 and 1967, their mid-1966 *Fifth Dimension* (issued a few months after the "Eight Miles High" single) marking the first album by major early folk-rockers to break away from folk-rock into folk-rock-psychedelia. And where they flew, many would follow.

6

folk-rockin'

around the world

ew York and Hollywood's domination of the record and entertainment industry translated into a concurrent domination of the folk-rock scene. It would be a mistake, however, to conclude that all of the important folk-rock artists and records of the mid-'60s sprung out of Greenwich Village and Sunset Strip, as unexpectedly and inexplicably as the stork delivers the newborn baby. It sometimes seemed that way, so sudden and overwhelming was the downpour from those two metropolises. In reality, within a year of "Mr. Tambourine Man" hitting #1, uncounted folk-rock artists and records—some excellent, some mediocre, some awful—had sprouted all across North America, and sometimes across the Atlantic. Many different breeds of performers tried their hand at folk-rock at one point or another, from the unlikeliest of celebrity pop stars and senior citizen folksingers to the humblest garage bands. Folk-rock had truly become an international language among youth, even among some who couldn't speak English.

"The folk-rock fusion of the '60s was many-layered, and also ushered in a revolution, one of lyric and subject," believes Donovan. "The folk scene had the message, the pop scene had the media; 'the media is the message' was a phrase then. But really, the frivolous entertainment of pop music was infiltrated consciously by me and others who saw the potential to reach millions of youths who were not in the bohemian worlds of London, Paris, Rome, Berlin, New York, San Francisco, and Los Angeles." Thus, he continues, he and others were able to advocate "free speech, and put down bigotry, hypocrisy, and all the other sicknesses of western society which had been able to continue due to control of the media by post-war propaganda governments. Folk-rock would change all this."

onovan was unquestionably the greatest ambassador of folk-rock from the British Isles, and indeed the only one from the UK who could rightly claim a place in the pantheon of the greatest mid-'60s folk-rockers from anywhere. Certainly his three dozen or so recordings from 1965 had already established him as a troubadour who could deliver the message of folk protest and poesy with a sharper acumen for pop crossover than any other British singer. Those tracks, including the hits "Catch the Wind" and "Colours," were still largely in an acoustic framework, though the "Catch the Wind" single had light strings.

Even at that time, however, he was starting to edge toward rock in the studio. Some basic, almost skifflish bass and drums are heard on cuts like "You're Gonna Need Somebody on Your Bond" (which he had performed live, with an electric band, as early as April 1965, on the televised *NME* Pollwinners Concert). The truest indicator of the balance between old and new that would make him an international superstar, however, lay in "Sunny Goodge Street," from his second British LP, *Fairytale* (released October 1965). The full band setting drew in flute, horn, cello, double bass, and brush drums, owing much to cool jazz-blues as well as to pop, folk, and rock.

"When I heard jazz, classical music, Billie Holiday and [classical cellist] Pablo Casals, and read poetry and new wave literature, I saw all these merging into one sound," he reminisces. "Musically, 'Sunny Goodge Street' was a jazz fusion even when I played it acoustic. The fusion of the musical styles announced the breaking down of barriers and categories in music. I not only introduced a Celtic-rock fusion. I absorbed and merged world music as a whole, in keeping with the truth that all music is one, as all humans are one race on the one planet." He'd given fair warning of his ambitions as early as August 1965, when he told *Melody Maker* he was "doing a modern jazz record. I will be singing blues over French horns and it will be a Charlie Mingus–style arrangement."

"'Sunny Goodge Street' anticipates the spiritual journey which generations would follow," Donovan adds. "The lyric may just be the first mention of a spiritual path in popular music, with the lines 'the magician he sparkles in satin and velvet, you gaze at his splendour with eyes you've not used yet'—referring to the opening of awareness which was growing in the generation of the late '50s and early '60s. Folk-rock is not only a sound. It is a manifesto of change."

Donovan's utopianism would flower, and reward him with an American #1 single in the summer of 1966, when he made the jump from near-acoustic folk-pop to fully electric psychedelic folk-rock in nearly one bound on "Sunshine Superman." Originally titled "For John and Paul" in honor of the Beatles' principal singer-songwriters, it portrayed a protagonist as indestructible and omniscient as the Beatles themselves were regarded by this time. Bongos, booming bass, harpsichord, and scorching electric guitar swoops by then-session man Jimmy Page gave supercharged force to Donovan's new persona as super-suave avatar of good vibes. Hot on its heels was another hippie manifesto, "Mellow Yellow," which made #2 in 1966 and incited more experimental banana-peel smoking than any old wives' tale could. Just as "Eight Miles High" had wholly unshackled the Byrds from lingering suspicions that they wouldn't have gotten anywhere without Dylan's repertoire, so did "Sunshine Superman" finally lay to rest accusations that Donovan was a mere Dylan imitator. Donovan Leitch was now lord of his own realm, a magical fairyland-type kingdom that reached back to the prehistoric Celtic past and forward to a brilliant future, allowing for some harsh blasts of reality from time to time.

The *Sunshine Superman* album, also released in 1966 (and begun in late 1965), was a keystone of both folk-rock and early psychedelia in its spinning wheel of musical colors and moods. At heart, Donovan was still a folk minstrel, with his odes to long-lost medieval fiefdoms ("Guinevere"),

Ferris wheels, and three king fishers. But there were also cynical, hard-edged takes on the trendy exploitation of the burgeoning hippie counterculture ("Season of the Witch") and the breakneck pace of Sunset Strip ("The Trip"); swinging jazz-blues on "Bert's Blues," its title inspired by the great British folk-blues guitarist Bert Jansch; dreamy meditations on a mysterious psychedelic guru, "The Fat Angel" (written for Cass Elliot), which name-checked Jefferson Airplane long before that upcoming California folk-rock group became famous; and "Celeste," which was simply one of the most delicate, enchanting romantic songs in all of folk-rock, one that evoked a mythical muse rather than a real-life woman. At various points, the folk-based tunes were embroidered with sitars, violins, horns, crackling blues-rock guitar, tinkling harpsichords, and buzzing organs. Arranger John Cameron, producer Mickie Most, and sidemen like Shawn Phillips were instrumental to the beauty of the final work. But Donovan's songs and benign, breathy vocals were always the focal points.

"I wanted a pop sensibility in my records which would appeal to the mass, and introduce my unique vocals and lyrics of a curious call to adventure," Donovan explains. "Mickie was the best pop producer around [Most also worked with the Animals, Herman's Hermits, and Lulu], and he saw immediately I needed an arranger of experimental talent. Shawn Phillips particularly was my sideman for the fusion of the sitar and my music; Shawn also is an excellent 12-string player. Mickie would choose the singles, and I would explore the albums with John. Like mini-movies, each song took the listener into the strange world I create in my art. Before the Beatles' *Sgt. Pepper* album used film score arrangements to Beatle songs, I was doing it on my *Sunshine Superman* album in my Abbey Road sessions I did with Mickie Most and John Cameron, in the same Studio One the Beatles would use for their coming masterpieces." In fact Donovan recalls Most asking him not to play *Sunshine Superman* to McCartney in advance of its release, fearing that the Beatles might be influenced by some of its ideas, though "of course I did.

"There were folk purists who would not dream of plugging a banjo into an amp, let alone a guitar, [as] I did on *Sunshine Superman* in May of 1966. It would take Dylan and me to break the mold that year—he with direct blues-gospel-soul organ and electric guitar, me with my Celtic-rock guitar fusion: electric violins, classical instruments, and Latin-rock-jazz grooves."

"We decided that a change of style and appearance was necessary to start with," said Most of the *Sunshine Superman* era in 1968 in *Record Mirror*. "Off went the cap, jeans, jacket and harmonica in favor of more varied clothes. We continued the acoustic guitar sound, but gave Donovan more scope in available backings. The first session was really a sight. There were flowers and incense distributed throughout the studio, odd characters with zapata moustaches sprawled majestically in all corners of the room and Don right in the center. This was years before the San Francisco scene began [Most was exaggerating somewhat; Jefferson Airplane were already recording by this time and were only a year or so away from their first American hits], so these fellows were somewhat ahead."

"My influence with Don is that I would play the guitar, and create a set of chord structures," says Phillips, who had already recorded a couple of folk albums of note in Britain as an expatriate American folksinger, and would go on to create his own eclectic body of work, though mostly after the 1960s. "I would be playing, and he'd start making up words. This happened five or six times. 'Guinevere,' 'Fat Angel,' 'Season of the Witch,' 'King Fishers,' that's the way they came about. Don sort of worked pretty much like I do. I have a basic structure, and then I go to the different people and say, 'Here's my vision. Now put your vision to it.' Because I only used absolutely the best players I could find, I trust their judgement implicitly. It was due to the producer and the arranger that a lot of those tunes turned out the way they did. Also, you know, they were definitely going for a commercial market. I have exactly the opposite problem. I keep going in the studio and going, 'Man, we gotta get commercial.' And it turns out so fucking esoteric. But I love it, so I leave it."

Donovan would never make another album as consistent as *Sunshine Superman*. But it did establish the format he would explore in various shades throughout the rest of the 1960s: gentle, optimistic minstrelsy, embellished by imaginative florid production, sometimes leaving the songs to stand alone as acoustic works, other times unleashing some ferocious psychedelic hard rock guitars. Some revisionist critics have come down hard on his work, dismissing him as a doe-eyed innocent whose philosophies were not nearly as pertinent and enduring as those of the more hard-nosed, skeptical songwriters. It is important to realize, however, that not only is that stereotype inaccurate (as listening to "Season of the Witch" and "Hurdy Gurdy Man" verifies), but that at the time, Donovan was considered very much a big deal, revered almost on the level of Dylan. He ate up more ink than almost anyone else in the British music weeklies, which gave the impression of a Renaissance man of the counterculture.

According to various reports in the last half of the 1960s, Donovan was writing music for a modern psychedelic love ballet, with choreography by Toni Basil (yes, the same woman who would have a bubblegum new wave hit with "Micky" 15 years later). Donovan was writing the script and entire musical score for a film in which he was to star, playing the role of a wandering minstrel, with Paul McCartney likely to make a guest appearance. Donovan was being invited to write the music and narration for a film about the Maharishi. Donovan wanted to do vaudeville in a West End Theater, with "a combination of musicians with me which would enable me to get virtually any sound which I wanted" (reported *Record Mirror*). Donovan was playing with a 28-member orchestra in the Royal Festival Hall. Donovan was everywhere. All the while he kept on scoring Transatlantic hits, with "Wear Your Love Like Heaven," "There Is a Mountain," "Jennifer Juniper," "Hurdy Gurdy Man," "Epistle to Dippy," and "Atlantis." And not everyone gave automatic precedence to Dylan's more misanthropic outings of the period, some finding in Donovan a more humanistic prophet. As Graham Nash, then of the Hollies, told *NME* in 1966, "Donovan's new compositions to me excel Dylan's because Don has this tremendous ability to transmit tenderness and kindness through his work."

Donovan's reputation suffered somewhat in his homeland due to a complicated contractual/management dispute that found him unable to release any records during the first half of 1966. Unusually, "Sunshine Superman" (and the attendant album) were cleared for American release by the summer, but the singer remained unable to put out records in Britain until December 1966, by which time "Sunshine Superman" had already topped and left the American charts. "Sunshine Superman" did make #2 in the UK nonetheless, but both the *Sunshine Superman* (some of which had actually been recorded in Hollywood) and *Mellow Yellow* LPs were chopped up for piecemeal British consumption. (This was a reversal of the usual practice, where British LPs were chopped

Donovan

up for piecemeal consumption in America.) So fast was rock music on the move in late 1966 and early 1967 that the delay in release of some of his best material in the UK created the misleading impression in Britain that Donovan was following trends, rather than helping to set them.

As a consequence Donovan's innovations were not properly appreciated in the UK, and he'd always be more popular in the States. "A man or woman is always treated with more respect outside his or her own land," he speculates. "I was appreciated in the States better than anywhere. It is known that to make it in the USA is to be truly arrived, as the varied eclectic musical tastes of America have trained American audiences to be very aware of what's really innovative, and what's derivative and shallow." As a land with many acoustic folksingers, it could have been expected that droves of British musicians would follow Donovan's lead by amplifying and diversifying, much as had been the case in the United States, leading to similar international acclaim. Remarkably, this did not happen.

ther than Donovan, there was not a single other major standout folk-rock performer to emerge from the British Isles in the mid-'60s. Or, at least, folk-rock as that label is usually applied by Yankees. That's to say, music that borrowed large amounts from both folk and rock, often in roughly equal doses, with an end product that synthesized both genres, admittedly falling closer to rock than to folk. Donovan did this. No one else in Britain did so with similar quality and consistency until the emergence of Fairport Convention and some similar artists two or three years later, an eternity in 1960s pop annals.

That's not an entirely welcome appraisal to some rock and folk fans and critics, who would point to a thriving British mid-'60s folk scene. Folk clubs dotted around the country were hosting standout emerging and veteran performers like Bert Jansch, Davy Graham, John Renbourn, Al Stewart, the nucleus of the Incredible String Band, Roy Harper, Sandy Denny, Dave Cousins, Shirley Collins, and others. Most of those artists were beginning to write original material, sometimes of striking quality. Bert Jansch did so on his stark, haunting debut album, featuring the chilling lament for the death of a friend from heroin, "Needle of Death." All of those musicians would eventually move into folk-rock for a while or for good, making some fine-to-great music. What they were recording in 1965 and 1966, however, was with rare exceptions acoustic folk music, not rock or folk-rock. It is no more satisfying to dub *Bert Jansch* a folk-rock album, on the tenuous grounds that it was rock in spirit, than it is to use the same criteria to call *The Freewheelin' Bob Dylan* a rock record.

Davy Graham, in the studio at any rate, was the figure making the boldest moves to more expansive musical backdrops. His January 1965 album *Folk, Blues and Beyond* boasted a lean, snazzy full jazz-blues rhythm section, including drums, and melded blues, folk, jazz, and Middle Eastern music together in an invigorating fashion. Undoubtedly Graham was influential on expanding the eclecticism of both folk guitarists and British rock axemen such as Richard Thompson and Jimmy Page. Certainly he impressed Paul Simon during his stint in Britain, as Simon & Garfunkel adapted one of Graham's set pieces, the instrumental "Anji," for their *Sounds of Silence* album. Graham would continue to mine this world-folk-fusion on other obscure, more erratic 1960s albums, making sure to throw in imaginative covers of Beatles songs. But they weren't quite rock records, lacking the brash electrified guitars and rock-slanted material that would push them over that border, even as they were akin in some respects to the risk-taking of many of the era's folk-rock and psychedelic musicians. (It did not help, either, that Graham's vocals were colorless and adequate at best.)

There were various flop attempts, half-assed and half-hearted, to manage some kind of folk-rock blend in Britain in 1965 and 1966. Wagnerian chanteuse Nico, the year before joining the Velvet Underground, had done a cover of Gordon Lightfoot's "I'm Not Saying" whose dancing strings emulated the mid-'60s pop recordings of Marianne Faithfull. Like Faithfull's earliest recordings, "I'm Not Saying" had been produced by Andrew Loog Oldham, who says it was "an effort by me to cop that Bob Lind 'Elusive Butterfly' sound," though in fact Nico's single came out a couple of months before Lind's. Its B-side, the wholly acoustic "The Last Mile," was a true oddity, co-written by Oldham and Jimmy Page, the latter of whom produced and played guitar, along with Brian Jones (who had played on "I'm Not Saying").

Faithfull herself had some pop-folk crossover hits with pastoral, orchestral arrangements and backup vocal choirs that were really too mild to qualify as folk-rock, although some were decent. She did get into rootsier folk on the albums *Come My Way* and *North Country Maid*. The latter LP, from 1966, was an overlooked, surprisingly respectable effort mixing traditional folk tunes with covers of tunes by Donovan, Bert Jansch, Tom Paxton, and Ewan MacColl. On the more fully arranged cuts, there was a folk-blues swing that anticipated similar work done in the style a bit later by the group Jansch was soon to form with John Renbourn, the Pentangle; her readings of the trad folk classics "She Moved Through the Fair" and "Wild Mountain Thyme" were bolstered by adventurous sitar. Faithfull's recording career sputtered through the rest of the decade, though, as she got caught up in a volatile romance with Mick Jagger. It wasn't until the 1970s, her voice lowered by about a full octave and her life scarred by personal traumas, that she would emerge as a truly personal singer-songwriter.

There were also pop-folk hits with a mild beat by the Seekers and the Silkie, a Peter, Paul & Mary–like combo who took the Beatles' "You've Got to Hide Your Love Away" into the American Top Ten. There were tentative gropes at pop-folk-rock on rare singles by Roy Harper (whose "Take Me Into Your Eyes" sounds more like the Zombies than folk-rock) and Al Stewart (on "The Elf"). There were crummy Dylan covers, like Jonathan King's "Just Like a Woman." There was forced George Martin–produced jug band-pop with "Babe I'm Leaving" by the Levee Breakers, who featured John Martyn's future wife Beverley. There were utterly bland sub-Donovan outings by Belfast singer-songwriter David McWilliams, who was to Donovan what David Blue was to Dylan in the States, getting photographed in wardrobes that seemed pinched from outtakes of Donovan LP sleeves. There were, of course, covers of Donovan songs, Deena Webster's "Summer Day Reflection Song" being one of the better ones.

Donovan's associates made some little-heard ventures into rock as well. Mick Softley, who'd written some standout songs on Donovan's 1965 recordings, was one of the few acoustic singer-songwriters to get into electrified music on some obscure singles that were interesting but not exceptional. Mac MacLeod, who had taught Donovan in finger-picking and clawhammer guitar techniques, made some even more obscure recordings, sometimes with electric bands, that never saw wide distribution. Shawn Phillips, as noted actually an American living in Britain, made his odd fusion of pop-folk-rock with dramatic *West Side Story*–type vocals in "Summer Came," and then did a single, "Stargazer," that took *Sunshine Superman*–style sounds to more frenzied raga-rock pitch.

At the end of the day, however, you'd have a hard time assembling a first-rate CD anthology of pre-1967 material by thoroughbred British folk-rock artists not named Donovan. The reasons for this have much to do not just with the differences between US and UK folk, but also the differing evolutions of British and American rock. In a sense, the path American musicians like Roger McGuinn and the Byrds had taken from folk to rock in 1964 and 1965 had already been negotiated by British musicians in their teenage years. During the late-'50s skiffle boom, British teenagers had learned to play folk-based music on acoustic instruments, then expanding into rock with electric equipment by the beginning of the '60s. The Beatles were the most famous examples, but there were hundreds of others. In that manner, the transition from folk to rock had already happened in the UK in the late '50s and early '60s, albeit among musicians that were mostly years away from making their recording debuts. Many leading talents of the British Invasion had already been playing electric rock for five years or so by the time the Beatles had made it in the States. The blinding revelations of the glories of playing electric music were lessons that had already been learned and put into action.

Pete Frame, who founded the British rock magazine *Zigzag* in the late '60s (and is now well known as the writer/illustrator behind the *Family Trees* series of rock history books and television shows), was among the relatively few British music fans who was a zealous fan of both rock and folk in the mid-'60s. "You had gospel and hillbilly and stuff on the radio in America, rhythm and blues and so on," explains Frame, who ran a folk club in Luton that hosted appearances by Jansch, Renbourn, Paxton, Maddy Prior (later of Steeleye Span), and others. "We had absolutely none of that. We had no kind of ethnic world music at all.

"Skiffle was like *our* rock 'n' roll. It was based on hillbilly music, Carter Family, Woody Guthrie, with blues, Leadbelly, and whoever else thrown in. Our skiffle was partly acoustic, where people were just playing with acoustic guitars and tea chest basses and so on. The most popular exponent skiffle was Lonnie Donegan, and he had an electric rock band, basically. He was playing what you would call folk-rock in 1956, because he had an electric guitar in his band, and got the drum kit, and was singing Woody Guthrie songs and Leadbelly songs, 'Rock Island Line' and 'Grand Coulee Dam.' So he was what you might call the progenitor of folk-rock.

"Lots of people in my generation grew up liking folk music and rock music, and certainly a lot of those Liverpool groups and the Animals. 'House of the Rising Sun,' all the skiffle groups used to sing that. So even though they got it from Dylan or whatever, they would have been familiar with the song anyway. But [then] skiffle went two ways. Some went into rhythm and blues, like Alexis Korner, who'd been in skiffle, and some went into traditional English folk music." Consequently, by the time American folkies began plugging in, Frame says, "in England, it had all happened already. Buddy Holly was a huge influence in turning people onto electric; he played three chords and everyone could copy them. The guitar solo in the middle of 'Peggy Sue' was dead easy to copy. So all the bands in Liverpool certainly were bashing away and playing electrically." Those who had chosen folk over rock and R&B when the skiffle era closed, having made their choice and stuck with it, were more rigid in their ways than their American counterparts when faced with the opportunity to combine folk and rock years later. Most of them passed, at least initially.

"The next big division came when the folk boom came," Frame continues. "People took sides then. People like Donovan were despised, because they represented a very unpleasant, sort of commercial angle. I loved Donovan, I thought he was fantastic. But to a lot of people, he represented the sort of commercial end of folk music." Apart from concern over flak from purists, why didn't singer-songwriters like Al Stewart, who weren't writing material that was poles apart from Donovan, follow him into rock right away? "Because they were kind of johnny-came-latelys. They hadn't been around for that long. And they'd found a little niche, which was acoustic folk music. They knew they could go play the clubs. I guess they just were singer-songwriters, and saw themselves as such, and didn't want to expand into a band situation." Perhaps Stewart didn't want to jeopardize an opportunity he'd found in folk that he couldn't get in rock, which he'd actually played in groups such as Tony Blackburn & the Sabres in the early '60s. It wasn't until he memorized everything from Dylan's *Freewheelin'* and *Times They Are A-Changin'* albums to get a residency at Bunjies coffee bar in London in early 1965 that his career really started to advance.

Some note that divisions between purists and more open-minded upcomers could be so sharp as to even discourage the performance of any newly penned material, let alone electric music. "In England it seems there exists a unique phenomena whereby people are very much into their own persuasion of music to the exclusion of all others, and have very little time for anything that doesn't fit into their particular pigeonhole," says Mac MacLeod. "On this side of the Atlantic, prior to Davy Graham, it was either the Cecil Sharp folk collections or performers and songwriters such as Ewan MacColl who dominated the scene, with material very much with a traditional bias. There was one occasion when I was touring the West Country with John Renbourn in '64 when a fight nearly developed at a club in Exeter between the audience and ourselves because we weren't sticking to English traditional roots!

"I can still remember my sentiments up until 1965 when anything folk or blues-orientated would be completely unacceptable unless accompanied by acoustic instruments, and this seemed to be shared by most of my contemporaries. This period marked a change in myself and many of my contemporaries' approach as the influences broadened to such new wave talents as Davy Graham, Bert Jansch, Paul Simon, and the trailblazer, Dylan. With the advent of American artists playing in English clubs it brought a freshness to the folk process of traditional songs and styles doing the two-way Atlantic crossing."

There was some influence working the other way as well. On his first visit to England, Dylan had learned the traditional songs "Scarborough Fair" and "Lord Franklin" from Martin Carthy, using the tunes as the basis for two tracks on his *Freewheelin'* album ("Girl from the North Country" and "Bob Dylan's Dream" respectively). "Masters of War," from the same LP, lifted the melody from the British trad song "Nottamun Town," while the tune of "With God on Our Side" was taken from British folksinger Dominic Behan's "The Patriot's Game." ("I don't want to hear nobody like Dominic Behan, man!" grimaces Dylan after Behan's name is mentioned in the hotel party scene in *Don't Look Back*.) Paul Simon and Bruce Woodley of the Seekers wrote a few songs together, including "Red Rubber Ball," made into a bouncy pop hit by American group the Cyrkle. Simon & Garfunkel covered both Graham's "Anji" and, much more controversially, "Scarborough Fair," using Martin Carthy's arrangement. That in turn generated a feud between Simon and Carthy that lasted until they finally buried the hatchet by dueting together on the song at a 2000 Simon concert in London. Simon did, Carthy told Matt Swaine of *Guitarist* in 1999, make a tragicomic one-off payment to him after Simon & Garfunkel's rendition had become famous with its inclusion on *Parsley, Sage, Rosemary and Thyme*: "After splitting up with my first wife, I rang Paul asking if the money had come through. I told him I wanted to buy a house for £1800. 'That's amazing,' he said, 'The payout is exactly £1800.'"

In all, though, the influence of British folk on American folk-rock was minimal. It would not be until the end of the 1960s that spates of UK groups and singer-songwriters—foremost among them Fairport Convention, Pentangle, the Strawbs, Al Stewart, Nick Drake, and the Incredible String Band, many of whom had roots in the acoustic mid-'60s British folk scene—came up with distinctly British spins on folk-rock. Though most of the American folk-rock giants had big hits in the old country in the mid-'60s, "our folk-rock boom, such as it was, was pitiful," bewails Frame. "It was just a bunch of beat groups who sang Dylan songs for a couple of months, just because it was fashionable. They would do a really bad recording of 'She Belongs to Me' or something like that."

In a further dispiriting twist, some American folk-rock hits made the UK charts not in their original versions, but in far inferior, watered-down middle-of-the-road pop covers by British singers. The originators were not amused. Bob Lind had to share Top Five honors with Val Doonican (Lind: "He was like Andy Williams") for "Elusive Butterfly." The Bachelors, not Simon & Garfunkel, had a hit with "The Sound of Silence," prompting Paul Simon to diplomatically inform *NME*, "I think it strange that the Bachelors should choose to record a very hip song when their style is so conflicting." (They weren't done with the Simon catalog, covering "Punky's Dilemma" in 1969.) Crispian St. Peters had a Transatlantic Top Five with "The Pied Piper," originally an obscure single by the Changin' Times, a New York duo including future Woodstock Festival co-organizer Artie Kornfeld.

St. Peters also took a sluggish reading of "You Were on My Mind," which he actually learned from Barry McGuire's cover rather than the We Five hit or the Ian & Sylvia original, to #2 in Britain. "The thing that really pissed me off was that he put his name on it," carps the song's author, Sylvia Tyson. "He claimed he'd written it. I think it got straightened out pretty quickly, but I thought it was pretty stupid on his part." What's more, some chowderheads on a subsequent Ian & Sylvia British tour booed the couple when they played "You Were on My Mind" in concert. The "folk Nazis," as Sylvia Tyson calls them, were upset at the pair for including a song that had been such a big pop hit, even though Sylvia had written the tune and Ian & Sylvia had not gotten the hit themselves, on either side of the ocean.

"There is a simple answer to this," states Donovan when asked why so few of his acoustic folk peers followed him into full-blown folk-rock. "In the States, Roger McGuinn was influenced by the Beatles and his own folk roots. McGuinn did *not* play the electric as an amplified acoustic. This allowed him to use electric guitar in a powerful way, while the fewer UK folk stars who went electric used the electric guitar as an amplified acoustic. I was the exception as I also heard what the Beatles had done in breaking the pop band mold in 1963, and the Kinks and the Who. I was not shy in developing a power-riff Celtic-rock fusion, while most other UK folk stars were not into raising the level like McGuinn and I would naturally do.

"It is also true that to leave behind a tradition is a bold act, and the American folk-rock stars were brave enough to try it out and act the rock star with folk commitment. The radio is our friend, [but] many folk purists still had an aversion to governmental institutions, a kind of class consciousness that prevented them from actually leaving the folk club in their head and storming the establishment citadels to take over the radio media. Americans, with their revolutionary past, could do just this, and I did in Europe. It is a question of boldness and expression."

Pete Frame has a warier take on the influence of class on British folk and rock. Folk purist snobbery, he thinks, "wasn't to do with working class or middle class or upper class. It was more to do with being aloof and feeling superior and exclusive, and feeling that rock music was beneath one. It was kid stuff, whereas folk music had great heritage and tradition and was worthy and was historically important. For intelligent grammar school kids or public school kids to go into the music business was unheard of. You just did not do it. You went into a secure job." By 1965, he adds, this had changed, a shift not fully appreciated by folk elitists. "People like Mick Jagger, Paul Jones, John Lennon, they were the first generation of sharp kids who could have gone on to university and got degrees, but dropped out and became musicians. The Zombies were extremely clever kids who were sort of like the Genesis of their day. They dumped out of school and decided, instead of going off to university, they'd be in a band. And that was a great innovation. Pete Seeger had been doing that in the '30s in America [when Seeger had dropped out of Harvard, where he had been in the same class as future president John F. Kennedy]."

Donovan aside, as usual, folk-rock's main presence in British mid-'60s pop was not via bona fide folk-rock artists, but in British groups that used folk-rock as one more paint in which to occasionally dip their brushes, thereby adding to their rapidly widening musical mosaics. Manfred Mann never was a folk-rock band per se but, as previously discussed, made some very effective Dylan covers. The Animals weren't folk-rock either, but did much to get the style started with "House of the Rising Sun," and later did a cool cover of Donovan's "Hey Gyp." The Beatles flirted with folk-rock magnificently in several 1965 recordings, particularly the *Rubber Soul* album, though by 1966 they were off on other brilliant tangents with *Revolver*. The Rolling Stones, as much as they cultivated an image of roughhouse blues-rock bad boys, made exquisite and stately folk-rock on "Lady Jane," with its Brian Jones-stroked dulcimer. "To me, 'Lady Jane' is very Elizabethan," Keith Richards told *Rolling Stone* in 1971. "Brian was getting into dulcimer then. Because he dug Richard Fariña. We were also listening to a lot of Appalachian music then too," as can be heard on another superb folky Jagger-Richards original of that time, "Sittin' on a Fence."

And the list goes on. The Kinks had hit singles with wry social commentary and folky strummed guitars on "Well Respected Man" and "Dedicated Follower of Fashion," around the same time their lead guitarist Dave Davies enthused to *NME* in January 1966 about American folk guitarist Spider John Koerner: "He gets these fantastically weird chords by having the extra string on his guitar. A friend of mine recently lent me some of his records and I was fascinated by the hypnotic tempos he uses on the numbers." (Davies also inferred those techniques would be used on an unnamed future Kinks single, possibly the one that turned out to be "Dedicated Follower of Fashion.") Incidentally, in case it's tempting to view "Well Respected Man" as composer Ray Davies's putdown of the establishment in general, Kinks producer Shel Talmy reveals that it was actually about one stuffed shirt in particular: "'Well Respected Man' was written, of course, about one of their managers. And to this day, I'm not sure he even knows about it. We were all in on the joke at the time, but"—Talmy laughs—"I'm not sure *he* was."

Them, with Van Morrison on vocals, did a corking cover of Paul Simon's "Richard Cory," as well as taking on "It's All Over Now, Baby Blue." A Morrison-less Them spinoff band, the Belfast Gypsies, did a tense, howling version of the latter song that qualifies as one of the greatest unknown Dylan covers ever. The Pretty Things did a convincing job on "London Town," a folk song that Donovan had done on a 1964 demo. The Hollies spent time at Simon & Garfunkel recording sessions, and did Simon's "I Am a Rock," as well as rocking up Peter, Paul & Mary's "Very Last Day" and making their own naive attempt to write brisk, vaguely malcontent folk-rock on "Too Many People." The Searchers had folk-rock hits in 1966 with P.F. Sloan's "Take Me for What I'm Worth" and Jagger-Richards's "Take It or Leave It," and Searchers' guitarist John McNally regrets that they and their management did not take songwriting more seriously: "If you'd had said, like Andrew Loog Oldham did to the

Stones, 'Go and write some songs, and don't come out 'til you've written 'em' to us, we'd have been a much better act."

As excellent as some of them were, all of these folk-rock outings were detours rather than the main course. Folk-rock's true importance to British Invasion rock was to elevate the lyrical ambitions and social consciousness of its greatest artists. That was apparent even in some songs that had no sonic debts to folk or folk-rock, such as the Yardbirds' proto-psychedelic "Shapes of Things," which decried war and environmental devastation. "It's really an observation song. Along the lines of the type of things Bob Lind is writing, which I admire very much," remarked one of the song's cowriters, Yardbirds bassist Paul Samwell-Smith, to *NME* at the time. "I like to think it's a little above the rut. You need some poetry inside you, sure, although I didn't really do any of it at school; nothing you could really write about. Dylan has been my main inspiration. Before Dylan, would anybody have appreciated the lyrics of our hit 'Shapes of Things'? People seemed to like the things I was trying to express but before Dylan came along they wouldn't have thought twice. You see, Dylan made lyrics *important*."

I t wasn't just the British Invasion bands that were motivated to occasionally adopt folk-rock postures. Back in the States, there were a host of unlikely folk-rockers for a day, or at least for a single. Sometimes they were awful; sometimes they were hugely entertaining; and sometimes they created skeletons in the closets of performers that would eventually make their mark in far different styles. Perhaps many, or most, of them were insincere. Together, they formed an overlooked testament to just how huge folk-rock's influence was in the mid-'60s, and, admittedly, just how desperate the industry was to capitalize on the trend while it lasted.

In Michigan, a young Bob Seger hurled forth a terrific derivation of Bob Dylan's "Tombstone Blues" on his double-timed single "Persecution Smith." ("Make your goal the first foxhole!" he screamed with delight at one point.) That radical stance was somewhat undercut by another Seger single of the time, "Ballad of the Yellow Beret" (issued under the name the Beach Bums), a wretched poke in the eyes of draft dodgers. In Texas, a young Johnny Winter wove a hypnotic, surreal folk-rock tale of what a statue would think if it could come to life on "Birds Don't Row Boats"—gotta love that title—which had extremely attractive Byrdsian guitar lines and harmonies. Also in Texas, the Loose Ends came up with a strong single, "A Free Soul," that matched a late 1965-Beatles/Kinks influence with adamant I've-gotta-do-my-own-thing lyrics. Their guitarist, a teenaged T-Bone Burnett, would within a decade be backing Bob Dylan himself on the Rolling Thunder Revue tour. The Sir Douglas Quintet, the unclassifiably diverse Texas roots-rock band led by Doug Sahm, did an Animals-like arrangement of "It Was in the Pines," the desperate folk lament recorded by everyone (under different titles) from Leadbelly to Nirvana. Sahm, a friend of Dylan's, had jammed with Dylan and Brian Jones in late 1965, and it was even reported (in *Record Mirror*) that they had wanted to record, but couldn't find a studio that was open.

In Hollywood, Leon Russell, not content to limit himself to session work on recordings by folk-rockers and others, got in on the game early with the August 1965 single "Everybody's Talking 'Bout the Young." This was everything-but-the-kitchen-sink-folk-rock, co-produced by Russell himself, the lyrics scooting over themes of the assertion of youthful identity, anti-Vietnam War protest, and nuclear detonation angst, backed by snarling Dylanesque vocals and angry high-pitched distorted guitars. The single passed unnoticed, and it wasn't until the very end of the 1960s that Russell truly launched his career as a singer-songwriter and solo recording artist. Another struggling L.A. singer-songwriter, Warren Zevon, took a shot as half of the folk-rockish male-female duo Lyme & Cybelle, whose obscure 1966 single of Dylan's "If You Gotta Go, Go Now" seemed to be trying its hardest to make it into a clap-along good-time pop song.

Also in Hollywood, Byrds chum Peter Fonda recorded an entire unreleased album around late 1966, with input from Roger McGuinn, David Crosby, and South African jazz star Hugh Masekela. One Fonda single, "November Nights," did escape on Masekela's small Chisa label in 1967, written by a then-unknown Gram Parsons. The song, an average pop-folker with serviceable, characterless vocals by Fonda and some trumpet, perhaps by Masekela, did nothing commercially. Fonda's greatest musical contributions to folk-rock were destined not to be his records, but his selections of recordings by the Byrds, Roger McGuinn, the Band, and the Holy Modal Rounders for the *Easy Rider* soundtrack at the end of the decade.

Back in Michigan again, popular young DJ Terry Knight had quit radio to pursue a career as a folksinger, eventually hooking up with the Pack to record a string of singles that unapologetically mimicked various top artists of the day. Bob Dylan's "Positively 4th Street" was sliced and diced for "Dimestore Debutante"; the Lovin' Spoonful's good-time bounce appropriated for "What's on Your Mind"; and Donovan's *Sunshine Superman* mystique draped on "Dirty Lady." His best 45, "A Change on the Way," one of those "the new generation will usher in a new dawn for mankind" anthems, is thus probably about as sincere as a presidential campaign promise, but was a likable melancholy soft folk-rocker despite itself. Knight, a bland vocalist and thoroughly unoriginal songwriter, was making no bones about it: he wanted to be on the side that was winning. Financially speaking, that is, and he got his wish when he stepped behind the scenes to manage his former backup group, the Pack, who became Grand Funk Railroad.

Link Wray, the raunchy instrumental guitar gonzo of "Rumble" fame, did not limit his vocal folk-rock stint to his cover of Dylan's "Girl from the North Country." Its B-side, the Wray original "You Hurt Me So," was clearly inspired by the Beatles' "You've Got to Hide Your Love Away," albeit with a more countrified twang, and a guitar riff that oinked around like a cross between a wah-wah pedal and Jew's harp. (In fairness, Wray's interest in folkish music was not a one-off detour, as in the early 1970s he recorded several interesting low-key vocal albums for Polydor that were suffused with a heavy Band influence.) Captain Beefheart, before diving into defiantly inaccessible avant-garde blues-free jazz-rock, made his stab at folk-rock with the 1965 demo acetate "Call on Me." Unearthed for the Beefheart rarities box *Grow Fins*, it boasted a decidedly Byrdsy guitar line, an appealing melody, and a vocal so sweetly restrained that one is tempted to believe that it might not actually be Don Van Vliet singing (although the Captain is given the vocal credit). By the time it was revived for official release on the debut Beefheart album *Safe As Milk* (which featured the guitar of ex-Rising Sons virtuoso Ry Cooder), it was delivered with Van Vliet's habitual bluesy yowl.

In Nashville, a man as far in spirit from Captain Beefheart as was humanly imaginable, country star George Hamilton IV, became the first artist to release a Joni Mitchell composition with the Chet Atkins–produced "Urge for Going," recorded in late 1966 and a #7 country hit in early 1967. It's not a bad version, actually, the opening three-note burst of steel guitar strongly echoing the style of Bruce Langhorne, who played on Tom Rush's cover of the same song. Also in Nashville, Elvis Presley did an understated version of Dylan's "Tomorrow Is a Long Time" in mid-1966, five years before a Dylan recording of the song was first released. Said Dylan of Presley's interpretation of the song in *Rolling Stone*, "That's the one recording I treasure the most."

Non-American artists made some weird folk-rock one-offs as well. Chad & Jeremy, the sub-Peter & Gordon British Invasion duo that was always far more popular in the States than at home, put a parodic (and not incredibly amusing) sub-Dylan vocal and catalog-of-complaint lyrics onto their 1966 single "Teenage Failure." Like the song's protagonist, the single was a failure, reaching just #131 in the charts. In Canada, the Guess Who recorded what may have been the very first cover of a Neil Young song in early 1967 with "Flying on the Ground Is Wrong." The Guess Who, like Young, emerged as performers in Winnipeg, and knew Neil dating back to his pre-Buffalo Springfield days in his early band the Squires; when Young returned to the city in 1966 to visit his mother, the Guess Who learned the tune from an acetate of the first Buffalo Springfield LP. The arrangement, with AM radio-friendly flugelhorn and glockenspiel on the bridge, was inferior to the original, if undeniably more pop-slanted than the Springfield's version.

In late 1965, an 18-year-old Barry Gibb penned "And the Children Laughing" for his group, the Bee Gees, still based in Australia and more than a year away from sailing to London for their ultra-successful shot at international fame and fortune. Relegated to an October '65 B-side, this stab at social consciousness featured loud Byrdsy guitars and harmonies, as well as self-righteous castigation of a neighbor who won't shake hands with a "Negro," still an acceptable term for blacks even among liberals at the time. Rex Harrison's son Noel, better known as an actor on the TV series *The Girl from U.N.C.L.E.* than anything else, did a ridiculously jaunty cover of P.F. Sloan's "The Man Behind the Red Balloon" on a 1966 single. The following year Harrison, who had actually been performing in British folk clubs since the late '50s, gave many singles-buyers their first taste of a Leonard Cohen song when he took "Suzanne" to #56. The folk-rock celebrity-vocal connection spilled into nepotism, most likely, when the Rooney Brothers, all sons of Mickey Rooney, managed to issue an unmemorable folk-rock cover of the traditional song "Geordie" on a Columbia single. More successful were Dino, Desi & Billy, fronted by the sons of Dean Martin and Desi Arnaz. Their manifesto of revolutionary independence was the Lee Hazlewood–authored "The Rebel Kind," another late-1965 B-side. They probably didn't rebel against the older generation too hard, though, considering that their label, Reprise, was also home not only to Dean Martin, but his pal Frank Sinatra, who had founded the company.

Much more established artists, whether of their own volition or acceding to management/label pressure or both, also made their strange, little-noted dashes in and out of the folk-rock arena. *Johnny Rivers Rocks the Folk* might have spotlighted rocked-up versions of traditional folk songs, as well as "Catch the Wind" and "Mr. Tambourine Man." But in the end it was not so much an inspiring hybrid as an irresistible force meeting an immovable object, sounding like just another Johnny Rivers album, with its handclapping go-go rhythms, female vocals, and nightclub rock arrangements.

Jimmy Gilmer, whose "Sugar Shack" had been one of the last gargantuan squeaky-clean American rock hits before the Beatles arrived, made an inconsequential *Folkbeat* album in New Mexico in 1965 with Buddy Holly producer Norman Petty containing folk-rock covers of Dylan, Buffy Sainte-Marie, Tom Paxton, and trad folk tunes. Gilmer at least came by his folk connections honestly, having met Paxton in Greenwich Village through mutual friend Carolyn Hester. It was through Hester that Gilmer learned Paxton's "Bottle of Wine," and in 1968, Gilmer's band the Fireballs had an unexpected Top Ten hit with the song. Far from being offended, Paxton cackles, "That was such fun, because it was flat-out jukebox rock 'n' roll. It was really a kick to hear that. I think it would have gone to number one, except the one woman who oversaw the ABC radio station affiliates banned it, because it was about wine."

In mid-1965, the Beach Boys did a live-in-the-studio "unplugged" album of sorts, designed to simulate an informal recording at a *Beach Boys' Party!* Among the pseudo-hootenanny items was an unlikely cover of Bob Dylan's "The Times They Are A-Changin'," sung by Al Jardine, the one member of the band with some folk music experience prior to the formation of the Beach Boys. On that same album was Dennis Wilson's hoarse but heartfelt cover of the Beatles' own Dylanesque "You've Got to Hide Your Love Away." And let's not forget that the group had a #3 hit in 1966 with "Sloop John B," a 1920s song from the West Indies that Jardine had learned from a version on the Kingston Trio's first album (and which the Weavers had recorded in 1950).

Far more objectionable was Jan & Dean's *Folk 'n' Roll*. Its limply executed "Eve of Destruction," "It Ain't Me Babe," and "Turn! Turn! Turn!" (not to mention "Folk City," a contrived update of their classic "Surf City") were delivered with a suspicious condescension suggesting they felt not so much excited by the new trend as threatened by it. And threatened by it they were: they probably would have washed out of the charts by 1967 even if Jan Berry hadn't been severely injured in a car wreck.

Soul singers barely dipped into the folk-rock bag at all, but it did happen. Stevie Wonder made the Top Ten in 1966 with "Blowin' in the Wind," the first real indication that Motown was willing to admit lyrics of broad social concern into its stable. The Staple Singers, who had done their time on the folk circuit and heavily influenced folk-rock session guitarist supremo Bruce Langhorne, took a straightforward cover of the Buffalo Springfield protest folk-rock classic "For What It's Worth" to #66 in the pop charts in 1967. The Chambers Brothers, like the Staple Singers, had been popular on the folk circuit, even recording an album on Folkways with Barbara Dane, before moving into soul-gospel-psychedelic rock on their big hit "Time Has Come Today" and popular Columbia albums. And while most listeners would regard the Four Tops' "Reach Out (I'll Be There)" as an epic soul melodrama, the group's Lawrence Payton saw it otherwise at the time, telling *NME*, "We were talking to [Motown songwriter-producers] Holland-Dozier-Holland one day and we decided that what was needed was something in the folk-rock idiom. So they went away and came back with 'Reach Out (I'll Be There).' I think it's the best piece of folk-rock that's been around in a long time."

Although Dylan, the Byrds, and the like were big in many non-English-speaking countries, rock acts there had to struggle both with a language barrier and the long odds at making an impact in the British- and American-dominated international pop scene. Composing and singing in a foreign tongue didn't stop some of the best of them, like Holland's Outsiders, who like most rock bands from non-English-speaking territories recorded their discs in English. They not only absorbed influences from Peter, Paul & Mary, Love, and the Searchers, but also combined downcast Russian folk melodies (lead singer Wally Tax's mother was a Russian gypsy) with bluesy punk in songs like "Sun's Going Down." In contrast, their zither-driven, wistful "Summer Is Here," like many of their numbers, added a certain Continental folk breeze.

France's own Bob Dylan, engineering student Antoine, eschewed English in favor of his native tongue, with *Time* reporting that his "La Guerre" "sounds like a medley of 'Eve of Destruction' and 'Blowin in the Wind.'" At any rate his "Lucubrations" lyric wouldn't have stood a chance of collecting airplay in the States if it had been in English, detailing as it did a letter from the President's office asking, "What can we do to make the country richer?" Antoine's reply: "Put the pill on sale in the dime stores." Transatlantic folk-rock echoes went into comic overdrive when Marseilles band the Five Gentlemen gently mocked the idolization of Dylan and Donovan as prophets in "Dis-Nous Dylan." That prompted the Sandals, a Belgian group that had moved to Los Angeles, to record an English cover on World Pacific in late 1966, retitled "Tell Us Dylan." "Tell-us tell-us, Dee-lunn! Tell-us tell-us, Do-no-vunn!" they beseeched in their best Franglais.

T here was also the folk-rock sub-genre, sometimes grotesque and at its best only tolerable, of older folk revivalists finally crying uncle to the new order and recording with electric instruments. It is still not widely known that Odetta, Pete Seeger, Eric Von Schmidt, Bonnie Dobson, the Kingston Trio, Carolyn Hester, Randy Sparks, and Ramblin' Jack Elliott all eventually threw in the towel and made belated studio efforts in this regard by the end of the 1960s. Peter, Paul & Mary, still popular but starting to fade, used musicians from the Paul Butterfield Blues Band and, yet again, veterans of Dylan's 1965–66 sessions for their maiden rock venture, 1966's *The Peter, Paul and Mary Album*. Dave Van Ronk recorded an album for Verve/Forecast with a rock band, the Hudson Dusters, that included covers of "Chelsea Morning" and "Both Sides Now" before Joni Mitchell had become a national star. Bob Johnston even produced a Burl Ives LP, *The Times They Are A-Changin'*, with dismal full-band versions of songs by Dylan, Paul Simon, and Tim Hardin, including a ludicrous reading, literally, of the title track that degenerated into a pompous-beyond-belief spoken recitation of the lyrics. By 1970, Malvina Reynolds was recording with a rock band including Gene Parsons (then of the Byrds) on drums and harmonica. One of the songs from those sessions, "The World's Gone Beautiful," could have easily fit into the set list of a Jefferson Airplane–type group of the late '60s, as difficult as that might be to fathom.

For artists such as these, using rockish backup might not have been a choice. If they wanted to continue their recording careers at all for nonfolkloric labels, the acoustic format was simply considered outmoded. Yet sometimes, it has to be emphasized, it *was* the artist's choice. Seeger insists there was no pressure from Columbia to use electric backing, as he occasionally did, referring to it as "kind of another experiment. I'm always experimenting." Hester had tried without success to convince Norman Petty to record a rock album with her prior to re-signing with Columbia in 1966; Petty, described by Hester as "a Sunday go-to-meetin' type of guy," had nixed the release of her rock cover of "Bottle of Wine" as he "REALLY didn't want to think of me singing a song about alcohol." Only two singles came out of Hester's folk-rock stint with Columbia, one a cover of Tim Hardin's "Reason to Believe."

"I was not timid about folk-rock," she asserts. "I embraced it for the folk artists who felt so inclined and who were able to raise a band. What I was uncomfortable with in my return to Columbia Records was the fact that the sides with John Simon [later to produce the Band and Big Brother & the Holding Company] had such a wide focus. I walked away from the situation because I didn't think I was going to be able to target an audience with that particular project. Simon was and is a tremendous talent as a musician and producer/arranger, and it was a joy to share a studio project with him. I became concerned, however, when Simon wanted to add music by Mahler to an album that already included the writings of Ravi Shankar, Anthony Newley, Cat Stevens, Sandra Phelps and the Beatles."

"We were experimenting like everybody else," says Peter Yarrow of Peter, Paul & Mary's first ventures into recording with rock arrangements. "It was in the wind." He saw the best folk-rock, he emphasizes, as differing from folk music primarily as "a change in form, or a fusion of presentation styles, rather than a change in its spirit. [The Byrds'] 'Turn! Turn! Turn!,' although it utilized non-acoustic instruments, basically came from the same heart's place." When his trio incorporated folk-rock features in the late '60s, he adds, "It was very natural, and it wasn't simply a matter of rock. It was a matter of the appropriate approach to each song. You hear the Paul Butterfield Blues Band on 'The King of Names,' which is an extrapolation of 'There's a Man Going Around Taking Names,' which was a song about the blacklist. Then you hear one guitar and a bass with three voices singing 'Leaving on a Jet Plane'; then you hear 'I Dig Rock & Roll Music,' which was a fantasy of fun, delight, and homage. Every song found its own integrity in the instruments that were chosen, and the experiments that we used."

In other cases, the artists weren't stylistically or psychologically disposed to do anything other than what they'd been doing for years. "I consider working with Jack Elliott something that I probably really shouldn't have done," says Bruce Langhorne, who produced Elliott's first somewhat modernized album, 1968's *Young Brigham*. "Jack was very difficult, because he would not do the same song twice anything like the same way. The only ways you could be a good producer was to record exactly what Jack did, and if you loved Jack's music enough, you could extract those pieces that were really significant, real, and excellent. I just didn't really have the patience. If I were advising someone how to do it, I would tell them, just give Jack an audience and a mike, and just record and record and record and record and record and record and record, and get his best performances and knit them together to make a superb performance. Then take this Jack Elliott performance, and write bass parts or drum parts or string parts or kazoo parts or whatever, and put that out as a sophisticated Jack Elliott [record]. Because he would give you a core, but it would be difficult to extract to make into something that would have commercial viability." *Young Brigham* sold little, but did find an appreciative audience among one significant late-1960s folk-rocker's clique. According to Tim Buckley's songwriting partner Larry Beckett, "Buckley and all the gang used to play that album on almost a daily basis, loving it for its breadth of genres, and [its] Beat prose poem."

The standout good-bad novelty of old-school folkies sticking their feet so far into their mouth as to produce folk-rock lockjaw was the Mitchell Trio's "The Sound of Protest (Has Begun to Pay)," from its 1966 album *Violets of Dawn*. That track's full electric folk-rock arrangement, with its 12-string guitar and soaring harmonies, slavishly recreated the sound of the Byrds. This was not a tribute, however, but a mean-spirited swipe at folk-rock as a whole, the lyrics quite clearly intimating that the Byrds and their flock were strip-mining the social protest song with dollar signs in their eyes. The intention might have been humorous, but actually it came off as the last desperate gasps of drowning folk revivalists, bitterly bemoaning the tidal wave of electric folk-rock that was quite literally putting them out of business.

As in the worst mean-spirited gags, though, the joke was on them. *Violets of Dawn*, which other than "The Sound of Protest" stuck to passé acoustic folk, was just about the last of the unbearably wholesome, sterile commercial folk revival LPs, and the Mitchell Trio was soon history. Not all of those guilty of contributing to "The Sound of Protest (Has Begun to Pay)" would be gone for long, though. Mitchell Trio guitarist John Denver rose to superstardom as a mellow singer-songwriter in the 1970s, while one of the authors of the song, former Weaver Fred Hellerman, couldn't have taken the sentiments of his tune too close to heart; in just a year or two, he would be producing the first albums by folk-rock singer Arlo Guthrie.

There were those, quite few and far between in 1966, who proved that you could still play acoustic folk without either forcing yourself to adapt to the changing times or pretend that the times hadn't changed. The Charles River Valley Boys recorded an entire album of bluegrass versions of Lennon-McCartney songs on their critically acclaimed 1966 Elektra LP *Beatle Country*, playing the material as *bluegrass*, rather than compromised folk-rock. Charles River Valley Boys banjoist Bob Siggins sees this rapprochement as no big deal, as they thought the Beatles "had a lot of country twang in songs like 'I've Just Seen a Face' and 'What Goes On.' A lot of the folkies were into the Beatles big time, on the sly if nothing else, including us. We just thought a lot of [their songs] would adapt themselves to a country sound. As we got into learning the songs, we discovered that the singing they did lent itself well to bluegrass harmonies, and we discovered we liked the ones that weren't so country too. The only flak we got was from [the group's mandolinist] Joe Val initially. I think he was worried about what some of his friends might say, some of his hardcore bluegrass fans. Our approach was to do it as hardcore bluegrass as we could. And I think that kind of settled his mind on it a bit, and his friends too, for that matter."

A t the furthest corner away from the purist folk crowd that could be found in popular music, folk-rock made a deep impact upon the young garage bands, usually teenaged, on the rampage in almost every hamlet in America in the mid-'60s. Garage rock, or '60s punk as it was sometimes termed retroactively, is prized by aficionados above all for its naive energy, as teenagers coined crude variations of British Invasion bands like the Rolling Stones, Yardbirds, Animals, Them, and the Zombies. This almost exclusively male-dominated field was usually devoted to expressing hormonal rage. Its lyrics were usually obsessed either with scoring with girls or putting down girls who wouldn't put out. There was also a lot of rebellious fury against society in general involved, though, and not all of it was unconscious. In folk-rock, particularly the full-band guitar-oriented sort pioneered by the Byrds and Dylan, garage bands found another inspirational outlet for their bile, especially among the more sensitive and intelligent teens.

Hence the yet more esoteric sub-genre "folk-punk," in which young teenagers did to the Byrds what they were doing to the Rolling Stones, imitating their heroes in raw caricature. Much of what is now called "folk-punk" actually consists of typical teenage love songs, often lovesick and frustrated, wrapped in Byrds-like guitars, harmonies, and dragging tambourine beats. There will probably never be an accurate count of the huge numbers of obscure garage rock records, heard only on local radio if at all, that specifically mimicked Roger McGuinn's circular 12-string leads. Form often took precedence over lyrical substance, but that doesn't mean that some dynamite records didn't arise from these bastardizations.

There will never be a more dead-on emulation of McGuinn's breathlessly engaging vocal manner than Bristol, Connecticut's the Squires summoned on "Go Ahead." On the tiny Current label, Bakersfield, California's Avengers emulated the more psychedelic evolution of the Byrds on "Open Your Eyes," with interlocking guitar lines and harmonies nearly as heavenly as those of their obvious role models. From Chicago, the Knaves' "The Girl I Threw Away" might have had fairly standard boy-lost-girl lyrics, but is regarded by garage-rock zealots as the outstanding folk-punk single for its adroit hazy-shades-of-Byrds harmonies and ringing guitars. Also from Chicago, also in the sub-Byrds vein, and even better was the Ides of March's "I'll Keep Searching," with its riveting descending vocals and acoustic-electric riffs. (And yes, those were the same Ides of March that landed a huge 1970 hit with the blustery Blood, Sweat & Tears imitation "Vehicle.")

There were those garage bands, however, that aimed for something extra in their lyrics. Certainly the most notorious Bob Dylan imitation, and the best, was Mouse & the Traps' "A Public Execution," which bubbled under the *Billboard* Hot 100 briefly in early 1966. Its ascending, grinding "Like a Rolling Stone" organ riff, humorously surreal putdown of an ex-lover, and snide nasal vocals captured the essence of *Highway 61 Revisited* better than some of the actual songs on that album did. Mouse & the Traps were not Dylan operating under a pseudonym, however, but a real Tyler, Texas band fronted by Ronnie "Mouse" Weiss. They never recycled His Bobness as blatantly again, recording a wide variety of respectable singles mingling pop, country, R&B, and psychedelia.

And there were yet more oddities in a protest frame of mind by acts who went on to become known for something much different. A youngster billed as Link Cromwell did a credibly witty Sonny Bono homage/takeoff on "Crazy Like a Fox." Under the name Lenny Kaye, he would become lead guitarist in the Patti Smith Group (as well as the rock critic most responsible for launching the '60s garage band revival, with the *Nuggets* compilation). The Cowsills, prior to adding their mother to the lineup and setting the prototype for the Partridge Family, were a struggling New England garage band. Their obscure mid-'60s indie single, "All I Wanta Be Is Me," was a typically snarling raw rebellious adolescent folk-rocker, with a heavy Byrds influence to the guitars and P.F. Sloan/Sonny Bono flavor to the vocal and defiantly individualistic lyrics.

Back in New York, the Blues Magoos, later famous for the psychedelic garage-pop of "(We Ain't Got) Nothing Yet," actually began life as the Bloos Magoos, a folk-rock band. Their rare debut single, recorded for Verve/Folkways and issued under the Bloos Magoos spelling, was actually a fairly tasty, moody folk-rocker with all the hallmarks of youth newly awakened to the form circa late 1965: sullen vocalizing, a lumbering but appealing mid-tempo beat, and slightly surreal lyrics projecting social alienation. The threads connecting multiple levels of the industry and classes of individuals get especially labyrinthine with this 45, both sides of which were produced by Rick Shorter, who wrote the A-side and cowrote the flip. Shorter, one of the few African-American singer-songwriters to record in the folk-rock boom's early days, had a pretty respectable what-does-the-future-hold-for-me-in-this-messed-up-world folk-rock single of his own, "Last Thoughts of a Young Man." That single was produced by Teo Macero, who in turn was far more famous for producing Miles Davis, who had been instrumental in getting the Byrds on Columbia in the first place.

Folk-rock subversion also found its way into the upper-crust bastions of the privileged classes. Phillips Academy in Andover, Massachusetts, the prep school that counts among its graduates the first president named George Bush, was home to the Rising Storm, who filched rehearsal time in basements and closet-sized spaces whenever its members could. Just before graduation in 1967, the band recorded and pressed a vanity album, *Calm Before*, that eventually became one of the most highly valued collector's items of the 1960s. This was not due just to its rarity, but also the surprisingly high quality of some of its original material. Its delicate, brooding folk-rock ballads were strongly influenced by Love material such as "A Message to Pretty" (which they covered on the LP). On the otherworldly, dreamlike "Frozen Laughter," they even had the cheek to quote from T.S. Eliot's "The Love Song of J. Alfred Prufrock."

The message of Love (the band, and probably the concept too) had spread from small Hollywood clubs all the way up to the enclaves of the elite's offspring. In their dorms, Rising Storm leader Tony Thompson and bandmate Todd Cohen played the first Love LP over and over, learning nearly every song, performing "A Message to Pretty" and the first-person junkie narrative "Signed D.C." at every show they did. One does wonder exactly what the 14-year-old girls in the audience (not to mention their chaperones) thought of watching guys not much older than them wailing in despair over having sold their souls to drug dealers. "Even though we did that song for two years every week at every dance, it didn't occur to us that that was what it was about," confesses Thompson.

But they were not alone in covering controversial addiction confessions. Buffy Sainte-Marie's "Codine" was honored with several folk-rock covers (probably done first by the Matthew Moore Plus Four), some by bands so young they may have had yet to try anything stronger than cough syrup. "Signed D.C." itself was done on obscure singles in New Mexico (by Axis Brotherhood) and the nation's capital in Washington, DC (by December's Children Ltd.). Love might have been thought of as an "underground" band, but there were enough Love covers by '60s garage bands to fill up a 20-track compilation in 1993. And even that anthology didn't collect all of them.

Rising Storm, posing for the cover of their only album.

If using Love as a springboard to write songs around the poetry of T.S. Eliot was naive, it was nonetheless indicative of a genuine desire by teenagers to express themselves and expand their grasp of an increasingly chaotic world. Folk-rock put those tools in their hands, just as it had done for the considerably older musicians who were their mentors. "We tried to make statements about what was going on in our lives at the time, and how we felt about the world," says Thompson, now a Washington, DC lawyer, who, like the rest of the Rising Storm, abandoned music for collegiate studies after graduating from Andover. "We were relatively innocent kids in a sheltered prep school environment. We weren't really into folk music. But we were oriented toward doing things that were meaningful. I think maybe we felt that doing slower music which would allow the lyrics to stand out would be the best way to accomplish that.

"I was swept away by the sweet sad melodies, the gruff singing of Arthur Lee, and the simple arrangements and chord progressions. I do not remember feeling rebellious or angry about the state of the world. We were drug free. The word 'psychedelic' meant nothing to us. Later, in college, when the Vietnam War became a threat and a focus of concern, these same songs took on new meaning. We understood them better in hindsight, because we could see how they fit into a musical fabric of significant dimension. It was music that dealt with the issues of the day and, I think for all of us in the Rising Storm, the music deeply affected our political outlook."

The garage band explosion gave vent to regionalist representation on disc, even if most of those groups' singles were usually only available in their home city or state. This element, unfortunately, was missing from the more mature folk-rock scene. Undoubtedly there were interesting or at least promising folk-rock artists all over North America, just as there were interesting or at least promising young garage bands almost everywhere. But the odds were against even recording if you were not based in New York or California. There were some—admittedly, not many—outstanding acts operating outside of the Hollywood-Manhattan studio oligarchy that were almost overlooked at the time.

On the edge of the Mojave Desert north of L.A., Palmdale, California might have been only an hour or so from Hollywood's studios. But they may as well have been on the other coast when Merrell Fankhauser was recording his vocals there for the miniscule Glenn Records in a plastic military surplus jet cockpit. As the winsome-voiced singer-songwriter on releases credited to both Merrell and the Exiles and the much less conventionally monickered Fapardokly, Fankhauser crafted shimmering Byrdsy rockaballads like "Lila." There were also freakier cuts like the psychedelic folk-rock airline commercial "Super Market," and "Gone to Pot," with its gonzoid "Eight Miles High"–derived guitar breaks backing moaning first-person observations of astral projection. The psychedelic drugs presumably were really kicking in at this point, as the sessions cobbled together on the *Fapardokly* album (some done in L.A.) also contained songs addressed to a cuckoo clock and a glass chandelier.

Fankhauser himself sees the wild trajectory of his work as no big deal: "I always liked the Kingston Trio. They did these ballads that told stories, and I just took that to a more far-out approach with songs like 'Lila' and 'Super Market.'" Eventually Fankhauser would get a rabid cult following among collectors, both for Fapardokly and his subsequent work with H.M.S. Bounty, where he did about the best Donovan-type psych ballad ever, "A Visit with Ashiya." In the early 1970s he was still taking folk-rock to extremes with MU, who sang hippie odes to lost continents in work that matched the easygoing eclecticism of bands like the Grateful Dead with the freakier tinges of acts like his friend Captain Beefheart.

The Daily Flash, from Seattle, was another of the most talented mid-'60s folk-rock bands to form outside of the big recording centers. Playing 12-string and harmonizing with bassist Don MacAllister (formerly of a bluegrass trio, the Willow Creek Ramblers) was Steve Lalor, who'd played in both the Seattle and San Francisco folk scene with such luminaries as "Hey Joe" author Billy Roberts and Janis Joplin. Lalor rightly sees the Daily Flash's greatest strengths lying in its skills as interpreters, with "vocal precision and counterpoint coloring that took [Ian Tyson's] 'French Girl' from a Leonard Cohen–like lost love dirge into a baroque bittersweet epic love story. We took 'Jack of Diamonds' (a tune Billy Roberts picked up from the singing of Percy Heath in New Orleans) from a mournful blues to a melodious psychedelic swirl with as tense a guitar solo as I have ever heard." Indeed "Jack of Diamonds," released in mid-1966, was a flash forward to psychedelia, with its devastating shock waves of guitar feedback introducing a folk-rock-meets-the-Yardbirds raveup.

Yet just two singles were released by the group during its lifetime. Some other quality unreleased material, such as covers of Eric Andersen's "Violets of Dawn" and Billy Roberts's "The Girl from North Alberta," did show up on a compilation in the 1980s. Yet, as Lalor acknowledges, "MacAllister and I were vocal interpreters. Dan Hicks gave us a homemade reel-to-reel tape of his tunes. Danny O'Keefe gave us 'Goodtime Charlie' and some other tunes. Billy gave us 'North Alberta.' None of us were moved to compose. We felt pressured to produce product we had absolutely no interest in producing."

Specifically, there was pressure from managers Charlie Greene and Brian Stone, who Lalor thinks "only knew one way to launch artists. Make singles; teenyboppers buy the singles; then, make an album composed of the same singles, and so on." The Daily Flash did live and work in both San Francisco and Los Angeles for periods in a bid to make a splash: "We went to L.A. [in spring of 1966] to become stars. At the time, L.A. was THE only place to record. As soon as we moved from Seattle, our stock went up and we toured the northwest extensively, as well as several gigs at the Avalon [in San Francisco]." But in the end it couldn't compensate for their lack of strong original material. After several lineup shuffles, the group broke up, guitarist Doug Hastings serving a brief stint in Buffalo Springfield during one of Neil Young's extended periods of absence from that band.

In the twenty-first century, when Hollywood and Manhattan production facilities and publishers rule the industry with a somewhat lighter iron fist than they did in the 1960s, it can be difficult to appreciate just how difficult it was for folk-rockers to make headway if they weren't based in or near those cities. It might have seemed logical, for instance, for Cambridge to have developed a thriving folk-rock community, as it had been such a linchpin of the early-'60s folk revival. But there was little Boston folk-rock of note, in part because the Cambridge folk crowd was more rigid in its purity than the Village's, and in part because there weren't major studios or labels in the region. "The Cambridge scene was quite different from the New York scene," feels Tom Rush. "The Cambridge scene was basically a bunch of amateurs in the original, positive sense of the word, people playing for the love of it. We had psychofarmocologists, college students, typewriter repair men, and carpenters getting together just to play for the fun of it. Everybody had something else they were doing in real life.

"But I headed out and moved down to New York, probably [around] '66. And it wasn't entirely because that's where the folk-rock thing was happening. It was mainly that's where the *industry* was happening. I figured I had to be in town to keep an eye on my manager and my booking agent and my record company, and be where the scene was."

It was a similar deal in Toronto, whose Yorkville district was buzzing with folk and rock clubs as Canada's own Greenwich Village. Yet all the major Canadian folk-rock singer-songwriters—Ian & Sylvia, Neil Young, Gordon Lightfoot, Joni Mitchell, the Band (all but one of whom were Canadian), and Leonard Cohen—would need to record in the United States to make their international reputation, and usually need to move there for extended periods or permanently. Things, again, have changed decades later, but at the time Canadian studios didn't even possess some of the most rudimentary technological requirements necessary to compete with their New York counterparts. "We did try at one point to record in Toronto, very early on," says Sylvia Tyson. "It was a company called Arc Records. They assured us that they had four-track. When we went in to try to do the album, what they had was two Ampex two-tracks, kind of fastened together. And they were out of sync!"

There were no greater victims of regional bias than the Blue Things (sometimes spelled the Bluethings), who qualify as the great lost mid-'60s folk-rock group. Their sole album and handful of 1965–66 singles echoed some of the finest attributes of the early Byrds and Beau Brummels: scrumptious acoustic-electric guitar matings, quality original songs that drew from both folk and the Beatles, and jubilant three-part harmonies. Principal singer-songwriter Val Stecklein's husky, earnest voice had an attractive, slightly weary, yet compassionate tone that echoed the lived-in quality heard in the singing of peers like Roger McGuinn, Bob Dylan, John Lennon, Gene Clark, and Sal Valentino. He even had the good fortune to look like Paul McCartney. The Blue Things' misfortune, however, was that they were from Hays, Kansas, which was about as far from both the East Coast and West Coast action as they could have possibly gotten. Some of their records sold well in the Midwest and Texas, where they often toured. But they were basically unknown anywhere else, despite recording for one of America's biggest labels, RCA.

Although the Blue Things had formed in a small town in the Midwest, it's important to note that Kansas was not in Siberia. Underground coffeehouse culture existed there too, if not on the same flashy level as it did in New York, California, and Cambridge. Blue Things bassist Richard Scott, who also took the high vocal harmony parts, had been a fan of not just Peter, Paul & Mary, but also the Mugwumps, who had released just one poorly distributed 1964 single while Cass Elliot, Denny Doherty, and Zal Yanovsky were in that group. That gives some indication of just how close some had their ears to the ground in the heartland as folk-rock was in its embryonic state. "The trends generally start on either of the coasts, and work their way the other direction," Scott allows. "I was an art major. So that lends more toward the offbeat, or more toward that bohemian lifestyle. Val had been in that lifestyle for quite some time when he joined the group in 1964."

Indeed, the formation and fruition of the Blue Things is almost like a prototype of the road followed by folk-rock bands from coast-to-coast. Songwriter Stecklein, who had been weaned on the rock of Buddy Holly and the Everly Brothers, retreated into folk as a member of the Hi-Plains Singers in the early '60s, and then re-embraced his rock roots by teaming with the rock band the Blue Boys. From 1964 to 1966, the Blue Boys (soon to change their name to the Blue Things) made a blitzkrieg run from Buddy Holly and rockabilly covers to highly enjoyable Searchers and early Beatles derivations to thoughtful folk-rock with 12-string guitars. By their late-1966 singles, they'd rushed headlong into wildly innovative, off-kilter psychedelia.

Along the way were several great recordings: the lilting, seriocomic "I Must Be Doing Something Wrong," the down-in-the-dumps "I Can't Have Yesterday" (where the Byrds met the Righteous Brothers), and the heart-rending cautious optimism of "Now's the Time." Social consciousness figured into the proletarian protest of "The Man on the Street" (by Wayne Carson, famous as author of the Boxtops' "The Letter"), and "Doll House," with its sympathetic, subtle portrait of the social pressures leading its heroine into prostitution. "Desert Wind"—a compelling drama of a Colorado drifter unable to win the hand of a girl he loves, with a vague thematic similarity to Ian Tyson's "Four Strong Winds"—is folk-rock in the purest sense, in that it sounds as if it could have been an ageless, author-less ballad. (In fact Stecklein had written it, and recorded it in demo form as a wistful folk ditty with the Hi-Plains Singers prior to joining the Blue Things.) The declarative 12-string guitars, Stecklein's dignified-yet-urgent vocal, and the group's pleading harmonies planted it firmly in the present, however. Unbelievably, the Blue Things' version of it did not even find release at the time, though a previously unissued recording they made of the tune did finally surface on a compilation in the 1980s.

Scott puts some of the blame for the Blue Things' failure to sell well outside of the Midwest on RCA. The company might have been the most backward of the major labels in rushing to catch up with the rock revolution in the mid-'60s, though they did sign Jefferson Airplane and the Young-bloods around this time. "RCA's policy at that time was, 'We will not promote anything but a hit

The Blue Things. Left to right: Val Stecklein, Richard Scott, Bobby Day (standing), Mike Chapman (sitting)

record. And you cannot get a hit record without promotion. It's your manager's responsibility to promote you.' And our manager was saying, 'It's RCA's responsibility, they're the record company.' So as a result, we got almost no promotion at all."

Making the situation worse, "We were recording in Nashville. There was a lot of rivalry between RCA New York, RCA Los Angeles, and RCA Nashville. Because although Nashville wasn't as big, they were consistently in the black, because of their country artists. It was much more sporadic on the coasts with the Top 40 acts, because RCA New York would release something and it would sell, and they'd go in the black. Then they'd release a few other things and they wouldn't sell, and they'd go in the red. And California was the same way. So they didn't work together, basically. They considered anything that came out of Nashville to be country music, so they didn't promote it."

Musically, however, the Blue Things did find benefits to recording in Nashville under producer Felton Jarvis. Jarvis, most known for producing Elvis Presley in the late '60s, was more accustomed to working with country-pop artists like Skeeter Davis than with young, rather radical rock bands like the Blue Things. "But he was willing to explore new areas, which most of the A&R men there were not," points out Scott. "They were into country, and did not understand anything that didn't fit into that Nashville image. But he was more than willing to explore any direction, as long as he felt that it would turn to something positive. And he had a vast knowledge. He worked with *everybody* there. It wasn't at all unusual to see the president of RCA, Chet Atkins, just walk into a session, sit down, put his feet up on the rail, and say, 'Play it nice, boys.' They all supported us. 'Cause they knew we were trying to do something a little bit different than what they were used to.

"We were using Raleigh Music for our publishing in Nashville, and of course we knew all those people too. Nashville is actually a very small town. If you go into Recording Row, it's only a few blocks long, and all the publishing companies and studios are together. They were right across the alley from RCA Studio. So we'd walk over there, and they'd play demos for us—'Is there anything here you like?' The Raleigh man would bring something over and say, 'Hey guys. Listen to this. You might like this.' One time he brought us 'Doll House' and said, 'This is the first time I've ever had someone [writer Marge Barton] request that you do a song, or that a specific artist do it, other than some big name, like Elvis.'

"We had a lot of contact with a lot of studio musicians in Nashville, quite simply because the Nashville recording regulations for the union demand that they have one local musician on every session. So we had no choice. But we had some really good ones. We had a starving kid named Chip who was saving pennies, trying to get enough money to finish [his own recordings]. He played guitar on a number of our tracks, just because he had to be there. So we'd usually put him in with an acoustic guitar, just to do a straight rhythm pattern background, 'cause it would save us an overdub.

"Ray Stevens [the same singer famous for novelties like "Ahab the Arab" and "The Streak"] played organ on 'Orange Rooftop [of Your Mind],' and he also played the little toy piano at the end of 'Doll House.' We had the contrabass bassoon player from the Nashville Philharmonic come in and do some overdubbing on 'I Must Be Doing Something Wrong,' as well as a couple of other things. Just punching in a couple of notes, in parallel with the bass, just to give it a little extra depth.

Live, we couldn't do more than three-part [harmony]. But in the studio, we could do, four, five, even six parts."

For "I Must Be Doing Something Wrong," one of the Jordanaires, the vocal group most famous for backing Elvis, "was on that song, and it changed our whole direction. Because when we went in to cut, we were doing a lot of three- and four-part harmony. As far as we were concerned, it was done, but there was something lacking. And Felton came walking out with this little bitty short guy and said, 'Hey, guys, come and listen to this.' He had him sing this *real* high part. Just a few notes, just a few words, an octave above the lead voice. It was exactly what the record needed. And after that, we were sitting in the control room listening while he cut it, he came walking out, we said, 'Hey, that was really great. That's exactly what the song needed.' And he says"—Scott switches to a super-low gruff voice—"'Thank you.' He sang a four-octave range. After that, *I* had to sing all those parts, and I stretched my voice till I could clear up to G above high C. Clear up to the soprano range."

Nashville would by the end of the 1960s be a popular option for recording folk-rock and country-rock, and no one did more to make that happen than Bob Dylan. Producer Bob Johnston had been urging his most famous client to record in the country music capital from almost the time they started to work together. This was, at least in part, so they could escape the heavy breathing of those ostensibly in charge of Dylan's business affairs rather than his studio recordings. "I remember [Albert] Grossman, and the president of Columbia, when I was with [Dylan] doing *Highway 61*, leaning over the board," says Johnston. "And I said, 'Hey, man, if you ever get a chance you ought to come down to Nashville, 'cause those people are really great down there and there's no fucking clock and nobody watches anything.' Dylan, like always, went 'Hmmm.' Never said, 'Oh, well, that's a good idea,' or something. Then the next thing I knew, he went out in the studio and the president of Columbia and Al Grossman came around and said, 'If you ever mention Nashville to Dylan again, you're out of here. Period.' And I said, 'Good enough. You're the boss.'

"So," he continues without missing a beat, "I took him to Nashville, did *Blonde on Blonde*. 'Cause I would have been selling peanuts if I had to leave it up to the suits and the ties. Dylan, Johnny Cash, Leonard Cohen, Simon & Garfunkel—those people didn't need some goddamned attorney or accountant patting their foot out of time, whistling out of tune, trying to judge what they were doing so they could keep their jobs three months longer with their boss. That was all bullshit to me. Anybody that's a great artist should have complete and utter creative freedom."

Blonde on Blonde was not the first folk-rock record made in Nashville. The Blue Things had started recording there in 1965, and Tim Rose says he did five folk-rock tracks with Johnston that year as well that Columbia president Clive Davis "wouldn't release." *Blonde on Blonde*, however, was the first to make a major impact. Dylan had been recording in spurts with the Hawks (before they were called the Band) in New York in late 1965 and early 1966. These sessions did yield the eccentric not-quite-a-hit single "Can You Please Crawl Out Your Window?" and the sad breakup song "One of Us Most Know (Sooner or Later)," which was used on both a flop single and *Blonde on Blonde*. The album didn't properly get on its way, however, until Dylan laid down a double-LP's worth of tracks in Nashville in February and March. Old reliable Al Kooper and Hawks guitarist Robbie

Robertson were retained as links to the sound Dylan had forged in 1965. But for the most part, the players were Nashville session cats who were not deeply immersed in either folk or rock, including guitarist Charlie McCoy, bassist Joe South (soon to become a recording star under his own steam), and drummer Kenneth Buttrey.

Blonde on Blonde was Dylan's best album—and along with the Mothers of Invention's *Freak Out*, the first double album in rock, incidentally—not only because of the stellar musicianship. As both a songwriter and a vocalist, Dylan had tempered the gleeful misanthropy and misogyny that was threatening to get out of hand at some points during the *Highway 61* era. It was only tempered, not eliminated. Songs like "Absolutely Sweet Marie" and "Most Likely You Go Your Way and I'll Go Mine" still seethe with a mixture of sexual frustration, resentment, and a relieved I'm-better-off-without-you-anyway pose. Still, he invested songs like the Top 20 hit "I Want You" and the 11-minute, side-long "Sad Eyed Lady of the Lowlands" with some of his most seductive vocal and melodic sweetness, though his words and imagery remained as complex as ever. "Just Like a Woman" is one of popular music's finest portraits of fragile femininity; "Stuck Inside of Mobile with the Memphis Blues Again" one of his most exhilarating, humorous stream-of-consciousness narratives of impressions along his unique on-the-surreal-road.

"The closest I ever got to the sound I hear in my mind was on individual bands in the *Blonde on Blonde* album," Dylan told *Playboy* in 1978. "It's that thin, that wild mercury sound. It's metallic and bright gold, with whatever that conjures up. That's my particular sound. I haven't been able to succeed in getting it all the time." Whatever Dylan meant by his now-famous reference to a thin wild mercury sound, it probably had something to do with the combination of Kooper's luminous organ parts, the delicate accents of Nashville guitar pickers on cuts like "Just Like a Woman" and "Fourth Time Around," and the "direct blues-gospel-soul" vibe that Donovan has praised. Given the spontaneity of Dylan's methods, he was fortunate it clicked so well. By way of illustration, Charlie McCoy describes how "Sad Eyed Lady of the Lowlands" was recorded: "He came in and didn't have his song finished. He said, 'You guys just be patient while I finish this song.' We came in at two, and he started to write the song, and four A.M. the next morning he said, 'Okay, I'm ready to record.' After you've tried to stay awake 'til four o'clock in the morning, to play something so slow and long was really, really tough."

His album in the can, Dylan was ready to embark on his first world tour as a rock 'n' roll musician in April 1966. He was still, as he had been ever since introducing electric music into his onstage repertoire in mid-1965, dividing his sets into acoustic and electric halves, even though some of the songs in the acoustic half (such as "Just Like a Woman" and "Fourth Time Around") had been recorded in rock arrangements for *Blonde on Blonde*. For the electric half, he would front the Hawks. Mickey Jones, formerly drummer with Trini Lopez and Johnny Rivers, filled in for a disillusioned Levon Helm, who would not return to the group until late 1967.

The tour began in Hawaii and swept through Australia on the way to Britain and Ireland, fitting in a few European dates as well. Mystery surrounds many phases of the Dylan legend, and the 1966 world tour is no exception. Accounts are usually scarred with intimations of musicians pushing themselves to the limit both on and offstage, many suggesting the pace was fueled by inordinate drug use.

The most famous scene in the rarely screened tour documentary *Eat the Document* shows a miserably dazed and confused Dylan rambling incomprehensibly for ten minutes before, it seems, preparing to throw up out of or all over a limousine. (Sharing the back seat was a stiff, embarrassed John Lennon, who looked like he'd rather be anywhere else than within five feet of his companion.) Onstage, he followed his taut and masterly acoustic sets with deafening, full-bore rock, interjecting electric versions of "I Don't Believe You," "One Too Many Mornings," and "Baby, Let Me Follow You Down" (all of which he'd recorded acoustically on his early albums) with newer material from his 1965–66 LPs.

If Dylan thought the issue of whether he was entitled to play rock 'n' roll had been settled by the wide acceptance of folk-rock records by himself and others in the past year, he wasn't quite right. Dylan had already released one-and-a-half no-doubt-about-it electric rock albums; already had two massive folk-rock hit singles; and already been, as noted, playing rock live for almost a year. Unbelievably, a large, vocal minority of his British audiences seemed to expect to see the same acoustic solo folk protest singer that had been pictured on the cover to *The Times They Are A-Changin'*. Disappointed concert-goers slow hand-clapped and booed to make their displeasure known. At his show in Manchester on May 17, one wag shouted "Judas!" Dylan's response was to snarl, "I don't believe you. You're a liar!" before closing the show with a tornado-force "Like a Rolling Stone." That concert, preceding dialogue included, became the biggest-selling bootleg of all time (usually erroneously billed as Dylan's '66 show at the Royal Albert Hall) before finally seeing official release in 1998.

There's been almost as much controversial speculation about just what British audiences thought of Dylan and the Hawks as there has been regarding his 1965 Newport Folk Festival appearance. As at Newport, even when reading contemporary accounts, one wonders if the listeners were watching the same event. "Before the end of the concert, about 25 percent of the total audience had walked out," wrote Norman Jopling of Dylan's Royal Albert Hall show in *Record Mirror*. "Another 25 percent stayed under sufferance and didn't show overmuch enthusiasm." In contrast, at the same concert, *Melody Maker* found "very few boos and a raving audience, Beatles included, yelling for more punishment." Claimed John Lennon in the same magazine, "All that stuff about Dylan being booed has been exaggerated. I saw the London concerts and about five or six people booed. That's all—and everyone else in the audience were shutting them up. The newspaper writers got it completely wrong. They didn't know what they were talking about."

And, as with Newport, interest in what did and didn't take place failed to dim over the next 35 years. C.P. Lee centered an entire book, *Like the Night: Bob Dylan and the Road to the Manchester Free Trade Hall*, around what's sometimes called the "Judas" concert. In 1998, the man who cried Judas, Keith Butler, finally came forward and identified himself. It turned out that he was also the angry young man interviewed in *Eat the Document* who proclaims, "Any pop group could produce better rubbish than that. It was a bloody disgrace, it was. He wants shooting. He's a traitor."

D.A. Pennebaker, who had filmed Dylan's '65 British tour for his documentary *Don't Look Back*, was also on hand to film some of the '66 jaunt for *Eat the Document*, though as a cinematographer and not as director. "The first thing I noticed the next year when he was with the

Band onstage was how excited he was with the music," says Pennebaker. "His whole attitude was so different. The second half, when the curtain opened and there was the Band standing around with electrical instruments, and then he walked out on stage and joined them . . . I think they knew something different was gonna happen. There were probably people that were outraged. But I must say, maybe it was because I was on stage and didn't hear, I never really heard much of that. Mickey [Jones] said he could hear it sometimes."

Ian Anderson, a musician (not the same Ian Anderson as the Jethro Tull leader) and now the editor of Britain's leading roots music magazine, *fRoots* (formerly *Folk Roots*), saw Dylan play on that tour as a young fan. "I'll tell you the really stupid thing about that tour, is that anybody who was a Dylan fan already knew what he was doing on record," he exclaims. "They already knew that he was touring with an electric band. And a lot of people—it was like, they came along to be offended. They came along to make their protest. 'Cause it wasn't like it was a big shock.

"The thing that *was* a big shock was the fact that the sound was absolutely crappy. They were playing *loud*. The PAs they had were being driven absolutely flat out. It was distortion, and not intentional distortion. The other thing with Dylan was that of course so much was dependent on the words. And you couldn't hear the words. I mean, not only was he stoned out of his gourd and slurring everything into kind of another language anyway, but on top of that, the sheer awfulness of the sound completely wiped out any chance of hearing what he was singing. So people were upset by that, for sure."

As in the States a year earlier, Dylan was bearing the brunt of dissatisfaction among hard-line British folk fans, who were at least as purist and traditional in their thinking as those in America. It now seems as nonsensical to go to a Dylan 1966 show and expect only acoustic folk songs as it would be to go to a David Bowie show in 1975 and throw tomatoes at him for not wearing the glam clothes he'd sported a few years earlier in his Ziggy Stardust incarnation. Dylan's protest songs had meant so much to some British fans, however, that they saw his new guise as a betrayal. Never mind that some of the new electric versions were truly scarifying in their intensity. He retooled "I Don't Believe You" from plaintive ballad to full-tilt rocker. The Hawks' coruscating attack on "Ballad of a Thin Man" took their leader's bottom-of-my-soul howl to new levels of anguish, amplified by the deft interplay between Dylan's pounding piano and Garth Hudson's organ.

The malice borne by some fans to the contrary, Dylan felt no obligation to ingratiate himself with his audience, or to live up to anyone's hopes that he would act as a spokesman for progressive liberal causes. In Melbourne, reported *Variety*, he declared he "wouldn't write for Negroes if you paid me $1,000." Asked if he was shocked at the "horror of young boys being killed in wars," he replied, "this doesn't disturb me in the least," adding for good measure, "in fact I'm quite happy about the state of the world. I don't want to change it." In France, wrote *Billboard*, he took ten minutes between each number to tune his guitar and refused to acknowledge applause, inciting shouts of "Go home!" "I'm just as anxious to go home as you are," he retorted. The punishing pace of superstardom was taking its toll. When French star Françoise Hardy paid a visit to Dylan at his Paris Olympia concert, as she recounts in the biography *Françoise Hardy: Superstar et Ermite*, she found his sickly appearance so alarming that she feared he was about to die.

Dylan wasn't in such good shape after he did go home, either. He didn't have much time to recuperate before his next anticipated tour, this one of the States later in 1966. Deadlines were facing him from multiple directions. His novel, *Tarantula*, was getting pushed toward publication (though it would not come out for about five years). He frantically worked on editing *Eat the Document*, originally planned as an hour-long ABC television special (which was never broadcast). His Columbia contract was due to expire soon, with Albert Grossman getting ready to renegotiate or open a bidding war. All of these commitments were put on hold when he was injured in a motorcycle accident in Woodstock on July 29. The tour was canceled. No one could have predicted that it would be seven-and-a-half years before Dylan would tour again, using the same backup musicians, who by that time would be stars in their own right.

ylan and the folk-rock revolution he'd helped spearhead had done much to change the world in the mere 18 months prior to his accident. But much of the world, it must be emphasized, was determined to resist that change. In the summer of 1966, Dylan's own "Rainy Day Women #12 & 35" (*Blonde on Blonde*'s lead-off single) was one of several songs singled out for censorship by the media as the establishment fought back. Certainly the song gave it a wide target, with its insistent inebriated chorus "everybody must get stoned!" It, along with "Eight Miles High," was targeted by the *Gavin Report* as condoning marijuana and LSD use. The radio trade periodical concluded, "We cannot conscientiously recommend such records for airplay, despite their acknowledged sales." Presumably "everybody must get stoned" was ambiguous enough to leave those ever-alert guardians of the airwaves in some doubt. Huffed *Time*, in all seriousness, "What cinched it for the radio men was the title: a 'rainy-day woman,' as any junkie knows, is a marijuana cigarette." Presumably they did not ask any pot smokers for a translation (or did not know any to ask), as no one from that era seems to recall that term.

Though "Rainy Day Women" was banned by some stations, that had little effect on its sales. It became (in tandem with "Like a Rolling Stone") Dylan's highest-charting single, peaking at #2. The Byrds were not so lucky, with "Eight Miles High," as previously noted, stopping at #14 as a result of radio reluctance, sending them into a commercial downturn they never reversed. "We could have called the song '42,240 Feet,'" an exasperated Roger McGuinn told *NME*. "But somehow this didn't seem to be a very commercial song title and it certainly wouldn't have been scanned.... It seems extraordinary that a very pretty lyric about an intriguing city should be condemned because the phrases are couched in some sort of poetry."

The singles' roadblocks were not limited to the US, with Birmingham Councilor Colin Beardwood demanding that the British home secretary ban both songs in the UK as well. "Don't get me wrong—I'm not a fuddy duddy and, in fact, I'm a Dylan fan," he claimed to *Disc*. "But both these songs have a subtle message encouraging drug taking and influence of this kind can't be particularly good for young people." Dylan answered the charges in his inimitable fashion, from the stage during his Royal Albert Hall Concert, where he introduced "Visions of Johanna" as follows: "I'd just like to say this next song is what your English musical papers call a 'drug song.' I never have and never will write a 'drug song.' I don't know how to. It's not a 'drug song.' It's just vulgar."

Censorship of rock and indeed all facets of pop songs was nothing new, and certainly not limited to folk-rock or the mid-'60s. The Kingsmen's "Louie, Louie," after all, had been considered filthy enough to warrant an FBI investigation. The *Time* article that cited "Rainy Day Women," bearing the headline "Going to Pot," went on to insinuate all manner of ridiculous inferences into then-current releases. "Straight Shooter" could be "junkie argot for someone who takes heroin intravenously." "Norwegian Wood" "has been interpreted by some as the tale of a man trying to seduce a lesbian." Non-folk-rock hits came under the speculative gun too, like Frank Sinatra's "Strangers in the Night," which, it was inferred, could be "a song about a homosexual pickup." But the article made the linkage of drugs and sex to folk-rock clear by intoning, "What is happening is that the folk-rock movement, heady with the success of its big-message-with-a-big-beat songs, has been prompted to try racier, more exciting themes. It is no longer down with the P.T.A. and conformism, but—whee!—onward with LSD and lechery.... For variety, high-schoolers can also contemplate the problem of suicide in [Simon & Garfunkel's] 'A Most Peculiar Man' or search for the supposed reference to an unwed mother in 'Little Girl' or a whorehouse in [the Blue Things'] 'Doll House.'"

If it all seems laughable in retrospect, it was anything but funny to some artists tarred as disreputables at the time, such as the Byrds and the Blue Things. "We cut 'Doll House,' and *Time* said it was a piece of smut, which it wasn't," says Richard Scott. "There was no objectionable language in the entire song. In fact, it was a very moralistic song about a house of prostitution. There was no even questionable language in it. But there was a questionable moral. We were saying, 'Don't blame the girls that live there, because if the people didn't come there, there would be no reason for them to be there. Blame everybody that's a part of it, not just the girls.'

"But one week after this magazine article came out [on July 1, 1966], our record wasn't being played. We called station after station that had sent us strip charts of their Top 40, saying that our record was in the Top 40, and they'd say they never heard of it. Until finally, we called a station where we knew some of the DJs, and we knew they liked us. And we said, 'What's going on here? All of a sudden our record's not being played.' And they said, quite simply, 'The station owner's wife called down after that article in *Time* magazine and said that anyone that played that piece of smut would be fired.' So that was the end of it. The wrong place at the wrong time. If that article had come out two weeks later, [the single] would have been high enough in the charts it wouldn't have hurt it. It killed the record, and it shouldn't have."

There were other incidents, mostly with less serious consequences. Manfred Mann wanted to play Paul Jones's anti-Vietnam War protest song "Paul's Dream" (which the group never recorded) on a 1965 New Year's Eve broadcast for the BBC, but were refused, a BBC spokesman told the *National Guardian*, on the grounds that it was not "lighthearted" enough. After *Variety* ran a story about controversial songs in mid-1966, Lovin' Spoonful manager Bob Cavallo wrote a heated letter to the magazine in defense of his clients. "You imply that America's top new pop group have selected a name which alludes to narcotics," he steamed. "I have known the Lovin' Spoonful since long before their formation, and I can assure you that they are too mature and too intelligent to engage in this particular form of nonsense." The name, it was pointed out, was actually inspired by a lyric by bluesman Mississippi John Hurt, who offered affection by the lovin' spoonful in the song "Coffee Blues." "Over here, they think that everything sung by young people is a drug song," John Sebastian complained to *Melody Maker*. "'Daydream' came under the same axe, too."

Janis Ian, already having battled industry and radio resistance to her debut single "Society's Child," found another of her songs caught in an especially tangled imbroglio in Britain in 1967. When British band the Shame (including a young Greg Lake) covered Ian's "Too Old to Go 'Way Little Girl," they rewrote a lyrical reference to rape so as not to discourage BBC airplay. Covering accusations of selling out, slightly, the group inserted slips with both the original and changed lyrics in 1,000 of the 45's record sleeves. Britain's W.H. Smith chain withdrew the slip from those sleeves, with BBC producer Denys Jones emphasizing to *Disc*, "I can't imagine any producer playing a song mentioning rape." As the Shame probably never came close to selling 1,000 copies of this release (which was their sole single) anyway, it seems possible that the whole thing was a stunt cooked up to get what turned out to be the band's only media publicity.

There was also self-censorship, tailored to avoid airplay problems. "House of the Rising Sun" and "You Were on My Mind" had already been toned down by the Animals and the We Five respectively. "Changes in my lyrics upset me some," Paul Simon informed *NME*. "The Hollies, for example, who I'm delighted to hear are interested in 'I Am a Rock,' have had to cut out the word 'womb' from one line in case it gets banned by the BBC or someone." Jefferson Airplane's first B-side, "Runnin' Round This World," was taken off its debut album at RCA's request after the disc's first pressing, for fear that a lyrical reference to trips would be construed as LSD promotion. For the second pressing, it also had the band rerecord lyrics to two other songs on the LP to tone down words the label feared might be taken as too sexually forthright.

Even folk-rock's most radical group and independent record label got into a tiff about a decidedly unambiguous phrase when ESP Records, Ed Sanders of the Fugs recalls, "tried to remix 'Doin' All Right.' Ted Berrigan's line, 'I'm not ever gonna go to Vietnam, I'd prefer to stay right here and screw your mom'— 'screw your mom' was a big problem with the owner of ESP. Because I think the woman bankrolling this whole shot *was* his mom. She was always around. I know that when we signed with ESP, I think Mom was right there in the room. He wanted to dip 'screw your mom' [Sanders's voice lowers an octave or two] *way* down there, sort of underneath the bass. That was the only censorship the Fugs ever suffered."

And they paid the price, saleswise. "At one point, our distributor in Indiana called me, or I called him," says the ESP boss in question, Bernard Stollman. "He was a very genteel, very nice man. But he said, 'Bernard, I got a problem. I was playing golf the other day with the governor. And he turned to me as we were on the links and said, 'I don't want those dirty Fugs in my state.' There were no sales."

In some cases censorship extended to government surveillance and interference. The FBI, the New York City Attorney's Office, and the Postal Service conducted an investigation of the Fugs, as Sanders learned more than a decade later after getting access to some files under the Freedom of Information Act. "We were very controversial," says Sanders. "People forget *how* controversial. People would call in bomb threats, they would raid my bookstore. Somebody sent me a fake bomb. Right-wing nurses picketing us. We would get thrown out of theaters. Carnegie Hall wouldn't rent to us. We played Santa Monica Civic, and they wouldn't rent to us again. We were always in trouble. My phone sounded like Miriam Makeba sometimes. So we ran a close ship. I learned that James Brown wouldn't let his band carry drugs, and I did the same thing, because I knew how close we were to being arrested at any point." The FBI also kept files on Cass Elliot and Phil Ochs, apparently without turning up anything that jeopardized national security.

"By the late '60s, like Eartha Kitt, Taj Mahal and other outspoken artists of color, I was pretty much hamstrung by the Lyndon Johnson blacklist which also had a side effect on the direction of folk-rock/electric rock," says Buffy Sainte-Marie. "A radio broadcaster named Joe Forester in Toronto made me aware of the situation. He surprised me by beginning what I thought was to be a routine interview with a ten-years-too-late apology for having gone along with a request from the Lyndon Johnson White House ten years before to suppress my music, which 'deserved to be suppressed.'

"This was a huge surprise to me. Until Joe brought up this mystery I had figured that American show biz is fickle, and that music tastes change with the times, and that my continued success in other parts of the world was what was pretty amazing. After Joe's on-air apology to me, I received a similar one from a DJ in Cleveland, and from time to time broadcasters have mentioned it. At the time I reviewed my FBI files from the period and although there were a lot of pages to go through, there was so much crossed out in fat indelible marker that there was nothing to be learned about this matter or anything else except that they kept files on me and corresponded with other people. Conversations with long-term friend Taj Mahal (with whom I attended college) let me know I wasn't the only one who had experienced blacklisting. I really have no idea of how big a deal it was, but I've always wished someone had the time to investigate it properly.

"The television side of the same period affected me too," Sainte-Marie goes on. "Because I had a following, I would be invited to the *Tonight Show* but told not to sing 'Universal Soldier' or talk about Native rights issues, because 'it was unhip' at the time. However, Harry Belafonte as guest host supported me and told me to sing anything I wanted. The next *Tonight* invitation I had to turn down because it was made very clear to me that I was to follow *Tonight*'s policy, which felt like censorship, so I declined. Regarding records, I came back from months in Europe to full house concerts, and audiences complaining that they couldn't find my records in the stores any more. I blamed Vanguard, but they always said that the records had been shipped, so I have no explanation.

"At the time, without strong management or business clout to investigate further, I felt that the disappearing records phenomenon was probably just the normal career decline that happens with most artists after a few years. However, Taj had spoken with other artists who had experienced the same kind of thing re: media airplay and variable record counts. Less naive than I am, he and others took a guess at why, and came back to their own experiences with blacklisting from the Johnson White House. He said that LBJ wanted to take personal credit for the Great Society, which had already been going on, spearheaded by lots of us prior to his election. Those of us who were loose cannon/loner types, unaffiliated with corporate or partisan organization control, and able to show up on television and include LBJ on the wrong side of his preferred public image would, according to Taj's logic, be subject to radio euthanasia (my term). In my evaluation, in

The core trio of Fugs at the Peace Eye Bookstore in New York City, 1967.
Left to right: Ed Sanders, Tuli Kupferberg, Ken Weaver

show business you only have to hold somebody underwater for about five minutes for them to be dead for a long time."

There was also a small backlash of antiprotest songs emanating from the same industry selling millions of folk-rock records. There were pro-Vietnam intervention records by country artists Dave Dudley ("What We're Fighting For") and Don Reno & Benny Martin ("Soldier's Prayer in Vietnam"). Staff Sergeant Barry Sadler's "The Ballad of the Green Berets" topped the charts for RCA for five weeks running in early 1966, at around the same time the label was recording the Blue Things' "Doll House" and Jefferson Airplane's "Runnin' Round This World." There may have been innumerable teens and young adults tuning in to the likes of the Byrds and Dylan, but as Sadler's single proved, there were probably at least as many people in the country who wanted to reaffirm the status quo.

There were also turncoats within rock's own ranks, with a rash of unfunny semi-satirical, semi-folk-rock antiprotest efforts that were most likely aiming for parody and fell flat on their face. Among them were the previously noted Spokesmen's "Eve of Destruction" answer single "Dawn of Correction" and draft dodger taunts by Bob Seger ("Ballad of the Yellow Beret") and Mike Nesmith ("The New Recruit"). The worst of the lot was Jan & Dean's "Universal Soldier" satire "The Universal Coward," which was not just as politically unhip as could be at a time when antiwar protest was heating up, but musically terrible and lyrically inane to boot. According to Steve Kolanjian's liner notes to *Jan & Dean's All the Hits—From Surf City to Drag City*, Jan's partner Dean Torrance "felt Jan & Dean should be apolitical and didn't want to release it," leading to it getting credited solely to Jan Berry when it was issued as a 45. Perhaps it was just Hollywood mercenary business as usual. Its anti-protest-folk-rock stance didn't stop one of Jan Berry's cowriters on this noncharting single, then-girlfriend Jill Gibson, from replacing Michelle Phillips in the Mamas & the Papas shortly afterward, when Phillips was briefly fired for various indiscretions.

But at the same time the establishment was fighting back, the establishment itself was changing. The Fugs' second album, probably the most up-front expression of free love and antiwar protest that had been recorded in rock 'n' roll up to that point, crept inside the *Billboard* Top 100 albums chart in July 1966. "I don't think there was any airplay," speculates Bernard Stollman. "I think it was all word of mouth. With respect to the chart activity, it was interesting, because our sales did not reflect that. So it must have had admirers or supporters." Under an October article titled "Record Companies Battling for Underground Artists," *Billboard* noted, "The unique thing about this is that the group has received very little exposure on radio, perhaps none, and never had a hit single to push the LP. The material on their first LP doesn't fit in with programming policies of most stations." Nevertheless, MGM and Atlantic were now bidding with ESP for the Fugs' next record, and executives were already on the lookout for something even newer and bolder than folk-rock to sell. Said Marty Hoffman of Mercury Records, "Our generation has fostered rock 'n' roll, folk and folk-rock. Now this generation is searching for these new forms with which to identify."

And truth be told, despite the false readings into songs like "Eight Miles High" and the substantial damage they wreaked on some careers, there *was* a lot of drugs and sex being talked about in folk-rock, to a franker degree than had ever before been heard in rock music. One of the songs targeted by *Time*'s article was on the B-side of a noncharting debut single by a new band that had yet to even release an album. Marty Balin, lead singer of Jefferson Airplane, did not shirk from *Time*'s assessment of "Runnin' Round This World" (which, incidentally, the ever-trustworthy magazine mistitled as "Running Around the World") as one of their "trips songs," saying it celebrated the "fantastic experience of making love while under LSD." Drugs would fuel part of the inspiration for taking folk-rock into its next phase, as a foundation for psychedelia. California would be its crucible, and the next big leap forward for both folk-rock and the counterculture would be concentrated not in New York or Los Angeles, but in Jefferson Airplane's hometown, San Francisco.

olk-rock would head down several different, fascinating avenues over the next 18 months. But it would do so without Bob Dylan, though he continued to write and record in private, as the world would eventually learn. For the year and a half following his serious, then mysterious motorcycle crash in July 1966, Dylan virtually disappeared from public view. Rumors that he was near death, that he was disfigured, or even that the mishap had never taken place ran rampant. Rumors about how the motorcycle crashed, what exactly Dylan did over the next few weeks and months, and indeed whether the accident happened *still* continue to circulate. Dylan, apparently, did not (and does not) care.

For many Dylan fans and rock critics, the motorcycle accident has taken on mythical significance, as the easily defined precise moment at which his first incarnation as folkie-blazing-to-rock-superstardom ended, and his reincarnation as calmer and wiser singer-songwriter began. Some would go even further and contend that the calamity marked the end of the greatest, most feverishly inventive era not just in Dylan's career, but in rock itself. Without Dylan's leadership, such pundits opined, the rock juggernaut began to fragment into scattered, more self-indulgent pieces, without Dylan around to set the ultimate standard for which to shoot.

Unquestionably the motorcycle accident *did* slow down the blazing trajectory of Dylan's meteor. So much had been accomplished, for him and folk-rock, since the beginning of 1965: his transition to rock 'n' roll, first in the studio and then live, that apocalyptic summer night at the '65 Newport Folk Festival; the charge of his songs to the top of the hit parade, first in the voices of other rock 'n' rollers, then in his own; and the world tour with what might have been the loudest band on the planet.

Whether due to Dylan's vanishing act or not, the accident did also seem to mark the end of folk-rock's first golden age. The Byrds, Simon & Garfunkel, the Mamas & the Papas, Donovan, the Lovin' Spoonful—all had been through similarly lightning transformations from folkies to rock stars during roughly the same time as Dylan. And all, around mid-1966, were settling into their new rock personas as the initial shock and controversy wore off, among themselves as well as their audiences.

Yet it was only the end of the first golden age of folk-rock, with more golden ages just around the corner. For what Dylan had done so much to set in motion was now far, far bigger than what any individual could steer with a single hand. Folk-rock was now ready to sprout many offshoots that were just as exciting as what happened when the Beatles met America's folk troubadours. Just eleven days before Dylan's accident, the Byrds had released *Fifth Dimension*, whose synthesis of folk-rock with jazz, Indian music, and electronics would help jump-start psychedelic rock and indeed take folk-rock into an entirely new dimension. The folk-rock revolution had been won. But it was far from over.

epilogue

eight miles high

folk-rock's flight from haight-ashbury to woodstock

From mid-1966 to the end of the 1960s, folk-rock would continue to evolve and profoundly alter the course of popular music. That story is told in the author's sequel to this book, *Eight Miles High: Folk-Rock's Flight from Haight-Ashbury to Woodstock* (Backbeat Books, 2003). It portrays the mutation of folk-rock into psychedelia via California bands like the Byrds and Jefferson Airplane; the maturation of folk-rock composers in the birth of the singer-songwriter movement; the comeback of Bob Dylan and the inception of country-rock; the rise of folk-rock's first supergroup from the ashes of the Byrds and Buffalo Springfield; the origination of a truly British form of folk-rock; and the growth of the live folk-to-rock music festival, from Newport to Woodstock.

discography

T here were many albums and singles made in the mid-'60s that contained quality folk-rock. What follows is a selected list of the best and most important of those releases that include music discussed in this book, with some possible additional releases to explore mentioned in the capsule reviews. Bear in mind that this discography, in line with the rest of the book, covers the music made by the generation of performers that shaped 1960s folk-rock. With just a few exceptions of particularly important pre-1964 recordings, and a couple of '67 releases that sneak in because they're covered in the section on East Coast folkies going electric circa 1966, the records listed here reflect the 1964–66 era that celebrated the birth and rise of folk-rock. To keep the list within that focus, important pre-1960s folk recordings, such as the Harry Smith– and Alan Lomax–compiled anthologies, are not listed. Nor are acoustic folk records from before and during the 1960s by such major folk performers as Woody Guthrie, Odetta, and Martin Carthy, though anyone interested in the traditional folk roots of and influences on folk-rock should investigate some of those.

The record labels listed for these entries are the most recent known labels on which the albums have been reissued or maintained in print. For reviews of many folk-rock albums not listed here, and additional, detailed reviews of many folk-rock albums that *are* listed here, readers are encouraged to check out the largest online database of album reviews and artist discographies, the All Music Guide, at www.allmusic.com.

Links to Web sites with all sorts of weird and wonderful details about folk-rockers featured in this book, as well as some additional lists of wonderful and weird 1960s folk-rock recordings and other folk-rock miscellany, can be found on the author's Web site, at www.richieunterberger.com.

Eight Miles High: Folk-Rock's Flight from Haight-Ashbury to Woodstock (published by Backbeat Books, in 2003), the sequel to *Turn! Turn! Turn!*, has a critical discography of the most important folk-rock recordings from approximately mid-1966 through the end of the 1960s. Some of the best-ofs and compilations in the following discography will include some of that music. It seemed inappropriate to be too rigorous in dividing such anthologies chronologically; the main purpose is to direct listeners to the best music described in the text, even if it sometimes shares space with tracks from a later vintage.

The complete discography of the author's recommended 1960s folk-rock recordings—covering the entire decade—can be viewed online at www.richieunterberger.com/folkrockdisc.html.

Eric Andersen, *Violets of Dawn* (1999, Vanguard). A sampler of the best of Andersen's early recordings, including his best early songs: "Violets of Dawn," "Close the Door Lightly When You Go," "Thirsty Boots," and "The Hustler." The track selection is almost the same as on Vanguard's *The Best of Eric Andersen*, but the sound on this CD is better.

The Beatles, *Meet the Beatles* (1964, Capitol). Not a folk-rock album, but the one record that more than any other awakened young American folk musicians to the possibilities of electric rock music. The *Meet the Beatles* LP—as opposed to *With the Beatles* (their second British LP, which has much of the same material and is the one that was reissued on CD)—is what you need to re-create the impact. It is almost wholly devoted to original songs, including two great ones ("I Want to Hold Your Hand" and "I Saw Her Standing There") that don't appear on *With the Beatles*.

The Beatles, *A Hard Day's Night* (1964, Capitol). Songs from and recorded before, during, and after the making of the movie of the same name, which was about as influential on early folk-rock musicians as the *Meet the Beatles* album. You can hear some folky influences creeping into their work, too, on songs like "Things We Said Today" and "I'll Be Back."

The Beatles, *Beatles for Sale* (1964, Capitol). More music that, if only unconsciously, continued to help bring folk and rock closer together, explicitly so on "I'm a Loser" and "I'll Follow the Sun."

The Beatles, *Help!* (1965, Capitol). A fine album on any terms, as all Beatles albums are. Within the context of folk-rock, it's notable for several songs that show a definite folk-rock influence, like "You've Got to Hide Your Love Away" and "I've Just Seen a Face," as well as the appearance (*not* influenced by the Byrds) of a prototypical ringing 12-string electric guitar riff in "Ticket to Ride."

The Beatles, *Rubber Soul* (1965, Capitol). The Beatles' most strongly folk-rock-influenced album, from Lennon-McCartney songs like "Norwegian Wood" and "I'm Looking Through You" to George Harrison's homage to the Byrds, "If I Needed Someone."

The Beau Brummels, *The Best of the Beau Brummels* (1987, Rhino). A good 18-song survey of their 1960s tracks, though not perfect in its song selection, particularly with the omission of "I Want You." It does have their key hits "Just a Little" and "Laugh, Laugh," as well as standout lesser-known singles like "Sad Little Girl." There's much to enjoy on some other Beau Brummels releases if you like what you hear here, such as 1965's *Vol. 2*, Sundazed's three-CD mid-'60s rarities collection *San Fran Sessions*, and the more reflective 1967 album *Triangle*.

The Blue Things, *The Blue Things* (2001, Rewind). A reissue of the great lost folk-rock group's 1966 RCA album, with six bonus tracks from 1966-67 singles (including some very cool psychedelic ones like "Orange Rooftop of Your Mind"). Highly recommended to anyone who enjoys the early Byrds and Beau Brummels, though it has an earnest longing appeal of its own. The getting-harder-to-find Cicadelic LPs *Story Vol. 1–3* fill out the picture with numerous outtakes and early singles, as do the Collectables CDs *Story Vol. 1–2*.

Buffalo Springfield, *Buffalo Springfield* (1966, Elektra/Asylum). The Springfield's first album is stellar California folk-rock, with great harmonies, songwriting (by Stephen Stills and Neil Young), and electric-acoustic guitar interplay. The hit single "For What It's Worth" is here, but there are plenty of other gems from Stills ("Everybody's Wrong," "Pay the Price," "Go and Say Goodbye") and Young ("Nowadays Clancy Can't Even Sing," "Out of My Mind," "Flying on the Ground Is Wrong"). Origi-nally issued on Atco, this somehow ended up on Elektra for its 1997 CD reissue, which includes both stereo and mono versions of the album.

Buffalo Springfield, *Buffalo Springfield Box Set* (2001, Rhino). This "definitive" four-CD box set isn't quite definitive, and could have been done better. It's missing some tracks from their final album *Last Time Around*, and disc four, comprised of songs from the first two albums in their orig-inal sequence, is a waste, as all the tracks appear on other discs in the package, in all cases but two in identical versions. Still…it has almost everything the group issued, and dozens of cool demos, outtakes, and alternates, and as such must be considered a great collection of music.

The Byrds, *The Preflyte Sessions* (2001, Sundazed). There is no more important collection of pre-1965 folk-rock than this two-CD set of early Byrds demos and rehearsals. Not only is it historically important, it's for the most part immensely enjoyable as well, if less mature and more Beatles-influenced than their early Columbia recordings. The addition of four pre-Byrds David Crosby solo rock recordings is a nice bonus. Note that the versions of the tracks on their first sin-gle (credited to the Beefeaters), "Please Let Me Love You" and "Don't Be Long," that appear here are almost identical to the takes used on the Elektra 45, but not the exact same ones—those are available on the Collectors' Choice Music various-artists compilation *Buried Treasure*.

The Byrds, *Mr. Tambourine Man* (1965, Columbia/Legacy). If there is one album that neo-phytes to 1960s folk-rock should start with after reading this book, this is it. Their 1965 debut fea-tures the hit single title track—the most important *song* covered in this book—and standout covers of more Bob Dylan songs ("All I Really Want to Do," "Chimes of Freedom") and Pete Seeger's "The Bells of Rhymney," as well as quality original material such as "Here Without You," "I Knew I'd Want You," and "It's No Use." Like all of the Columbia/Legacy Byrds CD reissues, it's bolstered with sev-eral bonus tracks of rarities and previously unissued outtakes and alternate versions.

The Byrds, *Turn! Turn! Turn!* (1965, Columbia/Legacy). Not as good as the preceding *Mr. Tam-bourine Man*, but still high-quality early folk-rock, particularly on the title smash. Gene Clark's songs, especially "Set You Free This Time," show their original material starting to mature, though this would be the last album that Clark recorded with the group before leaving in 1966.

The Byrds, *Greatest Hits* (Columbia). You won't go wrong with any of the first five proper Byrds albums. But as an introduction, *Greatest Hits* covers their 1965-67 recordings in splendid fash-ion. "Eight Miles High," released as a single before its inclusion on the 1966 *Fifth Dimension* album (just outside the scope of this book), is here. If you want to hear the original single version of its raga-rock B-side, "Why," that's on both the expanded *Fifth Dimension* CD and the compilation *The Original Singles 1965-1967*.

Judy Collins, #3 (1963, Elektra). Though a folk album and not a folk-rock album, this was vital in expanding folk's parameters to contemporary songwriters and full multi-instrumental arrangements. The presence of Roger McGuinn as guitarist-banjoist-arranger, as well as pre-Byrds versions of "Turn! Turn! Turn!" and "The Bells of Rhymney," further cements its role as an important folk-rock antecedent.

Judy Collins, *In My Life* (1966, Elektra). The album that brought Collins into folk-rock was also the flagship of the folk-rock sub-genre baroque folk, with fine covers of songs by Dylan, Richard Fariña, Leonard Cohen, Donovan, the Beatles, and others, often with classical-influenced arrangements.

Judy Collins, *Forever: An Anthology* (1997, Elektra). Certainly this suffers from a lack of chronological sequencing, and not all of it covers the 1960s. Still, the 35 songs include most of her key 1960s folk-rock recordings, among them "Both Sides Now," "Who Knows Where the Time Goes?," "Hard Lovin' Loser," "Suzanne," "First Boy I Loved," and "My Father," not to mention her 1963 recording of "Turn! Turn! Turn!"

The Daily Flash, *I Flash Daily* (1984, Psycho). Side one of this posthumous album has four singles from 1966–67 by this good Seattle folk-rock group, as well as some quality unreleased material. These have solid West Coast 12-string-guitar-and-harmony folk-rock arrangements, highlighted by covers of Ian & Sylvia's "The French Girl" and Eric Andersen's "Violets of Dawn." But side two, whose two live recordings are dominated by a long cover of a Herbie Hancock song, is far less worthwhile.

Jackie DeShannon, *What the World Needs Now...The Definitive Collection* (1994, EMI). DeShannon only periodically did folk-rock, or more properly proto-folk-rock, in 1963-65. This 28-track best-of compilation, though, has her important efforts in that style, like "Needles and Pins," "When You Walk in the Room," and "Don't Turn Your Back on Me."

Jackie DeShannon, *1965 Metric Music Demo* (1965, Metric Music Co.). Probably the most fiendishly rare item referred to in this discography, this album of publisher demos was only circulated within the music industry. With a solitary acoustic guitar serving as accompaniment, it features strong, movingly sung, and—from the sounds of things—Bob Dylan-influenced personal songs that approximate the approach frequently tapped by early folk-rock composers. Among them is a version of "Don't Doubt Yourself, Babe," which the Byrds covered on their first album.

Dion, *The Road I'm On: A Retrospective* (1997, Columbia/Legacy). Though some of this double-CD of Dion's 1962–66 Columbia recordings contains the pop-rock and doo wop for which he's most famous, the majority of it is given over to his initial forays into blues and folk-rock. That includes rare mid-'60s Tom Wilson–produced tracks that are unsurprisingly close in arrangement to some of Dylan's 1965 cuts. Unfortunately, his best such track, a ripping 1965 cover of the rare Dylan composition "Baby, I'm in the Mood for You," is only available on a different, less wide-ranging CD, *Bronx Blues: The Columbia Recordings (1962–1965)*.

Donovan, *Summer Day Reflection Songs* (2000, Castle). Donovan's highly underrated 1965, pre-electric rock period is fully documented by this fine two-CD release, which contains everything he recorded prior to "Sunshine Superman," including some real rarities. The hit singles "Catch the Wind," "Universal Soldier," and "Colours" are here, as are some good little-known originals, like "Summer Day Reflection Song."

Donovan, *Sunshine Superman* (1966, Epic). Donovan's best album, and his first full electric rock one, gets off to a great start with the "Sunshine Superman" hit, and stays in exhilarating early folk-rock-psychedelia gear the whole way. "Season of the Witch," "Bert's Blues," "Guinevere," "The Trip," and "The Fat Angel" are all nearly up to the level of his best hit singles, and "Celeste" is the great overlooked Donovan LP track.

Donovan, *Troubadour: The Definitive Collection 1964–1976* (1992, Epic/Legacy). The absence of "Celeste" from this two-CD best-of is inexcusable. But for the most part it does a good job in compiling his strongest material, including all of his hit singles, numerous standout album tracks, and a handful of previously unreleased cuts.

Bob Dylan, *The Freewheelin' Bob Dylan* (1962, Columbia). Though there's no rock 'n' roll here (except perhaps, to the slightest of degrees, on the cover of "Corinna, Corinna"), this merits inclusion as the pre-1964 folk album with perhaps the most influence on the first folk-rock generation. This was the album on which Dylan laid out much of the songwriting approach that would carry over to the birth of folk-rock, including such classics as "Blowin' in the Wind," "Girl of the North Country," "Don't Think Twice, It's All Right," and "A Hard Rain's A-Gonna Fall."

Bob Dylan, *The Freewheelin' Bob Dylan Outtakes* (Vigotone, bootleg). Twenty-five outtakes recorded around the time of *Freewheelin'*, which would be interesting enough under its own steam. As it relates to folk-rock, though, it's particularly intriguing for the inclusion of multiple takes of "Mixed Up Confusion," "That's All Right," "Rocks and Gravel," and "Corrina, Corrina," all of them recorded in 1962 with rock arrangements.

Bob Dylan, *Bringing It All Back Home* (1965, Columbia). Half of this has the man's first full entry into rock music, in a basic bluesy mode on "Subterranean Homesick Blues" and "Maggie's Farm," but in a more romantic and melodic frame of mind on "Love Minus Zero/No Limit" and "She Belongs to Me." The acoustic-dominated songs are just as important, including his own version of "Mr. Tambourine Man" and "It's All Over Now, Baby Blue."

Bob Dylan, *Highway 61 Revisited* (1965, Columbia). For "Like a Rolling Stone" alone, this would be considered a major folk-rock album. "Tombstone Blues," "Queen Jane Approximately," "Desolation Row," and "Ballad of a Thin Man" ensured that Dylan's first all-out rock album would be subject to more critical analysis than almost any other popular music recording.

Bob Dylan, *Blonde on Blonde* (1966, Columbia). His greatest album (though many would argue for others), with greater melodic and emotional depth than his previous folk-rock recordings. Includes the classic hits "Just Like a Woman," "I Want You," and "Rainy Day Women #12 & 35," but also other songs of a similar caliber, like "Sad Eyed Lady of the Lowlands," "Stuck Inside of Mobile with the Memphis Blues Again," and "Absolutely Sweet Marie."

Bob Dylan, *The Bootleg Series Vol. 4: Live 1966: The "Royal Albert Hall" Concert* (1998, Columbia/Legacy). The title's about as unwieldy and confusing as they come for a major label superstar release. What you need to know: this is a double-CD live set of his May 17, 1966 Manchester concert, frequently bootlegged as having been recorded at the Royal Albert hall. The first disc contains fine solo acoustic versions of songs from 1965–66 releases. But it's more renowned for the second disc, with his fiery electric rock performances backed by the Hawks aka the Band, including the famous shout of "Judas!" from the crowd.

Bob Dylan, *Biograph* (1985, Columbia). This five-record box set covers Dylan's work through the early '80s, but not unexpectedly features much material from the 1960s. It's valuable not only for the inclusion of all his major hits and several vital LP tracks, but also a number of important non-LP folk-rock singles, live versions, and outtakes from the 1960s, like "Mixed Up Confusion," "Positively 4th Street," "Can You Please Crawl Out Your Window?," and "Quinn the Eskimo" (aka "The Mighty Quinn"). Other important 1960s rarities appear on Columbia's three-CD *The Bootleg Series Vol. 1–3*, and too many Dylan bootlegs to count. The 1965 Newport Folk Festival set discussed in detail in the prologue appears on numerous boots.

Marianne Faithfull, *North Country Maid* (1966, Deram). A surprisingly credible rock-tinged folk album from a star whose 1960s work is usually dismissed as superfluous. It approximates a Pentangle-like swing on cuts like "Sally Free and Easy," and uses sitar on the traditional folk numbers "She Moves Through the Fair" and "Wild Mountain Thyme." The 1990 Deram CD reissue has three worthwhile bonus cuts, but is now about as hard to find as the original LP.

Fapardokly, *Fapardokly* (1967, Sundazed). Though this is a hodgepodge of mid-'60s sessions rather than a proper album, about half of it's among the finest little-known early Byrds-influenced folk-rock, paced by Merrell Fankhauser's light, optimistic singing and songwriting. He offered some more good stuff, in a more pop-psychedelic vein, on the 1968 *Things* album by Merrell Fankhauser & H.M.S. Bounty, also reissued on Sundazed.

Richard & Mimi Fariña, *Celebrations for a Grey Day* (1965, Vanguard). A seminal nearly-folk-rock album from early 1965, though it's folkier than their second LP, including several guitar-dulcimer-dominated instrumentals. "Pack Up Your Sorrows," "One-Way Ticket," and "Reno Nevada," however, all cross the border into early folk-rock, with a poetic flair not far below the standards of Dylan's contemporaneous work.

Richard & Mimi Fariña, *Reflections in a Crystal Wind* (1965, Vanguard). The duo's second album definitely took their music in a more decisive folk-rock direction, even if it still retained an Appalachian flavor (particularly in Richard Fariña's dulcimer) not heard in much other folk-rock music. "Sell-Out Agitation Waltz" is their best cut with full rock accompaniment, and "Bold Marauder," "Raven Girl," and "Children of Darkness" are all exceptional melancholic songs.

Richard & Mimi Fariña, *The Complete Vanguard Recordings* (2001, Vanguard). The title of this three-CD set is a bit inaccurate as a few stray items (none particularly essential) are missing. But it does include everything from their first two albums, as well as most of their posthumous LP *Memories* (also available separately). *Memories* actually contained some of their best songs, like "Joy 'Round My Brain," "Morgan the Pirate," and "The Quiet Joys of Brotherhood" (all on this compilation too), as well as material from their appearance at the 1965 Newport Folk Festival, and the Richard Fariña–produced Joan Baez track "All the World Has Gone By" (perhaps the greatest thing she ever recorded). If this collection sounds like too much for the casual investor, there's also a good 75-minute anthology, *Pack Up Your Sorrows: Best of the Vanguard Years.*

The Fugs, *The Fugs First Album* (1965, Fantasy). The jug band-into-pre-punk rock phase of the Fugs is documented by their debut album, featuring such sex-drugs-subversion odes as "Slum Goddess," "I Couldn't Get High," and "Boobs a Lot." The CD reissue on Fantasy doubles the length of the album with outtakes and live recordings, and yet more outtakes from the LP sessions (in a yet more primitive style) are found on *Virgin Fugs.*

The Fugs, *The Fugs Second Album* (1966, Fantasy). Originally titled *The Fugs* when it first came out on ESP, this remains their finest hour, with both lust- and politically-charged rockers ("Frenzy" and "Kill for Peace") and gentler melodic, poetic folk-rock ("Morning Morning" and "I Want to Know"). The CD reissue on Fantasy adds a couple of live 1967 performances and three songs from their rejected 1967 Atlantic album.

Gale Garnett, *We'll Sing in the Sunshine* (1997, Collectables). The hit title track is all virtually anyone remembers of Garnett these days. It's on this album, which repackages her 1964 LP *My Kind of Folk Songs* with some additional bonus tracks from the mid-'60s. There are surprisingly strong cuts that oh-so-slightly mesh commercial folk with rock rhythm, like the nuclear danger warning "I Came to the City" and the cover of the well-traveled "I Know You Rider."

Davy Graham, *Folk Blues and Beyond* (1965, Topic). The cult British guitarist's groundbreaking album combined blues, folk, Indian, middle-eastern, and jazz music, working with a rhythm section. Though not quite folk-rock, it anticipates much of what colored arrangements by British folk-rockers like the Pentangle.

Tim Hardin, *Hang on to a Dream: The Verve Recordings* (1994, Polygram). Hardin, for all his influence, only recorded three studio albums during the 1960s. The first and best two of those, *Tim Hardin 1* and *Tim Hardin 2*, are found on the first disc of this set; the second disc features mid-'60s demos—some from as early as May 1964—which are largely given over to blues, illustrating his first excursions into electric music. There is additional material of merit to be found on the various demo and live albums Hardin put out in the 1960s, as well as 1969's *Suite for Susan Moore and Damion: We Are One, One, All in One.* But the first disc of this set contains what is inarguably his most focused work, including "If I Were a Carpenter," "How Can We Hang on to a Dream," "Misty Roses," "Lady Came from Baltimore," and "Reason to Believe."

Judy Henske, *High Flying Bird* (1964, Collectors' Choice Music). For folk-rock purposes, the important track here is the magnificent title song, as close to folk-rock as anything recorded prior to 1964. The rest of the album has some good folk-blues too, but never in as progressive a fashion. The hard-to-categorize Henske made about five albums of interesting music in the 1960s—sometimes dovetailing with folk-rock—and an intelligently compiled best-of is overdue.

Janis Ian, *Society's Child: The Verve Recordings* (1995, Polydor). While hearing all of her first four albums at once might seem excessive if you're not a devoted fan, actually the price of this two-CD set—which has everything from those records—isn't that much more than a single-disc 1960s best-of would entail. These albums are better than some critics have made them out to be, too, with more shades of soul and blues than some have admitted.

Ian & Sylvia, *Northern Journey* (1964, Vanguard). It says here that there are simply no Ian & Sylvia compilations (although several best-ofs have been attempted) that represent the best of their material well, due to erratic song selection and poor sequencing that lumps in some pedestrian late-'60s recordings with prime gems. Most of their albums have at least several strong tracks to recommend them. 1964's *Northern Journey* might be a good one to start with because it captures how they sounded just before the folk-rock they influenced got properly started. Plus, it has the original version of "You Were on My Mind," as well as one of Ian Tyson's best songs, "Someday Soon."

Ian & Sylvia, *The Complete Vanguard Studio Recordings* (2001, Vanguard). And if you do want to take the plunge and find all of their worthy 1960s cuts—and there were many, though some frustratingly mediocre ones were mixed in—this four-CD box set contains all seven of the albums they issued on Vanguard in the 1960s, with four rare tracks added. "You Were on My Mind," "Four Strong Winds," "Early Morning Rain," "Tomorrow Is a Long Time," "The French Girl," "Twenty Four Hours from Tulsa," "Circle Game"—all are here, as well as numerous other goodies, though it'll cost you. Unfortunately, it doesn't have the two albums they did for MGM in the late '60s.

Ian & Sylvia, *Lovin' Sound* (1967, MGM). A typically erratic Ian & Sylvia folk-rock album, but about half of it is very good, and much lesser known than their Vanguard material. The brooding title track is one of the best overlooked 1960s folk-rock cuts in general, and the uncharacteristically happy-go-lucky "Sunday" sounds halfway between a Mamas & the Papas imitation and a Mamas & the Papas satire.

Jim & Jean, *Changes* (1966, Verve/Forecast). Even if Jim & Jean sounded a lot like Ian & Sylvia and didn't have nearly as much of an artistic personality as most early folk-rockers did, the *Changes* album has much good music, particularly in the covers of Phil Ochs's "Crucifixion" and David Blue's "Strangers in a Strange Land," as well as the original "One Sure Thing." Unlike most of the albums in this discography, this long-out-of-print LP has never been reissued.

The Leaves, *…Are Happening! The Best of the Leaves* (2000, Sundazed). Though often derivative of the Byrds, Rolling Stones, and the Beatles, this is a highly enjoyable compilation of material by one of the best just-post-Byrds Los Angeles folk-rock bands. No less than three versions of their hit "Hey Joe" are here, along with other good garageish folk-rock (or folk-rockish garage rock) like "Be with You," "Love Minus Zero," "Just a Memory," and "Too Many People."

Bob Lind, *The Best of Bob Lind: You Might Have Heard My Footsteps* (1993, EMI). The 25-track compilation of the lushly produced, earnest singer-songwriter's 1965–67 recordings features his sole hit "Elusive Butterfly," but also several songs covered by other rock and folk-rock artists: "Cheryl's Goin' Home," "Mister Zero," "Counting," and "Drifter's Sunrise." The previously unreleased baroque-folk "English Afternoon" is actually a match for anything he recorded.

Love, *Love* (1966, Elektra). There's too much derivative recycling of Byrds riffs on this debut to qualify it as a great album. But it's good, including as it does such class folk-rockers as "Mushroom Clouds," "Signed D.C.," "A Message to Pretty," and "Softly to Me," as well as their garage rock classic "My Little Red Book."

Love, *Love Story 1966–1972* (1995, Rhino). A double-CD compilation that includes everything from their 1967 album *Forever Changes*, most (but not everything) from *Love*, and all of the good material from the band's second album, *Da Capo*, which is great music though it's less strongly folk-rock based than the other recordings by the group's first incarnation. The post-Bryan MacLean–era material is a bore, though. The two Sundazed CDs of MacLean acoustic demos, *IfYouBelieveIn* and *Candy's Waltz*, are recommended further listening, though much of the material was recorded after the 1960s.

The Lovin' Spoonful, *Anthology* (1990, Rhino). Though a major folk-rock group, the Lovin' Spoonful's albums are patchy enough to make a best-of the preferred point of entry. And *Anthology* is the best best-of, its 26 tracks including all their hit singles, as well as outstanding album tracks like "Younger Girl."

The Mamas & the Papas, *Creeque Alley* (1991, MCA). Like the Lovin' Spoonful, the Mamas & the Papas' best output can be succinctly boiled down to a good best-of that serves them better than their individual albums. The two-CD *Creeque Alley* does this, including all of their hit singles, outstanding B-sides and LP tracks like "Got a Feelin'," some pre-Mamas & the Papas cuts by the Big Three and the Mugwumps, and some post-Mamas & the Papas solo efforts.

The Mugwumps, *The Mugwumps: An Historic Recording* (1967, Warner Brothers). More interesting as an historical document than as rock music, this nonetheless has 1964 pre-Mamas & the Papas/Lovin' Spoonful sides by the group to feature Cass Elliot, Denny Doherty, and Zal Yanovsky. Some of this is mediocre rock 'n' roll, but on other cuts, particularly "Here It Is Another Day," you can hear precedents to the more famous groups they would soon found.

Fred Neil, *Bleecker & MacDougal* (1965, Collectors' Choice Music). Even if the folk-rock here is more hinted at than fully realized, this *is* Neil's first fully realized set of original material. And fine songs these are too, blending folk, rock, blues, country, and pop on "Little Bit of Rain," "Blues on the Ceiling," and the much-covered "Other Side of This Life."

Phil Ochs, *Farewells & Fantasies* (1997, Elektra). A bit pricey for an anthology, perhaps, but this three-CD box set does a good job of covering highlights from both his acoustic and electric periods. Some rarities are here too, the most important of them being the 1966 electric rock version of "I Ain't Marching Anymore," released only on a UK 45 and *Sing Out!* flexi-disc at the time.

Tom Paxton, *The Best of Tom Paxton* (1999, Elektra). A smartly chosen, good-value (26-song) single-disc compilation covering his 1964–71 recordings for Elektra. It's true that his late-'60s electric albums are lightly represented, but this does include the songs for which he's most famous: "The Last Thing on My Mind," "Ramblin' Boy," "I Can't Help But Wonder Where I'm Bound," "Victoria Dines Alone," "Bottle of Wine," and, yes, "Goin' to the Zoo."

Peter & Gordon, *The EP Collection* (1995, See For Miles). Though this happens to have been compiled from European EPs (hence the title), it serves as a good best-of collection for this British Invasion duo, an underrated influence on the likes of the Byrds. All of their hits are here, along with some cuts that expose their little-appreciated folk leanings, like a cover of Phil Ochs's "The Flower Lady."

Peter, Paul & Mary, *Ten Years Together: The Best of Peter, Paul & Mary* (1970, Warner Brothers). Indeed this has the best of their records from both the early '60s folk boom and the later 1960s folk-rock era. From the former, we hear "Blowin' in the Wind," "If I Had a Hammer," and "Don't Think Twice, It's All Right"; from the latter, there's "I Dig Rock & Roll Music" and Dylan's "Too Much of Nothing"; and there are also the Gordon Lightfoot covers "For Lovin' Me" and "Early Mornin' Rain."

The Rising Sons, *Rising Sons Featuring Taj Mahal and Ry Cooder* (1992, Columbia/Legacy). The Rising Sons only put out one official single while they were in existence, their legacy thankfully retrieved by this 22-track CD. It includes that single and much or all of what would have been on their unreleased album, and is good if slightly schizophrenic folk-blues-pop-rock, somewhat ahead of its time in its anticipation of aspects of groups such as Moby Grape and Buffalo Springfield.

Tim Rose, *Morning Dew* (1988, Demon). Actually a retitled reissue of his 1967 solo debut *Tim Rose*, this is a little stylistically inconsistent, including some shots at pop-soul as well as folk-rock. Rose came across strongest in his gravelly folk-rock updates of tunes that started as folk songs, particularly "Morning Dew," "Come Away, Melinda," and his slow arrangement of "Hey Joe."

Tom Rush, *Take a Little Walk with Me* (1966, Collectors' Choice Music). Rush's second Elektra album isn't nearly as strong or original a collection as his next LP for the label, *The Circle Game*, which was instrumental in starting the singer-songwriter genre. It's still an interesting early leap of an acoustic folkie into flat-out R&B-heavy rock 'n' roll, albeit only on half the record, and primarily on rock oldies covers.

Buffy Sainte-Marie, *The Best of Buffy Sainte-Marie* (1970, Vanguard). This 24-song survey of her early work includes most of the songs she's most famous for (and that were frequently covered, by folk-rockers and others): "Codine," "Universal Soldier," "Until It's Time for You to Go," "My Country 'Tis Of Thy People You're Dying," and "Now That the Buffalo's Gone." Plus there's her most concentrated effort to crack the folk-rock singles market, a cover of Joni Mitchell's "The Circle Game."

The Searchers, *Greatest Hits* (1985, Rhino). A fine summary of the American and British hits by the band that did much to influence folk-rock's guitar arrangements, including "Needles and Pins," "What Have They Done to the Rain," "When You Walk in the Room," and "Take Me for What I'm Worth." Their albums are dotted with folk covers like "Where Have All the Flowers Gone" and "Four Strong Winds," should you want to dig further.

Simon & Garfunkel, *Sounds of Silence* (1966, Columbia). A very good record considering it needed to be thrown together in haste when "The Sound of Silence" single became an unexpected chart-topper. Besides that classic, the early hit "I Am a Rock" is here, as well as good early Simon originals like "Richard Cory" and "April Come She Will."

Simon & Garfunkel, *Parsley, Sage, Rosemary and Thyme* (1966, Columbia). The two continued to improve on their third album, highlighted by the hit single "Homeward Bound," and also including numerous songs that were almost as good and popular as their 45s: "Scarborough Fair/Canticle," "Patterns," "The 59th Street Bridge Song (Feelin' Groovy)," and "For Emily, Whenever I May Find Her."

Simon & Garfunkel, *The Columbia Studio Recordings 1964–1970* (2001, Columbia/Legacy). A well-packaged five-CD box set of all of Simon & Garfunkel's studio albums. Even if you have the old LPs, you might find this worth consideration due to the addition of a few bonus tracks, from non-LP cuts and previously unreleased outtakes, tagged onto the end of each album.

P.F. Sloan, *Anthology* (1993, One Way). This is a decent selection of 18 tracks from his mid-'60s recordings, although there are a few other good songs on his first pair of albums and the non-LP single "I Can't Help But Wonder, Elizabeth." For more, if less vital, material from the same era by the songwriter most adept at combining youthful folk-rock yearning with L.A. pop-rock, the demo collection *Child of Our Times: The Trousdale Demo Sessions, 1965–1967* is also recommended.

The Springfields, *Over the Hills & Far Away* (1997, Philips). Unquestionably some will find this too poppy and wimpy for consideration as core folk-rock. However, the sides by this British group (featuring Dusty Springfield) were among the few records made in the early '60s to anticipate the fusion of folk and rock. There's considerable piffle on this two-CD set, but there's also their American hit "Silver Threads & Golden Needles," as well as others that are vague folk-rock forerunners, like "Allentown Jail."

Jesse Colin Young, *Young Blood* (1965, Edsel). Obscure but notable early-1965 album that started to tilt toward folk-rock in some of the arrangements, before folk-rock had become established. Young's fine singing, shaded with soul, folk, blues, pop, and country, *was* already well established.

Various Artists, *Before They Were the Mamas & the Papas…The Magic Circle* (1999, Varese Sarabande). This grab bag of pre-Mamas & the Papas recordings—quite a few of them previously unreleased—on which some members participated might be more interesting than great. But it's *very* interesting, particularly for the inclusion of several 1964 Erik Jacobsen electric tracks in which Cass Elliot, Zal Yanovsky, and Jerry Yester participated. There are also items by the Big Three (with Elliot and Denny Doherty), several pre-Mamas & the Papas groups featuring John Phillips, and previously unreleased 1965 songs by the New Journeymen (with Doherty and John and Michelle Phillips), including a cover of "Mr. Tambourine Man."

Various Artists, *The Best of Broadside 1962–1988* (2000, Smithsonian Folkways). Mostly from the 1960s, this five-CD box set includes numerous, sometimes rare, early sides by artists who recorded for or had songs published in *Broadside*: Bob Dylan, Buffy Sainte-Marie, Tom Paxton, Janis Ian, Richard Fariña, Phil Ochs, Eric Andersen, Happy Traum, the Fugs. Most of these are acoustic, but they give a good insight into the singer-songwriters' folk roots, surrounded by cuts from some older folk figures like Pete Seeger. Very early versions of the folk-rock standards "Morning Dew" (by Bonnie Dobson) and "Society's Child" (by Janis Ian) are included.

Various Artists, *Casey Kasem Presents America's Top Ten: The 60s—The Folk Years* (2002, Top Sail). This sticks to Top Ten singles exclusively, but contains some of the folk-rock hits most important to spreading the folk-rock gospel to the mainstream: the Byrds' "Mr. Tambourine Man," Barry McGuire's "Eve of Destruction," the Mamas & the Papas' "California Dreamin'," the Lovin' Spoonful's "Daydream," the We Five's "You Were on My Mind," Donovan's "Mellow Yellow," Judy Collins's "Both Sides Now," Scott McKenzie's "San Francisco," and the Youngbloods' "Get Together." It also has the pre-British Invasion folk hit by the Rooftop Singers, "Walk Right In," and folk-pop and pop-rock hits bearing folk-rock influences, like the Seekers' "I'll Never Find Another You" and Nilsson's cover of Fred Neil's "Everybody's Talkin'."

Various Artists, *Nuggets Vol. 10: Folk-Rock* (Rhino). An odd mix (issued in the mid-'80s, though it doesn't bear a release date) of huge folk-rock hits (the Byrds' "Mr. Tambourine Man," the Turtles' "It Ain't Me Babe," Barry McGuire's "Eve of Destruction," Scott McKenzie's "San Francisco"), pop-leaning minor hits (the Sunshine Company's "Back on the Street Again," the Nitty Gritty Dirt Band's "Buy for Me the Rain"), and rarities by Jake Holmes (the original version of "Dazed and Confused"), the Modern Folk Quartet, and the Deep Six.

Various Artists, *Songs of Protest* (1991, Rhino). Though it's only about half folk-rock, this is a good place to pick up on some major hits in the protest folk-rock bag. Barry McGuire's "Eve of Destruction," Sonny Bono's "Laugh at Me," Janis Ian's "Society's Child," Dion's "Abraham, Martin and John," the Turtles' "Let Me Be," Donovan's "Universal Soldier," Phil Ochs's electric version of "I Ain't Marchin' Anymore," and Country Joe & the Fish's "I-Feel-Like-I'm-Fixin'-to-Die-Rag" are all here, as well as the notable early Dylan cover by Manfred Mann, "With God on Our Side."

Various Artists, *Washington Square Memoirs: The Great Urban Folk Boom 1950–1970* (2001, Rhino). Less than a third of this is genuine folk-rock, but this three-CD box set is a great way to follow the transition of urban folk from its just-post-World World II manifestation through the early-'60s folk boom to the onset of folk-rock. Many major North American folk performers of the period, or folk-rock performers of the era with heavy roots in the folk boom, are represented here, including Bob Dylan, Ian & Sylvia, Judy Collins, Judy Henske, Richie Havens, Tim Hardin, Gordon Lightfoot, Richard & Mimi Fariña, Phil Ochs, Fred Neil, Tim Buckley, Buffy Sainte-Marie, Arlo Guthrie, Barry McGuire (as part of Barry & Barry), and Jesse Colin Young.

interviewees

●●

Turn! Turn! Turn! draws upon firsthand author interviews with the following musicians, producers, managers, journalists, venue owners, folklorists, filmmakers, and promoters (primary mid-'60s affiliations noted in parentheses). My thanks go to:

Lou Adler (producer, the Mamas & the Papas
   and Barry McGuire)
Eric Andersen
Ian Anderson (British musician, present-day
   editor of *fRoots* magazine)
Peter Asher (Peter & Gordon)
Larry Beckett (songwriting partner of Tim
   Buckley)
Steve Boone (the Lovin' Spoonful)
Joe Boyd (1965 Newport Folk Festival produc-
   tion manager, head of Elektra Records
   UK division)
Hamilton Camp
Dick Campbell
Tom Campbell
Morgan Cavett (manager, the New Balladeer
   coffeehouse, Los Angeles)
Anna Chairetakis (daughter of folklorist Alan
   Lomax, present-day head of the Alan Lomax
   Archive)
Judy Collins
Chris Darrow (Kaleidoscope)
Jim Dickson (manager/producer, the Byrds and
   the Dillards)
Rodney Dillard (the Dillards)
Art D'Lugoff (owner, the Village Gate club, New
   York City)
Denny Doherty (the Mamas & the Papas)
Donovan
Kenny Edwards (the Stone Poneys)

Ron Elliott (the Beau Brummels)
Merrell Fankhauser (Merrell & the Exiles,
   Fapardokly)
Mimi Fariña (Richard & Mimi Fariña)
Cyrus Faryar (the Modern Folk Quartet)
John Forsha (session guitarist, Judy Henske)
Pete Frame (administrator, Luton folk club,
   England; founder, *ZigZag* magazine)
David Freiberg (Quicksilver Messenger Service)
Barry Friedman aka Frazier Mohawk (producer,
   Kaleidoscope and the Paul Butterfield Blues
   Band; mentor, Buffalo Springfield)
Richie Furay (Buffalo Springfield)
Steve Gillette
Arthur Gorson (manager/producer, Phil Ochs,
   Tom Rush, David Blue, and Jim & Jean)
Vern Gosdin (the Gosdin Brothers, the Hillmen)
Arlo Guthrie
Roy Halee (engineer/producer, Simon &
   Garfunkel)
Judy Henske
Carolyn Hester
Chris Hillman (the Byrds)
Jac Holzman (president, Elektra Records)
Janis Ian
Erik Jacobsen (producer, the Lovin' Spoonful
   and Tim Hardin)
Billy James (publicist, Columbia Records)
Bob Johnston (producer, Bob Dylan and Simon
   & Garfunkel)

Carol Kaye (session guitarist and bassist, Sonny & Cher, Simon & Garfunkel, Bob Lind, and others)

Howard Kaylan (the Turtles)

Jesse Kincaid (the Rising Sons)

Ken Koblun (the Squires)

Al Kooper (the Blues Project)

Tuli Kupferberg (the Fugs)

Steve Lalor (the Daily Flash)

Bruce Langhorne (session guitarist, Bob Dylan, Richard & Mimi Fariña, Tom Rush, Carolyn Hester, and others)

Sam Lay (the Paul Butterfield Blues Band)

Murray Lerner (director, Newport Folk Festival documentary film *Festival*)

Banana Levinger (the Youngbloods)

Bob Lind

Trini Lopez

Mac MacLeod (guitarist, Donovan)

Manfred Mann

Roy Marinell

Gary Marker (the Rising Sons)

Joe Marra (owner, the Night Owl Cafe, New York City)

Charlie McCoy (session musician, Bob Dylan)

John McEuen (the Nitty Gritty Dirt Band)

Roger McGuinn (the Byrds)

Barry McGuire

John McNally (the Searchers)

Barry Melton (Country Joe & the Fish)

Geoff Muldaur (Jim Kweskin & the Jug Band)

Larry Murray (Hearts & Flowers)

Paul Nelson (managing editor, *Sing Out!* magazine)

Michael Ochs (manager, Phil Ochs)

Andrew Oldham (manager/producer, the Rolling Stones, Marianne Faithfull, and the Poets)

Tom Paxton

D.A. Pennebaker (director, Bob Dylan documentary film *Don't Look Back*; cinematographer, Bob Dylan documentary film *Eat the Document*)

Shawn Phillips

Pamela Polland (the Gentle Soul)

Jim Pons (the Leaves)

Tim Rose

Tom Rush

Buffy Sainte-Marie

Ed Sanders (the Fugs)

Richard Scott (the Blue Things)

John Sebastian (the Lovin' Spoonful)

Pete Seeger

Bob Siggins (the Charles River Valley Boys)

Irwin Silber (editor, *Sing Out!* magazine)

Marc Silber (the Children of Paradise)

Howard Solomon (owner, the Cafe Au Go Go club, New York City)

Peter Stampfel (the Holy Modal Rounders, the Fugs)

John Steel (the Animals)

Bernard Stollman (owner, ESP Records)

Shel Talmy (producer, the Kinks and the Who)

Barry Tashian (the Remains)

Tony Thompson (the Rising Storm)

Happy Traum

Rick Turner (guitarist, Ian & Sylvia)

Sylvia Tyson (Ian & Sylvia)

Sal Valentino (the Beau Brummels)

Gordon Waller (Peter & Gordon)

Dean Webb (the Dillards)

Frank Werber (manager/producer, the Kingston Trio and the We Five)

Paul Williams (founder and editor, *Crawdaddy* magazine)

Peter Yarrow (Peter, Paul & Mary)

Jerry Yester (the Modern Folk Quartet)

Jim Yester (the Association)

Izzy Young (proprietor, the Folklore Center in Greenwich Village, columnist for *Sing Out!*)

bibliography

Babiuk, Andy. *Beatles Gear*. San Francisco: Backbeat Books, 2001.

Bacon, Tony, and Paul Day. *The Rickenbacker Book*. London: Balafon Books, 1994.

Beatles, The. *The Beatles Anthology*. San Francisco: Chronicle Books, 2000.

Brend, Mark. *American Troubadours: Groundbreaking Singer Songwriters of the 60s*. San Francisco: Backbeat Books, 2001.

Brunning, Bob. *Blues: The British Connection*. Poole, England: Blandford Press, 1986.

Cable, Paul. *Bob Dylan: His Unreleased Recordings*. New York: Schirmer, 1978.

Collins, Judy. *Singing Lessons: A Memoir of Love, Loss, Hope, and Healing*. New York: Pocket Books, 1998.

Cunningham, Agnes, and Gordon Friesen. *Red Dust and Broadsides: A Joint Autobiography*. Amherst: University of Massachusetts Press, 2000.

Daho, Étienne, and Jérôme Soligny. *Françoise Hardy: Superstar et Ermite*. Paris: Jacques Grancher, 1986.

Davis, Clive, with James Willwerth. *Clive: Inside the Record Business*. New York: William Morrow & Co., 1974.

DeCurtis, Anthony, and James Henke with Holly George-Warren, eds., original editor Jim Miller. *The Rolling Stone Illustrated History of Rock & Roll*. New York: Random House, 1992.

DiMucci, Dion, with Davin Seay. *The Wanderer: Dion's Story*. New York: Beech Tree Books, 1988.

Dunaway, David. *Pete Seeger: How Can I Keep from Singing*. New York: Da Capo Press, 1981.

Egan, Sean. *Animals Tracks: The Story of the Animals: Newcastle's Rising Sons*. London: Helter Skelter Publishing, 2001.

Einarson, John. *Desperados: The Roots of Country Rock*. New York: Cooper Square Press, 2001.

———. *Neil Young: The Canadian Years: Don't Be Denied*. New York: Omnibus Press, 1993.

Einarson, John, and Richie Furay. *There's Something Happening Here: The Story of Buffalo Springfield: For What It's Worth*. Kingston, Canada: Quarry Press, 1997.

Eliot, Marc. *Death of a Rebel: A Biography of Phil Ochs*. New York: Franklin Watts, 1989.

Fonda, Peter. *Don't Tell Dad: A Memoir*. New York: Hyperion, 1998.

Frame, Pete. *The Complete Rock Family Trees*. New York: Omnibus Press, 1980.

————. *More Rock Family Trees*. New York: Omnibus Press, 1998.

Gibson, Bob, and Carole Bender. *Bob Gibson: I Come for to Sing*. Naperville, IL: Kingston Korner, 1999.

Gill, Andy. *Don't Think Twice, It's All Right: Bob Dylan, the Early Years*. New York: Thunder's Mouth Press, 1998.

Goldsmith, Peter D. *Making People's Music: Moe Asch and Folkways Records*. Washington, DC: Smithsonian Institution Press, 1998.

Gray, Michael, and John Bauldie (eds.). *All Across the Telegraph: A Bob Dylan Handbook*. London: Futura Publications, 1988.

Hajdu, David. *Positively 4th Street: The Lives and Times of Joan Baez, Bob Dylan, Mimi Baez Fariña and Richard Fariña*. New York: Farrar, Straux and Giroux, 2001.

Harper, Colin. *Dazzling Stranger: Bert Jansch & the British Folk and Blues Revival*. London: Bloomsbury Publishing, 2000.

Havens, Richie, with Steve Davidowitz. *They Can't Hide Us Anymore*. New York: Spike Books, 1999.

Helm, Levon. *This Wheel's on Fire: Levon Helm and the Story of the Band*. New York: William Morrow, 1993.

Heylin, Clinton. *Bob Dylan: A Life in Stolen Moments: Day By Day: 1941–1995*. New York: Schirmer Books, 1996.

————. *Bob Dylan: Behind the Shades: The Biography—Take Two*. London: Viking, 2000.

————. *Bob Dylan: The Recording Sessions 1960–1994*. New York: St. Martin's Press, 1996.

————. *Bootleg: The Secret History of the Other Recording Industry*. New York: St. Martin's Press, 1994.

Hodkinson, Mark. *As Tears Go By: Marianne Faithfull*. New York: Omnibus Press, 1991.

Holzman, Jac, and Gavan Daws. *Follow the Music: The Life and High Times of Elektra Records in the Great Years of American Pop Culture*. Santa Monica, CA: FirstMedia Books, 1998.

Hoskyns, Barney. *Across the Great Divide: The Band and America*. New York: Hyperion, 1993.

————. *Waiting for the Sun: Strange Days, Weird Scenes, and the Sound of Los Angeles*. New York: St. Martin's Press, 1996.

Humphries, Patrick. *Paul Simon*. New York: Doubleday, 1988.

Jahn, Mike. *Rock*. New York: Quadrangle Press, 1973.

Jennings, Nicholas. *Before the Gold Rush: Flashbacks to the Dawn of the Canadian Sound*. Toronto: Penguin Books, 1997.

Kooper, Al. *Backstage Passes & Backstabbing Bastards*. New York: Billboard Books, 1998.

Lee, C.P. *Like the Night: Bob Dylan and the Road to the Manchester Free Trade Hall*. London: Helter Skelter Publishing, 1998.

Lefcowitz, Eric. *The Monkees Tale*. Berkeley, CA: Last Gasp, 1985.

Lewisohn, Mark. *The Complete Beatles Chronicle*. New York: Harmony Books, 1992.

McDermott, John, with Eddie Kramer. *Hendrix: Setting the Record Straight*. New York: Warner Books, 1992.

McParland, Stephen J. *P.F.: Travelling Barefoot on a Rocky Road*. North Stratfield, Australia: CMusic Books, 2000.

Miles, Barry. *Paul McCartney: Many Years from Now*. New York: Henry Holt & Co., 1997.

Phillips, John, with Jim Jerome. *Papa John*. Garden City, NY: Dolphin Books, 1986.

Phillips, Michelle. *California Dreamin'*. New York: Warner Books, 1986.

Ribowsky, Mark. *He's a Rebel: The Truth About Phil Spector—Rock and Roll's Legendary Madman*. New York: E.P. Dutton, 1989.

Rogan, Johnny. *Neil Young: Zero to Sixty: A Critical Biography*. London: Calidore Books, 2000.

———. *The Byrds: Timeless Flight Revisited: The Sequel*. London: Rogan House, 1997.

Russo, Greg. *Mannerisms: The Five Phases of Manfred Mann*. Floral Park, NY: Crossfire Publications, 1995.

Scaduto, Anthony. *Bob Dylan: An Intimate Biography*. New York: Grosset and Dunlap, 1971.

Schumacher, Michael. *There But for Fortune: A Life of Phil Ochs*. New York: Hyperion, 1996.

Seeger, Pete. *Where Have All the Flowers Gone*. Bethlehem, PA: *Sing Out!*, 1993.

Shannon, Bob and John Javna. *Behind the Hits*. New York: Warner Books, 1986.

Shapiro, Harry. *Alexis Korner*. London: Bloomsbury Publishing, 1996.

Shelton, Robert. *No Direction Home: The Life and Music of Bob Dylan*. New York: Beech Tree Books, 1986.

Sounes, Howard. *Down the Highway: The Life of Bob Dylan*. New York: Grove Press, 2001.

Turner, Steve. *A Hard Day's Write: The Stories Behind Every Beatles' Song*. New York: Harper-Perennial, 1994.

Von Schmidt, Eric, and Jim Rooney. *Baby, Let Me Follow You Down*. Garden City, NJ: Anchor Books, 1979.

Wald, Elijah. *Josh White: Society Blues*. Amherst: University of Massachusetts, 2000.

Whitcomb, Ian. *After the Ball: Pop Music from Rag to Rock*. New York: Simon and Schuster, 1973.

Willens, Doris. *Lonesome Traveler: The Life of Lee Hays*. New York: W.W. Norton & Co., 1988.

Witts, Richard. *Nico: The Life & Lies of an Icon*. London: Virgin Books, 1993.

Woliver, Robbie. *Bringing It All Back Home: Twenty-Five Years of American Music at Folk City*. New York: Pantheon Books, 1986.

Wolkin, Jan Mark, and Bill Keenom. *Michael Bloomfield: If You Love These Blues*. San Francisco: Backbeat Books, 2000.

acknowledgments

W hen I decided to write the history of 1960s folk-rock, I had the feeling that I would face the most daunting writing project I had ever undertaken. I was right. Over the three years it has taken to research and write *Turn! Turn! Turn!*, dozens of friends, fans, fellow writers, and music professionals have provided vital contact information; assistance in setting up interviews, rare recordings and videos; leads to unearthed information; and just plain moral support. This book could not have been completed without their help.

Special thanks go to those friends who let me stay in their homes on my out-of-town research trips. Susan Mallett and Curt Lamberth cheerfully gave me accommodation and other amenities at their house in Oxford, England, as they have for other lengthy stays while I have worked on other books. In New York, Jason Gross and Bob Maresca were second-time-around hosts for book-related sojourns, as were Gordon Anderson and Lisa Kotin in Los Angeles. In London, Nora McCormick and Dana Mayer made me welcome to stay in their flats while I worked in that city.

In the San Francisco Bay Area, extra-special thanks go to these fellow folk-rock fanatics who spent many hours discussing, playing, and displaying items in their archives that I would never have heard or located otherwise: Joel Bernstein, Alec Palao, and Pat Thomas. In London, Ian Anderson of *fRoots* magazine generously allowed me to look through his office's large collection of 1960s folk periodicals. Jeff Davis of Flat Plastic Sound in San Francisco let me borrow numerous recordings, many of them out of print and hard to find.

Many thanks as well to all of the following individuals for their help with acquiring music, interviews, and other useful information, often going to great lengths to make sure I had copies of numerous rarities and the contacts I needed: Rene Aagaard, Gene Aguilera, Jim Allen, Bill Allerton of Stand Out Records in London, Joel Bellman, Bill Belmont, Pirmin Bossart, Paul Bradshaw of Mod Lang Records in Berkeley, Mark Brend, Denny Bruce, Ron Cabral, Richard Campbell, Phil Carson, Douglas Cooke, Jud Cost, Steve Davidowitz, Jeff Davis of Niagara, Fred Dellar, Dawn Eden, Sean Egan, Joe Ehrbar, John Einarson, Tom Erikson, Trudy Fisher, Don Fleming, Tim Forster, Bill Allen George of the Jackie DeShannon Appreciation Society, Charlie Gillett, George Gimarc, Joe Goldmark, Giorgio Gomelsky, Dick Greener, Matt Greenwald, Randy Haecker of Legacy Media Relations, Matt Hanks, Colin Harper, Karl Ikola, Jeff Jarema, Elliot Kendall, Alan Korn, Harvey Kubernik, Spencer Leigh, Andy Linehan, Tim Livingston of Sundazed Records, Jeff March, Debi Moss, Mark Moss, Ric O'Barry, Domenic Priore, Ben Sandstrom, Michael Scully, Will Shade, Doug Sheppard, Phil Smee, Pat Smith, Steve Stanley, Mike Stax of *Ugly Things* magazine, Armin Steiner, Anatol Sucher, Denise Sullivan,

Jeff Tamarkin, Bryan Thomas, Jennifer Vineyard, Ed Ward, Steven Ward, Jeff Watt, Kurt Wolff, Chris Woodstra of the All Music Guide Web site, Reinhard Zierke, and Alan Zollner.

Janet Rosen of San Francisco, and her husband Stuart Kremsky, provided especially valuable friendship and critical counsel from the book's inception through its completion. In New York, agent Sheree Bykofsky, and her assistant Janet Rosen (no relation to the San Francisco Janet Rosen!), provided professional and sympathetic representation. Agent Robert Shepard offered useful advice in the proposal's formative stages. My parents, Sue and Elliot, were again fully supportive of my endeavors.

As they have done with my books *Unknown Legends of Rock 'n' roll* and *Urban Spacemen & Wayfaring Strangers: Overlooked Innovators and Eccentric Visionaries of '60s Rock*, Backbeat Books have eagerly applied their best resources to ensure the publication of a book that seeks to dig deep into the riches of rock history. Thanks need to be spread around to editors Dorothy Cox and Richard Johnston, and publisher Matt Kelsey; managing editor Nancy Tabor; production editors Amanda Johnson and Michael Baughan; marketing communications manager Nina Lesowitz; sales and marketing associate Kevin Becketti; sales manager Jay Kahn; copy editor Julie Herrod-Lumsden; text designer and compositor Leigh McLellan; cover designer Doug Gordon; and proofreader Larissa Berry. Also to these boosters at Backbeat UK: Nigel Osborne, Tony Bacon, Doug Chandler, and Holly Willis.

The greatest thanks go to the more than 100 musicians, producers, promoters, and journalists who graciously granted the interviews upon which much of this volume is based. Folk-rock couldn't have happened without them, for which we should all be grateful. This book certainly would not have happened without their participation, for which I will be eternally grateful.

about the author

R ichie Unterberger's books include *Unknown Legends of Rock 'n' roll* (Backbeat Books, 1998), which profiles 60 underappreciated cult rock artists of all styles and eras. His *Urban Spacemen & Wayfaring Strangers: Overlooked Innovators & Eccentric Visionaries of '60s Rock* (Backbeat Books, 2000) contains more in-depth surveys of 20 underrated greats of the era, again drawing on dozens of firsthand interviews. Unterberger is also author of *The Rough Guide to Music USA*, a guidebook to the evolution of regional popular music styles throughout America in the twentieth century, and the travel guidebook *The Rough Guide to Seattle*. A senior editor for the All Music Guide, the largest online database of music biographies and album reviews, he lives in San Francisco.

The second half of the history of the 1960s folk-rock movement documented in *Turn! Turn! Turn!* is covered in its sequel, *Eight Miles High: Folk-Rock's Flight from Haight-Ashbury to Woodstock*, to be published by Backbeat Books in 2003. Detailing the period from mid-1966 to the end of the 1960s, Unterberger portrays the mutation of folk-rock into psychedelia via California bands like the Byrds and Jefferson Airplane; the maturation of folk-rock composers in the birth of the singer-songwriter movement; the reemergence of Bob Dylan and the inception of country-rock; the rise of folk-rock's first supergroup from the ashes of the Byrds and Buffalo Springfield; the origination of a truly British form of folk-rock; and the growth of the live folk-to-rock music festival, from Newport to Woodstock.

More information about Richie Unterberger, his books, and the music he documents (including the 1960s folk-rock covered in this volume) can be found on his Web site at: www.richieunterberger.com. E-mail can be sent to him at richie@richieunterberger.com.

photo credits

Courtesy of Vanguard Records: page 7

©David Gahr: page 13

Michael Ochs Archives.com, ©Alice Ochs: page 19

Courtesy of Holzman Archives: page 27

Sylvia Tyson: page 57

Courtesy of Capitol Records: page 121

Courtesy of Gary Marker; photo by Guy Wet: page 141

Don Paulsen: page 145

Courtesy of Rhino Records: page 217

Courtesy of Donovan: page 235

Courtesy of Erik Lindgren: page 251

Courtesy of Cicadelic Records: page 255

Courtesy of Fantasy Records, photo ©1994, The Fugs: page 265

Michael Ochs Archives.com: pages 45, 73, 85, 89, 107, 127, 169, 189, 201, 223, 227

index

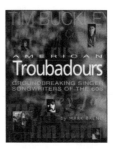
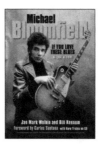